THE STUDY OF MANKIND

Anthropology—from the Greek *anthropos* (man) and *logia* (study)—is the systematic wonder about and the scientific study of man. At its heart are questions such as: "What is mankind's essential nature?" and "Where is our place in the universal scheme of things?"

Divided into sections on reconstructing the past, fieldwork, human communication, sex and sex roles, understanding "culture," marriage and kinship, magic and religion, and politics, law, and war, this fascinating collection of essays explores everything from the impact of the introduction of steel into a stone-age culture to the special language of drunks and the ritualized role-playing games of doctors and nurses. Here is a volume that places anthropology precisely where it belongs—within the reach of anyone who is intrigued by the variety and potential of human beings.

THE PLEASURES
OF ANTHROPOLOGY

MORRIS FREILICH, Professor of Anthropology at Northeastern University in Boston, Massachusetts, is the editor of *Marginal Natives at Work; Anthropologists in the Field* and *The Meaning of Culture*.

WITHDRAWN

The Study of Man from MENTOR and SIGNET Books

THE PLEASURES OF ANTHROPOLOGY

EDITED AND
WITH AN INTRODUCTION
AND NOTES BY

Morris Freilich

A MENTOR BOOK
NEW AMERICAN LIBRARY
TIMES MIRROR
New York and Scarborough, Ontario

**To Sura Freilich
With love**

NAL BOOKS ARE AVAILABLE AT QUANTITY DISCOUNTS WHEN USED
TO PROMOTE PRODUCTS OR SERVICES. FOR INFORMATION PLEASE
WRITE TO PREMIUM MARKETING DIVISION, THE NEW AMERICAN
LIBRARY, INC., 1633 BROADWAY, NEW YORK, NEW YORK 10019.

Library of Congress Catalog Card Number: 83-60242

 MENTOR TRADEMARK REG. U.S. PAT. OFF. AND FOREIGN COUNTRIES
REGISTERED TRADEMARK—MARCA REGISTRADA
HECHO EN CHICAGO, U.S.A.

SIGNET, SIGNET CLASSIC, MENTOR, PLUME, MERIDIAN and NAL BOOKS
are published by The New American Library, Inc.,
1633 Broadway, New York, New York 10019

First Printing, September, 1983

1 2 3 4 5 6 7 8 9

PRINTED IN THE UNITED STATES OF AMERICA

ACKNOWLEDGMENTS

I am pleased to acknowledge valuable comments on earlier drafts of this book by C. Paul Dredge, Carole Hall, Nancy Jaffee, Alan Klein, and Ronald McAllister.

CONTENTS

INTRODUCTION
BEAUTY IN
THE BEAST

Man is an animal that can
make promises.

Nietzsche

Time is to man what water
is to fish.

Heidegger

ANTHROPOLOGY—FROM GREEK *anthropos* (man) and *logia* (study)—is the systematic wonder about and the scientific study of humans. Wonder about humans is probably as old as man, *Homo sapiens*. Universally such wonder has triggered unempirical questions, such as: "Where do I stand? Where is my place in the universe? Why is there a world as such and why and how do I exist?" Such questions continue to be asked, and old answers still have a powerful appeal. Indeed, old answers *must have* a powerful appeal.

Traditional answers to questions about the essential nature of man differ markedly. Polar views present man either as almost divine or as a mere animal. Taking the almost-divine view, the psalmist wrote poetically:

> What is man that Thou art mindful of him?
> And the son of man that Thou thinkest of him?
> Yet Thou hast made him little less than divine.
> And hast crowned him with glory and honor.

The Platonists presented man as a mere animal. As Ralph Borsodi reminds us in *The Definition of Definition*, they rigidly maintained this position even when confronted with contradictory evidence:

At one meeting of the Academy in ancient Athens, the Platonists are said to have defined man as "a featherless animal with two feet." When Diogenes heard the definition, he plucked all the feathers off a cock, took the poor bird to the Academy where the Platonists were in solemn conclave, threw it down among them and said, "Plato's man." Whereupon the members put their heads together again and after appropriate consideration of the matter added to the definition the phrase "without claws."

In the spirit of Diogenes, anthropologists avoid simplistic, animalistic views of man.[1] But they recognize man's membership in the animal kingdom. Anthropologists consider humans as peculiar primates, strange animals who transform themselves and their environments with culture. Studying humans as primates makes anthropologists biological scientists. Studying humans as cultural beings makes anthropologists social scientists. This involvement with both biological and social sciences (with frequent glances toward the humanities) puts anthropologists into an intellectual no-man's land where problems of data collection, analysis, and synthesis become gargantuan.

Of necessity, anthropologists become specialists in archaeology, biological anthropology, linguistics, and social or cultural anthropology, to name but the major branches of the evolutionary and comparative study of humans.

Archaeologists and biological anthropologists study the past with dug-up rather than written data. The past, for them, stretches back for more than 20 million years. Archaeologists select digging sites that are rich in information, develop techniques for dating their finds, and build models to interpret their data. Biological anthropologists study human evolution and human variation, do field studies of living primates, and analyze primate fossils.

This research has revealed ever more complex forms alongside ever more complex technology, and shows that in dealing with nature, humans have progressed from crude tools to precision instruments, from simple fire-making techniques to the control of atomic energy. Evolution seems to have a direction: to create a form of life capable of mastering nature.

Evolution is now undeniable. Humans share more structural and behavioral characteristics with other animals than most subjects of Queen Victoria would have dared to imagine. Humans are *generalized primates*. Unlike *specialized primates*, humans are not preadapted to a particular environment or life-style. This categorization is useful for most, not all, discussions of human

---

[1] Diogenes' confrontation with Platonists illustrates the validity of Moq's Law: *Decisions Arrived at by a Committee are More than a Match for Mere Data.*

life, because humans do have a rather strange specialization—information. Indeed, specialization understates the human fascination with and constant juggling of information. As information addicts, humans send information and keep requesting feedback (e.g., "Do you see what I mean?" Or, "Get it?" "O.K.?"). The human attachment to information seems to be a function of language—a sound system which uses symbols to hide and reveal information and sentiments.

Anthropologists who study humans as information addicts, information revealers, and information hiders are called linguists. Linguists listen to people talk. They also listen and watch as people communicate without language—with body movements, hand waving, eye contact, and avoidance of eye contact; with laughter, tears, sighs, and grunts; with stony silence and raised eyebrows; with clothes, perfumes, scents, and adornments. Like all anthropologists, linguists ask questions about man's essential nature. For example, is language an intellectual prison forcing us to see reality in given, rigid ways? And if it is, can we ever escape? Is language an evolutionary advance? And if it is, then do we need nonlinguistic forms to communicate with? Children get linguistic fluency largely by hanging around. Why does linguistic fluency often elude adults even when (or perhaps because) professionals teach them? Can nonhuman animals be taught language? And if they can, will they have anything to say that is interesting?

One of anthropologists' favorite ways at getting at answers is through fieldwork. Like nonprofessionals who travel, anthropologists often arrive in a foreign society lacking linguistic fluency. Like most weaknesses, this too has some advantages. While it is true that informants initially laugh at the way many anthropologists "maul" their words, such laughter at the researcher tends to change quickly to laughter with the stranger. The role of "student of language" provides a smooth transition to the role of "student of culture." Once made, this transition moves a project from "passive" fieldwork to "active" fieldwork. "Fieldwork," a Britisher once remarked, "keeps you anthropologists running around the world seeking goodies you call culture." He had discovered the curious relationship between anthropologists and their mode of doing research.

Life "in the field" is an orgy of discovery. Undreamed-of traits are discovered, both in ourselves and in our informants. Multiple images must be invented to fully comprehend the complexities. If fieldwork concentrates on symbolism, then humans appear to be much like digital computers because much of human reality is symbolically reduced to binary pairs—male/ female, young/old, fat/thin, tall/short, alive/dead, we/they, etc. If the focus is on sexual life, then humans appear to be sexy primates often ready to perform and often fascinated by variety. If fieldwork is primarily concerned with marriage and kinship, then humans appear as beings fascinated by their own ancestry and concerned with those who share a common descent line. Research on magic and religion spotlights human talents in discovering and "solving" dilemmas and paradoxes relating to unempirical phenomena. Research on politics, law, and war presents humans as power-seeking, justice-loving, or just aggressive. These and other images (that of "economic man," for example) are often subsumed under one grand image. Humans, wheresoever found, it is often said correctly, seem to be *cultural beings*.

The simplicity of the grand image is, however, illusory. Beings with culture own a precious commodity which seems to resist definition, and provides many different conceptions of what it means to live "the good life." How different such conceptions can be was well described by Benjamin Franklin:

At the treaty of Lancaster, in Pennsylvania, *anno* 1744, between the Government of Virginia and the Six Nations, the commissioners from Virginia acquainted the Indians by a speech, that there was at Williamsburg a college with a fund for educating Indian youth; and that if the chiefs of the Six Nations would send down half a dozen of their sons to that college, the government would take care that they be well provided for, and instructed in all the learning of the white people.

The Indians' spokesman replied:

. . . We are convinced . . . that you mean to do us good by your proposal and we thank you heartily. But you, who are wise, must know that different nations have different conceptions of things; and you will not therefore take it amiss, if our ideas of this kind of education happen not to be the same with yours. We have had some experience of it; several of our young people were formerly brought up at the colleges of northern provinces; they were instructed in all your sciences; but, when they came back to us, they were bad runners, ignorant of every means of living in the woods, unable to bear either cold or hunger, knew neither how to build a cabin, take a deer, nor kill an enemy, spoke our language imperfectly, were therefore neither fit for hunters, warriors, nor counsellors; they were totally good for nothing.

We are however not the less obligated by your kind offer, though we decline accepting it; and, to show our grateful sense of it, if the gentlemen of Virginia will send us a dozen of their sons, we will take care of their education, instruct them in all we know, and make men of them.

Culture, like a successful actor, hides behind many disguises and makes us wonder about its true identity. What are its essential characteristics? In 1871, Edward Tylor presented an answer which is the most frequently quoted definition of culture: "Culture or civilization, taken in its wide ethnographic sense, is that complex whole which includes knowledge, belief, art, morals, law, custom and any other capabilities and habits acquired by man as a member of society." Sir Edward wrote when anthropology was yet in its infancy, still cutting its first conceptual teeth. Given the primitive state of anthropological knowledge, Sir Edward's definition must be admired for its productive vagueness. It leaves us unclear whether "culture" is a synonym for "civilization" or whether all humans—no matter how primitive their technology or how underdeveloped their economy—have "culture." It leaves us uncertain whether culture refers to *behavior*, *to rules for behavior*, or to both. And "complex whole" cleverly avoids the issue: "What kind of system is culture?" Fuzziness such as this stimulated many scholars to produce their own definitions, which today number in the hundreds. Let me suggest a synthesis: culture is a humanly produced guidance system for *proper* belief, action, explanation, and sentiment. Culture guides humans to near and far-off futures just as computers guide missiles to near and far-off targets.

Is it possible that culture and computer—both children of the human mind—are essentially similar systems? If they are, then anthropology can share in the fascinating developments of modern computer science. Even the differences between culture and computer suggest profound similarities. For example, humans program, but they do so neither quickly nor peacefully, tending to avoid cultural programs as often as they submit to them.

The relationship between culture and computer bears watching. It may be a temporary flirtation or it may represent real love. If the relationship turns out to be serious and permanent, what kinds of offspring will it produce? Will the computer dominate the mind and produce culture in its own image? If the computer gains absolute power, will it banish culture's old and intimate companions—myth, ritual, illusion, and vision? Or will culture's friends adapt and meet the demands of the cold, logical, and unemotional computer? As usual, we have more questions than we have answers. One certainty, though, is that the computer has become man's ally in his attempt to master nature.

Will humans ever master nature? Will such power mean a total escape from nature's powers? These foxy questions hide a strange paradox. How can humans escape nature when they themselves are part of nature? Perhaps behind the noble brow and upright form sits a Beast whose nature is still unclear. Will the Beast submit to Beauty (that inseparable companion, also called Culture)? Beauty's relationship with the Beast, the subject of numerous stories, legends, and myths, needs to be understood today, more than ever before. Must Beauty and Beast be in constant conflict, as depicted in *Dr. Jekyll and Mr. Hyde?* Or, can Beast and Beauty live in harmony, as described in the myths of many South American Indians? Evolutionary studies, clearly, are relevant to modern problems. Peculiar primates have thumbs that hover over nuclear buttons. A small error or miscalculation can wipe out our planet.

To understand the essential nature of humans we must dig out the meaning of the Beast within us. What precisely is our Beast nature? A currently popular group of writers believe that the Beast is a direct descendant of killer apes. Our ancestors, they say, killed to survive and learned to enjoy the experience. Other writers describe our ancestors as hunters who killed but who never became killers. For them the Beast is a cooperative animal who rarely revels in conflict. Yet others describe our ancestors as peaceful vegetarians who lived together harmoniously. This last group would take strong exception to the very existence of a Beast within us. In sum, whether we shelter a killer Beast, a hunter Beast, or a primitive flower child is as uncertain as the nature of Beauty (i.e., Culture). Those composing on human nature or Beast nature might do well to copy Alison Jolly's style:

> We are primates by our loves and fears and hatred, by the crook of our thumbs and by the size of our big toes. Our thumbs have been modified to hold precision tools; our big toes have been flattened to walk upon the ground; our loves and hatreds are shaped to the needs of human groups. But above all we are *Homo sapiens*. . . . We exchanged instinctive certainty for adaptive complexity, and in our myths bought knowledge at the price of innocence.

It is proper that a book dedicated to pleasure should end its introduction with a gift. My gift is the unanswered question: How is man's relationship to culture best conceptualized? This question demands no immediate answer. This question, if left hanging, will create no mental anguish, no pressure for instant certainty. Those who accept it, therefore, can take it free of any worries.

But it will be a useful companion while reading *The Pleasures of Anthropology* and provide much additional pleasure.

We children of modern, "instant-process" society want fast understanding; instant insight. Looking for insights, though, I strongly suggest, is in itself a slow-brewing pleasure that stays with us. Unlike instant pleasure, it does not instantly disappear.

REFERENCES

Borsodi, Ralph. *The Definition of Definition*. Boston: Porter Sargent Publishing Co., 1979.

Franklin, Benjamin. "Remarks Concerning the Savages of North America." In *The Works of Benjamin Franklin*, Volume II, Boston: Tappan and Dennet Publishing Co., 1844 (Pamphlet 1784).

Jolly, Alison. *The Evolution of Primate Behavior*. New York: Macmillan, Inc., 1972.

Tylor, Edward (Sir). *Primitive Culture*. Reprinted in 2 volumes: 1. *The Origins of Culture*, 2. *Religion in Primitive Culture*. New York: Harper Torch books, 1958 (original 1871).

I

RECONSTRUCTING
THE PAST

The past should be considered as a political and psychological treasure from which we draw the resources to cope with the future.

Christopher Lasch

RECONSTRUCTING THE PAST is an anthropological preoccupation. Anthropologists want to discover ancestors, origins, and processes. We (*Homo sapiens*) belong to the order Primates, that group of mammals which also includes lemurs, monkeys, and apes. The evolutionary history of the Primates exceeds seventy million years. Those who search for human ancestry, therefore, must be willing to cover a considerable amount of "history." Scholars such as William W. Howells ("Homo Sapiens: Twenty Million Years in the Making") limit their research to the time when the first "real ancestors" emerged. They are interested in creatures like *Ramapithecus*, which had just branched off from the group of our nearest relatives, the apes. Compared to the study of the history of the earth (about four billion years), finding "real ancestors" may not appear so impressive. However, when we realize that written history goes back only about five thousand years, this anthropological task comes into sharper perspective. The study of four thousand times as much history as has been written by historians, clearly, is a huge endeavor.

In searching for ancestors, along with Howells, it is useful to remember what we are physically. Humans have brains which are large and rounded; the average volume of the braincase, or human skull, is fourteen hundred cubic centimeters. Humans have small teeth, arranged in jaws in a parabolic curve. The third molar is the smallest in the series and the canines do not project. Humans stand upright and walk with a bipedal, striding gait. The human thumb is "opposable." Its length is about 65 percent the length of the forefinger; this permits both the *power grip* (grasping objects with strength) and the *precision grip* (grasping objects with delicacy and exactness).

2

How did we become what we are? Howells instructs us on the many problems which prevent this question from being answered easily and quickly. He takes us backstage to reveal the hidden trappings of scientific investigation. We are granted the rare privilege of seeing the naked scientist—without halo, costume, or makeup.

Humans attempt to escape from nature. One form this "escapism" takes is a desire to live in the past. Archaeology supports and nourishes this odd human interest. Understandably, therefore, people tend to find archaeology entertaining and engrossing. So fascinating is this escape into the past that people are ready to believe almost anything if it is labeled "archaeology." It is important, therefore, to distinguish between pseudoarchaeology and scholarly archaeology.

Pseudoarchaeologists are nonspecialists. They write about archaeological matters with neither a commitment to nor a training in the scientific method. They produce exciting theories which may include visitors from outer space bringing advanced technology to "backward" earthlings. They assume, for example, that the Maya Indians were too primitive to have perfected a sophisticated writing system. Therefore, they argue, some foreign group, perhaps an extraterrestrial one, taught the Maya much of their "advanced" knowledge.

Scholarly archaeologists form a very diverse category. It is useful to distinguish between those who do *classical, historical,* and *prehistoric archaeology*. Classical archaeologists study Egyptian pyramids and mummies and (among other things) Greek and Roman temples. Their work generally dovetails with that of documentary historians. Historical archaeologists study sites that date to historical times. Much of their work is concerned with reconstructing the material, social and cultural life of the historic period. Their labors cover a wide range of activities—from the analysis of colonial cemeteries to the reconstruction of nineteenth-century towns in Pennsylvania.

Prehistoric archaeologists are anthropologists. They want to understand the structure of past social organizations by analyzing the artifacts of past human activities. They attempt to build a theory of cultural evolution and are therefore concerned with the interaction between different cultures and their respective environments. Current attempts to develop more sophisticated theory and methodology include much argumentation: there is "a wide range of opinion as to the nature of relevant theory and appropriate methodology, and much work needs to be done on even the most extensively discussed points in these matters."[1]

Prehistoric archaeologists, although well trained in scientific method, theory, and archaeological technique, still disagree on fundamental issues. Their argumentation is presented by Kent Flannery ("The Golden Marshalltown") in a manner understandable to nonprofessionals. "Real" archaeologists passionately argue under assumed names—the Born-Again Philosopher, the Child of the Seventies, the Old Timer. Each of these subtypes of prehistoric archaeology preaches for a specific approach. They are shown as flesh-and-blood people working for science and for themselves.

For the first two or three million years of his existence, *Homo* (man) lived in bands or villages which were probably completely autonomous.[2] *Homo sapiens* (modern man) continued this form of life, which included surviving by means of hunting and gathering. Around ten thousand years ago, on the hillsides and tablelands adjoining the Fertile Crescent, humans invented a new mode of survival: agriculture. The wide expansion of the zone of original agricultural activity did not occur until about six thousand years ago. Migrations then took four directions—toward Europe, Africa, India, and China. And the migrants brought along their knowledge of agriculture. Agriculture provides a surplus of food capable of feeding people who do not work at food production. An agricultural base, many people believe, is a necessity for state formation. An important question therefore becomes: "Must agriculture, once invented, necessarily lead to the formation of the state?" Robert L. Carneiro's answer, no, is based on the fact that agriculture does not automatically create a surplus.

Carneiro's essay includes a controlled comparison of the coastal valleys of Peru with the Amazon basin. In Amazonia, although warfare was frequent, "losers" were not (generally) incorporated into a larger social system. Here, because of the availabil-

[1] Robert Whallon, *"Editorial Opinion," Journal of Anthropological Archaeology*, vol. 1, no. 1 (March 1982), pp. 1–4.

[2] The anthropological answer to the question: "How old is man, *Homo*?" is both vague and subject to considerable dispute. Recent work in Ethiopia indicates that the upper chart (in Howells' paper) is probably superior to the lower chart. This work has also identified what some believe to be a new ancestor, *Australopithecus Afarensis*, who lived around three and a half million years ago (See Don Johanson and Maitland A. Edey, *Lucy* (New York: Simon and Schuster, 1981).

ity of all the forest land needed, the rule was "fight and (for losers) flight." In the narrow valleys of the Peruvian coast, in sharp contrast, a village that lost a war was allowed to survive if it accepted political subordination to the victor. In short, Carneiro presents a very plausible theory of conquest under given ecological conditions as explaining the origin of the state.

Howells, Flannery, and Carneiro teach an important lesson: the kind of detective work required for reconstructing our past is a curious mixture of elements. Fads and fashions, philosophies and personalities, strivings for truth and strivings for fame intermingle with careful methodology, respect for data, and much sweat. Given the latter, and a little luck, we somehow manage to understand a bit about our past.

REFERENCES

Cazeau, Charles J., and Stuart D. Scott, Jr. *Exploring the Unknown: Great Mysteries Reexamined*. New York: Plenum, 1979.

Fagen, Brian M. *Archaeology: A Brief Introduction*. Boston: Little, Brown, 1983.

Fried, Morton. *The Evolution of Political Society*. New York: Random House, 1967.

Mendelssohn, Kurt. *The Riddle of the Pyramids*. New York: Praeger, 1974.

Sagan, Carl. *Broca's Brain*. New York: Ballantine, 1980.

Homo Sapiens: Twenty Million Years in the Making

by
William W. Howells

TODAY WE CAN almost point to the first real "ancestor" of man. By this ancestor I mean a creature who, among the evolving primates of twenty million or more years ago, had just branched off from the group of our nearest relatives, the apes—a creature, still very much like an ape himself, whose descendants nevertheless evolved continuously in a different direction from that point on. We are quite sure we have the fossil jaws of such a creature—his name is *Ramapithecus* (named romantically for the Indian god Rama)—who lived about fourteen million years ago, and the story of our knowledge of him is an interesting story about science itself.

We have realized for some time that man arose in this way, from animals leading to the apes on one side and to ourselves on the other. After Darwin's great book, *On the Origin of Species*, had made inevitable the acceptance of evolution (including human evolution), Thomas Huxley almost at once showed how closely, in every way, we resemble the great apes. He said, in fact, that they, the apes, are closer to us than they are to monkeys.

This led to a lot of public jokes and private dismay, and the idea was resisted in many ways, by scientists as well as others. But now, after a hundred years, all the study of anatomy and, quite late, of such things as the molecular structure of proteins has only shown more and more positively that Huxley was right. Indeed we can go a step beyond Huxley and say that apes of Africa, the gorilla and chimpanzee, are more closely related to man than is any of the three to the orang-untan of Indonesia.

Reprinted from *UNESCO Courier*, August–September 1972, pp. 5–13, by permission of The Unesco Courier.

After Huxley's time, some anatomists pointed to the fact that apes are adapted in body form for brachiating, or hanging and swinging from their arms. This is a particularly good and safe way for a large animal to move in trees. Pointing also to our own broad shoulders and flat, broad chests, as well as to details of our elbow and wrist joints, and arrangements of muscles, they argued that our ancestors were likewise adapted to a considerable degree for brachiation, and for life in trees. This was one more argument for close relationship to the apes.

Here again, other anatomists resisted the idea, arguing that the resemblances were not very significant, and perhaps had evolved in parallel with the apes. They preferred to think of an ancestral line which had been separate from apes, or even monkeys, for a very long time. (Always in the background there seems to have been an unconscious revulsion against relating ourselves to chimpanzees, by people who looked on them as "animals," not noticing how large-brained and intelligent these same animals really are.)

They had arguments: we do indeed stand upright, and our feet are very different from an ape's; and our jaws are now quite different, particularly with small eye teeth which do not project above the other teeth in the obvious way an ape's do. Could these larger teeth have evolved backwards to smaller ones? Could the handlike foot of an ape have been made over into a human foot?

These difficulties are not as great as they once seemed. Such changes are almost commonplace in animal evolution, with teeth being diminished or lost, and limbs modified in drastic ways. In addition, we must not try to picture our common ancestor as though he were a chimpanzee or gorilla; these animals have been evolving too. As study has gone on, and fact is piled on fact, most anthropologists have become convinced that our forebears did indeed use trees like the African apes, who actually live more on the forest floor than in trees.

Still later, fossil jaws of the ancestral ape *Dryopithecus* drew attention to the very close likeness of the molar teeth in ourselves and apes. Though the first specimen was found in France in 1856, it was during the early part of this century that such fragments were discovered in greater numbers, from fossil-bearing beds of Miocene and Pliocene age, and in the time range of about twenty million to eight million years ago.

The fossils have come from other parts of Europe and from India, and later from East Africa, Georgia (U.S.S.R.) and China. With all this, the web of evidence has drawn tighter around our connection with the apes. For *Dryopithecus* was evidently the ancestor of the large apes, and his remains are so widespread that we can now hardly expect to find a new and different fossil group in the future from which we ourselves might have come.

Another important fossil "ape," *Oreopithecus* of Italy and East Africa, who lived at the same time, became well known a few years ago. But, while his body form was rather like a chimpanzee's, showing a similar kind of adaptation to trees in a related animal, his teeth are quite different from a chimpanzee's and from ours as well, a fact which only links our descent still more closely to the apes of Africa.

It was out of the *Dryopithecus* stock that man emerged, and in fact it was from among the fossils of *Dryopithecus* fossils that our ancestor *Ramapithecus* became known. G. E. Lewis of Yale in 1934 described the first upper jaw, found in India's Siwalik Hills, and pointed to some manlike features.

Your own mouth will show you these things, where you can feel them with your finger. Your dental arch is short and rounded in front, while that of apes has become increasingly longer and broad across the front, with large canine teeth and broad incisors. Your molar teeth have the cusp and furrow pattern of *Dryopithecus*, but are square; an ape's are longer. This length makes an ape's face projecting; yours is straighter.

Approaches to the human shape could be seen in the small fragment of *Ramapithecus* as though he had just set his foot on a path diverging from *Dryopithecus*, although unfortunately we have not found the foot, only the jaw. So Lewis thought *Ramapithecus* might belong in our ancestry.

But the tide of scientific opinion—and such tides are apt to influence, not facts, but the way we see facts—was against *Ramapithecus*, and the fossil was put away in a drawer as simply one more kind of *Dryopithecus*. After almost thirty years, however, L. S. B. Leakey found a very similar fossil at Fort Ternan in Kenya, which he could date as being fourteen million years old.

It happened that at the same time, Elwyn Simons at Yale was looking once again at *Ramapithecus*. He was impressed with what Lewis had pointed to, and saw the same features in Leakey's new specimen.

Perhaps more important, Simons rescued other pieces of *Ramapithecus* from burial in museum drawers. He began examining old collections in various places from the U.S.A. to India, and recognized a few more fragments with the same special features, fragments which had previously been misnamed and ignored, but which he identified as fossils of *Ramapithecus*.

This careful sorting out made it easier to see the slight distinctions between *Ramapithecus* on one hand and *Dryopithecus*, ancestor of the apes, on the other. Thus we also see the beginnings of the separating paths of human and ape evolution, or between animals properly called pongids (apes) and those called hominids (anything on the human side of the same group). So palaeontology is not all looking for fossils in old river banks.

What brought the split about? Evolution has "reasons"—it follows lines of successful adaptation—but we know so little about *Ramapithecus*, having only his jaws and teeth, that we cannot see the "reason." We cannot simply say that it is better or more successful to be "human," because that really means nothing, and *Ramapithecus* certainly resembled the ancestral apes far more than he resembled man. Like some chimpanzee populations he seems to have lived in an open wood and, again like chimpanzees, it is probable that he was still a tree-user.

Professors Simons and Keith Jolly, however, think he had begun to differ in diet from chimpanzees (who eat much coarse wild fruit) by using tough but nutritious foods like nuts, seeds and hard roots. This is because his teeth had thicker enamel than an ape's, and showed signs of heavy wear. He seems to have used his molars as grinders, more than his front teeth, and this would be related to his shorter face.

Ramapithecus lived from some time before fourteen million years ago down at least as far as eight million. Then, simply because no fossils have yet been found, there is a gap in knowledge until five million years ago. But surprising changes must have taken place: by this time much more obvious human ancestors had appeared, and they are fairly well known from the time between about 4 million and 1.5 million B.C. Here also, however, there was a long wait for recognition in the face of doubt.

It was in 1924 that Raymond Dart in South Africa saw the first skull, of a young child, in a box of fossils brought from Taung. He thought from its face and teeth that it stood halfway between man and ape, and he named it *Australopithecus* ("ape of the south"). But he had not found—and we never do find—a complete skeleton, adult, and exactly dated; and his colleagues rejected his idea, believing this juvenile, still with its milk teeth, to be merely an interesting new ape. Much later, and slowly, did the many finds arrive which showed that Dart himself had been too cautious. (The further fossils were found years ago by Dart and Robert Broom in South Africa. New ones are found every year, greatly added to by discoveries in East Africa by Dr. and Mrs. Leakey, at Olduvai Gorge, and their son Richard, in northern Kenya, as well as by Professors Camille Arambourg and F. Clark Howell.)

In the jaws of these australopithecines, the large (but human) back teeth also strongly suggest powerful chewing for tough foods. The front teeth (canines and incisors) were small and entirely hominid in nature, not something partly apelike. For several million years there were two lines of these australopiths: *Australopithicus*, barely the size of a modern pygmy, and *Paranthropus*, who was a little larger but had jaws as powerful as a gorilla's, though the jaws were short and deep (for grinding with the back teeth), not long, with a gorilla's large canines (for stripping forest vegetable food).

The australopiths, we know, were bipeds like modern man, capable of running in the open plains. Their hip and leg bones differ from ours today in some ways, showing that they were less efficient walkers. Nevertheless, some time before five million years ago they had passed a major milestone of change, from tree-hanging, and from using the arms when walking on the ground (like apes), to a free upright gait on an arched foot with an erect torso. Apes can walk this way but poorly: their feet are flat, their great toes protrude and do not help in pushing forward, their knees will not straighten (except in orangs) and their long, high pelvic bones make them top-heavy.

So we now know that definite hominids go back before 5 million B.C., while at the same time our strong likeness to the African apes means that we have a common ancestor at a time not too remote. *Ramapithecus* looks like the beginning of our line, and if he seems very apelike we must remember that it is the human side, not the ape, which has been changing most rapidly. We can be sure our ancestors abandoned trees and a diet of fruit and coarse vegetable matter, perhaps only in the last ten million years or less.

The reasons why we became bipeds are far from clear, though many have speculated. Even now we cannot run very fast: on uneven ground a gorilla, using the knuckles of his hands in running, can go as fast. We can, however, cover long distances in hunting, but could the first bipeds do so? Carrying food in the arms to a safe eating place might have encouraged uprightness: so might the need of a small animal to rise and peer over tall grass.

Perhaps, in our tree life, we became adapted to uprightness, as did apes, but not to such a degree that, as in apes, a heavy torso and long arms encouraged throwing part of our weight on our

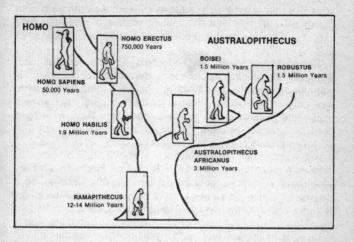

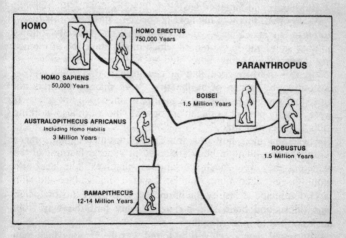

Figure 1. Two views of the phylogenetic (evolutionary) relationships of the australopithecines to *Homo*. Upper chart shows the australopithecines as an extinct dead end, paralleling the evolution of *Ramapithecus* to *Homo habilis* and thence on to true humans, *Homo erectus*. Lower chart shows one kind of australopithecine, africanus (also including *Homo habilis*) as ancestral to *Homo erectus*, with the more robust australopithecines as off the main line of evolution. New "habilis" discoveries make the upper chart more likely than previously believed.

arms. Perhaps several such factors combined; we cannot say. But bipeds we were by about five million years ago, with important changes still going on in hip bones and feet to make this kind of gait more effective.

The australopiths are our undoubted ancestors at that time; there are no other possible candidates. Once again, there is controversy over the actual path of evolution. Some think there was only one varied species of australopith, not two distinct lines. And in former days it was assumed that there must have been a "cerebral rubicon," a magic brain size of about 750 cubic centimeters below which an ancestor could not be "human."

But simple stone tools, which are over two million years old, have now been found near Lake Rudolf in East Africa. They could have been made only by the australopiths since no more "advanced" men are known to have existed then; and the brains of these australopiths were not larger than a chimpanzee's. So shaped stone tools did not wait for "man" to make them, and it is thought likely that tools actually helped the australopiths to become "man," by accenting the evolutionary advantages of skilful hands and larger brains.[1]

At any rate, this was the next major step, the advent of *Homo erectus*. His appearance, about 1 million B.C., probably follows another small gap in the record which might make the difference from *Australopithecus* more obvious. "*Homo*," a new genus, recognizes the difference, and the new group. Also *Homo erectus* is commonly spoken of as the first "true man," but it is not clear that such an expression is justified, since many of his traits were already present in the australopiths, who were also working tools at an earlier time.

These new men, however, must have presented an appearance more like our own. In body size, and in general features of the skeleton, they were much the same as ourselves. The head also would have looked more "human," with a smaller face and with jaws dominated at last by the braincase. However, this braincase was thick, and brain size had come only half the way from australopiths to modern man.

The first *Homo erectus* to be found was the famous Java man (originally named *Pithecanthropus*), of 1891. He caused a scientific explosion, as the first really primitive man to come to light,

[1] Some of these same australopiths, before the tools were found, had already been classed by Leaky and others as very early "men," or *Homo*, and, following a suggestion of Professor Dart, were named *Homo habilis*, with the sense of being "good with the hands." We shall come back to this.

and even his own discoverer came to think that he was really a large tree-living ape. He reigned virtually alone (very recently five new examples of his skull have been found) until the Peking men of north China were discovered, but *Homo erectus* is now recognized from East and North Africa, and in Hungary (Vértesszöllös) and Germany (the Heidelberg jaw).

We know little about the transition to *Homo erectus*, or where it took place. Writers like to argue for either Africa or Asia as the "home of man," but this may not be important. *Ramapithecus* probably reached India from Africa ten million years ago at least, and after that there must have been hominids in both continents, at the stage of *Australopithecus*. It happens that their remains so far have been found mostly in Africa, in favourable spots like Olduvai Gorge.

We have a few suggestions of what occurred. The large-jawed *Paranthropus* seems to have changed hardly at all during three million years or more. The site of Swartkrans, in South Africa, yielded many of his known fossil parts. It also provided two or three jaw fragments, of the same age, which Broom and Robinson twenty years ago believed to be different from *Paranthropus*, and more advanced in form. They christened the type "Telanthropus," though Robinson later decided that the parts belonged to *Homo erectus*. In either case, two different hominids were there together, one being *Paranthropus* and the other a more advanced kind. Here is a powerful argument for the real existence of two different forms at the same time.

A few years ago, by an almost magic piece of luck, three men were looking over these and other fragments in the collections in Pretoria when they noticed broken edges which could be fitted together to make larger pieces, where this had not been seen before.

They were able to join the "Telanthropus" upper jaw to much of a face, an ear region, and a bit of forehead. (Palaeontology, I said, is not just a matter of looking in river banks.) This gave most of the face and front of the skull, to which the lower jaw of "Telanthropus" would have been a fairly good fit. The whole thing suggests *Homo* even more strongly than before, but seems to be too small in size.

At about the same time Mrs. Leakey found a small crushed skull in the lowest levels of Olduvai Gorge, below the well-known *Zinjanthropus* (a *Paranthropus*) and dated to not quite two million years. This was only the latest in a series of similar finds from Olduvai, all of which had been called *Homo habilis* by Leakey and his associates. Though fragmentary, they were obviously not *Paranthropus*, having higher skulls and smaller jaws, and to many they suggested the smaller South African form *Australopithecus*.

After a great deal of work, the new skull was put together. This and the reconstructed "Telanthropus" give us a better picture; they are somewhat more advanced than the known *Australopithecus* but are still very small for *Homo*. They may well be showing us the ancestor who had just begun to make stone tools and who, in the next million years, turned into *Homo*.

Again, controversy. Some prefer to call this little person *Homo habilis*, in the belief that both *Australopithecus* and *Paranthropus* became extinct, and that this graceful little creature developed directly into high-skulled, large-brained *Homo sapiens* without passing through the stage of low-browed, thick-skulled *Homo erectus*.

But this raises the problem of who might have been the ancestor of *Homo habilis*, unless it was *Australopithecus*, whom he greatly resembles; and also the problem of why remains of only *Homo erectus* have been found for the period immediately after. It seems safer to assume, for the present, that the *Australopithecus* line began making simple tools nearly two and one-half million years ago and, during a time from which we have almost no fossils, grew larger in size and advanced to the *erectus* stage, while *Paranthropus* continued contentedly munching coarse vegetable food with his great jaws, ignoring tools, until he became extinct.

If the first *Homo erectus* to be found, the Java Man, was considered in the 1890s to be very subhuman, we know better now. In Africa, and evidently in Europe, he made large stone handaxes, or coups de poing, increasingly well-shaped in comparison with the earlier pebble tools.

We do not really know about how he used them. All we can say is that he occupied the warmer parts of the Old World for at least half a million years (and even some cool places in Europe and China), as the major glacial periods were beginning; and that in this time he showed some evolutionary progress in brains which became larger and skulls and jaws which became less massive.

At the moment, he may now seem more like a well-defined "stage" than he should, because we not only lack fossils from the period just before, but also have very few from the hundreds of thousands of years following the second (Mindel) glaciation.

Change doubtless went on by small steps during these times, but we cannot see the steps just now.

The Swanscombe and Steinheim skulls, of the Second Inter-glacial, perhaps 250,000 years ago, and the new Tautavel skull from the early Third Glacial, are important. They are much advanced over the known *erectus* men, but they are still too few to help us much, or show what was happening worldwide. It is only in the Third Interglacial and the last, or Fourth Glacial, mainly within the last hundred thousand years, that we come again to a wealth of fossil men, and to the Neanderthal problem, the greatest controversy of all.

When the first of the Neanderthals was reported in 1856, he too was thought to be subhuman by some, but only an exceptional modern man, possibly a diseased person, by others (the first controversy, now forgotten). A Neanderthal skull is indeed exceptional, being very long and low, with a continuous protruding bony browridge across the forehead containing well-developed sinuses or air spaces. But the skull contours are not those of *Homo erectus*, and the brain was at least as large as our own.

Neanderthal man's face was equally remarkable; it was long, protruding sharply forward in the midline from the top of the nose on down. Had his nose not been so broad we might call him "hatchet-faced," but modern "hatchet-faced" north Europeans are apt to be tall and slender, while the Neanderthals of Europe were short and stocky.

Controversy over primitiveness and antiquity did not last long. Today we know that Neanderthal man occupied Europe in the Third Interglacial and much of the Fourth Glacial periods (perhaps between 150,000 and 35,000 B.C.), and that he was the author of the Mousterian varieties of retouched flake stone tool, which were technically far advanced over something like a handaxe. These tools in some ways foreshadowed those of the Upper Paleolithic, which were made from blade-like flakes and were used by Cro-Magnon man among others.

For a hundred years now, discoveries of skeletons of the European Neanderthals have given rise to a conception of his "classic" form as I have described it. They have also reinforced the conclusion that he gave way, with seeming abruptness, about 35,000 B.C. to men who were entirely modern in physique, though robust, and who were in fact like living Europeans.

This is the heart of the modern controversy, with strong opinions on both sides. I have stated the distinctiveness of Neanderthal man too simply and sharply, in order to begin with a contrast. In North Africa there were other Neanderthal-like men, more modern, in some ways, lacking the typical facial projection of the Europeans. They too were followed by modern men of rugged build, apparently coming from the east about the same time (35,000 B.C.), or perhaps earlier.

The Near East is more puzzling. Men with Neanderthal faces, and with Neanderthal peculiarities of the skeleton, existed in the early Fourth Glacial, with Mousterian tools. But their skulls were not as "classic" as the Europeans, and some of them were remarkably tall, like the Amud man of Israel, found by Japanese excavators. (Here we must remember that modern men vary greatly—Scots and Eskimos might be compared to these Neanderthals in body size.)

The argument is over whether the Neanderthals, in Europe or elsewhere, were in fact replaced by invaders, with really new Upper Palaeolithic methods of tool-making, in a brief period (a few thousand years); or whether the Neanderthals simply evolved into modern man on the spot, while his stoneworking, adopting new techniques, made the changes from what is termed Mousterian to what is termed Upper Palaeolithic.

It is a complex argument, and is based partly on assumptions (and, I believe, partly on tides of scientific opinion, like older arguments). In spite of all that is known, ways of convincing opponents have not been found. Some archaeologists emphasize transition in tool-making. Other archaeologists grant that there are important Mousterian survivals in the early Perigordian culture of the Upper Palaeolithic of France. But they see a clear break with the coming of a second culture, the Aurignacian, which has different tool-making techniques and also a wealth of decorative objects previously lacking. This they view as something entirely new, an intrusion; and they cannot imagine a simple cultural evolution.

Similarly, some anthropologists cannot imagine biological evolution so swift as to produce a modern face and skull from that of Neanderthal man in a few thousand years. Others are doubtful about the shortness of period, and emphasize intergradation in shape between Neanderthal and modern man, especially in the east. They hold that evolution, not replacement, presents fewer difficulties. They note that if there was an invasion, the source of the "modern" Upper Palaeolithic men has not been found and that, if the European Neanderthals are rather special, the Near Eastern Neanderthals are more intermediate and "progressive."

These scholars would paint a rather simple picture of human history, probably too simple. They suggest that there was everywhere a "Neanderthal phase" of human evolution in the last glacial period, out of which all of us—Eskimos and Scots alike—emerged as modern man. This broad view assumes that there were Neanderthal men everywhere in the Old World, as there certainly were throughout Europe and apparently around its edges.

Carleton Coon, in a well-known book, *The Origin of Races*, has argued for another theory something like this one. Modern races appeared in different parts of the Old World, not from a single Neanderthal population, but from different races of *Homo erectus* already present in these places.

There are difficulties here, but the theory does recognize something important which the other scholars neglect: that there were other kinds of Ice Age men, such as Solo Man of Java and Broken Hill Man ("Rhodesian Man") of southern Africa, who had some of the primitive traits of Neanderthal man but were really quite different. They are less well known: they are discoveries, or facts, which are still hard to interpret. Solo Man, though living at the same time as the Neanderthals, had a much thicker and cruder skull, more like *Homo erectus*.

There is a final chapter to all this. What *do* we know about modern man himself? Living races seem very different, some with very dark skin, some with blond hair, some with narrowed eye openings. But in form of skull (and this is what we can compare with early man) they are really much alike, with smaller faces and higher, narrower braincases. This is my own conclusion, after having worked with skulls from all parts of the globe. I believe, as do many colleagues, that all must have some common source. But where, and when?

Here we are in a shadowland lighted by too few discoveries. Outside of Europe, where we observe the disappearance of Neanderthal man, remains are especially scanty. Nevertheless, striking recent finds seem to mean that *Homo sapiens* of our own kind existed elsewhere, in Africa and Asia, in the same period as the Neanderthals of Europe.

They are different from those "progressive" Neanderthals I spoke of. Several skeletons from Jebel Qafzeh, in Israel, have no radiocarbon date but come from cave levels in which the tools and the soils indicate a time fairly early in the last glacial period, probably well before forty thousand years ago. And the skulls are surprisingly modern—not completely so, but being quite different from Neanderthals. Only the large bony brows, and perhaps larger front teeth, in some of them, suggest Neanderthal man, and others of the tribe had quite small teeth, and smaller, modern brows and faces as well, as far as is now known.

Two skulls found by Richard Leakey in Kenya, of modern form or close to it—and not Neanderthal—are surely older than thirty seven thousand years. Some authorities think they may be very much older. Far to the east a skull from the Niah Cave in Sarawak (Borneo) has been dated by two methods to about 40,000 B.C., and it looks like a Melanesian or possibly an Australian.

Modern men of the same general kind had made the difficult water crossings (difficult for early men) to Australia before 30,000 B.C., and many recent discoveries attest the presence of such people there and in New Guinea over the next ten thousand years. In the New World, recent finds prove the Indians were in South America about twenty thousand years ago, much earlier than had been generally believed, so that men had come to the Americas from Asia probably several thousand years before. No American skeletons are as old as this, but we can only suppose that these earlier men were like the later.

Now here is the important thing. All the known skeletons I have mentioned were of modern form. In addition, the European Upper Palaeolithic people had the nature of later Europeans; the early Australians were recognizably like later Australians or Melanesians; and we can only suppose that the first Indians of America were the same kind of proto-Mongoloid we see in them today.

The Omo skulls of Africa cannot be recognized yet, and otherwise there are no African skulls quite so old. But the signs are that, by the time the Neanderthals vanished, or before, not only was modern man fairly widespread, but the races we see today had already taken shape.

We still cannot say how this happened. It is strange that we should know so little of our nearest ancestors. But we cannot expect to have the whole story after only one century of searching. There are blank parts of our history now, but they will be filled: we have hundreds of years of exploration ahead of us.

The Golden Marshalltown:
A Parable for the Archeology
of the 1980s

by
Kent V. Flannery

> I am happily too busy *doing* science to have time to
> worry about philosophizing about it.
>   Arno Penzias, nobel laureate, 1978

THIS IS A story about archeological goals and rewards, and no
one should look for anything too profound in it. It's really just
the story of a ride I took on an airplane from San Diego to
Detroit. That may not sound very exciting to those of you who
fly a lot, but this particular trip was memorable for me. For
one thing, it was my first time on a 747. For another, I met
someone on that plane who became one of the most unforgetta-
ble characters I've ever run across.

The flight was taking me home to Ann Arbor after the Society
for American Archaeology meetings in May of 1981. I was
leaving San Diego a day early because I had endured all the
physical stress I could stand. I didn't particularly feel like watching the movie, so as soon as the plane was airborne and the seat
belt sign had been turned off, I went forward to the lounge area
of the plane. There were only two people there, both archeologists,
and both recognized me from the meetings. So I had no choice
but to sit down and have a beer with them.

I want to begin by telling you a little about my two companions,
but you have to understand, I'm not going to give their actual
names. Besides, their real identities aren't important, because
each considers himself the spokesman for a large group of
people.

Reprinted from *American Anthropologist*, 84 (1982), pp. 265–278, by
permission of the author and the American Anthropological Association.

The first guy, I suppose, came out of graduate school in the late 1960s, and he teaches now at a major department in the western United States. He began as a traditional archeologist, interested in Pueblo ruins and Southwestern prehistory, and he went on digs and surveys like the rest of us. Unlike the rest of us, he saw those digs and surveys not as an end in themselves, but as a means to an end, and a means that proved to be too slow. After a few years of dusty holes in hot, dreary valleys he was no closer to the top than when he had started, and in fact, he was showing signs of lamentable fallibility. In fifty tries at laying out a five-ft square, he had never come closer than four feet ten inches by five feet three inches, and he'd missed more floors than the elevator in the World Trade Center. And then, just when all seemed darkest, he discovered Philosophy of Science, and was born again.

Suddenly he found the world would beat a path to his door if he criticized everyone else's epistemology. Suddenly he discovered that so long as his research design was superb, he never had to do the research; just publish the design, and it would be held up as a model, a brass ring hanging unattainable beyond the clumsy fingers of those who actually survey and dig. No more dust, no more heat, no more five-ft squares. He worked in an office now, generating hypotheses and laws and models which an endless stream of graduate students was sent out to test; for he himself no longer did any fieldwork.

And it was just as well, for as one of his former professors had said, "That poor wimp couldn't dig his way out of a kitty litter box."

In all fairness to the Born-Again Philosopher, he was in large measure a product of the 1960s, and there are lots more like him where he came from. And let us not judge him too harshly until we have examined my other companion in the lounge, a young man whose degree came not from 1968, but from 1978. I will refer to him simply as the Child of the Seventies.

Like so many of his academic generation, the Child of the Seventies had but one outstanding characteristic: blind ambition. He had neither the commitment to culture history of my generation nor the devotion to theory of the generation of the 1960s. His goals were simple: to be famous, to be well paid, to be stroked, and to receive immediate gratification. How he got there did not matter. Who he stepped on along the way did not matter. Indeed, the data of prehistory did not matter. For him, archeology was only a vehicle— one carefully selected, because he had discovered early that people will put up with almost anything in the guise of archeology.

As a graduate student, the Child of the Seventies had taken a course in introductory archeology from a man I will simply refer to as Professor H. Professor H. worked very hard on the course, synthesizing the literature, adding original ideas and a lot of his own unpublished data. The Child of the Seventies took copious notes. Sometimes he asked questions to draw the instructor out, and sometimes he asked if he could copy Professor H.'s slides. When the professor used handouts, he bound them in his notebook.

At graduation, the Child of the Seventies went off to his first job at Springboard University. The day he arrived, he went directly to Springboard University Press and asked if they would like a textbook on introductory archeology. Of course they did. The Child polished his notes from Professor H.'s course and submitted them as a book. It was published to rave reviews. Today it is the only textbook on the subject that Professor H. really likes, and he requires it in his course. The faculty at Springboard overwhelmingly voted the Child of the Seventies tenure. Professor H., on the other hand, has been held back because he hasn't published enough. "He's a great teacher," his colleagues say. "If only he could write more. Like that student of his at Springboard U."

To his credit as an anthropologist, the child had merely discerned that our subculture not only tolerates this sort of behavior, it *rewards* people for it. But the story doesn't end there.

The Child of the Seventies had written a six-chapter doctoral dissertation. Now he xeroxed each chapter and provided it with an introduction and conclusion, making it a separate article. Each was submitted to a different journal, and all were published within a year. He then persuaded Springboard University Press to publish a reader composed of his six reprinted works. In that reader, the chapters of his dissertation were at last reunited between hard covers. He added an overview, recounting the ways his perspective had changed as he looked back over the full sweep of his eighteen months as a professional archeologist.

His publisher asked him to do another reader. This time, he invited six colleagues to write the various chapters. Some were flattered. Some were desperate. All accepted. He wrote a three-page introduction and put his name on the cover as editor. The book sold. And suddenly, his path to the top was clear: he could turn out a book a year, using the original ideas of others, without ever having an original idea himself. And in the long run, he would be better known and better paid than any of his contributors, even though they worked twice as hard.

I ordered a Michelob, and paid my buck-fifty a can, and sat wondering exactly what I could say to these two guys. It isn't easy when you know that one will criticize any idea you put forth, and the other will incorporate it into his next book. Fortunately I never had to say anything, for it was at exactly that moment that the third, and most important, character of this story entered the lounge.

He stood for a moment with his battered carryon bag in his hand, looking down at the three of us. He was an Old Timer—no question about that—but how old would have been anybody's guess. When you're that tanned and weather-beaten you could be fifty, or sixty, or even seventy, and no one could really tell. His jeans had been through the mud and the barbed-wire fences of countless field seasons, his hat had faded in the prairie sun, and his eyes had the kind of crow's feet known locally as the High Plains squint. I could tell he was an archeologist by his boots, and I could tell he was still a good archeologist by the muscle tone in his legs.

(You see, I have a colleague at Michigan—an ethnologist—who claims that since archeologists have strong backs and weak minds, when an archeologist starts to fade, it's the legs that go first. On the other hand, his wife informs me that when an ethnologist starts to fade, the first thing to go is not his legs.)

The Old Timer settled into the seat next to me, stowed his carryon bag, and turned to introduce himself. I failed to catch his name because the stewardess, somewhat out of breath, caught up with him at that moment and pressed a bourbon and water into his hand. "Thank you, ma'am," he said, sipping it down; and he stared for a moment, and said, "I needed that. And that's the God's truth."

"I know what you mean," I said. "The meetings can do that to you. Six hundred people crammed into the lobby of a hotel. Two hundred are talking down to you as if you're an idiot. Two hundred are sucking up to you as if you're a movie star. Two hundred are telling you lies, and all the while they're looking over your shoulder, hoping they'll meet somebody more important."

"This year it was worse than that, son. Last night my department retired me. Turned me out to pasture."

"I wouldn't have guessed you were retirement age," I lied.

"I'm not. I had two years to go. But they retired me early. Mostly because of an article in the *New York Times Sunday Magazine* by an ethnologist, Eric Wolf. You remember that one?"

"I read it," I said, "but I don't remember him calling for your retirement."

The Old Timer reached into his pocket, past a half-empty pouch of Bull Durham, and brought out a yellowed clipping from the *Sunday Times* of November 30, 1980. I caught a glimpse of Wolf's byline, and below it, several paragraphs outlined in red ink. "See what he says here," said the Old Timer.

An earlier anthropology had achieved unity under the aegis of the culture concept. It was culture, in the view of anthropologists, that distinguished humankind from all the rest of the universe, and it was the possession of varying cultures that differentiated one society from another. . . . The past quarter-century has undermined this intellectual sense of security. The relatively inchoate concept of "culture" was attacked from several theoretical directions. As the social sciences transformed themselves into "behavioral" sciences, explanations for behavior were no longer traced to culture; behavior was to be understood in terms of psychological encounters, strategies of economic choice, strivings for payoffs in games of power. Culture, once extended to all acts and ideas employed in social life, was now relegated to the margins as "world view" or "values." [Wolf 1980]

"Isn't that something?" said the Old Timer. "The day that came out my department called me in. The chairman says, 'It has come to our attention that you still believe in culture as the central paradigm in archeology.' I told him yes, I supposed I did. Then he says, 'We've talked about it, and we all think you ought to take early retirement.' "

"But that's terrible. You should have fought it."

"I *did* fight it," he said. "But they got my file together and sent it out for an outside review. Lord, they sent it to all these distinguished anthropologists. Marvin Harris. Clifford Geertz. And aren't there a couple of guys at Harvard with hyphenated names?"

"At least a couple," I assured him.

"Well, they sent my file to one of them. And to some Big Honcho social anthropologist at the University of Chicago. And the letters started coming back.

"Harris said he was shocked to see that in spite of the fact that I was an archeologist, I had paid so little attention to the techno-eco-demo-environmental variables. Geertz said as far as he could tell, all I was doing was Thick Description. The guy from Harvard said he wasn't sure he could evaluate me, because he'd never even heard of our department."

"And how about the guy from Chicago?"

"He said that he felt archeology could best be handled by one of the local trade schools."

There was a moment of silence while we all contemplated the heartbreak of an archeologist forced into early retirement by his belief in culture. In the background we could hear our pilot announcing that the Salton Sea was visible off to the right of the aircraft.

"They sure gave me a nice retirement party, though," said the Old Timer. "Rented a whole suite at the hotel. And I want to show you what they gave me as a going-away present."

His hand groped for a moment in the depths of his battle-scarred overnight bag, and suddenly he produced a trowel. A trowel such as no one had ever seen. A trowel that turned to yellow flame in the rays of the setting sun as he held it up to the window of the 747.

"This was my first Marshalltown trowel," he said. "You know what an archeologist's first Marshalltown is like? Like a major leaguer's first Wilson glove. I dug at Pecos with this trowel, under A. V. Kidder. And at Aztec Ruin with Earl Morris. And at Kincaid with Fay-Cooper Cole. And at Lindenmeier with Frank Roberts. Son, this trowel's been at Snaketown, and Angel Mound, and at the Dalles of the Columbia with Luther Cressman.

"And then one night, these guys from my department broke into my office and borrowed it, so to speak. And the next time I saw it, they'd had that sucker plated in 24-karat gold.

"It sure is pretty now. And that's the God's truth."

The trowel passed from hand to hand around our little group before returning to the depths of the Old Timer's bag. And for each of us, I suppose, it made that unimaginably far-off day of retirement just a little bit less remote.

"What do you think you'll do now?" asked the Child of the Seventies, for whom retirement would not come until the year 2018.

"Well," said the Old Timer, "so far the only thing that's opened up for me are some offers to do contract archeology."

The Born-Again Philosopher snickered condescendingly.

"I take it," said the Old Timer, "you have some reservations about contract archeology."

"Oh, it's all right, I suppose," said the Philosopher. "I just don't think it has much of a contribution to make to *my* field."

"And what would that field be?"

"Method and theory."

"No particular region or time period?"

"No. I wouldn't want to be tied down to a specific region. I work on a higher level of abstraction."

"I'll bet you do," said the Old Timer. "Well, son, there are some things about contract archeology I don't like either. Occasional compromises between scientific goals and industrial goals. Too many reports that get mimeographed for the president of some construction company, rather than being published where archeologists can read them. But in all fairness, most of the contract archeologists I know express just as strong an interest in method and theory as you do."

"But they're law *consumers*," said the Philosopher. "I'm committed to being a law *producer*."

The Old Timer took a thoughtful drag on his bourbon. "Son," he said, "I admire a man who dispenses with false modesty. But you've overlooked what I see as one of the strengths of contract archeologists: they still deal directly with what happened in prehistory. If I want to know what happened in Glen Canyon, or when agriculture reached the Missouri Basin, or how long the mammoth hunters lasted in Pennsylvania, often as not I need to talk to a contract archeologist. Because the answers to the cultural-historical questions don't always lie on a 'higher level of abstraction.' "

"No," said the Born-Again Philosopher. "Only the *important* questions lie on that level."

There was an interruption as the stewardess reappeared before us, pushing an aluminum beverage cart. We ordered another round of beer, and she picked up our empty cans, depositing them in a plastic trash bag attached to the cart.

"I'd like to ask a favor," said the Born-Again Philosopher. "Before our 10-minute stopover in Tucson, I'd like to examine the contents of that bag."

"Now I've heard everything," said the stewardess.

"No, it's not a come-on," said the Philosopher. "It's a favor for a friend. I have a colleague, Bill Rathje, who's doing a study of garbage disposal patterns in the city of Tucson [Rathje 1974]. He's got the internal system pretty well mapped out, but he realizes that Tucson is not a closed system: garbage enters and leaves via planes, cars, and backpacks. I promised him if I were ever on a plane landing or taking off from Tucson, I'd sample the refuse on board."

The stewardess struggled to remove all trace of emotion from her face. "Well," she said, "I suppose if you clean up everything when you're done—."

"I'll be checking the refuse in the tourist-class cabin," said the Philosopher, "while my friend here" (indicating the Child of the Seventies) "will be checking the first-class cabin, and coauthoring the paper with me."

"And what do you call your profession?" she asked.

"Archeology."

"You guys are weird," she called over her shoulder as she and the cart disappeared down the aisle.

The Born-Again Philosopher settled back in his seat with a pleased smile on his face. "Now there's a perfect example of why archeologists should not restrict themselves to the study of ancient objects lying on the surface or underneath the ground. If we're to develop a truly universal set of covering laws, we must be free to derive them from any source we can.

"In my opinion," he said, "the greatest legacy we can leave the next generation is a body of robust archeological theory."

"Well, son, I'll give you my opinion," said the Old Timer. "I don't believe there's any such thing as 'archeological theory.' For me there's only *anthropological* theory. Archeologists have their own methodology, and ethnologists have theirs; but when it comes to theory, we all ought to sound like anthropologists."

"My God, are you out of it!" said the Born-Again Philosopher. "For ten years we've been building up a body of purely archeological laws. I myself have contributed ten or twenty."

"I'd love to hear a few," I said. And I could see I was not the only one: the Child of the Seventies was getting ready to write them down unobtrusively on his cocktail napkin.

"Number One," said the Philosopher: "Prehistoric people did not leave behind in the site examples of everything they made. Number Two: Some of the things they did leave behind disintegrated, and cannot be found by archeologists."

"I don't want to sound unappreciative," I said, "but I believe Schliemann already knew that when he was digging at Troy."

"If he did," said the B.A.P., "he never made it *explicit*. I have made it *explicit*."

"Son," said the Old Timer, "I guess we can all sleep easier tonight because of that."

"I also came up with the following," the Philosopher went on. "Number Three: Objects left on a sloping archeological site wash downhill. Number Four: Lighter objects wash downhill farther than heavy objects."

"Hold it right there, son," said the Old Timer, "because you've just illustrated a point I was hoping to make. So often these things you fellows call archeological laws turn out not to be laws of human behavior, but examples of the physical processes involved in the formation of sites. And son, those are no more than the products of *geological* laws."

The Born-Again Philosopher's face lit up in a triumphant smile. "That objection has been raised many times before," he said, "and it was disposed of definitively by Richard Watson, who is both a geologist and a philosopher. In his 1976 *American Antiquity* article, Watson (1976:65) makes it clear (and here I am paraphrasing) that even when hypotheses are directly dependent on laws of geology, they are specifically archeological *when they pertain to archeological materials.*"

Now it was the Old Timer's turn to smile. "Oh. Well. That's different," he said. "In that case, I guess, archeology just barely missed out on a major law."

"How's that?" asked the Child of the Seventies earnestly, his pencil at the ready.

"Well, following your argument, the Law of Uniform Acceleration could have been an archeological law if only Galileo had dropped a metate and mano from the Leaning Tower of Pisa."

"I don't think you're taking this seriously," the Born-Again Philosopher complained.

"Son," said the Old Timer, "I'm taking it fully as seriously as it deserves to be taken. And as far as I'm concerned, so far the only legitimate archeological law I know of is the Moss-Bennett Bill."

The Born-Again Philosopher drew himself erect. "I think I'd better go back and start my inventory of the tourist-class trash," he said, and he began working his way down the aisle toward the galley.

"You're being awfully hard on him," said the Child of the Seventies. "You have to remember that he's the spokesman for a large number of theoretical archeologists who hope to increase archeology's contribution to science and philosophy."

The Old Timer took a long, slow pull on his bourbon. "Son, do you watch Monday Night Football?" he asked.

"Occasionally," said the Child. "When I'm not correcting page proofs."

"I have a reason for asking," said the Old Timer. "I just want to try out an analogy on you.

"During Monday Night Football there are twenty-two players on the field, two coaches on the sidelines, and three people in the broadcast booth. Two of the people in the booth are former players who can no longer play. One of the people in the booth never played a lick in his life. And who do you suppose talks the loudest and is the most critical of the players on the field?''

"The guy who never played a lick," I interrupted. "And the guys with him, the former players, are always saying things like, 'Well, it's easy to criticize from up here, but it's different when you're down on the field.' "

"Well said, son," the Old Timer chuckled. "And I want you to consider the symbolism for a moment. The field is lower than everything else; it's physical, it's sweaty, it's a place where people follow orders. The press box is high, detached, Olympian, cerebral. And it's verbal. Lord, is it verbal.

"Now football is a game of strategy, of game plans (or 'research designs,' if you will), and what are called differing philosophies. In our lifetime we've witnessed great innovations in strategy: the nickel defense, the flex, the shotgun, the wishbone—and the list goes on. How many of them were created in the press box?"

"None," I said. "They were created by coaches."

"By coaches, many of them former players, who are still personally involved in the game, and who diligently study their own mistakes, create new strategies, and return to the field to test them in combat," said the Old Timer.

"I think I see what you're driving at," said the Child of the Seventies, but we knew he was lying.

"There are estimated to be more than four thousand practicing archeologists in the United States," said the Old Timer. "Most of them are players. Sure, many of us are second- or third-string, but when we're called upon to go in, we do the best we can. And we rely on the advice and strategy of a fair number of archeological 'coaches'—veterans, people we respect because they've paid their dues the same as we have.

"What's happening now is that we're getting a new breed of archeologist. A kind of archeological Howard Cosell. He sits in a booth high above the field, and cites Hempel and Kuhn and Karl Popper. He second-guesses our strategy, and tells us when we don't live up to his expectations. 'Lew Binford,' he says, 'once the fastest mind in the field, but frankly, this season he may have lost a step or two.' Or, 'It's shocking to see a veteran like Struever make a rookie mistake like that.'

"What I worry about, son, is that every year there'll be fewer people down on the field and more up in the booth. There's a great living to be made in the booth, but it's a place that breeds a great deal of arrogance. No one in the booth ever fumbles a punt or, for that matter, misclassifies a potsherd or screws up a profile

drawing. They pass judgment on others, but never expose themselves to criticism. The guys in the booth get a lot of exposure,
and some even achieve celebrity status. What rarely gets pointed
out is that the guys in the booth have had little if any strategic
and theoretical impact on the game, because they're too far
removed from the field of play.

"But the players know that. Especially the contract archeologists,
and those of us who perennially work in the field. Because we
have the feeling the guys in the booth look down on us as a
bunch of dumb, sweaty jocks. And we're damn sick of it, son,
and that's the God's truth."

"But you surely don't deny the importance of theory in
archeology," said the Child of the Seventies. "I'm sure you've
used what Binford [1977] calls middle-range theory in your own
work."

"Of course," said the Old Timer. "I've used it to organize
and make sense out of my data. Which is, when you stop to
think about it, one of the main purposes for theory. The problem
came when the guys in the booth began to think of 'archeological
theory' as a subdiscipline in its own right—a higher and more
prestigious calling than the pursuit of data on prehistory, which
they see as a form of manual labor. As if that weren't bad
enough, some of them are now beginning to think of themselves
as philosophers of science."

"I find that exciting," said the Child of the Seventies.

"Son," said the Old Timer, "it *would* be exciting, if they
were any good at it. Unfortunately, in most cases, it's the only
thing they're worse at than field archeology."

"But some are establishing a dialogue with philosophers,"
said the Child.

"That's right," said the Old Timer. "Now we're going to
have philosophers who don't know anything about archeology,
advising archeologists who don't know anything about philosophy."

"They want archeology to make a contribution to philosophy,"
said the Child.

"I'll tell you what," said the Old Timer. "I'd settle for
making a contribution to *archeology*. I guess I'd rather be a
second-rate archeologist than a third-rate philosopher."

"But doesn't archeology have more to offer the world than
that?"

The Old Timer leaned back in his seat and sipped at his
bourbon. "That's a good question," he said. "We hear a lot
about archeology's relevance to anthropology in general. To the
social sciences. To the world. And of course, we're all waiting

for our recently departed friend to come up with his first Great Law. But I'd like to turn the question around and ask What does the world really want from archeology?

"If I turn on television, or walk through a paperback bookstore, I'll tell you what I see. I see that what the world wants is for archeology to teach it something about humanity's past. The world doesn't want epistemology from us. They want to hear about Olduvai Gorge, and Stonehenge, and Macchu Picchu. People are gradually becoming aware that their first three million years took place before written history, and they look to archeology as the only science—the *only one*—with the power to uncover that past.

"I remember Bill Sanders telling me once that the only legitimate reason to do archeology was to satisfy your intellectual curiosity. And I suspect that if we just try to do a good job at that, the more general contributions will follow naturally. I don't think Isaac Newton or Gregor Mendel ran around saying 'I'm a law producer.' Their laws grew unself-consciously out of their efforts to satisfy their own curiosity.

"Son, if the world wants philosophy, it will surely turn to philosophers, not archeologists, to get it. I'd hate to see us get so confused about what the world wants from archeology that we turn our backs on what we do best. In my opinion, our major responsibility to the rest of the world is to do good, basic archeological research."

"You know," said the Child of the Seventies, "as I listen to you talk, I'm thinking how nice it would be to have you write an overview for the book I'm editing right now. A book on future directions in archeology."

"I'm not sure how excited I am about some of the future directions," said the Old Timer.

"That's why your overview would give us needed balance," said the Child. "Why, you're our link with the past. You've stepped right out of the pages of archeology's rich, much maligned empiricist tradition."

"You overestimate me, son."

"No. You're too modest," said the Child, who was not used to being turned down. "I feel that you may well be the most significant figure of your generation, and I'd consider myself deeply honored to have your overview in my book."

"Horsefeathers," said the Old Timer.

The Child of the Seventies stood up with a gesture of frustration. "I've got to inventory the trash in the first-class cabin, or I won't get to coauthor that article," he said. "But think over what I said. And don't say anything important until I get back."

We watched him disappear through the curtain into the first-class section.

"You must have been inoculated against soft soap," I told the Old Timer.

"Son," he said, "if that young fellow's nose were any browner, we'd need a Munsell Soil Color Chart to classify it."

"If you think he's at all atypical," I suggested, "take a good look around you at the next archeology meeting."

"And you know," said the Old Timer, "we're partly to blame for that. All of us in academic departments.

"We hire a young guy, right out of graduate school, and we give him all our introductory courses to teach. Then we tell him it's publish or perish. His only choices are to write something half-baked, or make an article out of an attack on some already established figure. You take those two kinds of papers out of *American Antiquity*, and you got nothing left but the book reviews.

"What we *ought* to do, if we really want these young people to grow, is give them their first year off, so they can go collect their own data and make their own positive contribution. How can we give them eight courses to teach and then put pressure on them to publish?"

"You're right," I said. "But our two friends here have discovered how to beat the system. One has created a specialty that never requires him to leave his office, and the other has figured out how to get other people to write his books for him. And we reward both of them for it."

"But not without some reservations," said the Old Timer. "You know, archeologists don't really like having a colleague who's so ambitious he'd kick his own grandmother's teeth in to get ahead. Businessmen, or perhaps show-business people, will tolerate it. They'll say, 'He's a real S.O.B., but he gets things done.' But archeologists don't want a colleague who's a real S.O.B. They're funny that way."

The stewardess with the beverage cart paused by our seats for a moment to see if we needed a refill. We did. And I took that opportunity to ask how our friends were coming with their inventory of her garbage.

"The one in the aft cabin seems to have hit a snag," she said thoughtfully. "I think he ran into a couple of airsickness bags."

"Well," said the Old Timer, "nobody said fieldwork was easy."

"What are those guys trying to find out, anyway?" she asked.

"As I understand it," I said, "they're trying to provide us with a better basis for archeological interpretation. Since archeologists study the garbage of ancient peoples, they hope to discover principles of garbage discard that will guide us in our work."

The Old Timer's eyes followed the stewardess as she passed through the curtain into the next cabin.

"Son," he said, "I want to hit you with a hypothetical question. Let's say you're working on a sixteenth-century Arikara site in South Dakota. There's lots of garbage—bison scapula hoes, Catlinite pipes, Bijou Hills quartzite, cord-marked pottery— you know the kind of stuff. You got to interpret it. You got an eighteenth-century French account of the Arikara, and you got a report on Tucson's garbage in 1981. Which would you use?"

"I think you already know the answer to that one," I smiled.

"Then why do I have the distinct impression that these two kids would use the report on Tucson's garbage?" he demanded.

"Because *you* still believe in *culture*," I said, "and these kids are only concerned with *behavior*."

"I guess that's right," he said thoughtfully. "I guess I believe in something called 'Arikara culture,' and I think you ought to know something about it if you work on Arikara sites."

"But suppose, as Eric Wolf suggests in that *Times* article, you're one of those people who no longer looks to culture as an explanation for behavior," I suggested. "Suppose you believe that behavior is explained by universal laws, or psychological encounters, or strategies of economic choice. Then it really doesn't matter whether your interpretive framework comes from tribal ethnohistory or twentieth-century industrial America, does it?"

"Nope. And that's sure going to simplify archeology," said the Old Timer. "For one thing, we can forget about having to master the anthropological literature."

He fell silent as the Born-Again Philosopher and the Child of the Seventies returned to their seats, their notebooks filled with behavioral data and their faces flushed with success.

"Did we miss much?" asked the Child.

"Not much," said the Old Timer. "I was just fixing to ask my friend here where he thinks anthropology will go next, now that it no longer has culture as its central paradigm."

"I'm kind of worried about it," I admitted. "Right now I have the impression that anthropology is sort of drifting, like a rudderless ship. I have the feeling it could fragment into a dozen lesser disciplines, with everybody going his own way. Somehow it's not as exciting as it used to be. Enrollments are down all over the country. The job market sucks. I suspect one reason is that anthropology is so lacking in consensus as to what it has to offer, it just can't sell itself compared to more unified and aggressive fields.''

''Doesn't Wolf tell you in his *Times* article what the next central paradigm will be?'' asked the Child of the Seventies. He was hoping for a title for his next book.

''No,'' said the Old Timer. ''He mentions other things people have tried, like cultural materialism, cultural ecology, French structuralism, cognitive and symbolic anthropology, and so on. But you know, none of those approaches involves more than a fraction of the people in the field.''

''But it's useful to have all those approaches,'' I suggested.

''That's the God's truth,'' he agreed. ''But what holds us all together? What keeps us all from pursuing those things until each becomes a separate field in its own right? What is it that makes a guy who works on Maori creation myths continue to talk to a guy who works mainly on Paleoindian stone tools?''

''In my department,'' I said, ''they *don't* talk any more.''

''Nor in mine,'' he said. ''But they used to. And they *used* to talk because however obscure their specialties, they all believe in that 'integrated whole,' that 'body of shared customs, beliefs, and values' that we called culture.''

''That's right,'' I said. ''But now the Paleoindian archeologist would tell you his stone tools were best explained by Optimal Foraging Strategy. And the Maori ethnologist would tell you his creation myths are the expression of a universal logic inside his informants' heads.''

''You know,'' said the Old Timer, ''we've got an ethnologist like that on our faculty. He told me once, 'I'm not interested in anything you can feel, smell, taste, weigh, measure, or count. None of that is real. What's real is in my head.' Kept talking and talking about how what was in his head was what was important. For a long time, I couldn't figure it out.

''Then one day he published his ethnography, and I understood why what was in his head was so important. He'd made up all his data.''

The Born-Again Philosopher stirred restlessly in his seat. ''It's incredible to me,'' he said, ''that you people haven't realized that for more than a decade now the new paradigm has been Logical Positivism. It's hard to see how you can do problem-oriented archeology without it.''

Slowly the Old Timer rolled himself a cigarette. The Child of the Seventies sat up momentarily, leaned forward to watch, then slumped back in his seat with disappointment when he realized it was only Bull Durham.

"Have you considered," said the Old Timer deliberately, "the implications of doing problem-oriented archeology without the concept of culture?"

"Now you're putting us on," said the Philosopher.

For just a moment, the Old Timer allowed himself a smile. "Consider this," he said. "An ethnologist can say, 'I'm only interested in myth and symbolism, and I'm not going to collect data on subsistence.' He can go to a village in the Philippines and ignore the terraced hillsides and the rice paddies and the tilapia ponds, and just ask people about their dreams and the spirits of their ancestors. Whatever he does, however selective he is in what he collects, when he leaves the village, it's still there. And next year, if a Hal Conklin or an Aram Yengoyan comes along, those terraces and paddies and fish ponds will still be there to study.

"But suppose an archeologist were to say, 'I'm only interested in Anasazi myth and symbolism, and I'm not going to collect data on subsistence.' Off he goes to a prehistoric cliff dwelling and begins to dig. He goes for the pictographs, and figurines, and ceremonial staffs, and wooden bird effigies. What, then, does he do with all the digging sticks, and tumplines, and deer bones that he finds while he's digging for all the other stuff? Does he ignore them because they don't relate to his 'research problem'? Does he shovel them onto the dump? Or does he pack them up and put them in dead storage, in the hope that he can farm them out to a student some day to ease his conscience? Because, unlike the situation in ethnology, no archeologist will be able to come along later and find that stuff in its original context. It's *gone*, son."

"It's as if—well, as if your Philippine ethnologist were to interview an informant on religion, and then kill him so no one could ever interview him on agriculture," I ventured.

"Exactly, son," he said. "Archeology is the only branch of anthropology where we kill our informants in the process of studying them."

"Except for a few careless physical anthropologists," I said.

"Well, yes, except for that."

"But hasn't that always been the conflict between 'problem-oriented' archeology and traditional archeology?" asked the Born-Again Philosopher. "Surely you have to have a specific hypothesis to test, and stick pretty much to the data relevant to that hypothesis, rather than trying to record everything.''

"And what about other archeologists with other hypotheses?" I asked. "Don't you feel a little uncomfortable destroying data relevant to their problem while you're solving yours?"

"Well, *I* don't, because I really don't do any digging now," said the Philosopher. "I see my role as providing the hypotheses that will direct the research efforts of others. There are lots of archeologists around who can't do anything *but* dig. Let *them* do the digging.

"Look," he said, "I can't say it any better than Schiffer [1978:247] said it in Dick Gould's 1978 volume on ethnoarcheology. To paraphrase him: I feel free to pursue the study of laws wherever it leads. I do *not* feel the need to break the soil periodically in order to reaffirm my status as archeologist.''

"Son," said the Old Timer, "I think I just heard ten thousand archeological sites breathe a sigh of relief.''

There was a moment of air turbulence, and we all reached for our drinks. The sleek ribbon of the Colorado River shimmered below us, and over the audio system we could hear the captain advise us to keep our seat belts loosely fastened. Hunched in his seat, reflective, perhaps just a little sad, the Old Timer whispered in my ear: "That's what the ethnologists will never understand, son. There's a basic conflict between problem-oriented archeology and archeological ethics. Problem orientation tells you to pick a specific topic to investigate. Archeological ethics tell you you *must* record everything, because no one will ever see it in context again. The problem is that except for certain extraordinary sites, archeological data don't come packaged as 'cognitive' or 'religious' or 'environmental' or 'economic.' They're all together in the ground—integrated in complex ways, perhaps, but integrated. That's why the old concept of culture made sense as a paradigm for archeology. And it still does, son. That's the God's truth.''

I wish I could tell you how the rest of the conversation went, but at this point I could no longer keep my eyes open. After all, you wear a guy out at the meetings, and then give him six beers and start talking archeological theory, and that guy's going to fall asleep. So I slept even through those bumpy landings in the desert where the Child of the Seventies and the Born-Again Philosopher retired to their respective universities, and then somewhere between St. Louis and Detroit, I started to dream.

Now, I don't know whether it was because of the beer or the heated discussion we'd had, but my dream was a nightmare. I don't really know what it means, but my friends who work with the Walbiri and the Pitjandjara tell me that Dream Time is when you get your most important messages. So let me talk about it for a minute.

In this dream, I'd been released by the University of Michigan—whether for moral turpitude or believing in culture is really not clear. No job had opened up anywhere, and the only work I could find was with Bill Rathje's Garbage Project in Tucson. And not as a supervisor, just as a debagger. Sorting through the refuse of a thousand nameless homes, Anglo and Chicano, Pima and Papago, hoping against hope for that discarded wallet or diamond ring that could underwrite my retirement program.

And then, one day, I'm standing on the loading dock with my gauze mask on, and my pink rubber gloves, and my white lab coat with "Le Projet du Garbage" embroidered on the pocket, and this *huge* garbage truck pulls up to the dock and unloads a 30-gallon Hefty Bag. The thing is heavy as the dickens, and I wrestle it onto a dolly, and wheel it inside the lab; and we dump it onto the lab table, where the thing splits under its own weight and its contents come out all over the place.

And you know what's in it?

Reprints.

Reprints of *my* articles. Every single reprint I ever mailed out. All of them. And I'm not just talking reprints; I'm talking *autographed* reprints. The kind where I'd written something in the upper right-hand corner like, "Dear Dr. Willey, I hope you find this of interest."

You know, you can mail 'em out, but you never know whether they *keep* 'em or not.

And I suddenly realize that my whole career—my entire professional output—is in that Hefty Bag. Along with a couple of disposable diapers, and a pair of pantyhose, and a copy of *Penthouse* with the Jerry Falwell interview torn out.

But that's not the worst part.

The worst part is that the form Rathje's people fill out doesn't have a space for "discarded reprints." So my whole career, my entire professional output, simply has to be recorded as "other."

And that's where the nightmare ended, and I woke up on the runway at Detroit. I was grabbing my carryon bag as I bumped into the stewardess on her way down the aisle. "The Old Timer who was sitting next to me," I said. "What stop did he get off at?"

"What Old Timer?" she asked.

"The old guy in the boots and the faded hat with the rattle-snake hatband."

"I didn't see anybody like that," she said. "The only 'old guy' in the lounge was you."

"Have a nice day," I said sweetly. And I caught the limousine to Ann Arbor, and all the way home to my front door I kept wondering whether I had dreamed the whole thing.

Now I'll bet some of you don't think this all really happened. And I was beginning to doubt it myself until I started to unpack my carryon bag, and I was almost blinded by a gleam. A twenty-four-karat gleam.

And there, hastily stuffed into my bag with a note wrapped around the handle, was the golden Marshalltown.

And the note read: "Son, where I'm going, I won't be needing this. I know you and I see eye to eye on a lot of things, so I'm going to ask a favor. I want you to save it for—well, just the right person.

"First off, I don't see any paradigm out there right now that's going to replace culture as a unifying theme in archeology. If some ethnologists want to go their separate ways—into sociobiology, or applied semiotics, or social psychology—well, fine, they can call themselves something else, and let *us* be the anthropologists. I sort of felt that the concept of culture was what distinguished us from those other fields and kept us all from drifting apart for good.

"Because of the way our data come packaged in the ground, we pretty much have to deal with all of them to deal with any of them. It's harder for us to abandon the traditional concerns of anthropology, and we can't afford sudden fads, or quixotic changes in what's 'in' this year. We need long-term stability. And because we kill our informants as we question them, we have to question them in ways that are less idiosyncratic and more universally interpretable. And we have to share data in ways they don't.

"Because of that, we have to have a kind of integrity most fields don't need. I need your data, and you need mine, and we have to be able to trust each other on some basic level. There can't be any backstabbing, or working in total isolation, or any of this sitting on a rock in the forest interpreting culture in ways no colleague can duplicate.

"That's why we can't afford too many S.O.B.s. We can't afford guys whose lives are spent sitting in a press box criticizing other people's contributions. Son, all of prehistory is hidden in a vast darkness, and my generation was taught that it was better to light one tiny candle than curse the darkness. Never did I dream we'd have people whose whole career was based on cursing our *candles*.

"In the old days we mainly had one kind of archeologist: a guy who scratched around for a grant, went to the field, surveyed or excavated to the best of his ability, and published the results. Some guys labored patiently, in obscurity, for years. And one day, their colleagues would look up and say, 'You know, old Harry's doing good, solid work. Nothing spectacular, mind you, but you know—I'd trust him to dig on my site.' I believe that's the highest compliment one archeologist can pay another. And that's the God's truth.

"Now that doesn't sound like much, son, but today we got archeologists that can't even do that. What's more, they're too damn ambitious to labor in obscurity. So they've decided to create a whole new set of specialties around the margins of the field. Each defines himself (or herself) as the founder of that specialty, and then sets out to con the rest of us into believing that's where all the action is.

"And because archeologists will believe *anything*, pretty soon you've got a mass migration to the margins of the field. And pretty soon that's where the greatest noise is coming from.

"Now, don't get me wrong. A lot of these kids are shrewd and savvy, and they'll make a contribution one way or another. But that's one out of ten. The other nine are at the margins because things weren't moving fast enough for them in the main stream. You know, some of these kids think archeology is a one hundred-meter dash, and they're shocked and angry when no one pins a medal on them after the first one hundred meters. But I'll tell you a secret: archeology is a marathon, and you don't win marathons with speed. You win them with character.

"Son, after our talk this afternoon, I got to wondering about what archeology needed the most.

"I decided there probably isn't an urgent need for one more young person who makes a living editing other people's original ideas. I decided there probably wasn't an urgent need for one more kid who criticizes everyone else's research design while he or she never goes to the field. And I decided we probably didn't need a lot more of our archeological flat tires recapped as philosophers. There seem to be enough around to handle the available work.

"What I don't see enough of, son, is first-rate archeology.

"Now that's sad, because after all, archeology is fun. Hell, I don't break the soil periodically to 'reaffirm my status.' I do it because archeology is still the most fun you can have with your pants on.

"You know, there are a lot of awards in archeology. The Viking Fund Medal, the Kidder Medal, the Aztec Eagle, the Order of the Quetzal. But those awards are for intellectual contributions. I'd like to establish an award just for commitment to plain, old-fashioned basic research and professional ethics. And that's what this trowel is for.

"So, son, some day when you meet a kid who still believes in culture, and in hard work, and in the history of humanity; a kid who's in the field because he or she loves it, and not because they want to be famous; a kid who'd never fatten up on somebody else's data, or cut down a colleague just to get ahead; a kid who knows the literature, and respects the generations who went before—you give that kid this golden Marshalltown."

And the note ended there, with no signature, no address, and no reply required.

So that, I guess, is what I'm really here for tonight: to announce an award for someone who may not exist. But if any of you out there know of such a kid coming along—a kid who still depends on his own guts and brains instead of everyone else's—a kid who can stand on the shoulders of giants, and not be tempted to relieve himself on their heads—have *I* got an award for *him*.

And that's the God's truth.

REFERENCES

Binford, Lewis R. "General Introduction." In *For Theory Building in Archaeology: Essays on Faunal Remains, Aquatic Resources, Spatial Analysis, and Systemic Modeling,* Lewis R. Binford, ed. New York: Academic Press, 1977. pp. 1–10.

Rathje, William L. "The Garbage Project: A New Way of Looking at the Problems of Archaeology." *Archaeology,* 1974, 27:236–241.

Schiffer, Michael B. "Methodological Issues in Ethnoarchaeology." In *Explorations in Ethnoarchaeology,* pp. 229–247. Richard A. Gould, ed. Albuquerque: University of New Mexico Press (for the School of American Research), 1978.

Watson, Richard A. "Inference in Archaeology." *American Antiquity,* 1976, 41(1):58–66.

Wolf, Eric. "They Divide and Subdivide, and Call It Anthropology." *New York Times Sunday Magazine,* Nov. 30, 1980.

A Theory of the Origin of the State

by
Robert L. Carneiro

FOR THE FIRST two million years of his existence, man lived in bands or villages which, as far as we can tell, were completely autonomous. Not until perhaps 5000 B.C. did villages begin to aggregate into larger political units. But, once this process of aggregation began, it continued at a progressively faster pace and led, around 4000 B.C., to the formation of the first state in history. (When I speak of a state I mean an autonomous political unit, encompassing many communities within its territory and having a centralized government with the power to collect taxes, draft men for work or war, and decree and enforce laws.)

Although it was by all odds the most far-reaching political development in human history, the origin of the state is still very imperfectly understood.

Explicit theories of the origin of the state are relatively modern. Classical writers like Aristotle, unfamiliar with other forms of political organization, tended to think of the state as "natural," and therefore as not requiring an explanation. However, the age of exploration, by making Europeans aware that many peoples throughout the world lived, not in states, but in independent villages or tribes, made the state seem less natural, and thus more in need of explanation.

Of the many modern theories of state origins that have been proposed, we can consider only a few. Those with a racial basis, for example, are now so thoroughly discredited that they need not be dealt with here. We can also reject the belief that the state is an expression of the "genius" of a people or that it arose through a "historical accident." Such notions make the state

Adapted from *Science*, vol. 169 (August 21, 1970), by permission of the American Association for the Advancement of Science and the author.

appear to be something metaphysical or adventitious, and thus place it beyond scientific understanding. In my opinion, the origin of the state was neither mysterious nor fortuitous. It was not the product of "genius" or the result of chance, but the outcome of a regular and determinate cultural process. Moreover, it was not a unique event but a recurring phenomenon: states arose independently in different places and at different times. Where the appropriate conditions existed, the state emerged.

VOLUNTARISTIC THEORIES

Serious theories of state origins are of two general types: *voluntaristic* and *coercive*. Voluntaristic theories hold that, at some point in their history, certain peoples spontaneously, rationally, and voluntarily gave up their individual sovereignties and united with other communities to form a larger political unit deserving to be called a state. Of such theories the best known is the old Social Contract theory, which was associated especially with the name of Rousseau. We now know that no such compact was ever subscribed to by human groups, and the Social Contract theory is today nothing more than a historical curiosity.

The most widely accepted of modern voluntaristic theories is the one I call the "automatic" theory. According to this theory, the invention of agriculture automatically brought into being a surplus of food, enabling some individuals to divorce themselves from food production and to become potters, weavers, smiths, masons, and so on, thus creating an extensive division of labor. Out of this occupational specialization there developed a political integration which united a number of previously independent communities into a state. This argument was set forth most frequently by the late British archeologist V. Gordon Childe.[1]

The principal difficulty with this theory is that agriculture does *not* automatically create a food surplus. We know this because many agricultural peoples of the world produce no such surplus. Virtually all Amazonian Indians, for example, were agricultural, but in aboriginal times they did not produce a food surplus. That it was *technically feasible* for them to produce such a surplus is shown by the fact that, under the stimulus of European settlers' desire for food, a number of tribes did raise manioc in amounts

[1] See, for example, V. G. Childe, *Man Makes Himself* (London: Watts, 1936), pp. 82–83; *Town Planning Rev.* 21, 3 (1950), p. 6.

well above their own needs, for the purpose of trading.[2] Thus the technical means for generating a food surplus were there; it was the social mechanisms needed to actualize it that were lacking.

Another current voluntaristic theory of state origins is Karl Wittfogel's "hydraulic hypothesis." As I understand him, Wittfogel sees the state arising in the following way. In certain arid and semiarid areas of the world, where village farmers had to struggle to support themselves by means of small-scale irrigation, a time arrived when they saw that it would be to the advantage of all concerned to set aside their individual autonomies and merge their villages into a single large political unit capable of carrying out irrigation on a broad scale. The body of officials they created to devise and administer such extensive irrigation works brought the state into being.

This theory has recently run into difficulties. Archeological evidence now makes it appear that in at least three of the areas that Wittfogel cites as exemplifying his "hydraulic hypothesis" —Mesopotamia, China, and Mexico—full-fledged states developed well before large-scale irrigation. Thus, irrigation did not play the causal role in the rise of the state that Wittfogel appears to attribute to it.

This and all other voluntaristic theories of the rise of the state founder on the same rock: the demonstrated inability of autonomous political units to relinquish their sovereignty in the absence of overriding external constraints. We see this inability manifested again and again by political units ranging from tiny villages to great empires. Indeed, one can scan the pages of history without finding a single genuine exception to this rule. Thus, in order to account for the origin of the state we must set aside voluntaristic theories and look elsewhere.

COERCIVE THEORIES

A close examination of history indicates that only a coercive theory can account for the rise of the state. Force, and not enlightened self-interest, is the mechanism by which political evolution has led, step by step, from autonomous villages to the state.

The view that war lies at the root of the state is by no means

---

[2] I have in my files recorded instances of surplus food production by such Amazonian tribes as the Tupinambá, Jevero, Mundurucú, Tucano, Desana, Cubeo, and Canela.

new. Twenty-five hundred years ago Heraclitus wrote that "war is the father of all things." The first careful study of the role of warfare in the rise of the state, however, was made less than a hundred years ago, by Herbert Spencer in his *Principles of Sociology*.[3] Perhaps better known than Spencer's writings on war and the state are the conquest theories of continental writers such as Franz Oppenheimer.[4]

Oppenheimer argued that the state emerged when the productive capacity of settled agriculturists was combined with the energy of pastoral nomads through the conquest of the former by the latter. This theory, however, has two serious defects. First, it fails to account for the rise of states in aboriginal America, where pastoral nomadism was unknown. Second, it is now well established that pastoral nomadism did not arise in the Old World until after the earliest states had emerged.

Regardless of deficiencies in particular coercive theories, however, there is little question that, in one way or another, war played a decisive role in the rise of the state. Historical or archeological evidence of war is found in the early stages of state formation in Mesopotamia, Egypt, India, China, Japan, Greece, Rome, northern Europe, central Africa, Polynesia, Middle America, Peru, and Colombia, to name only the most prominent examples.

Thus, with the Germanic kingdoms of northern Europe especially in mind, Edward Jenks observed that, "historically speaking, there is not the slightest difficulty in proving that all political communities of the modern type [that is, states] owe their existence to successful warfare."[5] And in reading Jan Vansina's *Kingdoms of the Savanna*,[6] a book with no theoretical ax to grind, one finds that state after state in central Africa arose in the same manner.

But is it really true that there is no exception to this rule? Might there not be, somewhere in the world, an example of a state which arose without the agency of war?

Until a few years ago, anthropologists generally believed that

[3]See *The Evolution of Society; Selections from Herbert Spencer's Principles of Sociology*, R. L. Carneiro, ed. (Chicago: Univ. of Chicago Press, 1967), pp. 32–47, 63–96, 153–165.

[4]F. Oppenheimer, *The State*, trans. J. M. Gitterman (New York: Vanguard, 1926).

[5]E. Jenks, *A History of Politics* (New York: Macmillan, 1900), p. 73.

[6]J. Vansina, *Kingdoms of the Savanna* (Madison: University of Wisconsin Press, 1966).

the Classic Maya provided such an instance. The archeological evidence then available gave no hint of warfare among the early Maya and led scholars to regard them as a peace-loving theocratic state which had arisen entirely without war. However, this view is no longer tenable. Recent archeological discoveries have placed the Classic Maya in a very different light. First came the discovery of the Bonampak murals, showing the early Maya at war and reveling in the torture of war captives. Then, excavations around Tikal revealed large earthworks partly surrounding that Classic Maya city, pointing clearly to a military rivalry with the neighboring city of Uaxactún. Summarizing present thinking on the subject, Michael D. Coe has observed that "the ancient Maya were just as warlike as the . . . bloodthirsty states of the Post-Classic."[7]

Yet, though warfare is surely a prime mover in the origin of the state, it cannot be the only factor. After all, wars have been fought in many parts of the world where the state never emerged. Thus, while warfare may be a necessary condition for the rise of the state, it is not a sufficient one. Or, to put it another way, while we can identify war as the *mechanism* of state formation, we need also to specify the *conditions* under which it gave rise to the state.

ENVIRONMENTAL CIRCUMSCRIPTION

How are we to determine these conditions? One promising approach is to look for those factors common to areas of the world in which states arose indigenously—areas such as the Nile, Tigris-Euphrates, and Indus valleys in the Old World and the Valley of Mexico and the mountain and coastal valleys of Peru in the New. These areas differ from one another in many ways—in altitude, temperature, rainfall, soil type, drainage pattern, and many other features. They do, however, have one thing in common: *they are all areas of circumscribed agricultural land*. Each of them is set off by mountains, seas, or deserts, and these environmental features sharply delimit the area that simple farming peoples could occupy and cultivate. In this respect these areas are very different from, say, the Amazon basin or the eastern woodlands of North America, where extensive and unbroken forests provided almost unlimited agricultural land.

But what is the significance of circumscribed agricultural land

[7]M. D. Coe, *The Maya* (New York: Praeger, 1966), p. 147.

for the origin of the state? Its significance can best be understood by comparing political development in two regions of the world having contrasting ecologies—one a region with circumscribed agricultural land and the other a region where there was extensive and unlimited land. The two areas I have chosen to use in making this comparison are the coastal valleys of Peru and the Amazon basin.

Our examination begins at the stage where agricultural communities were already present but where each was still completely autonomous. Looking first at the Amazon basin, we see that agricultural villages there were numerous, but widely dispersed. Even in areas with relatively dense clustering, like the Upper Xingú basin, villages were at least ten or fifteen miles apart. Thus, the typical Amazonian community, even though it practiced a simple form of shifting cultivation which required extensive amounts of land, still had around it all the forest land needed for its gardens. For Amazonia as a whole, then, population density was low and subsistence pressure on the land was slight.

Warfare was certainly frequent in Amazonia, but it was waged for reasons of revenge, the taking of women, the gaining of personal prestige, and motives of a similar sort. There being no shortage of land, there was, by and large, no warfare over land.

The consequences of the type of warfare that did occur in Amazonia were as follows. A defeated group was not, as a rule, driven from its land. Nor did the victor make any real effort to subject the vanquished, or to exact tribute from him. This would have been difficult to accomplish in any case, since there was no effective way to prevent the losers from fleeing to a distant part of the forest. Indeed, defeated villages often chose to do just this, not so much to avoid subjugation as to avoid further attack. With settlement so sparse in Amazonia, a new area of forest could be found and occupied with relative ease, and without trespassing on the territory of another village. Moreover, since virtually any area of forest is suitable for cultivation, subsistence agriculture could be carried on in the new habitat just about as well as in the old.

It was apparently by this process of fight and flight that horticultural tribes gradually spread out until they came to cover, thinly but extensively, almost the entire Amazon basin. Thus, under the conditions of unlimited agricultural land and low population density that prevailed in Amazonia, the effect of warfare was to disperse villages over a wide area, and to keep them autonomous. With only a very few exceptions, noted below, there was no tendency in Amazonia for villages to be held in place and to combine into larger political units.

In marked contrast to the situation in Amazonia were the events that transpired in the narrow valleys of the Peruvian coast. The reconstruction of these events that I present is admittedly inferential, but I think it is consistent with the archeological evidence.

Here too our account begins at the stage of small, dispersed, and autonomous farming communities. However, instead of being scattered over a vast expanse of rain forest as they were in Amazonia, villages here were confined to some 78 short and narrow valleys. Each of these valleys, moreover, was backed by the mountains, fronted by the sea, and flanked on either side by desert as dry as any in the world. Nowhere else, perhaps, can one find agricultural valleys more sharply circumscribed than these.

As with neolithic communities generally, villages of the Peruvian coastal valleys tended to grow in size. Since autonomous villages are likely to fission as they grow, as long as land is available for the settlement of splinter communities, these villages undoubtedly split from time to time. Thus, villages tended to increase in number faster than they grew in size. This increase in the number of villages occupying a valley probably continued, without giving rise to significant changes in subsistence practices, until all the readily arable land in the valley was being farmed.

At this point two changes in agricultural techniques began to occur: the tilling of land already under cultivation was intensified, and new, previously unusable land was brought under cultivation by means of terracing and irrigation.

Yet the rate at which new arable land was created failed to keep pace with the increasing demand for it. Even before the land shortage became so acute that irrigation began to be practiced systematically, villages were undoubtedly already fighting one another over land. Prior to this time, when agricultural villages were still few in number and well supplied with land, the warfare waged in the coastal valleys of Peru had probably been of much the same type as that described above for Amazonia. With increasing pressure of human population on the land, however, the major incentive for war changed from a desire for revenge to a need to acquire land. And, as the causes of war became predominantly economic, the frequency, intensity, and importance of war increased.

Once this stage was reached, a Peruvian village that lost a war faced consequences very different from those faced by a defeated village in Amazonia. There, as we have seen, the vanquished could flee to a new locale, subsisting there about as well as they had subsisted before, and retaining their independence. In Peru, however, this alternative was no longer open to the inhabitants of defeated villages. The mountains, the desert, and the sea—to say nothing of neighboring villages—blocked escape in every direction. A village defeated in war thus faced only grim prospects. If it was allowed to remain on its own land, instead of being exterminated or expelled, this concession came only at a price. And the price was political subordination to the victor. This subordination generally entailed at least the payment of a tribute or tax in kind, which the defeated village could provide only by producing more food than it had produced before. But subordination sometimes involved a further loss of autonomy on the part of the defeated village—namely, incorporation into the political unit dominated by the victor.

Through the recurrence of warfare of this type, we see arising in coastal Peru integrated territorial units transcending the village in size and in degree of organization. Political evolution was attaining the level of the chiefdom.

As land shortages continued and became even more acute, so did warfare. Now, however, the competing units were no longer small villages but, often, large chiefdoms. From this point on, through the conquest of chiefdom by chiefdom, the size of political units increased at a progressively faster rate. Naturally, as autonomous political units increased in size, they decreased in number, with the result that an entire valley was eventually unified under the banner of its strongest chiefdom. The political unit thus formed was undoubtedly sufficiently centralized and complex to warrant being called a state.

The political evolution I have described for one valley of Peru was also taking place in other valleys, in the highlands as well as on the coast. Once valley-wide kingdoms emerged, the next step was the formation of multivalley kingdoms through the conquest of weaker valleys by stronger ones. The culmination of this process was the conquest of all of Peru by its most powerful state, and the formation of a single great empire. Although this step may have occurred once or twice before in Andean history, it was achieved most notably, and for the last time, by the Incas.

POLITICAL EVOLUTION

While the aggregation of villages into chiefdoms, and of chiefdoms into kingdoms, was occurring by external acquisition,

the structure of these increasingly larger political units was being
elaborated by internal evolution. These inner changes were, of
course, closely related to outer events. The expansion of successful states brought within their borders conquered peoples and
territory which had to be administered. And it was the individuals who had distinguished themselves in war who were generally
appointed to political office and assigned the task of carrying out
this administration. Besides maintaining law and order and collecting taxes, the functions of this burgeoning class of administrators included mobilizing labor for building irrigation works,
roads, fortresses, palaces, and temples. Thus, their functions
helped to weld an assorted collection of petty states into a single
integrated and centralized political unit.

These same individuals, who owed their improved social position to their exploits in war, became, along with the ruler and his
kinsmen, the nucleus of an upper class. A lower class in turn
emerged from the prisoners taken in war and employed as servants and slaves by their captors. In this manner did war contribute to the rise of social classes.

I noted earlier that peoples attempt to acquire their neighbors'
land before they have made the fullest possible use of their own.
This implies that every autonomous village has an untapped
margin of food productivity, and that this margin is squeezed out
only when the village is subjugated and compelled to pay taxes
in kind. The surplus food extracted from conquered villages
through taxation, which in the aggregate attained very significant
proportions, went largely to support the ruler, his warriors and
retainers, officials, priests, and other members of the rising
upper class, who thus became completely divorced from food
production.

Finally, those made landless by war but not enslaved tended to
gravitate to settlements which, because of their specialized
administrative, commercial, or religious functions, were growing
into towns and cities. Here they were able to make a living as
workers and artisans, exchanging their labor or their wares for
part of the economic surplus exacted from village farmers by the
ruling class and spent by members of that class to raise their
standard of living.

The process of political evolution which I have outlined for
the coastal valleys of Peru was, in its essential features, by no
means unique to this region. Areas of circumscribed agricultural
land elsewhere in the world, such as the Valley of Mexico,
Mesopotamia, the Nile Valley, and the Indus Valley, saw the
process occur in much the same way and for essentially the same

reasons. In those areas, too, autonomous neolithic villages were succeeded by chiefdoms, chiefdoms by kingdoms, and kingdoms by empires. The last stage of this development was, of course, the most impressive. The scale and magnificence attained by the early empires overshadowed everything that had gone before. But, in a sense, empires were merely the logical culmination of the process. The really fundamental step, the one that had triggered the entire train of events that led to empires, was the change from village automony to supravillage integration. This step was a change in kind; everything that followed was, in a way, only a change in degree.

In addition to being pivotal, the step to supracommunity aggregation was difficult, for it took two million years to achieve. But, once it was achieved, once village autonomy was transcended, only two or three millennia were required for the rise of great empires and the flourishing of complex civilizations.

RESOURCE CONCENTRATION

Theories are first formulated on the basis of a limited number of facts. Eventually, though, a theory must confront all of the facts. And often new facts are stubborn and do not conform to the theory, or do not conform very well. What distinguishes a successful theory from an unsuccessful one is that it can be modified or elaborated to accommodate the entire range of facts. Let us see how well the "circumscription theory" holds up when it is brought face-to-face with certain facts that appear to be exceptions.

For the first test let us return to Amazonia. Early voyagers down the Amazon left written testimony of a culture along that river higher than the culture I have described for Amazonia generally. In the 1500's, the native population living on the banks of the Amazon was relatively dense, villages were fairly large and close together, and some degree of social stratification existed. Moreover, here and there a paramount chief held sway over many communities.

The question immediately arises: With unbroken stretches of arable land extending back from the Amazon for hundreds of miles, why were there chiefdoms here?

To answer this question we must look closely at the environmental conditions afforded by the Amazon. Along the margins of the river itself, and on islands within it, there is a type of land called *várzea*. The river floods this land every year, covering it with a layer of fertile silt. Because of this annual replenishment, *várzea* is agricultural land of first quality which can be cultivated year after year without ever having to lie fallow. Thus, among native farmers it was highly prized and greatly coveted. The waters of the Amazon were also extraordinarily bountiful, providing fish, manatees, turtles and turtle eggs, caimans, and other riverine foods in inexhaustible amounts. By virtue of this concentration of resources, the Amazon, as a habitat, was distinctly superior to its hinterlands.

Concentration of resources along the Amazon amounted almost to a kind of circumscription. While there was no sharp cleavage between productive and unproductive land, as there was in Peru, there was at least a steep ecological gradient. So much more rewarding was the Amazon River than adjacent areas, and so desirable did it become as a habitat, that peoples were drawn to it from surrounding regions. Eventually crowding occurred along many portions of the river, leading to warfare over sections of river front. And the losers in war, in order to retain access to the river, often had no choice but to submit to the victors. By this subordination of villages to a paramount chief there arose along the Amazon chiefdoms representing a higher step in political evolution than had occurred elsewhere in the basin.

The notion of resource concentration also helps to explain the surprising degree of political development apparently attained by peoples of the Peruvian coast while they were still depending primarily on fishing for subsistence, and only secondarily on agriculture. Of this seeming anomaly Lanning has written: "To the best of my knowledge, this is the only case in which so many of the characteristics of civilization have been found without a basically agricultural economic foundation."[8]

Armed with the concept of resource concentration, however, we can show that this development was not so anomalous after all. The explanation, it seems to me, runs as follows. Along the coast of Peru wild food sources occurred in considerable number and variety. However, they were restricted to a very narrow margin of land. Accordingly, while the *abundance* of food in this zone led to a sharp rise in population, the *restrictedness* of this food soon resulted in the almost complete occupation of exploitable areas. And when pressure on the available resources reached a critical level, competition over land ensued. The result

[8]E. P. Lanning, *Peru Before the Incas* (Englewood Cliffs, N.J.: Prentice-Hall, 1967), p. 59.

of this competition was to set in motion the sequence of events of political evolution that I have described.

Thus, it seems that we can safely add resource concentration to environmental circumscription as a factor leading to warfare over land, and thus to political integration beyond the village level.

SOCIAL CIRCUMSCRIPTION

But there is still another factor to be considered in accounting for the rise of the state.

In dealing with the theory of environmental circumscription while discussing the Yanomamö Indians of Venezuela, Napoleon A. Chagnon[9] has introduced the concept of "social circumscription." By this he means that a high density of population in an area can produce effects on peoples living near the center of the area that are similar to effects produced by environmental circumscription. This notion seems to me to be an important addition to our theory. Let us see how, according to Chagnon, social circumscription has operated among the Yanomamö.

The Yanomamö, who number some ten thousand, live in an extensive region of noncircumscribed rain forest, away from any large river. One might expect that Yanomamö villages would thus be more or less evenly spaced. However, Chagnon notes that, at the center of Yanomamö territory, villages are closer together than they are at the periphery. Because of this, they tend to impinge on one another more, with the result that warfare is more frequent and intense in the center than in peripheral areas. Moreover, it is more difficult for villages in the nuclear area to escape attack by moving away, since, unlike villages on the periphery, their ability to move is somewhat restricted.

The net result is that villages in the central area of Yanomamö territory are larger than villages in the other areas, since large village size is an advantage for both attack and defense. A further effect of more intense warfare in the nuclear area is that village headmen are stronger in that area. Yanomamö headmen are also the war leaders, and their influence increases in proportion to their village's participation in war. In addition, offensive and defensive alliances between villages are more common in the

[9]N. A. Chagnon, *Proceedings, VIIIth International Congress of Anthropological and Ethnological Sciences* (Tokyo and Kyoto, 1968), vol. 3 (*Ethnology and Archaeology*), p. 249 (esp. p. 251).

center of Yanomamö territory than in outlying areas. Thus, while still at the autonomous village level of political organization, those Yanomamö subject to social circumscription have clearly moved a step or two in the direction of higher political development.

Although the Yanomamö manifest social circumscription only to a modest degree, this amount of it has been enough to make a difference in their level of political organization. What the effects of social circumscription would be in areas where it was more fully expressed should, therefore, be clear. First would come a reduction in the size of the territory of each village. Then, as population pressure became more severe, warfare over land would ensue. But because adjacent land for miles around was already the property of other villages, a defeated village would have nowhere to flee. From this point on, the consequences of warfare for that village, and for political evolution in general, would be essentially as I have described them for the situation of environmental circumscription.

To return to Amazonia, it is clear that, if social circumscription is operative among the Yanomamö today, it was certainly operative among the tribes of the Amazon River four hundred years ago. And its effect would undoubtedly have been to give a further spur to political evolution in that region.

We see then that, even in the absence of sharp environmental circumscription, the factors of resource concentration and social circumscription may, by intensifying war and redirecting it toward the taking of land, give a strong impetus to political development.

With these auxiliary hypotheses incorporated into it, the circumscription theory is now better able to confront the entire range of test cases that can be brought before it. For example, it can now account for the rise of the state in the Hwang Valley of northern China, and even in the Petén region of the Maya lowlands, areas not characterized by strictly circumscribed agricultural land. In the case of the Hwang Valley, there is no question that resource concentration and social circumscription were present and active forces. In the lowland Maya area, resource concentration seems not to have been a major factor, but social circumscription may well have been.

Some archeologists may object that population density in the Petén during Formative times was too low to give rise to social circumscription. But, in assessing what constitutes a population dense enough to produce this effect, we must consider not so much the total land area occupied as the amount of land needed to support the existing population. And the size of this supporting area depends not only on the size of the population but also on the mode of subsistence. The shifting cultivation presumably practiced by the ancient Maya required considerably more land, per capita, than did the permanent field cultivation of say, the Valley of Mexico or the coast of Peru. Consequently, insofar as its effects are concerned, a relatively low population density in the Petén may have been equivalent to a much higher one in Mexico or Peru.

We have already learned from the Yanomamö example that social circumscription may begin to operate while population is still relatively sparse. And we can be sure that the Petén was far more densely peopled in Formative times than Yanomamö territory is today. Thus, population density among the lowland Maya, while giving a superficial appearance of sparseness, may actually have been high enough to provoke fighting over land, and thus provide the initial impetus for the formation of a state.

CONCLUSION

In summary, then, the circumscription theory in its elaborated form goes far toward accounting for the origin of the state. It explains why states arose where they did, and why they failed to arise elsewhere. It shows the state to be a predictable response to certain specific cultural, demographic, and ecological conditions. Thus, it helps to elucidate what was undoubtedly the most important single step ever taken in the political evolution of mankind.

II

FIELDWORK

Always behave as a gentleman.

> Haddon

Take ten grains of quinine every night and keep off the women.

> Seligman

Don't converse with an informant for more than twenty minutes, because if you aren't bored by that time, he will be.

> Westermarck

FIELDWORK IS ANTHROPOLOGY's answer to the question: "How are people best studied?" Fieldwork means living with and like those being studied. Fieldwork is full-involvement research, sometimes boring, often exciting, and always self-transforming. Fieldwork is done by "marginal natives" (researchers) who must solve a host of problems: master a strange language, prove they are not "spies," and (among many other problems) stay sane.

Fieldwork provides the rich data of "normal" daily interaction and the complex data of unusual happenings. It assumes that humans are not pathetic puppets programmed by "culture" but, rather, are decisionmakers playing with rules and not necessarily following them. The rules and the styles of "play" are different from society to society. To those who are not raised according to the ideas of a given tradition its dictates may appear strange and even inhuman. Is it possible to understand the lifestyles of those who do not share our beliefs, values, and goals? Can the marginal native (the anthropologist) get into the heads of the "real" natives (the locals)? The answer, considered debatable by some, depends on how we interpret "get into the heads of." Clifford Geertz's "From the Native's Point of View" is very helpful here. Geertz teaches us to distinguish *experience-near concepts* from *experience-distant concepts*. Fieldwork, in part, becomes the learning of local, experience-near concepts (say, our English word *fear*) and then translating them (for sharing with non-natives) to experience-distant concepts (say, our English word *phobia*).

How does one get the knowledge to make this translation? Geertz does it "not by imagining myself as someone else—a rice peasant or a tribal sheikh, and then seeing what I thought—but

56

by searching out and analyzing the symbolic forms—words, images, institutions, behaviors—in terms of which, in each place, people actually represent themselves to themselves and to one another." Understanding inner lives is, for Geertz, much like "grasping a proverb, catching an illusion or seeing a joke." Clearly, the how-to-do-it and the communication that it has been done is no simple matter. But no one ever said that really understanding people was simple.

Geertz's manner of catching the native's point of view is nicely supplemented by Mary Douglas, in a strategy called structural analysis. Douglas here follows in a path brilliantly developed by the French anthropologist, Claude Lévi-Strauss. While Lévi-Strauss, generally, is involved with digging out the structure or building-blocks underneath myths, Douglas uses the method to study food habits. Structural analysis, Douglas argues convincingly, can handle such strange (but important) questions as: "Why are fox and dog excluded from our menu?" The answers here provided go far beyond insights into the food habits of a given society. These answers help us discover a hidden set of postulates which provide the foundation (or "structure") of a culture.

To understand the work of marginal natives, to catch the native's point of view, and to see the point of structural analysis requires much effort. Such an investment is extremely sound. It provides something never offered on the stock market: assured profit in a currency called insight into the human condition.

REFERENCES

Douglas, Mary. *Implicit Meanings: Essays in Anthropology.* London and Boston: Routledge and Kegan Paul, 1975.

Freilich, Morris, ed. *Marginal Natives at Work: Anthropologists in the Field.* Cambridge, Mass.: Schenkman, 1977.

Powdermaker, Hortense. *Stranger and Friend.* New York: W. W. Norton, 1966.

"From the Native's Point of View": On the Nature of Anthropological Understanding

by
Clifford Geertz

SEVERAL YEARS AGO a minor scandal erupted in anthropology: one of its ancestral figures told the truth in a public place. As befits an ancestor, he did it posthumously and through his widow's decision rather than his own, with the result that a number of the sort of right-thinking types who are always with us immediately rose to cry that she—an in-marrier anyway—had betrayed clan secrets, profaned an idol, and let down the side. What will the children think, to say nothing of the laymen? But the disturbance was not much lessened by such ceremonial wringing of the hands; the damn thing was, after all, already printed. In much the same way that James Watson's *The Double Helix* exposed the nature of research in biophysics, Bronislaw Malinowski's *A Diary in the Strict Sense of the Term* rendered the established image of how anthropological work is conducted fairly well implausible. The myth of the chameleon field-worker perfectly self-tuned to his exotic surroundings—a walking miracle of empathy, tact, patience, and cosmopolitanism—was demolished by the man who had perhaps done the most to create it.

The squabble that surrounded the publication of the *Diary* concentrated, naturally, on inessentials and, as was only to be expected, missed the point. Most of the shock seems to have arisen from the mere discovery that Malinowski was not, to put it delicately, an unmitigated nice guy. He had rude things to say

Reprinted from Bulletin of the American Academy of Arts and Sciences, vol. 28, no. 1 (1974), by permission of the American Academy of Arts and Sciences, Boston.

about the natives he was living with and rude words to say it in. He spent a great deal of his time wishing he were elsewhere. And he projected an image of a man as little complaisant as the world has seen. (He also projected an image of a man consecrated to a strange vocation to the point of self-immolation, but that was less noted.)

The discussion eventually came down to Malinowski's moral character or lack of it; ignored was the genuinely profound question his book raised, namely, if anthropological understanding does not stem, as we have been taught to believe, from some sort of extraordinary sensibility, an almost preternatural capacity to think, feel, and perceive like a native (a word, I should hurry to say, I use here "in the strict sense of the term"), then how is anthropological knowledge of the way natives think, feel, and perceive possible? The issue the *Diary* presents, with a force perhaps only a working ethnographer can fully appreciate, is not moral; it is epistemological. If we are going to cling—as in my opinion, we must—to the injunction to see things from the native's point of view, what is our position when we can no longer claim some unique form of psychological closeness, a sort of transcultural identification, with our subjects: What happens to *verstehen* when *einfühlen* disappears?

As a matter of fact, this general problem has been exercising methodological discussion in anthropology for the last ten or fifteen years; Malinowski's voice from the grave merely dramatized it as a human dilemma over and above a professional one. The formulations have been various: "inside" versus "outside," or "first person" versus "third person" descriptions; "phenomenological" versus "objectivist," or "cognitive" versus "behavioral" theories; or, perhaps most commonly, "emic" versus "etic" analyses, this last deriving from the distinction in linguistics between phonemics and phonetics—phonemics classifying sounds according to their internal function in language, phonetics classifying them according to their acoustic properties as such. But perhaps the simplest and most directly appreciable way to put the matter is in terms of a distinction formulated, for his own purposes, by the psychoanalyst Heinz Kohut—a distinction between what he calls "experience-near" and "experience-distant" concepts.

An experience-near concept is, roughly, one which an individual—a patient, a subject, in our case an informant—might himself naturally and effortlessly use to define what he or his fellows see, feel, think, imagine, and so on, and which he would readily understand when similarly applied by others. An experience-

distant concept is one which various types of specialists—an
analyst, an experimenter, an ethnographer, even a priest or an
ideologist—employ to forward their scientific, philosophical, or
practical aims. "Love" is an experience-near concept; "object
cathexis" is an experience-distant one. "Social stratification"
and perhaps for most peoples in the world even "religion" (and
certainly, "religious system") are experience-distant; "caste"
and "nirvana" are experience-near, at least for Hindus and
Buddhists.

Clearly, the matter is one of degree, not polar opposition:
"fear" is experience-nearer than "phobia," and "phobia"
experience-nearer than "ego dyssyntonic." And the difference is
not, at least so far as anthropology is concerned (the matter is
otherwise in poetry and physics), a normative one, in the sense
that one sort of concept as such is to be preferred over the other.
Confinement to experience-near concepts leaves an ethnographer
awash in immediacies as well as entangled in vernacular. Confinement to experience-distant ones leaves him stranded in abstractions and smothered in jargon. The real question, and the
one Malinowski raised by demonstrating that, in the case of
"natives," you don't have to be one to know one, is what roles
the two kinds of concepts play in anthropological analysis. To be
more exact: How, in each case, should they be deployed so as to
produce an interpretation of the way a people live which is
neither imprisoned within their mental horizons, an ethnography
of witchcraft as written by a witch, nor systematically deaf to the
distinctive tonalities of their existence, an ethnography of witchcraft as written by a geometer?

Putting the matter this way—in terms of how anthropological
analysis is to be conducted and its results framed, rather than
what psychic constitution anthropologists need to have—reduces
the mystery of what "seeing things from the native's point of
view" means. But it does not make it any easier nor does it
lessen the demand for perceptiveness on the part of the fieldworker.
To grasp concepts which, for another people, are experience-
near, and to do so well enough to place them in illuminating
connection with those experience-distant concepts that theorists
have fashioned to capture the general features of social life, is
clearly a task at least as delicate, if a bit less magical, as putting
oneself into someone else's skin. The trick is not to achieve
some inner correspondence of spirit with your informants;
preferring, like the rest of us, to call their souls their own, they
are not going to be altogether keen about such an effort anyhow.
The trick is to figure out what the devil they think they are up to.

In one sense, of course, no one knows this better than they do themselves; hence the passion to swim in the stream of their experience, and the illusion afterward that one somehow has. But in another sense, that simple truism is simply not true. People use experience-near concepts spontaneously, unselfconsciously, as it were, colloquially; they do not, except fleetingly and on occasion, recognize that there are any "concepts" involved at all. That is what experience-near means—that ideas and the realities they disclose are naturally and indissolubly bound up together. What else could you call a hippopotamus? Of course the gods are powerful; why else would we fear them? The ethnographer does not, and in my opinion, largely cannot, perceive what his informants perceive. What he perceives—and that uncertainly enough—is what they perceive "with," or "by means of," or "through" or whatever word one may choose. In the country of the blind, who are not as unobservant as they appear, the one-eyed is not king but spectator.

Now, to make all this a bit more concrete I want to turn for a moment to my own work, which whatever its other faults has at least the virtue of being mine—a distinct advantage in discussions of this sort. In all three of the societies I have studied intensively, Javanese, Balinese, and Moroccan, I have been concerned, among other things, with attempting to determine how the people who live there define themselves as persons, what enters into the idea they have (but, as I say, only half-realize they have) of what a self, Javanese, Balinese, or Moroccan style, is. And in each case, I have tried to arrive at this most intimate of notions not by imagining myself as someone else—a rice peasant or a tribal sheikh, and then seeing what I thought—but by searching out and analyzing the symbolic forms—words, images, institutions, behaviors—in terms of which, in each place, people actually represent themselves to themselves and to one another.

The concept of person is, in fact, an excellent vehicle by which to examine this whole question of how to go about poking into another people's turn of mind. In the first place, some sort of concept of this kind, one feels reasonably safe in saying, exists in recognizable form within all social groups. Various notions of what persons are may be, from our point of view, more than a little odd. People may be conceived to dart about nervously at night, shaped like fireflies. Essential elements of their psyche, like hatred, may be thought to be lodged in granular black bodies within their livers, discoverable upon autopsy. They may share their fates with *doppelganger* beasts, so that when the beast sickens or dies they sicken or die too. But at least some conception of what a human individual is, as opposed to a rock, an animal, a rainstorm, or a god, is, so far as I can see, universal.

Yet, at the same time, as these offhand examples suggest, the actual conceptions involved vary, often quite sharply, from one group to the next. The Western conception of the person as a bounded, unique, more or less integrated motivational and cognitive universe, a dynamic center of awareness, emotion, judgment, and action organized into a distinctive whole and set contrastively both against other such wholes and against a social and natural background is, however incorrigible it may seem to us, a rather peculiar idea within the context of the world's cultures. Rather than attempt to place the experience of others within the framework of such a conception, which is what the extolled "empathy" in fact usually comes down to, we must, if we are to achieve understanding, set that conception aside and view their experiences within the framework of their own idea of what selfhood is. And for Java, Bali, and Morocco, at least, that idea differs markedly not only from our own but, no less dramatically and no less instructively, from one to the other.

MAKING THE SELF "SMOOTH"

In Java, where I worked in the fifties, I studied a small, shabby inland county-seat sort of place: two shadeless streets of whitewashed wooden shops and offices, with even less substantial bamboo shacks crammed in helter-skelter behind them, the whole surrounded by a great half-circle of densely packed rice-bowl villages. Land was short; jobs were scarce; politics was unstable; health was poor; prices were rising; and life was altogether far from promising, a kind of agitated stagnancy in which, as I once put it, thinking of the curious mixture of borrowed fragments of modernity and exhausted relics of tradition that characterized the place, the future seemed about as remote as the past. Yet, in the midst of this depressing scene, there was an absolutely astonishing intellectual vitality—a philosophical passion, and a popular one besides, to track the riddles of existence right down to the ground. Destitute peasants would discuss questions of freedom of the will; illiterate tradesmen discoursed on the properties of God; common laborers had theories about the relations between reason and passion, the nature of time, or the reliability of the senses. And, perhaps most important, the problem of the self—its nature, function, and mode of operation—was pursued with the sort of reflective intensity one could find among ourselves in only the most recherché settings indeed.

The central ideas in terms of which this reflection proceeded and which thus defined its boundaries and the Javanese sense of what a person is were arranged into two sets of, at base, religious contrasts: one between "inside" and "outside" and one between "refined" and "vulgar." These glosses are, of course, crude and imprecise; determining exactly what was signified by the terms involved and sorting out their shades of meaning was what all the discussion was about. But together they formed a distinctive conception of the self which, far from being merely theoretical, was the means by which Javanese in fact perceive one another, and, of course, themselves.

The "inside"/"outside" words, *batin* and *lair* (terms borrowed, as a matter of fact, from the Sufi tradition of Muslim mysticism, but locally reworked), refer on the one hand to the felt realm of human experience and on the other to the observed realm of human behavior. These have, one hastens to say, nothing to do with "soul" and "body" in our sense, for which there are quite other words with quite other implications. *Batin*, the "inside" word, does not refer to a separate seat of encapsulated spirituality detached or detachable from the body, or indeed to a bounded unit at all, but to the emotional life of human beings taken generally. It consists of the fuzzy, shifting flow of subjective feeling perceived directly in all its phenomenological immediacy but considered to be, at its roots at least, identical across all individuals, whose individuality it thus effaces. And, similarly, *lair*, the "outside" word, has nothing to do with the body as an object, even an experienced object. Rather, it refers to that part of human life which, in our culture, strict behaviorists limit themselves to studying—external actions, movements, postures, speech—again conceived as in its essence invariant from one individual to the next. Therefore, these two sets of phenomena—inward feelings and outward actions—are regarded not as functions of one another but as independent realms of being to be put in proper order independently.

It is in connection with this "proper ordering" that the contrast between *alus*, the word meaning "pure," "refined," "polished," "exquisite," "ethereal," "subtle," "civilized," "smooth," and *kasar*, the word meaning "impolite," "rough," "uncivilized," "coarse," "insensitive," "vulgar," comes into play. The goal is to be *alus* in both separated realms of the self.

In the inner realm this is to be achieved through religious discipline, much but not all of it mystical. In the outer realm, it is to be achieved through etiquette, the rules of which, in this instance, are not only extraordinarily elaborate but have something of the force of law. Through meditation the civilized man thins out his emotional life to a kind of constant hum; through etiquette, he both shields that life from external disruptions and regularizes his outer behavior in such a way that it appears to others as a predictable, undisturbing, elegant, and rather vacant set of choreographed motions and settled forms of speech.

There is much to all this because it connects up to both an ontology and an aesthetic. But so far as our problem is concerned, the result is a bifurcate conception of the self, half ungestured feeling and half unfelt gesture. An inner world of stilled emotion and an outer world of shaped behavior confront one another as sharply distinguished realms unto themselves, any particular person being but the momentary locus, so to speak, of that confrontation, a passing expression of their permanent existence, their permanent separation, and their permanent need to be kept in their own separate order. Only when you have seen, as I have, a young man whose wife—a woman he had raised from childhood and who had been the center of his life—has suddenly and inexplicably died, greeting everyone with a set smile and formal apologies for his wife's absence and trying, by mystical techniques, to flatten out, as he himself put it, the hills and valleys of his emotion into an even, level plain ("That is what you have to do," he said to me, "be smooth inside and out") can you come, in the face of our own notions of the intrinsic honesty of deep feeling and the moral importance of personal sincerity, to take the possibility of such a conception of selfhood seriously and to appreciate, however inaccessible it is to you, its own sort of force.

A THEATER OF STATUS

Bali, where I worked both in another small provincial town, though one rather less drifting and dispirited, and, later, in an upland village of highly skilled musical instrument makers, is in many ways similar to Java, with which it shared a common culture until the fifteenth century. But at a deeper level, having continued Hindu while Java was, nominally at least, Islamized, it is quite different. The intricate, obsessive ritual life, Hindu, Buddhist, and Polynesian in about equal proportions (the development of which was more or less cut off in Java, leaving its Indic spirit to turn reflective and phenomenological, even quietistic, in the way I've just described), flourished in Bali to reach levels of scale and flamboyance that have startled the world and made the Balinese a much more dramaturgical people with a self to match. What is philosophy in Java is theater in Bali.

As a result, there is in Bali a persistent and systematic attempt to stylize all aspects of personal expression to the point where anything idiosyncratic, anything characteristic of the individual merely because he is who he is physically, psychologically, or biographically, is muted in favor of his assigned place in the continuing and, so it is thought, never-changing pageant that is Balinese life. It is dramatis personae, not actors, that endure; indeed, it is dramatis personae, not actors, that in the proper sense really exist. Physically men come and go—mere incidents in a happenstance history of no genuine importance, even to themselves. But the masks they wear, the stage they occupy, the parts they play, and, most important, the spectacle they mount remain and constitute not the facade but the substance of things, not least the self. Shakespeare's old-trouper view of the vanity of action in the face of mortality—"all the world's a stage and we but poor players, content to strut our hour"—makes no sense here. There is no make-believe: of course players perish, but the play doesn't, and it is the latter, the performed rather than the performer, that really matters.

Again, all this is realized not in terms of some general mood the anthropologist in his spiritual versatility somehow captures, but through a set of readily observable symbolic forms: an elaborate repertoire of designations and titles. The Balinese have at least a half dozen major sorts of labels, ascriptive, fixed, and absolute, which one person can apply to another (or, of course, to himself) to place him among his fellows. There are birth-order markers, kinship terms, caste titles, sex indicators, teknonyms, and so on, each of which consists not of a mere collection of useful tags but a distinct and bounded, internally very complex, terminological system. To apply one of these designations or titles (or, as is more common, several at once) to a person is to define him as a determinate point in a fixed pattern, as the temporary occupant of a particular, quite untemporary, cultural locus. To identify someone, yourself or anyone else, in Bali is thus to locate him within the familiar cast of characters—"king," "grandmother," "third-born," "Brahman"—of which the social drama is, like some stock company roadshow piece—*Charley's Aunt* or *Springtime for Henry*—inevitably composed.

The drama is, of course, not farce, and especially not transvestite farce, though there are such elements in it. It is an enactment of hierarchy, a theater of status. But that, though critical, is unpursuable here. The immediate point is that, in both their structure and their mode of operation, the terminological systems conduce to a view of the human person as an appropriate representative of a generic type, not a unique creature with a private fate. To see how they do this, how they tend to obscure the mere materialities—biological, psychological, historical—of individual existence in favor of standardized status qualities would involve an extended analysis. But perhaps a single example, the simplest further simplified, will suffice to suggest the pattern.

All Balinese receive what might be called birth-order names. There are four of these, "first-born," "second-born," "third-born," and "fourth-born," after which they recycle, so that the fifth-born child is called again "first-born," the sixth "second-born," and so on. Further, these names are bestowed independently of the fates of the children. Dead children, even still-born ones, count, so that in this still high birth rate–high infant mortality society, the names don't really tell you anything very reliable about the birth-order relations of concrete individuals. Within a set of living siblings, someone called "first-born" may actually be first-, fifth-, or ninth-born, or, if somebody is missing, almost anything in between; and someone called "second-born" may in fact be older.

The birth-order naming system does not identify individuals as individuals nor is it intended to; what it does is to suggest that, for all procreating couples, births form a circular succession of "firsts," "seconds," "thirds," and "fourths," an endless four-stage replication of an imperishable form. Physically men appear and disappear as the ephemerae they are, but socially the acting figures remain eternally the same as new "firsts," "seconds," and so on; they emerge from the timeless world of the gods to replace those who, dying, dissolve once more into it. Thus I would argue that all the designation and title systems function in the same way: to represent the most time saturated aspects of the human condition as but ingredients in an eternal, footlight present.

Nor is this sense the Balinese have of always being on stage a vague and ineffable one either. It is, in fact, exactly summed up in what is surely one of their experience-nearest concepts: *lek*. *Lek* has been variously translated or mistranslated ("shame" is the most common attempt), but what it really means is close to what we call stage fright. Stage fright is the fear that, for want of skill or self-control, or perhaps by mere accident, an aesthetic illusion will not be maintained, the fear that the actor will show through his part. Aesthetic distance collapses; the audience (and the actor) loses sight of Hamlet and gains, uncomfortably for all concerned, a picture of bumbling John Smith painfully miscast as the Prince of Denmark.

In Bali, the case is the same: what is feared is that the public performance to which one's cultural location commits one will be blotched and that the personality (as we would call it but the Balinese, of course, not believing in such a thing, would not) of the individual will break through to dissolve his standardized public identity. When this occurs, as it sometimes does, the immediacy of the moment is felt with excruciating intensity, and men become suddenly and unwillingly creatural, locked in mutual embarrassment, as though they had happened upon each other's nakedness. It is the fear of *faux pas*, rendered only that much more probable by the extraordinary ritualization of daily life, that keeps social intercourse on its deliberately narrowed rails and protects the dramatistical sense of self against the disruptive threat implicit in the immediacy and spontaneity which even the most passionate ceremoniousness cannot fully eradicate from face-to-face encounters.

A PUBLIC CONTEXT FOR A PRIVATE LIFE

Morocco, mid-Eastern and dry rather than East Asian and wet, extrovert, fluid, activist, masculine, informal to a fault, a wild-west sort of place without the barrooms and the cattle drives, is another kettle of selves altogether. My work there, which began in the mid-sixties, has been centered in a moderately large town or small city in the foothills of the Middle Atlas, about twenty miles south of Fez. It is an old place, probably founded in the tenth century, conceivably even earlier. It has the walls, the gates, the narrow minarets rising to prayer-call platforms of a classical Muslim town, and, from a distance anyway, it is a rather pretty place, an irregular oval of blinding white set in the deep-sea green of an olive-grove oasis, the mountains, bronze and stony here, slanting up immediately behind it.

Close up, it is less prepossessing, though more exciting: a labyrinth of passages and alleyways, three-quarters of them blind, pressed in by wall-like buildings and curbside shops and filled with a simply astounding variety of very emphatic human beings. Arabs, Berbers, and Jews; tailors, herdsmen, and soldiers; people out of offices, people out of markets, people out of tribes;

rich, super-rich, poor, super-poor; locals, immigrants, mimic Frenchmen, unbending medievalists, and somewhere, according to the official government census for 1960, an unemployed Jewish airplane pilot—the town houses one of the finest collections of rugged individuals I, at least, have ever come up against. Next to Sefrou (the name of the place), Manhattan seems almost monotonous.

Yet, no society consists of anonymous eccentrics bouncing off one another like billiard balls, and Moroccans, too, have symbolic means by which to sort people out from one another and form an idea of what it is to be a person. The main such means—not the only one, but I think the most important and the one I want to talk about particularly here—is a peculiar linguistic form called in Arabic the *nisba*. The word derives from the triliteral root, *n-s-b*, for "ascription," "attribution," "imputation," "relationship," "affinity," "correlation," "connection," "kinship." *Nsib* means "in-law"; *nsab* means "to attribute or impute to"; *munasāba* means "a relation"; "an analogy," "a correspondence"; *mansūb* means "belonging to," "pertaining to"; and so on to at least a dozen derivatives from *nassāb*, "genealogist," to *nisbiya*, "(physical) relativity."

Nisba itself, then, refers to a combination morphological, grammatical, and semantic process which consists of transforming a noun into what we would call a relative adjective but what for Arabs becomes just another sort of noun by adding *ī* (f., *īya*): *Sefrū*/Sefrou—*Sefrūwī*/native son of Sefrou; *Sūs*/region of southwestern Morocco—*Sūsī*/man coming from that region; *Beni Yazġa*/a tribe near Sefrou—*Yazġī*/a member of that tribe; *Yahūd*/the Jews as a people, Jewry—*Yahūdī*/a Jew; *'Adlun*/surname of a prominent Sefrou family—*'Adlūnī*/a member of that family. Nor is the procedure confined to this more or less straightforward "ethnicizing" use but is employed, in a wide range of domains, to attribute relational properties to persons. For example, occupation (*hrār*/silk—*hrārī*/silk merchant); religious sect (*Darqāwā*/a mystical brotherhood—*Darqāwī*/an adept of that brotherhood); or spiritual status (*'Ali*/the Prophet's son-in-law—*'Alawī*/descendant of the Prophet's son-in-law, and thus of the Prophet).

Now, as once formed, nisbas tend to be incorporated into personal names—Umar Al-Buhadiwi/Umar of the Buhadu Tribe; Muhammed Al-Sussi/Muhammed from the Sus region; this sort of adjectival, attributive classification is quite publicly stamped upon an individual's identity. I was unable to find a single case in which an individual was generally known, or known about, but his (or her) nisba was not. Indeed, Sefrouis are far more likely to be ignorant of how well-off a man is, how long he has been around, what his personal character is, or where exactly he lives, than they are of what his nisba is—Sussi or Sefroui, Buhadiwi or Adluni, Harari or Darqawi. (Of women to whom he is not related, that is very likely to be all he knows—or, more exactly, is permitted to know.) The selves that bump and jostle each other in the alleys of Sefrou gain their definition from associative relations they are imputed to have with the society that surrounds them. They are contextualized persons.

But the situation is even more radical than this. Nisbas render men relative to their contexts, but as contexts themselves are relative, so too are nisbas, and the whole thing rises, so to speak, to the second power: relativism squared. Thus, at one level, everyone in Sefrou has the same nisba, or at least the potential of it—namely, Sefroui. However, within Sefrou such a nisba, precisely because it does not discriminate, will never be heard as part of an individual designation. It is only outside of Sefrou that the relationship to that particular context becomes identifying. Inside it, a man is an Adluni, Alawi, Meghrawi, Ngadi, or whatever; and similar distinctions exist within these categories: there are, for example, twelve different nisbas (Shakibis, Zuinis, etc.) by means of which, among themselves, Sefrou Alawis distinguish one another.

The whole matter is far from regular: what level or sort of nisba is used and seems relevant and appropriate (relevant and appropriate, that is, to the users) depends heavily on the situation. A man I knew who lived in Sefrou and worked in Fez but came from the Beni Yazgha tribe settled nearby—and from the Hima lineage of the Taghut subfraction of the Wulad Ben Ydir fraction within it—was known as a Sefroui to his work fellows in Fez; a Yazghi to all of us non-Yazghis in Sefrou; an Ydiri to other Beni Yazghis around, except for those who were themselves of the Wulad Ben Ydir fraction, who called him a Taghuti. As for the few other Taghutis, they called him a Himiwi. That's as far as things went here but not as far as they can go in either direction. Should, by chance, our friend journey to Egypt he would become a Maghrebi, the nisba formed from the Arabic word for North Africa. The social contextualization of persons is pervasive and, in its curiously unmethodical way, systematic. Men do not float as bounded psychic entities, detached from their backgrounds and singularly named. As individualistic, even willful, as the Moroccans in fact are, their identity is an attribute they borrow from their setting.

Now, as with the Javanese inside/outside, smooth/rough phe-

nomenological sort of reality-dividing, and the absolutizing Balinese
title systems, the nisba way of looking at persons—as though
they were outlines waiting to be filled in—is not an isolated
custom but part of a total pattern of social life. This pattern is, as
the others, difficult to characterize succinctly, but surely one of
its outstanding features is a promiscuous tumbling in public
settings of varieties of men kept carefully segregated in private
ones—all-out cosmopolitanism in the streets, strict communalism
(of which the famous secluded woman is only the most striking
index) in the home.

This is indeed the so-called mosaic system of social organization so often held to be characteristic of the Middle East generally:
differently shaped and colored chips jammed in irregularly together to generate an intricate overall design within which their
individual distinctiveness remains nonetheless intact. Nothing if
not diverse, Moroccan society does not cope with its diversity by
sealing it into castes, isolating it into tribes, dividing it into
ethnic groups, or covering it over with some common denominator concept of nationality, though, fitfully, all have now and then
been tried. It copes with it by distinguishing, with elaborate
precision, the contexts—marriage, worship, and to an extent
diet, law, and education—within which men are separated by
their dissimilitudes, from those—work, friendship, politics, trade—
within which, however warily and however conditionally, they
are connected by them.

To such a social pattern a concept of selfhood which marks
public identity contextually and relativistically, but yet does so in
terms—tribal, territorial, linguistic, religious, familial—which grow
out of the more private and settled arenas of life and have a deep
and permanent resonance there, would seem particularly appropriate. Indeed, it would virtually seem to create it; for it produces a situation in which people interact with one another in
terms of categories whose meaning is almost purely positional
—location in the general mosaic—leaving the substantive content of the categories, what they mean subjectively as experienced forms of life, aside as something properly concealed in
apartments, temples, and tents. Nisba discriminations can be
more or less specific; they can indicate location within the
mosaic roughly or finely; and they can be adapted to almost any
changes in circumstance. But they cannot carry with them more
than the most sketchy, outline implications concerning what men
so named as a rule are like. Calling a man a Sefroui is like
calling him a San Franciscan: it classifies him but it doesn't type
him; it places him without portraying him.

It is the capacity of the nisba system to do this—to create a framework within which persons can be identified in terms of supposedly immanent characteristics (speech, blood, faith, provenance, and the rest) and yet to minimize the impact of those characteristics in determining the practical relations among such persons in markets, shops, bureaus, fields, cafes, baths, and roadways—that makes it so central to the Moroccan idea of the self. Nisba-type categorization leads, paradoxically, to a hyperindividualism in public relationships because by providing only a vacant sketch (and that shifting) of who the actors are— Yazghis, Adlunis, Buhadiwis, or whatever—it leaves the rest, that is, almost everything, to be filled in by the process of interaction itself. What makes the mosaic work is the confidence that one can be as totally pragmatic, adaptive, opportunistic, and generally *ad hoc* in one's relations with others—a fox among foxes, a crocodile among crocodiles—as one wants without any risk of losing one's sense of who one is. Selfhood is never in danger because, outside the immediacies of procreation and prayer, only its coordinates are asserted.

RELATING PARTS AND WHOLES

Now, without trying to tie up the dozens of loose ends I have not only left dangling in these rather breathless accounts of the senses of selfhood of nearly ninety million people but have doubtless frazzled even more, let us return to the question of what all this can tell us, or could if it were done adequately, about "the native's point of view" in Java, Bali, and Morocco. In describing symbol uses, are we describing perceptions, sentiments, outlooks, experiences? If so, in what sense is this being done? What do we claim when we assert that we understand the semiotic means by which, in this case, persons are defined to one another? That we know words or that we know minds?

In answering this question, it is necessary I think first to notice the characteristic intellectual movement, the inward conceptual rhythm, in each of these analyses, and indeed in all similar analyses, including those of Malinowski—namely, a continuous dialectical tacking between the most local of local detail and the most global of global structure in such a way as to bring both into view simultaneously. In seeking to uncover the Javanese, Balinese, or Moroccan sense of self, one oscillates restlessly between the sort of exotic minutiae (lexical antitheses, categorical schemes, morphophonemic transformations) that makes even the best ethnographies a trial to read and the sort of sweeping characterizations ("quietism," "dramatism," "contextualism") that makes all but the most pedestrian of them somewhat implausible. Hopping back and forth between the whole conceived through the parts which actualize it and the parts conceived through the whole which motivates them, we seek to turn them, by a sort of intellectual perpetual motion, into explications of one another.

All this is, of course, but the now familiar trajectory of what Dilthey called the hermeneutic circle, and my argument here is merely that it is as central to ethnographic interpretation, and thus to the penetration of other people's modes of thought, as it is to literary, historical, philological, psychoanalytic, or biblical interpretation, or for that matter to the informal annotation of everyday experience we call common sense. In order to follow a baseball game one must understand what a bat, a hit, an inning, a left fielder, a squeeze play, a hanging curve, or a tightened infield are, and what the game in which these "things" are elements is all about.

When an *explication de texte* critic like Leo Spitzer attempts to interpret Keats' "Ode on a Grecian Urn," he does so by repetitively asking himself the alternating questions, "What is the whole poem about?" and "What exactly has Keats seen (or chosen to show us) depicted on the urn he is describing?" At the end of an advancing spiral of general observations and specific remarks he emerges with a reading of the poem as an assertion of the triumph of the aesthetic mode of perception over the historical.

In the same way, when a meanings-and-symbols ethnographer like myself attempts to find out what some pack of natives conceive a person to be, he moves back and forth between asking himself, "What is the general form of their life?" and "What exactly are the vehicles in which that form is embodied?" emerging at the end of a similar sort of spiral with the notion that they see the self as a composite, a persona, or a point in a pattern.

You can no more know what *lek* is if you don't know what Balinese dramatism is than you can know what a catcher's mitt is if you don't know what baseball is. And you can no more know what mosaic social organization is if you don't know what a nisba is than you can know what Keats' Platonism is if you are unable to grasp, to use Spitzer's own formulation, the "intellectual thread of thought" captured in such fragment phrases as "Attic shape," "silent form," "bride of quietness," "cold pastoral," "silence and slow time," "peaceful citadel," and "ditties of no tone."

In short, accounts of other peoples' subjectivities can be built up without recourse to pretensions to more-than-normal capacities for ego-effacement and fellow-feeling. Normal capacities in these respects are, of course, essential, as is their cultivation, if we expect people to tolerate our intrusions into their life at all and accept us as persons worth talking to. I am certainly not arguing for insensitivity here and hope I have not demonstrated it.

But whatever accurate or half-accurate sense one gets of what one's informants are "really like" comes not from the experience of that acceptance as such, which is part of one's own biography, not of theirs, but from the ability to construe their modes of expression, what I would call their symbol systems, which such an acceptance allows one to work toward developing. Understanding the form and pressure of, to use the dangerous word one more time, natives' inner lives is more like grasping a proverb, catching an allusion, seeing a joke—or, as I have suggested, reading a poem—than it is like achieving communion.

Culture and Food

by
Mary Douglas

PERCEPTIONS OF EDIBILITY

FOX NEVER APPEARS on our menu, nor dog. When I ask English
friends why fox is excluded I am told it is not edible; being
carnivorous its flesh tastes rank, or, more seriously, the meat of
carnivorous animals is likely to be poisonous because their own
food may be tainted. But in parts of Russia foxes were reckoned
a delicacy, likewise dogs in China. Evidently a local objection to
eating carnivores is not a universal revulsion. Sometimes we
admit that our strong rejection of certain meats is not founded in
physiology but in aesthetic feeling. We may shrink from the
thought of eating insects or singing birds, but we know that
grubs and grasshoppers, blackbirds and larks are served as food
elsewhere. No human activity more puzzlingly crosses the divide
between nature and culture than the selection of food. It is part
of the nurture of the body, but it is also very much a social
matter.

Anthropologists paying attention in recent years to the cultural
aspects of food have developed a structural approach.[1] According to this approach it is never useful to ask questions about one
item of culture lifted out of context. To question only why fox is
rejected from the diet leads to the single cause-and-effect chain
of reasoning which leads in the end to human physiology. But if
we are content to follow this line of reasoning we are faced with
the dubious conclusion that carnivores are indeed really danger-

Reprinted from *Culture: Essay on Culture Program*, Russell Sage Foundation,
Annual Report 1976–77, pp. 55–81, by permission of the author and the
Russell Sage Foundation

[1]Claude Lévi-Strauss, *The Raw and the Cooked: Introduction to a Science
of Mythology*, vol. 1, translated from the French by John and Doreen
Weighman (London: Jonathan Cape, 1970).

ous foods for humans. From that conclusion two other teasing questions arise. How are some human societies not clever enough to recognize the toxic effects of certain meats, while others recognize them? It is also intriguing to consider how those who ignorantly feast upon the dangerous foods have managed to survive. We might surmise that they only survive with a higher death rate, or a puny physique, but evidence suggests this is not so. Again, one would like to know the mechanisms by which the well-adapted diet is selected or how the maladaptive one is taken on. There might be some physiologically-based system of warning signals against dangerous meats (and some people might be genetically incapacitated from recognizing them). But if the warning system exists at all, it is mighty inefficient in the other direction, since fine nutritious foods get ruthlessly scrubbed off the menu. The selective principles by which humans choose their dietary sources are not likely to be physiological but cultural.

Quite apart from the problem of how humans classify some foods as inedible, there is an important difference between us and animals in the wild. The latter generally know when they have eaten enough. How humans ever learn that it is time to stop eating is a very speculative matter. The physical signals "enough" are certainly very weak, easily overriden by cultural pressures. Culture creates the system of communication among humans about edibility, toxicity and repleteness. Culture is the distinctively human cognitive activity of classifying, valuing and ranking. It organizes the environment into systems and subsystems, always changing. It has to be fluid to incorporate the shifting judgments people make about what their relations with each other should be. If we are to make sense of a given food taboo we have to set it in the full context of the society which observes the rule.

STRUCTURAL ANALYSIS OF DIETARY RULES

Three examples will illustrate how this analysis is conducted and the kind of answers it provides. The Mosaic dietary rules tell the Israelites that holiness requires them to avoid the flesh of pig, camel, hare and hyrax,[2] also certain denizens of the water and the air. The villagers of North East Thailand show extreme aversion to the merest contact with the otter and would never consider it as edible. The Lele, a Kasai tribe in Zaire, are

[2]Leviticus XI; Deuteronomy XIII.

extraordinarily fastidious about what they will and will not eat. In each of these wide-apart cases the local rules of edibility are modelled upon rules of social conduct. They can only be understood structurally, not by following the cause-and-effect implications of particular rules. A structural interpretation traces how rules of conduct match together to constitute an intelligible pattern. It is not enough to say that culture is evaluative activity. Values become relative to one another within an overall framework, as the result of judgments which distinguish and grade. The gradations do not live in thin air by themselves; they are sustained by the way people use them to measure and compare what they are doing. The examples may help here.

The ancient Mosaic rules for the table are part of a set of rules about worship and about ritual cleanliness, and also about correct behavior in sex and marriage. The food rules turn out to make sense as part of a general picture of the universe in which God's people were to be set apart for a special destiny. The physical world was divided into the three elements of water, land, air, each having its proper kind of denizens which were edible for Israelites. Those living beings which did not properly fit into the classification were barred from the table, in the same way as the Hebrews themselves were prohibited from marrying foreigners who worshipped strange gods.[3] To be holy meant to be set apart. Ultimately, the whole universe was divided between the circle of living beings which came under the protection of God's Covenant and the outsiders who did not. So the Israelites' flocks and herds were also made subject to the rules for observing the Sabbath and consecrating their first born, and were taken as the model of the most sacrificible and most edible kinds of meat. Among other land animals only their wild counterparts (mountain goats, wild sheep) were counted as edible. I have given the full account of this interpretation elsewhere.[4] Detail for detail, the Mosaic dietary rules turn out to be a consistent and logical part of the whole Mosaic law. They make sense where sense is understood to involve the whole of experience; taken alone they easily make nonsense.

The villagers of North East Thailand subscribe to a classification

[3]E. R. Leach, "The Legitimacy of Solomon: Some Structural Aspects of Old Testament History," in *Genesis as Myth and Other Essays* (London: Jonathan Cape, 1969), pp. 25–84. First appeared in *European Journal of Sociology*, vol. 23 (1962).

[4]Mary Douglas, *Purity and Danger: An Analysis of Concepts of Pollution and Taboo* (London: Routledge and Kegan Paul, 1966).

of living creatures which basically treats all land animals as edible. The exceptions are the animals which wander through the house as pets or vermin. Neither dogs nor cats nor lizards have a settled place allocated to them in the home. Their wild counterparts are also reckoned inedible. The rough and ready rule is that humans should not eat pets or vermin, whether tame or wild.[5] The anthropologist S. J. Tambiah sets this edibility rule in the context of a village life strongly organized by spatial boundaries. Just as humans should not trespass on one another's territory, so animals which invade the habitat of other species are suspect. Amphibians which may wander onto flooded rice fields are double trespassers; they cross the wild/cultivated boundary as well as the land/water boundary. The otter is classed as a water dog because of its dog-like face. The wild varieties of dogs are not edible because of the rule against eating pets and wild counterparts of pets. But otters also transgress in their very existence since they belong in the wild and in the water, but sometimes stray onto the domesticated land and create a stir by their presence in the wrong place. The rule which makes the otter out to be specially unfit for human consumption can now be seen as a straight and consistent extension of the rules of Thai village society.

My last example of the way that structural analysis provides an interpretation of food taboos is the Lele tribe. At the time of research every social category in their society was represented by a special dietary rule, sometimes by several. Women never ate this animal, pregnant women avoided that one, nursing mothers another. Men had to be initiated before they could safely eat carnivorous animals. Land animals were classed as generally edible unless they were burrowing, predatory, nocturnal or water-frequenting or somehow straddling between classifications. Any set of animals that was forbidden as dangerous for one set of humans was allowed as safe for another. The Lele's idea of toxicity in foods was based on their social categories and on the aptness of animal classes to symbolize them. When someone fell sick, it was suspected that he or she had broken these dietary rules.[6] If we were to follow such a system it would be as if we

[5]S. J. Tambiah, "Animals Are Good to Think and Good to Prohibit," *Ethnology*, vol. 8, no. 4 (1969), pp. 425–459; E. R. Leach, "Anthropological Aspects of Language: Animal Categories and Verbal Abuse," in E. J. Lennenberg, ed., *New Directions in the Study of Language* (Cambridge, Mass.: M.I.T. Press, 1964).

[6]Mary Douglas, *The Lele of the Kasai* (London: International African Institute, 1963; paperback, 1977).

associated children with a diet of milk and fruits, adolescents with burger and coke, women with salad and tea, men with steak and beer; we would attribute illness to a person's having strayed into the wrong gastronomic class.

Taken together, these examples illustrate the theme that food taboos are rooted in the way our whole experience of life is structured. However, it may well be objected that insights gained from the study of exotic cultures will not explain our own dietary behavior. Many claim that we eat what we eat for explicit nutritional reasons, or that what we eat is what we like, with no regularity or resounding cosmic equations coded into our practice. Some would say that we would eat what is good for us but for the persuasive powers of advertisers. So what can this method yield of understanding about ourselves? Agreed, agreed—I do not expect to find any explanations so tidy or so powerful when planning a program of research into the cultural aspects of food. But there is another kind of theoretical quarry to be sought, a by-product of the research into small remote societies just described. That research suggests that each individual, by cultural training, enters a sensory world that is presegmented and prejudged for him. If the same analytic techniques could be adapted to our own food habits we could hope to discover the principles of segmentation and ranking of tastes and smells. That would be a very interesting result, one never looked for before.

Nutritionists know that the palate is trained, that taste and smell are subject to cultural control. Yet for lack of other hypotheses, the notion persists that what makes an item of food acceptable is some quality inherent in the thing itself. Present research into palatability tends to concentrate on individual reactions to individual items. It seeks to screen out cultural effects as so much interference. Whereas, if the foregoing argument is accepted, the cultural controls on perception are precisely what need to be analyzed.

This program would seem too daunting if the cultural possibilities were taken to be infinite. At a later stage the focus of the research will be reduced to a manageable scale. There are some practical reasons why food habits deserve more systematic attention than they have received.

THE NEED TO STUDY FOOD HABITS

A rural population once adequately fed by multiple small resources tapped at different points in the seasonal cycle, when it turns over to imported foods or to cash-cropping and a less complex diet, loses its delicate balance with the environment. Grave nutritional disorders frequently result. Nowadays there is a widespread concern about imposing alien foods or introducing even small changes too hastily. The local food system needs to be understood and appreciated in the context of its interlinkage into the other family institutions, and the interlocking of the family with the larger social institutions of the community.

Recognizing the global food crisis, some urge that certain food supplies once despised be reinstated in esteem.[7] It may be easier to improve a traditional staple than to control the consequences of introducing a new one. But attempts to improve the quality of traditional foods may meet resistance from the local population. Some new nutrients slip into the traditional system very easily, while others (with only minute taste differences) are emphatically rejected. There are, therefore, direct nutritional reasons for concentrating on cultural aspects of gastronomy.

Two other important policy areas may be served by this research. Cultural analysis can make us aware of second-order benefits in other fields. For example, the sense of ethnic identity may depend very much on a distinctive culinary tradition. The introduction of French words for cooked animals in eleventh century Britain testifies to the dominance of a foreign cuisine: mutton for sheep, pork for pig, veal for calf. The idea that the natives are a bunch of barbarians comes across as plainly in the dietary as in the linguistic changes. So we should consider whether an agricultural program geared to producing protein more efficiently (and almost certainly intended to alter food habits) might undermine a sense of ethnic dignity as much as a forced adoption of a foreign language. At least it is important to know the possible results of suppressing ethnic food traditions.

Policies which foster major changes in the division of labor between the sexes have an impact on the household, on cooking, on timetabling and food. On the one hand, the policy which seeks to free women to play a fuller part in a wider community is bound to change the hours women spend in the kitchen. On the other hand, the movement to promote better nutrition criticizes the quality of mass-produced food. But the advance of women's status will hardly be effected without mass production. At least

[7]F. Le Gros Clark, "Food Habits as a Practical Nutrition Problem," *World Review of Nutrition and Dietetics*, no. 9 (1968), pp. 56–84; E. F. Moran, "Food, Development, and Man in the Tropics," in Margaret L. Arnott, ed., *Gastronomy: The Anthropology of Food and Food Habits* (Paris: Mouton, Mouton World Anthropology Series, 1975).

we can be sure that it will involve a parallel change in food habits, and even a radical change in the size and function of domestic units.

METHODOLOGY

As to method, our subject bristles with formidable difficulties which are hardy annuals in the history of anthropology. To elicit the rules of patterning in food systems, the first problem is how to establish criteria for units of comparison. A facile parallel with linguistic analysis might suggest that the mouthful could be equated with the phoneme. But criteria richer in their structural implications are used by the housewife and her family in constructing a meal, and the mouthful is not a clue to these. The housewife makes daily decisions about the elements she will need and how they can be combined. To get at the patterning of food, we should try to find the rules which guide her.

Three procedural pitfalls hamper research into the social aspects of diet. One is failure to disengage the physiological aspects of nutrition from the social. Subjects are questioned about the suitability of different foods for various ceremonial or other occasions, but in the same survey they are likely to be asked their views about the nutritional value of the foods. Consequently, their answers to the first kind of questions are cued by the nutritional concerns of the investigator, or vice-versa, their nutritional views may be disguised by a sense of what is socially the best idea of family food.

Second, the economic aspects of nutrition are not disengaged from social and nutritional concerns. Both physical needs and economic constraints are relevant to a housewife's choice of food. But since no theoretical principles as yet exist to guide us in distinguishing one from the other, the result is only too often a mish-mash which reflects the investigator's prejudices.

The third pitfall is the questionnaire method itself. However much care is taken to disguise the investigator's viewpoint, food is a subject so sensitive to social manipulation that inevitably, the answers to a questionnaire on food are suspect. Market researchers are fully aware of this difficulty and have evolved techniques for counteracting or discounting the misleading effects. But the questionnaire has to be structured in advance and it cannot but reflect the structure of thought which the investigators carry to their problem. The chance of new insights is thus reduced. The solution of actually sharing the meals of the subjects has been tried, only to find that the nutritionist's presence has called forth hospitality which distorts the usual pattern of eating in the home. There seems to be no completely satisfactory answer to these difficulties.

As a result of attending the nutrition subcommittee of The International Biology Panel of the Royal Society, I became aware of the gap between social concern and sociological information on the subject of nutrition. On the one hand, the Royal Society's committees and panels had been well served by biologists and medical researchers. A great deal of information about the physiology of nutrition has been amassed in response to the world-wide concern in the subject. But when it came to understanding the social factors affecting presentation and acceptability of new food, practically no general principles were established. The scientific members of the International Biology Panel were ready to agree that the very broad and often irrelevant categories in which sociological information is collected cause the results to be of very little use to them in interpreting surveys. I was much encouraged by the readiness of the biologists to recognize that food always has a social dimension of the utmost importance and therefore I prepared at the first opportunity to organize research which would open this neglected area. A grant from the UK Department of Health and Social Security in 1971 enabled me to engage Michael Nicod to undertake for his Master's Thesis a project on "Food as a System of Communication."[8]

To control for economic variation he aimed to stay as far as possible with subjects whose economic circumstances were similar: industrial working-class factory labor, families with children. Since the physiological aspects of nutrition have been so thoroughly investigated, he did not presume to be able to offer anything new on the subject. He adopted the modest project of developing a method by which the sociological dimension of food could be understood. The limited-target justified him in dealing more boldly with the usual problems of survey questionnaires; he simply eschewed all interpretive and other questions completely. He found four families in which he was accepted as a lodger and stayed in them for varying periods (the shortest was one month), watching every mouthful and sharing food whenever possible. The period of stay was much longer than pre-

[8]Michael Nicod, "A Method of Eliciting the Social Meaning of Food," report to Department of Health and Social Security, (from unpublished M.Phil. Thesis, London University, 1974).

viously undertaken in nutritional research. I reckon that after ten days of such a discreet presence the most hospitable and sensitive housewife, busy with her children, settles down to her routine menus, making special allowance for the lodger in perfectly obvious ways.

This study tried to meet the problems of imported assumptions by making our own assumptions completely explicit. We expected to find correlations between patterning of the food and patterning of the social relations among people who habitually ate the food together. We were looking for regularities that might appear between social and dietary behavior. Each family study was followed by a street survey to control for idiosyncrasy.

Our assumptions caused us to be specially interested in the capacity of food to mark social relations and to celebrate big and small occasions. Therefore we needed as wide a gamut of celebration as could be achieved. It was an integral part of our method, required by these assumptions, that the researcher be present on feast days, Sundays, national holidays, Christmas, weddings and christenings, whenever possible.

Though we were interested in tracing relations between the structures of the food system and the structure of family life, it soon became clear that the first part of the program was going to absorb all our time. Michael Nicod managed to develop a method of describing an extraordinarily compact and tightly structured food system.

The larger task of relating cultural patterns to social patterns lies ahead of us, and constitutes an integral part of the Russell Sage program on culture.

NICOD'S METHOD

The dietary system chosen for study, that practiced in English working-class families, is based upon two staple carbohydrates: potatoes and cereals. In this respect it is distinguished from upper- and middle-class English diet which tends to make use of a wider range of cereals, beans, and roots, as accompaniments to fish, eggs and meat. In the particular system under study alcohol is not taken with meals; normally cold water is drunk throughout and the meal may end with hot tea or coffee. Meals rank themselves according to joint criteria of quantity and ceremonial complexity. Quantity is an easy dimension to recognize. Ceremonial complexity is expressed by rules about plate changing, extra utensils, spoons, forks and knives. Those criteria go together, the more ceremonious, the more copious the meal.

Michael Nicod introduced and defined for his research purposes certain terms: food event; structured event; snack; meal. A food event is an occasion when food is taken, without prejudice as to whether it constitutes a meal or not. A structured event is a social occasion which is organized according to rules prescribing time, place and sequence of actions. If food is taken as part of a structured event, then we have a meal. The latter is distinguished from the snack according to the following definition: A snack is an unstructured food event in which one or more self-contained food items may be served. The event is unstructured insofar as there are no rules to prescribe which items should appear together and there is no strict order of sequence when more than one item appears. Snacks may be separable from but capable of accompanying a drink. The meal by contrast has no self-contained food items and is strongly rule-bound as to permitted combinations and sequences. Together with the distinction between special and common food events, these terms constitute the tools of the analysis. Simple Venn diagrams were used to record which members of the family and which categories of visitors were present for each kind of meal.

After some experimenting, it proved most useful to fasten attention upon sculptural and sensory qualities of the food and to compare its arrangement in the dimensions which seemed regularly used and valued: quantity; salt/sugar; temperature; dryness. (In English cooking a strong dichotomy between salty and sugary is central and explicitly referred to as savory or sweet.) Under this gross classification, the food served on the table was able to be correlated with the kinds of regular social events which marked a meal.

Ignoring the names for the meals and concentrating only on the ranking, there are three kinds of meals: A, a major meal, is served at roughly 6:00 P.M. on weekdays and early afternoon on weekends; B, a minor meal, usually follows this at 9:00 or 10:00 P.M. on weekdays, and at about 5:00 P.M. on weekends; C, a still less significant meal, a tertiary food event, consisting of a sweet biscuit and a hot drink, is available in this system to be used at different times, say at 4:00 P.M. on return from the factory on weekdays, to welcome a visitor at any time, and at bedtime on weekends. Breakfast does not enter into the system as a meal. If asked, Nicod's subjects said they never had breakfast, just a cup of tea, just a piece of toast, or that they had what they liked.

Table I. Structural Elements in Main Meal

Meal A

Food in Course 2 repeats structure of Course 1 in different materials.

Mode		Structure	Elements
Course 1	hot	staple	potato
		center	meat, fish, egg with green vegetable, stuffing, Yorkshire pudding
		dressing	thick brown gravy
Course 2	hot or cold sweet	staple	cereal
		center	fruit
		dressing	liquid custard or cream

This range of answers allows breakfast to stand as a snack according to our definition of the word. The great and famous English breakfast would seem to be outside the urban working-class tradition, if the evidence from these four families can be extended.

A close correspondence between the structure of the Sunday and the weekday evening meal A appears at once. In both cases the first course is the main course, and it is always hot and savory. It has a three-part structure based on a serving of potato, plus a centerpiece (meat, fish or eggs with one or more vegetable garnishes), the whole plate soused in rich, brown, thickened gravy (here called dressing). To celebrate visitors or feast days the special meal may have more than one dressing and the centerpiece is always meat; otherwise the rules of combination are the same.

The second course shows a repetition of the rules of combination of the first course, except that now everything is sweet not salty; sugar is on the table for sprinkling over the food in the same way as salt in the first course. There is also more freedom

Table II. Overall Pattern in Main Meal

Meal A
Varieties reveal an overall pattern.

Course 1	Course 2	Course 3
savory	sweet	sweet
potato staple	cereal staple	cereal staple
no discretion to omit elements	some discretion	optional
dressing runny	dressing thick	dressing solid
other sensory qualities of food dominate over visual pattern	visual pattern dominates until serving	visual pattern dominates until eating
solids not segregated from liquids		solids and liquids segregated
start hot	optionally hot or cold	cold

in the second course to serve one element and omit another in modifying for everyday occasions the three festive prototypes of dessert, i.e., plum pudding, trifle and fruit tart. The pudding course varies freely upon the theme of cereal, fruit and cream; on the one hand the fruit may be diminished to a thin layer of jam or a mere streak of color in the jelly of a trifle which consists mostly of juice-soaked cake and custard, and it may disappear completely in a rice pudding; on the other hand, the fruit may dominate over everything else, as in the fruit pie, or the cereal may be omitted, as in tinned fruit and custard. Ordinarily the sweet dressing, though thicker than gravy, is poured over the plate in the same way as the gravy in the first course. On Christmas Day the special "hard sauce" or "brandy butter" is too solid to pour. So we see a tendency for dressing to be thicker from the first course to the second and thicker between ordinary and celebratory occasions.

On Sundays and other special occasions, when the second course is nearly finished, preparations are made for the third part of the meal, the hot drink and biscuits. Hitherto only cold water has been drunk with the food; the variations of liquid and solid are carried out upon the plate of food. Now in the third course total segregation of liquids from solids appears; in the cup is a hot drink, on the plate a cold, dry solid, a reversal of the hot/cold pattern of the first course, when the cold drink is in the glass and the hot food upon the plate (Table I). These rules relate the three courses to one another in an overall pattern; the meal starts hot and finishes with cold solids; the quantity decreases with each course; formal patterning increases with each course. That is to say, regularity in a three-dimensional sculpted shape is not at all required or even appropriate for the first course. One might say that the meal begins by looking like a haphazard, natural pile of food on the plate, and moves on to a formally designed cultural artifact, the cathedral-like dome of the jelly mold, the geometrical design of cherries, colored sugar crystals patterned over the bowl of custardy cake, the smooth spherical sides of the plum pudding. Incidentally, the generic term for some of these sweet items is "shape" as in chocolate shape, pink shape. The almost solid cream dressing on feast days is also able to hold a shape. These differences between Course 1 and Course 2 themselves are reinforced in Course 3 so that they become themes which constrain all the courses into a single consistent structure (Table II).

It is no surprise to the native Englishman that the distinction between hot and cold is critical in this dietary system. For the third course the teapot is carefully heated before the water is poured in, actually on the boil; the plates for the first course are kept stacked on the rack above the cooker so that they are carried to the table warm. Apart from bottled sauces no addition of cold foods to a hot plate is permitted, nor vice-versa, so cold tomato is not compatible with hot meat.

Looking again at Table II we can see that the three courses of main meal A in some of their rules of combination present the same structure as do the three meals of Sunday, so that a unitary frame holds the pattern together right across the week. When we consider the rules governing meal B the same pattern is reinforced still more (Table III). The regularity of the pattern is so strong that it can be made to bear some weight of explanation. For example, before seeing the structure laid out, one could have asked reasonably why they never serve potatoes in meal B. The answer now would be that potatoes are the staple for meal A Course 1. That part of the pattern would lose its distinctiveness if potatoes were served in Course 2 or meal B. Or if one asked why

Table III. Correspondence Between First and Second Meals

Meal B
Meal B repeats meal A in course sequence but keeps to the staple of Course 2.

	Mode	Structure	Elements
Course 1	savory, hot or cold	staple	bread
		center	meat, fish or egg or baked beans
		dressing	butter
Course 2	sweet, cold	staple	bread
		center	jam
		dressing	butter
Course 3	sweet, cold		optional cake for Sundays or sweet biscuits[a]

[a]This word has a special meaning in England. It cuts the spectrum which runs between cake-to-cracker and the spectrum of desserts in a distinctive way. Sweet biscuits are small, dry, smooth confections, presented in highly contrived, regular geometric shapes.

Table IV. Pattern for First and Second Meals

Rules controlling relation of meal A and meal B bring both under a single pattern.

Between meal A and meal B through courses one, two, and three, the following rules hold:

    a) increasing dessication
    b) increasing dominance of visual pattern
    c) decreasing scale of quantity
    d) nonreversibility:
        i) of staple order
        ii) of savory/sweet order
        iii) of dessication order
        iv) of scale order
        v) of hot to cold order

the main meal starts with hot solids and ends with cold ones, the answer to "why" questioning has to be given in terms of a pattern that would lose its distinctive recognizability if a change were made (Table IV).

The sequence, ranking and rules of the three meals of Sunday are now mapped on to the three courses of the main meal: first the potato meal, second the main cereal meal, third the last cereal, sweet and dry. Scanning the rules we see that the last course of the first two meals and the only solid of the third meal is exactly the same item, except that it is progressively drier. Going from pudding to cake, the lavish dressing has originally been poured over the cake, but instead of being a viscous custard it is set in the form of soft frosting. The option to select any of the possible ingredients of a second course in the main meal is even more open in the minor meal, but working through the menus, week-by-week and month-by-month, the prototype puddings are recognizable in the second part of the minor meal in their dry forms, as plum cake and jam sponge cake. When it comes to the final course of the main meal or the last meal on Sunday night, the range of sweet biscuits reveals the pudding again, in its most dessicated forms: currant biscuits; sugar-coated biscuits; jam-centered biscuits. Insofar as the sweet biscuit that may be eaten last thing at night on Sunday is a dry version of the cake, and the cake a dry version of the pudding, we can regard it as a summary form, literally, of those courses. The biscuit is capable of standing for all the sequences of puddings through the year and of wedding cakes and christening cakes through the life cycle.

One meal, one day's eating, even one weekend does not give enough time to discern the pattern. In each dietary system the duration of the whole pattern is likely to vary. This particular British one comes to its great climax with the life-cycle event celebrated with the white, glittering three-tiered architecture of the wedding cake. Its frosting is so hard that it takes a sword-sized knife and the combined efforts of the bride and groom to cut into it. Our analysis is beginning to reveal a dietary system which has the mimetic and rhythmic qualities of other symbolic systems. The capacity to recall the whole by the structure of the parts is a well-known technique in music and poetry for arousing attention and sustaining interest.

The description of the principles adopted by an English house-wife for constituting her family meals can be summarized in a few rules. In the very simplicity and economy of the dietary system, the normal principles of recognition and stable structuring are at work. The housewife can serve a meal that will be acceptable to her family so long as she works within certain restrictive patternings of sequence and combination. Novelties do not present a challenge so long as they are introduced within the pattern. For example, spaghetti in tomato sauce cannot be served as a main course in the main meal in this British dietary system. But a small amount of spaghetti can be used as an addition to the centerpiece in the savory potato course without disturbing the general pattern.

In this dietary system the most distinctive underlying feature appears to be the increasingly clear geometry of forms which is not discernible in the first phases, but which quickly wins out through the temporal sequences, so that we end with complete units structured in such a way as to show in each the pattern that dominates them all. In spite of, or rather perhaps we should say because of the strict austerity of the resources, the sequence of meals forms a single recognizable system: the whole is modelled on the parts and vice-versa. The strong repetitive pattern may reveal the basis of conservatism in the system, and this kind of analysis may be a route that discovers principles of rejection and acceptable innovation in other dietary systems.

TRENDS

We can now return to the question of how humans learn that it is time to stop eating. Already Nicod's research suggests something about a cultural system of stop signals which normally warn humans that they have had enough. The tightly structured meal system has its beginning, its middle and progressive movements towards a known and anticipated ending. Easy to know one has had enough when the biscuits and tea arrive on the table. How do we know that a sonnet has come to an end? Or a sonata? Not all works of art are necessarily subject to such rulings. Not all food systems signal beginnings and conclusions so firmly as the one just described. The fact that the stop signal can be suppressed suggests how we may use this approach for understanding trends in food habits.

Patterns of consumption in the UK show that bread takes a declining share in the total expenditure on food. If advertising could make us eat more bread, the vast sums expended to that purpose would have surely secured the result. Advertisers seem only able to influence the choice as between different brands, and can do little to affect broad trends. There is a general trend,

Table V. Consumption of Varieties of Foods in the UK, 1955–1971[a]

Ounces of Food/Week Per 1000 Daily (KCAL)
Income Groups

		A	B	C
Cheese in oz.	1955	1.11	1.06	1.07
	1962	1.31	1.20	1.13
	1971	1.67 (+50%)	1.47 (+39%)	1.33 (+24%)
Meat in oz.	1955	13.73	12.99	12.69
	1962	15.38	14.30	14.16
	1971	17.09 (+24%)	15.30 (+18%)	14.86 (+17%)
Total milk and cream in pints	1955	2.24	1.95	1.82
	1962	2.28	2.05	1.89
	1971	2.31 (+3%)	2.09 (+7%)	1.94 (+7%)
Total fats in oz.	1955	4.61	4.50	4.46
	1962	4.64	4.57	4.50
	1971	4.50 (−2%)	4.60 (+2%)	4.55 (+2%)
Potatoes in oz.	1955	20.27	23.75	23.85
	1962	18.30	20.75	21.06
	1971	14.40 (−29%)	19.67 (−17%)	21.16 (−11%)
Bread in oz.	1955	17.53	20.40	21.88
	1962	13.56	16.06	17.67
	1971	11.47 (−35%)	13.52 (−34%)	15.36 (−30%)
Biscuits in oz.	1955	2.12	2.01	1.88
	1962	2.24	2.23	2.13
	1971	2.27 (+7%)	2.30 (+14%)	2.28 (+21%)
Sugar and preserves in oz.	1955	8.21	8.17	8.17
	1962	8.20	8.05	8.17
	1971	6.41 (−22%)	7.09 (−13%)	7.61 (−7%)
Total fruit in oz.	1955	14.56	10.79	8.91
	1962	15.67	12.00	9.49
	1971	18.46 (+27%)	13.10 (+21%)	10.61 (+19%)

[a]From the National Food Survey Committee Report, 1973.

shown by potatoes and rice as well as by bread, for carbohydrates to have a declining share of total food expenditure. But this itself is part of a bigger trend. Food as a category also has a declining share of total expenditure.

The UK National Food Survey Committee[9] reported that be-

[9]National Food Survey Committee, "Household Food Consumption and Expenditure, 1970 and 1971" (London: Her Majesty's Stationery Office, 1973).

tween 1955 and 1971 the total food expenditure as a percentage
of total consumers' expenditure on goods and services declined
steadily. As among kinds of food, for the top income group (see
Table V for income groups A, B and C) there was a dramatic
rise in consumption of meat and fruit, and a dramatic decline for
potatoes, bread and sugar; biscuits more than held their own with
a 7 percent increase in the top income group, 14 percent increase
in the next and 21 percent in the third. If it was advertising that
made biscuits so important in the diet of lower-income groups
we should be curious to know why it could work for biscuits
but not for bread.

Michael Nicod's structural analysis suggests an explanation of
the trend in which biscuits held their own. During the 15 years
before his research, the working classes were following slowly a
trend clearly set in the higher-income groups. Over the period
from 1955 through 1971 the proportion of energy derived from
fats as compared with carbohydrates was going up in all
groups. The diagram below[10] refers to the top income group, A,
and the third, C. For group A until 1964, the two lines were
converging, a larger proportion of fats and a declining proportion
of carbohydrates. After 1965, the two lines cross and the trends
continue.

The C income group shows the same trend with a nine-year lag
behind income group A. The intervening income group B, not
shown here, has the same trend with a five-year lag; the last
income group D also shows the trend with the longest lag of all.
So group C (while it was not keeping up with the increased
intake of fats in groups B and A) was greatly increasing the
quantity of biscuits consumed. Impossible to say why, without a
closer focus. Perhaps the biscuit operated as a stop signal against
the excessive cost of fats and oils in the family budget. Perhaps
the formalization of the British working-class meal in the pattern
described by Nicod crystallized in this period. Perhaps there was
more entertaining among families. Humans, like animals, know
what they like to eat, but unlike animals they do not know when
to stop. As incomes go up we do not necessarily choose what is
best for our health. Neither selection nor repletion is signalled to
the human feeder by automatic physiological mechanisms; there
is no natural stop sign. Nutritionists tend to disapprove of these
trends to eat more and more fats and oils. Admittedly there may

[10]J. W. Marr, and W. T. C. Berry, "Income, Secular Change and
Family Food Consumption Levels: A Review of the National Food Survey
1955–1971," *Nutrition*, vol. 28, no. 1 (1974), pp. 39–52.

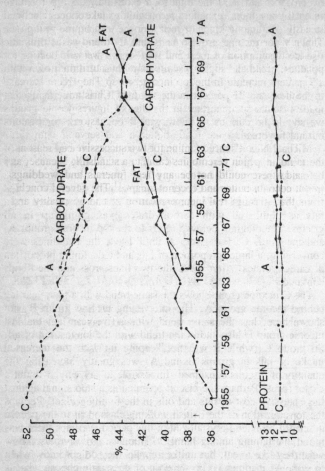

Figure I. Percentage of energy from carbohydrate, fat and protein, income groups A and C, 1955–1971. Income group C plotted with a nine-year time lag behind group A shows the same trends—a decrease in the percentage of energy from carbohydrate and an increase in the percentage from fat. These figures relate to food consumed in the home.[a]

[a]From Marr, J. W., and Berry, W. F. C., "Income, Secular Change and Family Food Consumption Levels: A Review of the National Food Survey, 1955–77," *Nutrition*, London, vol. 28, no. 1 (1974), fig. 2, p. 44.

be a physiological reason for them. We can only take in a given amount of dry food, so that if we decide to take more than we can easily stomach, we must wash it down with liquids and ease it down with oils. Spices also help salivation and so help us to eat more than is good for us. But why should we want to?

The fact is that food is only partly for nutrition and very largely for ceremonial and social purposes. The UK National Food Survey never takes information over Christmas. If it did so, how much more impressive would the figures for fats and oils have been! The more ceremonial the occasion, the greater the tendency to lard the food, butter it and serve it with oil. When Tikopia experienced famine for two successive bad seasons, life did not stop, but ceremonies came to a standstill, because, as they said, there could not be any real funerals and weddings without coconut butter and coconut cream.[11] The general conclusion is that a rise in real income means a rise in hospitality and celebration, and so in pressure to consume more, and so to a higher demand for fats. Instead of signalling "stop," the cultural pressures may signal the opposite.

COMPARATIVE RESEARCH INTO FAMILY SYSTEMS

Nicod's results are methodological. He shows how Sundays are distinguished from weekdays and how weddings are celebrated in the same idiom. But above all the value of his research is to show how a strong patterning can be traced. Using this experiment as a basis for comparative research, the method can be strengthened. In the future, the sociological background to the cultural aspects of food can be very much more explicitly researched. Since foods tend to be used for categorizing social occasions and statuses, the local ideas about food fit for visitors, for invalids, for children, for beggars, even for pets should be tracked. The finer distinctions between men's and women's food in each category will also be noted. For each distinctive food system, one expects to find a number of separate programs, each gaining its meaning by contrast with the other. Automatically the research will focus upon social pressures inside and outside the home. One would expect the same graded social categories to be manifest in other domestic arrangements: the division of labor between the sexes; the use of domestic space; the provision of

[11]Raymond Firth, *Social Change in Tikopia* (London: Allen and Unwin, 1960).

plates, cutlery and other accoutrements. A meal taken by women together is likely to be very different in all details from one taken by men together in a society where men and women live in very segregated social spheres; it is likely to be taken in a room with distinctive decoration, served with different utensils, judged by different criteria. The researchers, relying on observations based on continuous presence in the home and sharing of food presented in the day, will continually be trying to state the rule structure of each particular dietary system, with special attention for food chosen for ceremonial occasions.

Research into the cultural aspects of food should avoid the mistake of isolating one activity from the whole. The food system is only one of a number of family systems for caring for the body. These include the provision of rest, of cleaning and clothing, of care for the sick and the dying and of those giving birth. For example, the system for providing for rest consists of rules for allocating access to beds, seating and privacy. In any family with children there are conventions about whom the child may go to for comfort in the night. Sometimes it is to the bed of one or the other of the parents, sometimes to the grandmother, aunt, or nanny. There are questions which also get settled about precedence and priorities between members of the family as regards respecting each others' rights to sleep. Whose postprandial rest must be respected by tiptoe and whispers? Whose early bedtime similarly needs to be respected by hush in the rest of the house? The question of who gets the best seating spaces near or far from the window, the door, the television, etc., are settled by the exercise of authority or simply by bargaining or force, or appeals to principles such as: "Babies need sleep;" "The breadwinner needs rest."

As the medical profession gets more organized, the care for birth, death and sickness tends to be provided less and less by the family and more by professionals in specialized institutions. However, families vary on these points. When sickness is treated at home, the question of who is made responsible for the care of the sick and who is let off varies. In some families every single member of the family, not necessarily those living under the same roof, will be involved in a strict order; in other families it would all fall upon one person, say the youngest unmarried daughter, or maybe the mother or the father. As to the rules about regular bodily care, crises apart, questions of access to the taps and bathrooms have to be settled. Who has priority, who has to wait in line, and in what order, how often are individual preferences allowed to disturb the pattern of priorities? How much do the categories of sex and age, parental and child roles get expressed in terms of these rules? These priorities are also settled by indirect bargaining among the members of the family. An evolving system of body care is provided within the family, and at the same time it constitutes the pattern of relationships within the family.

By learning the rules of the different family systems we can get a way of characterizing family types. So we will be able to relate the food systems to the whole family system.

The family does not exist in a cultural vacuum. Information about food is continually pressed upon it by the media, advertising and friends. Theoretically this would seem to pose a major problem for our research if it were held to be necessary to distinguish the family or street as a subculture from the main culture of which it is a part. But fortunately there is no need in this program to make such distinctions. On the contrary, we hope to be able to identify the family types that are most receptive or most closed to outside influence. The research would seek to develop a method of relating society and culture. It would also need to take account of the social pressures to which the selected families are subject. Certain gastronomic patterns may be a universal response to given social conditions: for example, timetabling of food obviously responds to occupational timetabling. The dominance of carbohydrates tends to be a response to low-income urban conditions. It is likely that a closed repetitive pattern such as that revealed by Nicod may correspond to a closed network of social relations.

NEW DIRECTIONS FOR RESEARCH

Having painted the scene on a rather large canvas, we can now reduce the prospect to a few controllable perspectives. Certain dimensions for comparing the food-taking process will probably be applicable to all dietary systems: quantity, temporal sequencing, thermal, salt/sugar, liquid/solid, bland/spicy. Other bases of evaluation may turn out to be more significant, such as whole/chopped, roast/boiled, or color and smell. The following headings are proposed as guidelines for the research.

I. The relation of the gastronomic to other arts and orders of behavior in a particular cultural tradition. It would not be right to assume that gastronomy necessarily takes the same rank order of local esteem as music, dance, mythmaking, housebuilding, etc.

Attention should be paid to the interrelation of different cultural domains and the strength of their boundaries.

  II. Identification of relevant dimensions of comparison.
      A. Socioeconomic
      B. Esthetic
      C. Gastronomic

A. Socioeconomic

cost: in money; in labor $\begin{cases} \text{-male} \\ \text{-female;} \\ \text{-child} \end{cases}$ in time $\begin{cases} \text{-frequency of meals, etc.} \\ \text{-length of preparation} \end{cases}$

location: $\begin{cases} \text{-bedroom} \\ \text{-kitchen} \\ \text{-front room} \\ \text{-special dining area, etc.} \end{cases}$

What food is regarded as appropriate to these various locations may also relate to costs.

accoutrements: cutlery (numbers of items per person and specialization); textile (napkins, table cloth, doylies, etc.); ceramics and glass (numbers of changes of plates, etc.); lighting (dark, light, electric, candles, etc.); decoration (e.g., flowers, essential or not essential)

company: regular unit for eating together; unusual visitors; male/female/children; healthy/sick

B. Esthetic

    color relations: color combinations and sequencing rules; there may or may not be correspondence between these and gastronomic rules, but we would expect correlations with cost, time and company.

    color choices: distinctiveness of colors approved for gastronomic purposes (e.g., colors like or unlike those of flowers, floors, clothes, or the practice of using the same register for interior decoration as for food, e.g., cream walls with chocolate velvet curtains).

    formal pattern: the dominance of a clear geometric design in placement of food on dish, on plate, in mouthful sized item; three-dimensional sculptured effects:

-stiff edible container, natural/confected
-stiffened for sculptural effects (e.g., flour thickening,
  gelatin, eggs or by dessication)
-liquid with surface decoration
-liquid in layers (e.g., Irish coffee)
-liquid with regular or irregular solid elements (e.g.,
  spaghetti, etc.) floating in it.

part/whole (the large-whole/cut-part contrast against the
large-whole small-whole contrast): To make clear the
significance of this the anthropologist has to recall the
important suggestions made by Lévi-Strauss on the
significance of the roast as distinct from other kinds
of cooking. The large whole roast tends to be used
for big ceremonial occasions. But we note that the
large wedding cake must not be cut before the company arrives, and refer also to the custom of breaking
bread in the Jewish food system as part of the ceremony of food distribution. The distinction between
whole and cut parts may be important as an index of
formality.

These are only a few suggestions. There are many
other possible patternings. From this set of dimensions
can be derived a criterion on the relative segregation of
the gastronomic from other orders governing social
relations. This will help judgment of how high or low
gastronomy stands as a separate domain within the
local culture.

C. *Gastronomic*
  content: staples (one/two/none); meat/vegetarian; alco-
    holic/non-alcoholic. This will need to be related to
    costs and income.
  texture: liquid/solid; crisp, tough, tender, disintegrating,
    viscous, etc. Laboratory testing may be needed to
    identify these local terms and their reference. There
    are likely correlations between sticky foods needing
    many knives and forks and plates and napkins and a
    particular dining space and particular company. The
    distinction between wet and dry may be a regular
    marker for the social scale between intimacy and
    distance.
  taste: spicy/bland, savory/sweet; these distinctions are
    likely to be important markers of different social

statuses, as between children/adults (children's food is usually cheaper and blander), male/female, common/celebratory.

thermal: hot/cold/lukewarm; this applies to plates, napkins, drinks. There is special interest in asking whether the local culture recognizes a special thermal range appropriate to food, and the relation of this range to room and body temperatures.

olfactory: alleged and experimentally tested differences; expectations about appropriate olfactory perceptions in food as distinct from body smells, fecal, medicinal and deodorant smells. This item provides another measure of boundary strength between different cultural domains. The more a distinctive gastronomic domain appears to be clearly bounded from others, the more interesting it is to ask questions about the transfer or structure from one domain to another within a culture.

cooking medium: specialization of or mixing of preparatory oils and waters for different gastronomic classes, e.g., meat fat for savory cooking, mixture of fish and meat in same sauce, or nonmixture. This item clues the amount of internal segregation and specialization within a cultural domain and also permits comparison between cultural domains.

Industrialization has been accompanied by trends to disguise or screen off body odors. To this fact various trends in taste may be traced: there seems to be a trend to bland flavors, to separation of taste experiences, to repugnance from putrefaction and fetid smells. This may be part of a general tendency to prefer distinctive flavors unmixed. For example, it is now thought by some gourmets that the smoke of even a good cigar spoils the taste of good brandy, whereas traditionally they are complementary. Gorgonzola crawling with maggoty life is no longer so much appreciated as creamier fresh gorgonzola, and imported cheeses tend to be blander than those preferred in their place of origin, particularly on the farms where the smells of dairying and manure form part of the olfactory background. The same applies to malt whiskey: the peaty flavors come across both more clearly and more pleasingly in an air that is laden already with peaty smells and accompanying a diet cooked in peaty water. The medlar, grown and eaten in Shakespeare's England, never appears now, and it is surely not accidental in this context that it needs to be rotting before it is edible. Pheasants, grouse and beef are rarely hung long enough to get the rank, gamey flavor once prized. Asafoetida is not appreciated in Europe though prized as a flavoring in India; garlic has an interesting career, back and forth from Southern France and Italy among different social strata of other parts of Europe. This is a complex subject. But clearly, laboratory testing of taste should take account of background smells. It should be possible to take account of cultural conditioning. This research is planned to help to measure the cultural aspects of taste.

CONCLUSION

A set of field studies, closely coordinated, based on some perspective such as these, would have as one of its objects to improve the method and extend the range of questions about culture which can be broached. The culinary tradition is only part of the total cultural experience of an individual. This approach will provide a means of assessing the degree of insulation between cultural domains, and a way to map evaluative structures from one domain to another. Thus it will enable a serious comparison of cultural subsystems to be made in very general terms: the amount of internal cross-referencing, pattern repetition, the length of pattern rhythms, the placing of climax and cadence. It will be possible to develop hypotheses about the relation of such structural characteristics to the social structure. Theoretically, this is the most difficult and most interesting part of the whole research.

Those are technical problems very particular to anthropology. But this research will also help to understand what is happening to our food habits. As the years go on, we will surely become more deeply conscious of the pressure of population and the threat of widespread starvation. This consciousness has already started to exert a pressure of moral opinion on our food habits. We will surely also become more conscious of the artificial character of our restrictive rules. Once we realize that our ideas of edibility are mainly rooted in culture, not in nature, we can ask about possible food revolutions of the future. If hospitality were to become totally absorbed into social competitiveness it could continue to drive demand towards particularly prized animal meats,[12] to particularly tender and bloody cuts of meat, to extraordinary rare meats fetched from remote corners of the globe. Or the conscience of industrial society may sicken at the very thought of breeding and killing animals for food. Or it could make a complete turnabout in its attitude toward the edibility of vermin. Suppose we discovered some simple way of neutralizing the possible pathogenic associations of moths, spiders, worms and all the bugs. The human race could feed upon its own parasites and pests.

If we consciously overcame our aversion to eating bugs, the effort might lead us to treat nourishment as we do medicines, a part of private hygiene on the level of toothbrushing and defecating. Just imagine the shock to the catering industry, restaurant architecture and house decoration that such a futuristic view entails. Other equally unlikely difficulties might beset restaurants if, for instance, we conceived a horror of social exclusion and made every effort not to select our company. Then the street barbecue might gain social and moral superiority over the exclusive restaurant dinner. Restaurants might be forced to adapt to meet a radical judgment against private sumptuosity being indulged in public places, and good food guides would change their editorial tone.

Certainly new sources of nutrients would be developed as well as new sources of energy. This being so, we should ask how they will be presented at the tables of the future. Perhaps the new menus will be cautiously modelled on traditional ones. More interestingly, they might be presented in hitherto unimagined shapes and styles. Perhaps food could be designed for being consumed to the rhythm of music. A hundred radical changes in menu structure could be imagined. Whatever they may be, no doubt about it, there will be food revolutions in modern industrial society that are inconceivable now.

REFERENCES

Some of the material presented here is summarized from other scattered publications, to whose editors we are grateful for permission to reprint parts.
Douglas, Mary. "Food as an Art Form." *Studio International*, September 1974.

[12]Marshall Sahlins, *Culture and Practical Reason* (Chicago: University of Chicago Press, 1976).

————. "The Sociology of Bread." In A. Spicer, ed., *Bread*. London: Applied Science Publishers, 1975.

———— and Michael Nicod. "Taking the Biscuit: The Structure of British Meals." *New Society*, vol. 30, no. 637 (December 19, 1974), pp. 744–747. The help of the UK Department of Health and Social Security is acknowledged for supporting Michael Nicod's research.

III

HUMAN COMMUNICATION

There are only two things on which I cannot be trusted:
words and deeds.

Hindu saying

The limits of my language mean the limits of my
world.

Wittgenstein

ALL ANIMAL SPECIES communicate with each other—transfer information from one organism to another. Humans, however, have the richest and most versatile communication system of the animal kingdom. Humans have language, a system of vocal symbols capable of communicating anything we feel, believe, or know. Linguistic symbols stand for things and ideas. The thing "tree," for example, is something you can see, smell, touch, cut down, or whatever. Not so the symbol *tree*, which is attached to other symbols to form phrases, sentences, and so forth. The relationship between "tree" the thing and *tree* the symbol appears simple: one really exists while the other is only a representation. This simple explanation is, unfortunately, false. *Tree* (the word) is not just a passive, unimportant representation, for it conjures up a host of associations for us. *Tree* for English speakers is linked to *shade, fruit, forest, countryside, logs, fireside*, etc. The word *tree*, by describing something positive and pleasant, covers the thing "tree" with an aura. Hence when confronted with the thing "tree" it is difficult (perhaps impossible) to see it objectively. Similarly "bride," "baby," and "rose" are not seen objectively. *Bride* and *baby* are beautiful by definition. *Rose* is not only beautiful but a sweet-smelling symbol of purity and love.

Positive words such as *"tree," "bride" "baby,"* and *rose* contrast with negative words such as *rat* and *weed*. *Rat* reminds us of poverty and sewers. They are disloyal ("to smell a rat"), untrustworthy ("to rat on"), and extremely selfish ("like rats leaving a sinking ship"). *Weeds* are uncontrollable and therefore must be destroyed. As the Oxford Dictionary tells us, *weeds* are wild herbs springing up where they are not wanted. Natural

104

things, like weeds, which are uncontrollable are particularly obnoxious to English speakers. Nature, for us, is a passive agent to be molded to the human will. If we interact with nature and get into trouble, it is usually our fault. Thus we say, "I am drowning," for example, implying that a particular lack of control "is killing me." Whereas the Navaho, who believe that nature is more powerful than humans, would say, "The water is killing me."

Words, clearly, do more than just *represent* things. Words also *present* phenomena prejudicially. Words introduce things to us. Words "tell" us (very subtly yet most effectively): this is pleasant, that is unpleasant; this is valuable, that is valueless; this is to be feared, that is to be loved; and so forth. For one great anthropologist-linguist, Edward Sapir, this meant that "humans are very much at the mercy of that particular language which has become the medium of expression for their society." As shown by Thomas Kochman ("Rapping in the Black Ghetto") and by Earl Rubington ("The Language of 'Drunks' "), society consists of different subgroups each of which uses a special variation of the "particular language." These subgroups communicate with each other and share some bits of a common "reality." Those bits fully shared are represented and presented by several different words. Therefore, at least in a complex society such as the United States, there is no one-to-one relation between a word and a bit of "reality." Standing on the shoulders of a "giant," we are enabled to see further. This improved vision indicates that language is one of several subsystems that manipulates "reality." Such reality-manipulators include "culture," "social stratification," and "the individual."

Culture, social stratification, the individual, and language are all cleverly interrelated in Kochman's essay. Blacks in American society have been assigned a restrictive role subordinate to "the Man" (the white man, the establishment, or any authority figure). Real feelings have had to be concealed and words invented to work on the mind and heart of "Whitey." Having become expert in inventing word-games for use against "the Man," Blacks invented games to play against each other. "Word games" or encounters with a high degree of verbal structuring are found in many parts of the world. The stages and styles of discourse in a drinking encounter among the Subanun of the Philippines are presented in a fascinating paper by Charles Frake. In "How to Ask for a Drink in Subanun" we are shown again the close ties that exist between language and culture. Knowing functional sounds (phonemes), meaningful utterances (morphemes), and acceptable sentences will not insure an appropriate drinking encounter in Subanun. A special drinking code must be understood. It is necessary to manipulate a set of instructions which include a special sequence: "invitation," "jar talk," "discussion," and "display of verbal art."

In "The Language of Drunks" Earl Rubington provides a comparison between playing drinking games and living in order to drink. A special language helps "drunks" adapt to their hard, hazard-filled world. Getting rolled by toughs and having to deal with police, bad weather, or D.T.s (delirium tremens) are but few of the problems linked to drunk culture. Language here, as elsewhere, integrates a group and builds a wall between it and nonintimates.

Language, like every basic aspect of culture, can never be fully described in simple, functional terms. Yes, language presents and represents "reality." While at a given time the "limits of my language mean the limits of my world," at a later time my world has changed because my language has changed. I am still limited, but in a different way. Language, while ever limiting my world, permits me to carefully explore it. And language allows me to play one of the oldest roles in human history, that of gossip.[1]

Gossip is generally considered as nonserious and malicious conversation. In Western sexist terms, women gossip while men get together to have "bull sessions." Gossip produces pleasure while ruining reputations. Bull sessions produce bullshit, an earthy, fertilizing substance. Patricia Meyer Spacks artfully interweaves information from many disciplines in "In Praise of Gossip" to show us that both men and women gossip. And gossip need not be what my Chassidic informants call *loshon hara*, or "evil talk." Gossip can be and often is healing talk, a process which transforms a group of relative strangers into intimates. Yet, paradoxically, relative strangers tend *not to* gossip. Being allowed to join in is already a sign of some kind of intimacy. Why do intimates gossip if they are already "close"? Perhaps we should speak of "gossip for gossip's sake," the way we refer to "art for art's sake." Humans, as those who spend much time with babies know, are babbling primates. Perhaps the content does not really matter. We seem to be happier when we exercise our lips and related organs.

[1]It is generally believed that prostitution and surgery (Adam's rib being removed to form Eve) represent the really ancient roles. I would add "gossip."

REFERENCES

Burling, Robbins. *Man's Many Voices: Language in its Cultural Context*. New York: Holt, Rinehart and Winston, 1970.

Farb, Peter. *Word Play: What Happens When People Talk*. New York: Random House, 1973.

Sapir, Edward. *Selected Writings*. Edited by David G. Mandelbaum. Berkeley and Los Angeles: University of California Press, 1949.

"Rapping" in the Black Ghetto

by
Thomas Kochman

"RAPPING," "SHUCKING," "JIVING," "running it down," "gripping," "copping a plea," "signifying," and "sounding" are all part of the black ghetto idiom and describe different kinds of talking. Each has its own distinguishing features of form, style, and function; each is influenced by, and influences, the speaker, setting, and audience; and each sheds light on the black perspective and the black condition—on those orienting values and attitudes that will cause a speaker to speak or perform in his own way within the social context of the black community.

I was first introduced to black idiom in New York City, and, as a professional linguist interested in dialects, I began to compile a lexicon of such expressions. My real involvement, however, came in Chicago, while preparing a course on black idiom at the Center for Inner City studies, the southside branch of Northeastern Illinois State College.

Here I began to explore the full cultural significance of this kind of verbal behavior. My students and informants within black Chicago, through their knowledge of these terms, and their ability to recognize and categorize the techniques and to give examples, gave me much reliable data. When I turned for other or better examples to the literature—such as the writings of Malcom X, Robert Conot, and Iceberg Slim—my students and informants were able to recognize and confirm their authenticity.

While often used to mean ordinary conversation, rapping is distinctively a fluent and a lively way of talking, always characterized by a high degree of personal style. To one's own group, rapping may be descriptive of an interesting narration, a colorful rundown of some past event. An example of this kind of rap is

Adapted from *Trans*action, vol. 6 (February 1969), by permission of the author and Transaction, Inc.

the answer from a Chicago gang member to a youth worker who asked how his group became organized:

> Now I'm goin to tell you how the jive really started. I'm going to tell you how the club got this big. 'Bout 1956 there used to be a time when the Jackson Park show was open and the Stony show was open. Sixty-six street, Jeff, Gene, all of 'em, little bitty dudes, little bitty . . . Gene wasn't with 'em then. Gene was cribbin [living] over here. Jeff, all of 'em, real little bitty dudes, you dig? All of us were little.
>
> Sixty-six [the gang on Sixty-sixth street], they wouldn't allow us in the Jackson Park show. That was when the parky [?] was headin it. Everybody say, If we want to go to the show, we go! One day, who was it? Carl Robinson. He went up to the show . . . and Jeff fired on him. He came back and all this was swelled up 'bout yay big, you know. He come back over to the hood [neighborhood]. He told (name unclear) and them dudes went up there. That was when mostly all the main sixty-six boys was over here like Bett Riley. All of 'em was over here. People that quit gang-bangin [fighting, especially as a group], Marvell Gates, people like that.
>
> They went on up there, John, Roy and Skeeter went in there. And they start humbuggin [fighting] in there. That's how it all started. Sixty-six found out they couldn't beat us, at *that* time. They couldn't *whup* seven-o. Am I right Leroy? You was cribbin over here then. Am I right? We were dynamite! Used to be a time, you ain't have a passport, Man, you couldn't walk through here. And if didn't nobody know you it was worse than that. . . .

As a lively way of "running it down" the verbal element consists of personality and style plus information. To someone *reading* my example of the gang member's narration, the impression might be that the information would be more influential in directing the listener's response. The youth worker might be expected to say "So that's how the gang got so big," instead of "Man, that gang member is *bad* [strong, brave]" in which instance he would be responding to the personality and style of the rapper. However, if the reader would *listen* to the gang member on tape or could have been present when the gang member spoke he more likely would have reacted more to personality and style as my informants did.

Remember that in attendance with the youth worker were members of the gang who *already knew* how the gang got started (e.g., "Am I right Leroy? You was cribbin' over here then") and for whom the information itself would have little interest. Their attention was held by the *way* the information was presented.

The verbal element in "whupping the game" on someone, in the preceding example, was an integral part of an overall deception in which information and personality-style were skillfully manipulated for the purpose of controlling the "trick's" response. But again, greater weight must be given to personality-style. In the "murphy game" for example, it was this element which got the trick to trust the hustler and leave his money with him for "safekeeping."

The function of rapping in each of these forms is *expressive*. By this I mean that the speaker raps to project his personality onto the scene or to evoke a generally favorable response. When rapping is used to "ask for some pussy" or to "whup the game" on someone its function is *directive*. By this I mean that rapping becomes an instrument to manipulate and control people to get them to give up or to do something. The difference between rapping to a "fox" (pretty girl) for the purpose of "getting inside her pants" and rapping to a "lame" to get something from him is operational rather than functional. The latter rap contains a concealed motivation where the former does not.

"Shucking," "shucking it," "shucking and jiving," "S-ing" and "J-ing" or just "jiving," are terms that refer to language behavior practiced by the black when confronting "the Man" (the white man, the establishment, or *any* authority figure), and to another form of language behavior practiced by blacks with each other on the peer group level.

In the South, and later in the North, the black man learned that American society had assigned to him a restrictive role and status. Among whites his behavior had to conform to this imposed station and he was constantly reminded to "keep his place." He learned that it was not acceptable in the presence of white people to show feelings of indignation, frustration, discontent, pride, ambition, or desire; that real feelings had to be concealed behind a mask of innocence, ignorance, childishness, obedience, humility and deference. The terms used by the black to describe the role he played before white folks in the South was "tomming" or "jeffing." Failure to accommodate the white Southerner in this respect was almost certain to invite psychological and often physical brutality. A description related by a black psychiatrist, Alvin F. Poussaint, is typical and revealing:

Once last year as I was leaving my office in Jackson, Miss., with my Negro secretary, a White policeman yelled, "Hey, boy! Come here!" Somewhat bothered, I retorted: "I'm no boy!" He then rushed at me, inflamed, and stood towering over me, snorting "What d'ja say, boy?" Quickly he frisked me and demanded, "What's your name, boy?" Frightened, I replied, "Dr. Poussaint. I'm a physician." He angrily chuckled and hissed, "What's your first name, boy?" When I hesitated he assumed a threatening stance and clenched his fists. As my heart palpitated, I muttered in profound humiliation, "Alvin."

He continued his psychological brutality, bellowing, "Alvin, the next time I call you, you come right away, you hear? You hear?" I hesitated. "You hear me, boy?" My voice trembling with helplessness, but *following my instincts of self-preservation*, I murmured, "Yes, sir." *Now fully satisfied that I had performed and acquiesced to my "boy" status*, he dismissed me with, "Now, boy, go on and get out of here or next time we'll take you for a little ride down to the station house!" [Alvin F. Poussaint, "A Negro Psychiatrist Explains the Negro Psyche," *New York Times Magazine,* August 20, 1967 (emphasis mine)].

In the northern cities the black encountered authority figures equivalent to Southern "crackers": policemen, judges, probation officers, truant officers, teachers and "Mr. Charlies" (bosses), and soon learned that the way to get by and avoid difficulty was to shuck. Thus, he learned to accommodate "the Man," to use the total orchestration of speech, intonation, gesture and facial expression for the purpose of producing whatever appearance would be acceptable. It was a technique and ability that was developed from fear, a respect for power, and a will to survive. This type of accommodation is exemplified by the Uncle Tom with his "Yes sir, Mr. Charlie," or "Anything you say, Mr. Charlie."

Through accommodation, many blacks became adept at concealing and controlling their emotions and at assuming a variety of postures. They became competent actors. Many developed a keen perception of what affected, motivated, appeased or satisfied the authority figures with whom they came into contact. Shucking became an effective way for many blacks to stay out of trouble, and for others a useful artifice for avoiding arrest or getting out of trouble when apprehended. Shucking it with a judge, for example, would be to feign repentance in the hope of receiving a lighter or suspended sentence. Robert Conot reports an example of shucking in his book, *Rivers of Blood, Years of*

Darkness: Joe was found guilty of possession of narcotics. But he did an excellent job of shucking it with the probation officer.

The probation officer interceded for Joe with the judge: "His own attitude toward the present offense appears to be serious and responsible and it is believed that the defendant is an excellent subject for probation."

Some field illustrations of shucking to get out of trouble came from some seventh-grade children from an inner-city school in Chicago. The children were asked to talk their way out of a troublesome situation.

You are cursing at this old man and your mother comes walking down the stairs. She hears you.

To "talk your way out of this":

"I'd tell her that I was studying a scene in school for a play."

What if you were in a store stealing something and the manager caught you?

"I would start stuttering. Then I would say, 'Oh, Oh, I forgot. Here the money is.' "

A literary example of shucking comes from Iceberg Slim's autobiography. Iceberg, a pimp, shucks before "two red-faced Swede rollers (detectives)" who catch him in a motel room with his whore. My italics identify which elements of the passage constitute the shuck.

I put my shaking hands into the pajama pockets . . . *I hoped I was keeping the fear out of my face. I gave them a wide toothy smile.* They came in and stood in the middle of the room. Their eyes were racing about the room. Stacy was open mouthed in the bed.

I said, *"Yes, gentlemen, what can I do for you?"*

Lanky said, "We wanta see your I.D."

I went to the closet and got the phony John Cato Fredrickson I.D. I put it in his palm. I felt cold sweat running down my back. They looked at it, then looked at each other.

Lanky said, "You are in violation of the law. You signed the motel register improperly. Why didn't you sign your full name? What are you trying to hide? What are you doing here in town? It says here you're a dancer. We don't have a club in town that books entertainers."

I said, *"Officers, my professional name is Johnny Cato. I've got nothing to hide. My full name had always been too* long for the marquees. I've fallen into the habit of using the shorter version.

"My legs went out last year. I don't dance anymore: My wife and I decided to go into business. We are making a tour of this part of the country. We think that in your town we've found the ideal site for a Southern fried chicken shack. My wife has a secret recipe that should make us rich up here."
[Iceberg Slim, *Pimp: The Story of My Life.*]

Another example of shucking was related to me by a colleague. A black gang member was coming down the stairway from the club room with seven guns on him and encountered some policemen and detectives coming up the same stairs. If they stopped and frisked him he and others would have been arrested. A paraphrase of his shuck follows: "Man, I gotta get away from up there. There's gonna be some trouble and I don't want no part of it." This shuck worked on the minds of the policemen. It anticipated their questions as to why he was leaving the club room, and why he would be in a hurry. He also gave *them* a reason for wanting to get up to the room fast.

It ought to be mentioned at this point that there was not uniform agreement among my informants in characterizing the above examples as shucking. One informant used shucking only in the sense in which it is used among peers, e.g., bull-shitting, and characterized the above examples as jiving or whupping game. Others, however, identified the above examples as shucking, and reserved jiving and whupping game for more offensive maneuvers. In fact, one of the apparent features of shucking is that the posture of the black when acting with members of the establishment be a *defensive* one.

Frederick Douglass, in telling of how he taught himself to read, would challenge a white boy with whom he was playing, by saying that he could write as well as he. Whereupon he would write down all the letters he knew. The white boy would then write down more letters than Douglass did. In this way, Douglass eventually learned all the letters of the alphabet. Some of my informants regarded the example as whupping game. Others regarded it as shucking. The former were perhaps focusing on the maneuver rather than the language used. The latter may have felt that any maneuvers designed to learn to read were justifiably defensive. One of my informants said Douglass was "shucking *in order to* whup the game." This latter response seems to be the most revealing. Just as one can rap to whup the game on someone, so one can shuck or jive for the same purpose; that is, assume a guise or posture or perform some action in a certain way that is designed to work on someone's mind to get him to give up something.

"WHUPPING GAME" TO CON WHITEY

The following examples from Malcolm X illustrate the shucking and jiving in this context though jive is the term used. Today, whupping game might also be the term used to describe the operation. Whites who came at night got a better reception; the several Harlem nightclubs they patronized were geared to entertain and jive (flatter, cajole) the night white crowd to get their money (Malcolm X, *The Autobiography of Malcolm X*).

The maneuvers involved here are clearly designed to obtain some benefit or advantage.

Freddie got on the stand and went to work on his own shoes. Brush, liquid polish, brush, paste wax, shine rag, lacquer sole dressing . . . step by step, Freddie showed me what to do.

"But you got to get a whole lot faster. You can't waste time!" Freddie showed me how fast on my own shoes. Then because business was tapering off, he had time to give me a demonstration of how to make the shine rag pop like a firecracker. "Dig the action?" he asked. He did it in slow motion. I got down and tried it on his shoes. I had the principle of it. "Just got to do it, faster," Freddie said. *"It's a jive noise, that's all. Cats tip better, they figure you're knocking yourself out!"* [Malcolm X, *The Autobiography of Malcolm X*.]

An eight-year-boy whupped the game on me one day this way:

My colleague and I were sitting in a room listening to a tape. The door to the room was open and outside was a soda machine. Two boys came up in the elevator, stopped at the soda machine, and then came into the room.

"Do you have a dime for two nickels?" Presumably the soda machine would not accept nickels. I took out the change in my pocket, found a dime and gave it to the boy for two nickels.

After accepting the dime, he looked at the change in my hand and asked, "Can I have two cents? I need carfare to get home." I gave him the two cents.

At first I assumed the verbal component of the maneuver was the rather weak, transparently false reason for wanting the two cents. Actually, as was pointed out to me later, the maneuver began with the first question which was designed to get me to show my money. He could then ask me for something that he knew I had, making my refusal more difficult. He apparently felt that the reason need not be more than plausible because the amount he wanted was small. Were the amount larger, he would no doubt have elaborated on the verbal element of the game. The form of the verbal element could be in the direction of rapping or shucking and jiving. If he were to rap the eight-year-old might say, "Man, you know a cat needs to have a little bread to keep the girls in line." Were he to shuck and jive he might make the reason for needing the money more compelling, look hungry, etc.

The function of shucking and jiving as it refers to blacks and "the Man" is designed to work on the mind and emotions of the authority figure for the purpose of getting him to feel a certain way or give up something that will be to the other's advantage. Iceberg showed a "toothy smile" which said to the detective, "I'm glad to see you" and "Would I be glad to see you if I had something to hide?" When the maneuvers seem to be *defensive* most of my informants regarded the language behavior as shucking. When the maneuvers were *offensive* my informants tended to regard the behavior as "whupping the game."

Also significant is that the first form of shucking described, which developed out of accommodation, is becoming less frequently used today by many blacks, because of a new-found self-assertiveness and pride, challenging the system. The willingness on the part of many blacks to accept the psychological and physical brutality and general social consequences of not "keeping one's place" is indicative of the changing self-concept of the black man. Ironically, the shocked reaction of some whites to the present militancy of the black is partly due to the fact that the black was so successful at "putting Whitey on" via shucking in the past. This new attitude can be seen from a conversation I recently had with a shoe-shine attendant at O'Hare Airport in Chicago.

I was having my shoes shined and the black attendant was using a polishing machine instead of the rag that was generally used in the past. I asked whether the machine made his work any easier. He did not answer me until about ten seconds had passed and then responded in a loud voice that he "never had a job that was easy," that he would give me "one hundred dollars for any *easy* job" I could offer him, that the machine made his job "faster" but not "easier." I was startled at the response because it was so unexpected and I realized that here was a new "breed of cat" who was not going to shuck for a big tip or ingratiate himself with "Whitey" anymore. A few years ago his response probably would have been different.

The contrast between this "shoe-shine" scene and the one illustrated earlier from Malcolm X's autobiography, when "shucking Whitey" was the common practice, is striking.

Shucking, jiving, shucking and jiving, or S-ing and J-ing, when referring to language behavior practiced by blacks, is descriptive of the talk and gestures that are appropriate to "putting someone on" by creating a false impression. The terms seem to cover a range from simply telling a lie, to bullshitting, to subtly playing with someone's mind. An important difference between this form of shucking and that described earlier is that the same talk and gestures that are deceptive to "the Man" are often transparent to those members of one's own group who are able practitioners at shucking themselves. As Robert Conot has pointed out, "The Negro who often fools the White officer by 'shucking it' is much less likely to be successful with another Negro. . . ." Also, S-ing and J-ing within the group often has play overtones in which the person being "put on" is aware of the attempts being made and goes along with it for enjoyment or in appreciation of the style.

"Running it down" is the term used by speakers in the ghetto when it is their intention to give information, either by explanation, narrative, or giving advice. In the following literary example, Sweet Mac is "running this Edith broad down" to his friends:

> Edith is the "saved" broad who can't marry out of her religion . . . or do anything else out of her religion for that matter, especially what I wanted her to do. A bogue religion, man! So dig, for the last couple weeks I been quoting the Good Book and all that stuff to her; telling her I am now saved myself, you dig. [Woodie King, Jr., "The Game," *Liberator*, August, 1965.]

The following citation from Claude Brown uses the term with the additional sense of giving advice:

If I saw him (Claude's brother) hanging out with cats I knew were weak, who might be using drugs sooner or later, I'd run it down to him.

It seems clear that running it down has simply any informative function, that of telling somebody something that he doesn't already know.

"Gripping" is of fairly recent vintage, used by black high school students in Chicago to refer to the talk and facial expression that accompanies a *partial* loss of face or self-possession, or showing of fear. Its appearance alongside "copping a plea," which refers to a total loss of face, in which one begs one's adversary for mercy, is a significant new perception. In linking it with the street code which acclaims the ability to "look tough and inviolate, fearless, secure, 'cool,' " it suggests that even the slightest weakening of this posture will be held up to ridicule and contempt. There are always contemptuous overtones attached to the use of the term when applied to the others' behavior. One is tempted to link it with the violence and toughness required to survive on the street. The intensity of both seems to be increasing. As one of my informants noted, "Today, you're *lucky* if you end up in the hospital"—that is, are not killed.

REACTION TO FEAR AND SUPERIOR POWER

Both gripping and copping a plea refer to behavior produced from fear and a respect for superior power. An example of gripping comes from the record *"Street and Gangland Rhythms"* (Band 4 Dumb Boy). Lennie meets Calvin and asks him what happened to his lip. Calvin says that a boy named Pierre hit him for copying off him in school. Lennie, pretending to be Calvin's brother, goes to confront Pierre. Their dialogue follows:

Lennie: "Hey you! What you hit my little brother for?"
Pierre: "Did he tell you what happen man?"
Lennie: "Yeah, he told me what happened."
Pierre: "But you . . . but you . . . but you should tell your people to teach him to go to the school, man." [Pause] "I, I know, I know I didn't have a right to hit him."

Pierre, anticipating a fight with Lennie if he continued to justify his hitting of Calvin, tried to avoid it by "gripping" with the last line.

Copping a plea originally meant "to plead guilty to a lesser charge to save the state the cost of a trial" (with the hope of receiving a lesser or suspended sentence), but is now generally used to mean "to beg," "plead for mercy," as in the example "Please cop, don't hit me. I give." (*Street and Gangland Rhythms*, Band 1 "Gang Fight"). This change of meaning can be seen from its use by Piri Thomas in *Down These Mean Streets*.

> The night before my hearing, I decided to make a prayer. It had to be on my knees, 'cause if I was gonna cop a plea to God, I couldn't play it cheap.

The function of gripping and copping a plea is obviously to induce pity or to acknowledge the presence of superior strength. In so doing, one evinces noticeable feelings of fear and insecurity which also result in a loss of status among one's peers.

Signifying is the term used to describe the language behavior that, as Abrahams has defined it, attempts to "imply, goad, beg, boast by indirect verbal or gestural means" (Roger D. Abrahams, *Deep Down in the Jungle*). In Chicago it is also used as a synonym to describe language behavior more generally known as "sounding" elsewhere.

Some excellent examples of signifying as well as of other forms of language behavior come from the well known "toast" (narrative form) "The Signifying Monkey and the Lion" which was collected by Abrahams from Negro street-corner bards in Philadelphia. In the toast below the monkey is trying to get the lion involved in a fight with the elephant:

> Now the lion came through the jungle one peaceful day,
> When the signifying monkey stopped him, and that is what he started to say:
> He said, "Mr. Lion," he said, "A bad-assed mother-fucker down your way,"
> He said, "Yeah! The way he talks about your folks is a certain shame.
> I even heard him curse when he mentioned your grandmother's name."
> The lion's tail shot back like a forty-four
> When he went down that jungle in all uproar.

Thus the monkey has goaded the lion into a fight with the elephant by "signifying," that is, indicating that the elephant has been "sounding on" (insulting) the lion. When the lion comes back, thoroughly beaten up, the monkey again "signifies" by making fun of the lion:

> . . . lion came back through the jungle more dead than alive.
> When the monkey started some more of that signifying jive.
> He said, "Damn, Mr. Lion, you went through here
>   yesterday, the jungle rung.
> Now you come back today, damn near hung."

The monkey, of course, is delivering this taunt from a safe distance away on the limb of a tree when his foot slips and he falls to the ground, at which point,

> Like a bolt of lightning, a stripe of white heat,
> The lion was on the monkey, with all four feet.

In desperation the monkey quickly resorts to "copping a plea":

> The monkey looked up with a tear in his eyes,
> He said, "Please, Mr. Lion, I apologize."

His "plea" however, fails to move the lion to show any mercy so the monkey tries another verbal ruse, "shucking":

> He said, "You lemme get my head out of the sand,
> Ass out the grass, I'll fight you like a natural man."

In this he is more successful as,

> The lion jumped back and squared for a fight.
> The mother-fucking monkey jumped clear out of sight.

A safe distance away again, the monkey returns to "signifying":

> He said, "Yeah, you had me down, you had me at last,
> But you left me free, now you can still kiss my ass."

This example illustrates the methods of provocation, goading and taunting artfully practiced by a signifier.

Interestingly, when the *function* of signifying is *directive* the *tactic* employed is *indirection*, i.e., the signifier reports or repeats what someone else has said about the listener; the "report" is couched in plausible language designed to compel belief and arouse feelings of anger and hostility. There is also the implication that if the listener fails to do anything about it—what has to be "done" is usually quite clear—his status will be seriously compromised. Thus the lion is compelled to vindicate the honor of his family by fighting or else leave the impression that he is afraid, and that he is not "king" of the jungle. When used for the purpose of directing action, "signifying" is like "shucking" in also being deceptive and subtle in approach and depending for success on the naiveté or gullibility of the person being "put on."

When the function or signifying is to arouse feelings of embarrassment, shame, frustration or futility, to diminish someone's status, the tactic employed is direct in the form of a taunt, as in the example where the monkey is making fun of the lion.

"SOUNDING" TO RELIEVE TENSIONS

Sounding is the term which is today most widely known for the game of verbal insult known in the past as "Playing the Dozens," "The Dirty Dozens" or just "The Dozens." Other current names for the game have regional distribution: Signifying or "Sigging" (Chicago), Joning (Washington, D.C.), Screaming (Harrisburg), etc. In Chicago, the term "sounding" would be descriptive of the initial remarks which are designed to sound out the other person to see whether he will play the game. The verbal insult is also subdivided, the term "signifying" applying to insults which are hurled directly at the person and "the dozens" applying to results hurled at your opponent's family, especially the mother.

Sounding is often catalyzed by signifying remarks referred to earlier such as "Are you going to let him say that about your mama" to spur an exchange between members of the group. It is begun on a relatively low key and built up by verbal exchanges. The game goes like this:

One insults a member of another's family; others in the group make disapproving sounds to spur on the coming exchange. The one who has been insulted feels at this point that he must reply with a slur on the protagonist's family which is clever enough to defend his honor (and therefore that of his family). This, of course, leads the other (once again, more due to pressure from the crowd than actual insult) to make further jabs. This can proceed until everyone is bored with the whole affair, until one hits the other (fairly rare), or until some other subject comes up that interrupts the proceedings (the usual state of affairs). (Roger D. Abrahams, "Playing the Dozens," *Journal of American Folklore*, July–September, 1962.)

Mack McCormick describes the dozens as a verbal contest:

. . . in which the players strive to bury one another with vituperation. In the play, the opponent's mother is especially slandered. . . . Then, in turn fathers are identified as queer and syphilitic. Sisters are whores, brothers are defective, cousins are "funny" and the opponent is himself diseased. (Mack McCormick, "The Dirty Dozens," book jacket in the record album *The Unexpurgated Folksongs of Men*, Arhoolie Records.)

. . . The relatively high value placed on verbal ability must be clear to most black boys at an early age. Most boys begin their activity in sounding by compiling a repertoire of "one liners." When the game is played the one who has the greatest number of such remarks wins. Here are some examples of "one liners" collected from fifth- and sixth-grade black boys in Chicago:

Yo mama is so bowlegged, she looks like the bit out of a donut.

Yo mama sent her picture to the lonely hearts club, and they sent it back and said, "We ain't that lonely!"

Your family is so poor that rats and roaches eat lunch out.

Your house is so small the roaches walk single file.

I walked in your house and your family was running around the table. I said, "Why you doin that?" Your mama say, "First one drops, we eat."

Real proficiency in the game comes to only a small percentage of those who play it. These players have the special skill in being able to turn around what their opponents have said and attack them with it.

. . . The function of the "dozens" or "sounding" is to borrow status from an opponent through an exercise of verbal power. The opponent feels compelled to regain his status by "sounding" back on the speaker or other group member whom he regards as more vulnerable.

The presence of a group seems to be especially important in

controlling the game . . . one does not "play" with just anyone since the subject matter is concerned with things that in reality one is quite sensitive about.

. . . Significantly, the subject matter of sounding is changing with the changing self-concept of the black with regard to those physical characteristics that are characteristically "Negro," and which in the past were vulnerable points in the black psyche: blackness and "nappy" hair. It ought to be said that for many blacks, blackness was always highly esteemed and it might be more accurate to regard the present sentiment of the black community toward skin color as reflecting a shifted attitude for only a *portion* of the black community. This suggests that "sounding" on someone's light skin color is not new. Nevertheless, one can regard the previously favorable attitude toward light skin color and "good hair" as the prevailing one. "Other things being equal, the more closely a woman approached her white counterpart, the more attractive she was considered to be, by both men and women alike. 'Good hair' (hair that is long and soft) and light skin were the chief criteria." (Elliot Liebow, *Tally's Corner*.)

"The dozens" has been linked to the overall psycho-social growth of the black male. McCormick has stated that a "single round of a dozen or so exchanges frees more pent-up aggressions than will a dose of sodium pentothal." The fact that one permits a kind of abuse within the rules of the game and within the confines of the group which would otherwise not be tolerated, is filled with psychological import. It seems also important, however, to view its function from the perspective of the nonparticipating members of the group. Its function for them may be to incite and prod individual members of the group to combat for the purpose of energizing the elements, of simply relieving the boredom of just "hanging around" and the malaise of living in a static and restrictive environment.

A summary analysis of the different forms of language behavior which have been discussed above permit the following generalizations:

The prestige norms which influence black speech behavior are those which have been successful in manipulating and controlling people and situations. The function of all of the forms of language behavior discussed above, with the exception of "running it down," was to project personality, assert oneself, or arouse emotion, frequently with the additional purpose of getting the person to give up or do something which will be of some benefit to the speaker. Only running it down has as its primary function to communicate information and often here too, the personality and style of the speaker in the form of rapping is projected along with the information.

The purpose for which language is used suggests that the speaker views the social situations into which he moves as consisting of a series of transactions which require that he be continually ready to take advantage of a person or situation or defend himself against being victimized. He has absorbed what Horton has called "street rationality." As one of Horton's respondents put it: "The good hustler . . . conditions his mind and must never put his guard too far down, to relax, or he'll be taken."

I have carefully avoided limiting the group within the black community of whom the language behavior and perspective of their environment is characteristic. While I have no doubt that it is true of those who are generally called "street people" I am uncertain of the extent to which it is true of a much larger portion of the black community, especially the male segment. My informants consisted of street people, high school students, and blacks, who by their occupation as community and youth workers, possess what has been described as a "sharp sense of the streets." Yet it is difficult to find a black male in the community who has *not* witnessed or participated in "the dozens" or heard of signifying, or rapping, or shucking and jiving at some time during his growing up. It would be equally difficult to imagine a high school student in a Chicago inner-city school not being touched by what is generally regarded as "street culture."

In conclusion, by blending style and verbal power, through rapping, sounding and running it down, the black in the ghetto establishes his personality; through shucking, gripping and copping a plea, he shows his respect for power; through jiving and signifying he stirs up excitement. With all of the above, he hopes to manipulate and control people and situations to give himself a winning edge.

How to Ask for a Drink in Subanun

by
Charles O. Frake

WARD GOODENOUGH[1] HAS proposed that a description of a culture—an ethnography—should properly specify what it is that a stranger to a society would have to know in order appropriately to perform any role in any scene staged by the society. If an ethnographer of Subanun culture were to take this notion seriously, one of the most crucial sets of instructions to provide would be that specifying how to ask for a drink. Anyone who cannot perform this operation successfully will be automatically excluded from the stage upon which some of the most dramatic scenes of Subanun life are performed.

To ask appropriately for a drink among the Subanun it is not enough to know how to construct a grammatical utterance in Subanun translatable in English as a request for a drink. Rendering such an utterance might elicit praise for one's fluency in Subanun, but it probably would not get one a drink. To speak appropriately it is not enough to speak grammatically or even sensibly (in fact some speech settings may require the uttering of nonsense as is the case with the semantic-reversal type of speech play common in the Philippines.) Our stranger requires more than a grammar and a lexicon; he needs what Hymes[2] has called

Reprinted from *American Anthropologist* 66 (6, pt. 2), 1964, pp. 94–100, by permission of the author and the American Anthropological Association.

[1]Ward G. Goodenough, "Cultural Anthropology and Linguistics," in *Report of the Seventh Annual Round Table Meeting on Linguistics and Language Study*. Paul L. Garvin, ed., Georgetown University Monograph Series on Language and Linguistics, 9 (1957), pp. 167–173.

an ethnography of speaking: a specification of what kinds of things to say in what message forms to what kinds of people in what kinds of situations. Of course an ethnography of speaking cannot provide rules specifying exactly what message to select in a given situation. If messages were perfectly predictable from a knowledge of the culture, there would be little point in saying anything. But when a person selects a message, he does so from a set of appropriate alternatives. The task of an ethnographer of speaking is to specify what the appropriate alternatives are in a given situation and what the consequences are of selecting one alternative over another.

Drinking defined. Of the various substances which the Subanun consider "drinkable," we are here concerned only with a subset called *gasi,* a rice-yeast fermented beverage made of rice, manioc, maize, and/or Job's tears mash. *Gasi,* glossed in this paper as "beer," contrasts in linguistic labelling, drinking technique, and social context with all other Subanun beverages (*tebaq* "toddy," *sebug* "wine," *binu* "liquor," *sabaw* "juice-broth," *tubig* "water").

The context of drinking. Focused social gatherings among the Subanun fall into two sharply contrasted sets: festive gatherings or "festivities" and nonfestive or informal gatherings. The diagnostic feature of a festivity is the consumption of a festive meal as a necessary incident in the encounter. A "meal" among the Subanun necessarily comprises a serving of a cooked starchy-staple food, the "main dish," and ordinarily also includes a "side dish" of vegetables, fish, or meat. A festive meal, or "feast," is a meal with a meat side dish. A "festivity" comprises all socially relevant events occurring between the arrival and dispersal of participants in a feast. Apart from a feast, the necessary features of a festivity are (1) an occasioning event, (2) multi-family participation, and (3) beer. The drinking of beer, unlike the consumption of any other beverage, occurs only during a festivity and must occur as part of any festivity. It occupies a crucial position as a focus of formal social gatherings.

Drinking technique. "Beer," uniquely among Subanun drinks, is drunk with bamboo straws inserted to the bottom of a Chinese jar containing the fermented mash. Just prior to drinking, the jar is filled to the rim with water. Except in certain types of game

[2]Dell H. Hymes, "The Ethnography of Speaking," in *Anthropology and Human Behavior,* T. Gladwin and W. C. Sturtevant, eds. (Washington: Anthropological Society of Washington, 1962), pp. 15–53.

drinking, one person drinks at a time, after which another person replenishes the water from an agreed-upon "measure." As one sucks on the straw, the water disappears down through the mash where it picks up a surprising amount of alcohol and an indescribable taste. After initial rounds of tasting, drinking etiquette requires one to gauge his consumption so that when a full measure of water is added, the water level rises exactly even with the jar rim.

The drinking encounter. Each beer jar provided for a festivity becomes the focus of a gathering of persons who take turns drinking. A *turn* is a single period of continuous drinking by one person. Each change of drinkers marks a new turn. A circuit of turns through the gathering is a *round*. As drinking progresses, rounds change in character with regard to the number and length of constituent turns and to variations in drinking techniques. Differences in these features among successive sets of rounds mark three distinct stages of the drinking encounter: tasting, competitive drinking, and game drinking (Table I).

The first round is devoted to *tasting*, each person taking a brief turn with little regard to formal measurement of consumption. Successive turns become longer and the number of turns per round fewer, thus cutting out some of the participants in the encounter. These individuals go to other jars if available or withdraw from drinking during this stage of *competitive drinking*. Measurement is an important aspect of competitive rounds, participants keeping a mental record of each other's consumption. Within a round, successive drinkers must equal the consumption of the drinker who initiated the round. In later rounds, as the brew becomes weaker, the measure tends to be raised. Continued competitive drinking may assume an altered character signaled by accompanying music, dancing, and singing. The scope of the gathering may enlarge and turns become shorter. Special types of drinking games occur: "chugalug" (*san-gayuq*) and dual-drinking by opposite-sexed partners under the cover of a blanket. These rounds form a stage of *game drinking*.

Drinking talk. The Subanun expression for drinking talk, *taluq bwat dig beksuk* "talk from the straw," suggests an image of the drinking straw as a channel not only of the drink but also of drinking talk. The two activities, drinking and talking, are closely interrelated in that how one talks bears on how much one drinks and the converse is, quite obviously, also true. Except for "religious offerings," which must precede drinking, whatever business is to be transacted during a festivity occurs during drinking encounters. Consequently drinking talk is a major me-

Table I. Subanun Drinking Talk

Encounter stages	Discourse stages	Focus of speech acts	Function
1. Tasting	1. Invitation—permission	Role expression	Assignment of role distances and authority relations to participants
2. Competitive drinking	2. Jar talk	Role expression and context definition	Allocation of encounter resources (turns at drinking and talking)
	3. Discussion 3.1 Gossip 3.2 Deliberation	Topic	Exchange of information; disputation, arbitration; deciding issues on basis of cogent argument
3. Game drinking	4. Display of verbal art	Stylistic	Establishment of euphoria. Deciding issues on basis of skill in use of special styles of discourse (singing, verse)

Segments of a drinking encounter:

1. A turn (continuous drinking by one person)
2. A round (a set of related turns)
3. Encounter stage (a set of related rounds)

Segments of drinking talk:

1. An utterance (continuous speech by one person)
2. An exchange (a set of related utterances)
3. Discourse stage (a set of related exchanges)

dium of interfamily communication. Especially for an adult male, one's role in the society at large, insofar as it is subject to manipulation, depends to a considerable extent on one's verbal performance during drinking encounters.

Subanun society contains no absolute, society-wide status positions or offices which automatically entitle their holder to deference from and authority over others. The closest approximation to such a formal office is the status of religious specialist or "medium" who is deferred to in religious matters but who has no special voice in affairs outside his domain. Assumption of decision-making roles in legal, economic, and ecological domains depends not on acquisition of an office but on continuing demonstration of one's ability to make decisions within the context of social encounters. This ability in turn depends on the amount of deference one can evoke from other participants in the encounter. Although relevant, no external status attributes of sex, age, or wealth are sufficient to guarantee such deference; it must be elicited through one's skill in the use of speech. Apart from age, sex, and reputation from performances in previous encounters, the most salient external attributes brought to an encounter by a participant are his relational roles based on kinship, neighborhood, and friendship with specific other participants. Because of consanguineal endogamy and residential mobility, the relationship ties between an ego and any given alter are likely to be multiple and complex, giving wide latitude for manipulation of roles within particular encounters. Moreover, most kinship roles permit a range of interpretation depending upon other features of the relationship such as friendship and residential proximity.

The strategy of drinking talk is to manipulate the assignment of role relations among participants so that, within the limits of one's external status attributes, one can maximize his share of encounter resources (drink and talk), thereby having an opportunity to assume an esteem-attracting and authority-wielding role. Variations in the kinds of messages sent during periods devoted to different aspects of this strategic plan mark four distinct *discourse stages* within the drinking talk of the encounter: invitation-permission, jar talk, discussion, and display of verbal art (Table I). The constituents of a discourse stage are *exchanges:* sets of utterances with a common topic focus. (Boundaries of exchanges in American speech are often marked by such expressions as "Not to change the subject, but . . ." or "By the way, that reminds me. . . .") The constituents of exchanges are *utterances:* stretches of continuous speech by one person.

* * *

1. Invitation-Permission. The Subanun designate the discourse of the initial tasting round as "asking permission." The provider of the jar initiates the tasting round by inviting someone to drink, thereby signaling that this person is the one to whom he and those closest to him in the encounter owe the greatest initial deference on the basis of external status attributes. The invited drinker squats before the jar and asks permission to drink of the other participants. He has two variables to manipulate: the order in which he addresses the other participants and the terms of address he employs. Apart from the latter variable, message form remains relatively constant: *naa, A, sep pa u* "Well, *A*, I will be drinking." (*A* represents a term of address.) Role relations with persons who are not lineal consanguineal or lineal affinal kin (Mo, F, Ch, Sp, SpPr, ChSp, ChSpPr) permit a variety of forms of address each with different implications for social distance with respect to ego. The drinker's final opportunity to express role relations comes when he finishes tasting and invites another (ordinarily the person who invited him) to drink.

2. Jar talk. As competitive drinking begins, asking permission is reduced in scope and importance, and there is an increase in messages sent during drinking itself. The topic focus of these exchanges is the drink being consumed. The drinker responds to queries about the taste and strength of the beer, explanations are advanced for its virtues and defects, and the performance of drinkers is evaluated. During this stage the topic of messages is predictable. The informative aspect of the messages is the quantity and quality of verbal responses a drinker can elicit. This information signals the amount of drinking and talking time the gathering will allot him. Those who receive little encouragement drop out, and the encounter is reduced generally to less than half-a-dozen persons, who can thereby intensify their interaction with each other and with the beer straw.

3. Discussion. As the size and role-structure of the gathering becomes defined, discourse changes in topic to removed referents, usually beginning with relatively trivial gossip, proceeding to more important subjects of current interest, and, finally, in many cases arriving at litigation. Since there are no juro-political offices in Subanun society, a legal case is not only a contest between litigants, but also one between persons attempting to assume a role of legal authority by settling the case. Success in effecting legal decisions depends on achieving a commanding role in the encounter and on debating effectively from that position. Since there are no sanctions of force legally applicable

to back up a decision, the payment of a fine in compliance with a decision is final testimony to the prowess in verbal combat of the person who made the decision.

4. Display of verbal art. If drinking continues long enough, the focus of messages shifts from their topics to play with message forms themselves, following stylized patterns of song and verse composition. Songs and verses are composed on the spot to carry on discussions in an operetta-like setting. Even unsettled litigation may be continued in this manner, the basis for decision being shifted from cogent argument to verbal artistry. The most prestigious kinds of drinking songs require the mastery of an esoteric vocabulary by means of which each line is repeated with a semantically equivalent but formally different line. Game drinking is a frequent accompaniment to these displays of verbal art. Together they help assure that the festivity will end with good feelings among all participants, a goal which is explicitly stated by the Subanun. Participants who have displayed marked hostility toward each other during the course of drinking talk may be singled out for special ritual treatment designed to restore good feelings.

The Subanun drinking encounter thus provides a structured setting within which one's social relationships beyond his everyday associates can be extended, defined, and manipulated through the use of speech. The cultural patterning of drinking talk lays out an ordered scheme of role play through the use of terms of address, through discussion and argument, and through display of verbal art. The most skilled in "talking from the straw" are the de facto leaders of the society. In instructing our stranger to Subanun society how to ask for a drink, we have at the same time instructed him how to get ahead socially.

The Language of "Drunks"

by
Earl Rubington

LANGUAGE, IN PART, is composed of categories. These categories may be official and conventional, or unofficial and unconventional. Official categories are used in formal situations when people of divergent social statuses mix, e.g., writing, lectures, speeches. Conventional or informal categories are used in everyday life, most often when people meet as equals. Official terms can sometimes be used, but more often a set of terms emerges which make for common understanding among equals.

Unconventional categories exist for both equals and unequals who live outside the controls of either formal or everyday social life. Some of the users of unconventional speech are members of the underworld, jazz musicians, teen-agers, juvenile delinquents, narcotics users, hoboes, tramps, bums, Skid Row people, Negroes and members of other ethnic subcultures. But whether official, conventional or unconventional, categories organize social life.

At present, such a thing as an "alcohol language" exists. Formed in part by laymen and in part by professionals, it takes either an oral or a written form. For instance, there is a language of Alcoholics Anonymous which one can hear at A.A. meetings or read in the A.A. literature. Similarly, there is a whole set of terms which might be called "drinking slang," and this too is both oral and written, though probably more often oral than written. Finally, there is also a "drunk language" which is almost wholly oral. This is the language of people variously designated as Skid Row alcoholics, homeless men, chronic drunkenness offenders, "drunks," and the like.

Such social types participate, to greater or lesser degree, in

Reprinted from *Quarterly Journal of Studies on Alcohol* (Rutgers University Center of Alcohol Studies, New Brunswick, N.J.), vol. 32, no. 3, (September 1971), pp. 721–740.

deviant groups. To participate at all they need to learn some of the terms. Since the culture of "drunks" is relatively simple as compared with, say, the narcotics user, the number of terms and the array of people, places, things and events covered by them are not very diversified. Nonetheless the language, such as it is, exists and serves its purposes. Firstly, it is a vehicle for communication, particularly about drinking and its consequences. Secondly, it is a badge, revealing membership, including and excluding at one and the same time. And thirdly, it has its expressive uses.

Similarly, the language of "drunks" can have its purposes for those who are not members of groups which understand and use its terms: to students of language it can be of interest in its own right; for sociologists and anthropologists, it can be studied to learn exactly how "drunks" organize their lives and deal with the typically recurrent situations which make up those lives. It may also have possible uses in communication when nonmembers of "drunk groups" seek to persuade and influence members to defect from their peculiar style of life.

The present effort should serve all three groups. It lists the terms for those who have an intrinsic interest in language. It also lists them for sociologists and anthropologists interested in sociolinguistics, argots, deviant subcultures and the like. Finally, it also lists them in the hope that those who seek to help to rehabilitate "drunks" may find an understanding of these terms useful in their work.

THE VOCABULARY OF DRINK

Before listing the terms of "drunk" argot, some general remarks on the vocabulary are in order. At least two compilers of dictionaries of slang have noted that the act of drinking and its consequences have probably spawned more slang terms than any other social act (1, 2). A good deal of these terms are organized around drinking as an action system which has five phases: procurement, consumption, repair, punishment and reintegration (3). Many of the terms "drunks" use for discussing these phases, their cycles and their peculiar problems are not unknown to lay people.

This may well be the case because of the nature of slang and its social action. Slang deals with the immediate, the present, the colorful, the different, the novel. More often it is expressive rather than abstract or denotative like scientific language. For example, persons observing others who are intoxicated have had occasion to remark the effects of alcohol on behavior and to invent or borrow colorful terms for describing that behavior which departs from etiquette. Slang is particularly useful, when drinking is involved, as a language of disparagement. Persons who parade their worst selves before others open themselves to attack, criticism and ridicule. The terms of slang are especially helpful in handling these expressive problems and conveying the contempt and disgust the onlooker feels.

Slang itself represents a departure from cultural rules on how to use conventional language. As such, it says something about the person who uses it. Like obscenity and profanity, slang is a form of deviant behavior in its own right, from the point of view of those people who make and seek to enforce the rules on language. At the same time, slang creeps into common usage in time because it meets needs which conventional language often cannot supply. The officially appropriate language tends toward the abstract and the distant. Slang expressions make it possible to talk about matters of immediate importance about which there is strong feeling but some doubt about appropriate phrasing. These are the same conditions which seem to have produced obscenity and profanity.

The argot of the underworld, narcotics users, jazz musicians, and Skid Row alcoholics arose in response to a similar set of needs. This language is a basic part of the culture of deviant groups. Occupational subcultures, similarly, have their own special languages. For instance, one historical argument is that lawyers spoke in Latin so that their clients would not know what they were saying. The same reasoning applies to the development of underworld argot. As a matter of defense, so the argument runs, it became necessary to talk with colleagues without arousing the suspicions of legitimate people.

The vocabulary of "drunks" is made up of strands of all of these languages—lower-class idiom, underworld argot, and the vocabulary of drinking slang. However, because drinking is at the forefront, "drunks" think, feel and act mainly in terms of its categories. They have created a linguistic environment which largely influences the way they deal with alcohol and alcohol situations. This is an old, shared, linguistic tradition and not likely to die easily.

Some small elements of deceiving listeners or impressing them with a romantic way of life may be involved. But this will certainly be less often the case since "drunks," compared with participants in other deviant groups, are rather well aware of their low status. Turning their own language against their peers is perhaps the only way of deflecting attention from themselves.

More important, however, are the functions of this language within their own wide circle of drinking acquaintances. For this language not only deals with all the aspects of drinking episodes (including activities, objects, states of mind and body, and people involved in them) but likewise contains a moral evaluation of the objects so designated.

Some part of the language may arise out of the personality characteristics of alcoholics or the prolonged effects of drinking on speech functions and perhaps even on thinking—this hypothesis awaits clinical research. However, language is a group product and does not depend upon the properties of individuals. It has much more to do with the situation and the common problems that groups confront. It is one of the more important means of solving problems that were originally formulated in its own terms.

No small part of the success of A.A. depends on the fact that it has coined a special language by which alcoholics desirous of abstinence are able to communicate with one another with a simple set of terms which reveals a common understanding of the dilemmas of recovering alcoholics. New members are able to take on this way of thinking because it makes sense of their past and their immediate experience. Many nonalcoholics who have had intimate contact with alcoholics are able to understand and communicate with alcoholics very well. They do so because they put themselves in the place of the alcoholic by trying to see his world from his point of view. In the process, they cannot avoid using his language. This is how they put him at his ease, establish rapport, show quickly and immediately in the simplest way that they are aware of his situation: they speak his "lingo."

The mechanics of adopting "drunk talk" are probably no different from those underlying the acquisition of a new language in a new situation. Students do it all the time. Putting themselves in the place of their instructors, they now try to look upon the course materials through his eyes, which means employing his concepts, his language. As Bloomfield (4) pointed out, this is how elegant language is probably learned and transmitted in the first place. One admires and imitates, often unwittingly, another person and in so doing takes on his attitudes, his actions, his speech.

METHOD AND SETTING

On and off over a period of some six years, I conducted a case study of a halfway house for chronic drunkenness offenders (3, 5, 6, 7). The Connecticut State Commission on Alcoholism operated the Compass Club in New Haven. New Haven (155,000 population) is not large enough to sustain a traditional Skid Row quarter. Thus, institutions and establishments catering to homeless men are scattered in various pockets around the center of the city. All are within walking distance, rather than concentrated as in a typical Skid Row. Lodging houses, rooming houses, second-hand clothing stores, liquor stores that sell wine, restaurants and taverns catering to the homeless, missions and shelters all radiate from the center of the city. Important public places for the local and transient homeless are the Yale Hope Mission and a grassy common in the center known as the Green.

In the course of the study, I relied heavily on traditional methods of field work. The Commission asked me to study the facility and its effectiveness, its clientele, and their way of life. Being an employee hampered me from establishing the traditional role of independent field worker. To overcome these barriers I frequently alternated from a pure observer's role to a participant's role. For instance, I spoke informally with staff and members, I sat in on staff meetings, group discussions, counseling sessions, ate meals, drank coffee, lounged in and around the Compass Club. I conducted a series of Wednesday night meetings when a psychiatrist who formerly conducted them as supportive group therapy sessions dropped out. I drove men in need of treatment to the Blue Hills inpatient alcoholism clinic in Hartford, prowled the city, hung around on the Green to study bottle gangs, and passed some time in bars patronized by Compass Club men.

Primarily, then, the field work style I followed was that of the participant-observer. The bulk of my data, consequently, was recorded in field notes. Some use was made of Compass Club records, particularly in analyzing the relationship between source of referral and length of stay. But very early in the course of the study I became fascinated by "drunk language." Convinced that it was more than a curiosity, more likely a very important center around which the "drunks" understood and organized their lives, I set to work to collect information on and about this language as systematically as I could, given the field-work situation. Accordingly, whenever I heard anyone use a term I did not understand, I repeated it over to myself silently, tried to get its meaning from the context in which it was used, ultimately asked for a definition, and then listed each word together with its definition on an index card. Later I added to this another piece of information. I would list the name of the man who first used the term and the date of use. At the end of each period of field work I listed new terms and added the names of men who used old terms. This information is useful on two accounts: (*a*) it tells which persons are more immersed in "drunk culture" and (*b*) which are the key terms of that culture.

Before turning to the argot itself, five points ought to be made briefly. First, the present collection cannot be considered a complete dictionary, if only because of the method of collection and the region in which it was collected. Second, it has comparative value when examined alongside published (8, 9) and unpublished collections.[1] Third, the term "drunk" is used in the following list as an actual social role which people perform; hence, quotation marks will not be used therein for this or other slang terms. Fourth, I have attempted mainly to include only those terms (persons, places, things or events) which help to make some sense of the procurement, consumption, repair, punishment, and reintegration cycle. Fifth, in order to keep the collection to a size appropriate for publication in the *Quarterly Journal of Studies on Alcohol,* I have omitted all terms that are not directly or indirectly concerned with drinking.[2]

A.A. bum A member of Alcoholics Anonymous.

ace in the hole A person upon whom the drunk can count for help, for material as well as moral support. See also *cushion.*

alky (1) An alcoholic (2) Pure grain alcohol.

all bummed up Exhausted one's panhandling resources; e.g., "Mickey has got those bartenders all bummed up."

all rammed up Experiencing alcoholic convulsions.

all the way Complete abandon, as when "a real alcoholic goes on a drunk."

ammunition Alcohol in some form.

angle Any maneuver to obtain alcohol or money [either as verb or noun].

angle shooter One who is skilled in devious ways of obtaining drinks or money for drinks. Also ANGLESHOOTING.

antifreeze One of the many nonbeverage alcohol products men sometimes drink; automobile radiator fluid.

[1] J. F. Rooney, *Glossary of Skid Row and Seasonal and Casual Labor Terms,* unpublished MS., 1965.

[2] A separate publication of the nondrinking terms is in preparation.

babysitter Alcoholism counselor.

badass A dangerous, unpredictable person; one likely to use violence to gain his ends.

bad news A dangerous person; particularly one who becomes assaultive when intoxicated.

bag See *in the bag*.

ball, on the Abstinent.

ball and a half A 2-oz glass of whiskey and a 4-oz *chaser* of beer; sometimes shortened to *ball*.

bar drinker One who drinks only in bars.

barfly A person who frequents bars.

barreled up Intoxicated.

bat Extended drinking bout.

bathtub gin Gin produced illegally in bathtubs (or other large vessels) during Prohibition.

bats Delirium tremens; e.g., ". . . is in the bats."

belt A drink, usually from a bottle [either as verb or noun].

bend the elbow Imbibe freely.

bender Extended drinking bout.

B-girl A paid companion in certain bars who induces men to buy drinks and who may or may not engage in prostitution or other illegal activities.

big head Hangover. Also BIG SKULL.

bindle stiff A hobo who works, drinks socially if at all, and carries his belongings in a bedroll.

bing-bang Gasoline and milk cocktail, alleged to be popular on Philadelphia's Skid Row; also *gasso*.

binge Drinking bout.

bit of the hair Short for the *hair of the dog that bit you*.

blackout Alcoholic palimpsest, amnesia [either as verb or noun].

blase Intoxicated.

blind A respectable façade which conceals some illicit enterprise; e.g., a dry-cleaning store which is in reality a gambling office.

blind pig Illegal liquor outlet.

block and fall Inexpensive fortified wine. "So named because you walk a block after a drink of this wine and then fall." See also *Sneaky Pete*.

blood Port wine.

blotto Intoxicated.

boilermaker Same as a *ball and a half*.

bombed Intoxicated.

booster First drink in the morning, the *eye-opener*, the *starter*.

booze Any alcoholic beverage, especially distilled spirits.

booze fighter An alcoholic. Also BOOZEHOUND, BOOZER.

boozing Drinking alcoholic beverages.

booze talk, the booze talking Grandiose statements made only when the speaker is intoxicated.

bottle drinker Member of a *bottle gang;* one who does not drink in bars.

bottle gang Men who have pooled their resources in order to obtain alcohol for the group.

bottle off Same as *taper off*.

bottom Lowest limit of alcoholic degradation. See also *high-bottom, low-bottom*.

bouncing To be on a drinking bout; e.g., "I hear . . . is still bouncing."

Bowery bum Man who lives on the Bowery in New York City; by extension, any inhabitant of a Skid Row.

break a seal with Drink sociably; so called because it is necessary to break the seal on the bottle before drinking. Also *split a few seals with*.

break out Interrupt one's abstinence suddenly; also shortened to BREAK. See also *slip*.

bucket of blood Any rough-and-tumble bar.

bull pen The room adjoining the courtroom where men charged with drunkenness wait before they face the judge.

bum *v* To beg or panhandle. *n* Any man who prefers drinking to working. On Skid Row, synonymous with *drunk*. See also *all bummed up*. ON THE BUM = living as a bum.

bummology The theory, practice and study of life *on the bum*.

bust out Same as *break out*. Also, BUST OVER.

candy jag The occasional craving for sweets experienced by alcoholics when withdrawn from alcohol.

canned heat A commercial preparation used in portable cooking stoves. The methanol content is extracted from the paraffin wax by squeezing through a cloth. See also *squeeze*. The most common brand is *Sterno*. Also CAN OF SQUEEZE.

carry it Ability to tolerate alcohol without obvious effects.

carrying See *price*.

catch up Obtain parity in the number of drinks consumed by others in a drinking group.

character Same as *jail bait*.

charge *v* To take intoxicants with obvious effects. *n* Intoxicant. Also CHARGED UP = intoxicated.

chaser A 4-oz glass of beer drunk after a glass of whisky.

chemist The man in charge of squeezing the *canned heat* through the handkerchief, rag, etc. Also, PLAY THE CHEMIST.

chicken whisky Inferior whisky.

chuck horrors Sudden craving for food; frequently experienced by alcoholics when withdrawn from alcohol.

circuit The route one follows; the institutions one stops at in the course of the annual cycle of activities.

citizen (1) A person who will call the police when he or she sees someone publicly drunk. (2) In A.A., a person who is not a member of A.A.

civic-minded Same as a *citizen* (1).

clean-up Special drive by police to clear streets of drunks.

clip joint A bar or tavern which is suspected of diluting alcoholic beverages or overcharges for them.

closet drinker A secret drinker.

cocked Intoxicated. Also COCK-EYED.

cocktail bum (1) A "soft" drinker who has pretensions to "hard" drinker status. (2) A member of A.A.

coffee royale A cup of coffee laced with whisky.

cold turkey To stop or start something abruptly, without the customary preparation. Used most often for sudden withdrawal from alcohol.

come off it To end a sustained drinking bout. Also COME OFF ONE; COME OFF A DRINK, A DRUNK; COME OUT OF IT.

come up for air To be aware of others when sharing a bottle in a *bottle gang* and to regulate one's intake from the bottle.

con To gain an object by smooth talking; to *promote*. Also CON ARTIST = one who is skillful in raising money for drinks; CON JOB.

cook the pot To scheme about ways of obtaining money for drink.

corner Same as *heel*.

councilman Alcoholism counselor.

crock Jug or bottle of an alcoholic beverage. CROCKED = intoxicated.

crowd up To gather in such numbers around a bottle as to invite police attention. Also, *gang up*.

crumb bum Any derelict who appears to have lice on his person.

cuff Credit, usually from bartenders and usually for drinks.

cushion A source of material and moral support for the drunk. Also *ace in the hole*. From the point of view of an A.A. member the *cushion* prevents him from reaching *bottom;* from the point of view of the Skid Row alcoholic, the *cushion* encourages rehabilitation.

cushion bum A drunk with means.

dago Italian-type red wine.

delayed D.T.s The appearance of withdrawal symptoms from 4 to 10 days after termination of drinking.

Demon Rum Alcohol.

denatured Short for DENATURED ALCOHOL = ethanol made nonpotable by addition of, e.g., methanol.

Dick Smith A person who violates a trust. See *go south*.

ding A drinking bout.

dive Tavern of evil repute.

DK Drunkenness; from the abbreviation used in police forms.

dope Drugs.

double ball A 4-oz glass of whisky. Also DOUBLE HEADER, DOUBLE SHOT.

downs The name the *B-girl* gives to her drink, which is usually tea.

dragging Walking down a main street in search of money for drinks. Similar to *stemming* of hobo argot.

drinking joint Drinking place, tavern.

drinking man Heavy drinker, but not necessarily an alcoholic.

drown one's sorrows Drink heavily.

drunk (1) Heavy drinker, perhaps an alcoholic (2) A drinking bout.

drunk as a billy goat, as a hoot owl, as a lord Intoxicated.

drunk hole A *mission*.

drunk line Array of persons arrested on charges of public drunkenness who stand in a line in front of the judge in municipal court.

drunk money Funds earmarked for expenditure on drinking; usually, monthly compensation or social security or disability or retirement pensions. Known also as *rocking chair money*.

drunkard A man who drinks but who can still work.

drunked up Intoxicated.

dry Abstinent. Or, without alcohol in the organism. A.A.s mark their sobriety by saying, "I've been dry for . . . years now."

dry drunk A condition resembling alcohol intoxication experienced by some abstinent alcoholics. Also DRY STIFF.

dry heaves Acute gastritis attended by vomiting, induced by extended period of drinking while not eating. Also DRY REACHES.

dry out Detoxicate; rid one's system of alcohol and its aftereffects. DRYING-OUT JOINT = establishment for the treatment of intoxications, or the immediate aftereffects of a bout.

D.T.s Delirium tremens.

duck To hide or conceal some object; e.g., a drinker advised another to "duck it," meaning to conceal their bottle.

edge See *have an edge on*.

empty An empty bottle.

entrance fee A small amount of money which allows one to enter a bar, buy a drink and then wait for a *live one*. Also GATE MONEY.

eye-opener The first drink of the day, usually in the morning.

face the judge Appear before a judge usually on a charge of public intoxication.

fall To relapse from abstinence. Also FALL OFF = short for to fall off the *wagon*; e.g., "I was sober 6 weeks before I fell off." Also TOOK THE FALL, TOOK A FLIP.

feeling no pain Moderately intoxicated.

flip See *fall*.

floozie An older woman who frequents Skid Row bars; she may be an alcoholic, promiscuous, or both.

flop A cheap bed in a rooming house.

flop money The price of a night's lodging. Some men when panhandling are concerned about flop money first, money for drinks second. They usually put their flop money in their watch pockets, while the rest can then be used for drinking with the assurance that they will be able to pay for a night's rest. Also FLOP DOUGH.

fogged up Intoxicated.

fortified Protected by the effects of alcohol.

free-loader One who drinks from a bottle which he has not helped to purchase.

fried Intoxicated.

Frisco circle A circle drawn on the ground into which drinkers throw in what change they have toward the purchase of alcohol. West Coast practice. See also *tarpolian muster*.

front See *blind*.

front man Leader of transient group of alcoholics or bottle gang who plans the ways and means of procuring a supply of alcohol.

gang up Same as *crowd up*.

gas Alcohol. GASSED, GASSED UP = intoxicated.

gasso Same as *bing-bang*.

gate money Price of the first drink in a bar, employed to dispel the bartender's suspicion that the person is there to cadge drinks. Derived from term describing the funds given to prisoners on release.

geared up Intoxicated.

geesed up Intoxicated.

geographic cure In A.A., a move elsewhere in the hope that the alcoholic's drinking pattern will change or that he will regain control over his drinking in the new surroundings.

get a shithouse on Become intoxicated.

get off it Stop drinking. Also GET OFF THE BOOZE, GET RELIGION, GET STRAIGHT.

get stiff Become intoxicated.

get the monkey off the back To break the habit or control the addiction; term borrowed from argot of drug addicts.

gheed up, geed up Intoxicated.

gin mill A bar.

glow Pleasant effects of alcohol.

go south Abscond, violate a trust; specifically, failure to return from the package store with bottle purchased from group funds. See also *Dick Smith*.

good stuff Alcohol or alcoholic beverage of high quality.

goofballs Barbiturates. GOOFED UP = barbiturate intoxication. Also GOOFY.

gooned up Intoxicated.

grasshoppers Medications to treat alcohol intoxication.

grey paste Same as *wet brain*.

groove Abstinent; e.g., ". . . is in the groove."

Guinea red Italian-type red wine.

guzzle Drink large quantities.

hair of the dog that bit you A drink, as remedy for a hangover.

half a load on Moderately intoxicated. Also HALF-BARRELED-UP, HALF-CROCKED, HALF-GEARED-UP, HALF-GOOFED-UP, HALF-JACKED-UP, HALF-LIT-UP, HALF-LOADED, HALF-LOOPED, HALF-MOCUS, HALF-MULLED-UP, HALF-SHOT, HALF-SOUSED, HALF-STIFF.

hammer To solicit money for drinks, to *panhandle*. Also PUT THE HAMMER ON.

hanging paper Writing worthless checks for drinks.

hard stuff Distilled spirits.

have an edge on Moderately intoxicated to a pleasurable degree.

have you got the price? Typical request for funds when addressing another drunk. See *price*.

heat Short for *canned heat*.

heaves Vomiting induced by acute gastritis. See also *dry heaves*.

heel Dregs in the lower corner (or heel) of a tilted bottle. Also HEEL TAPS.

helpless drunk One who is unable to take care of himself; a complete dependent, even by Skid Row standards. Also *leaner*.

high Desirable state of intoxication.

high-bottom A.A. An A.A. member who did not hit *bottom*. Also HIGH-BOTTOM DRUNKS. See also *low-bottom*.

hit the skids Experience a serious decline in one's fortunes, mainly because of excessive drinking. Also ON THE SKIDS.

hitting the wine Drinking wine.

hold-out artist A man who has a reputation of not negotiating in good faith when contributions for group bottles are being solicited.

holding See *how much. . . .*

homeguard A drunk who rarely leaves the town or city in which he was born. Also HOME-TOWN BUM.

hooch Bootleg whisky.

hooker A 2-oz glass of whisky.

hop Drugs; e.g., ". . . acts like he's full of hop."

hophead Drug addict.

hopped up Intoxicated, usually with nonalcoholic intoxicants.

horrors Delirium tremens.

hot toddy Half hot black coffee, half whisky.

how much are you holding? How much money do you have? Phrase used in negotiation for contributions toward a group bottle.

hummer Drinking bout.

hung up Overextended credit, usually to other drinkers (done either in role of drinker, bartender, or both).

hungry horrors Same as *chuck horrors*.

hustler An energetic alcoholic who does not wait for drinks to come to him. Also ON THE HUSTLE.

in the bag (1) Intoxicated. (2) When the outcome of an event is certain. (3) When a case at law has been fixed in advance.

institutionalized When a person begins to rely upon hospitals or jails as the only agencies which can arrest his drinking, or relies on agencies for support, decision-making, etc.

Irish earache The consequence of listening to an Irishman who has become abstinent and now delights in informing the world of his accomplishment, which usually consists of two parts: one, how *dry* he is, and, two, how *wet* others are.

Irish toothache (1) A thirst for liquor. (2) Hangover.

jackroller One who robs drunks. See *roll*.

jail bait Men who are certain to be arrested (*sure pinches*) because they act indiscreetly after only a few drinks.

Joe Bum A bum. Also JOHN BUM.

John Alcoholic An alcoholic. Also JOHN DRUNK.

John Barleycorn Alcohol.

John Law The police.

John W. Lumberman Same as *ball and a half*.

joint A tavern or any place where men congregate. Also DRINKING JOINT.

jolt A drink.

jug (1) A bottle containing alcohol in some form; by extension, any container. (2) Jail. ON THE JUG = drinking.

jug juice Alcohol.

jugged up Intoxicated.

jugger An alcoholic.

juice Alcohol in any form. JUICED, JUICED UP = intoxicated.

junkin' Searching for discarded articles, such as empty bottles which can be resold.

kick Effects of drinking.

kicks (1) Trousers. (2) Exciting effects.

kill it Finish off a bottle.

king for a day. Euphoria from having enough money to buy a round of drinks for companions.

knockout drops Chloral hydrate; reputed to be used in certain taverns as a means of relieving patrons of their money.

lace it Add alcohol to (a beverage).

lace-curtain drinker A man who drinks in cocktail lounges.

lap dog A person who follows the *runner*, not so much out of distrust as out of haste and thirst.

leaner Homeless inebriate who is unable to obtain his own *flop money* or alcohol; completely dependent even by Skid Row standards. Also *helpless drunk*.

leech bum A clinging, dependent person.

level off (1) Attain a state of intoxicated well-being. (2) Descent from the peak of intoxication, approaching a plateau.

line-up (1) The line of prisoners who face the judge when court is opened, all arrested on charges of public drunkenness or related offenses. (2) The assemblage of *panhandlers* who gather around the *mission* at certain hours of the day.

lingo The Skid Row argot.

lit up Intoxicated.

live one A person who is willing to share his good fortune with those less fortunate. Also LIVE WIRE.

loaded Intoxicated. Also HAVE A LOAD ON.

lone eagle A solitary drinker. Often, the loner has been ostracized from the bottle gang because he "went south" (see *go south*) instead of *making the run* or violated bottle gang norms in some way. Thus, his solitary drinking is not necessarily from choice. Also LONER, LONE WOLF.

looped Intoxicated. LOOPED TO THE EYES = extremely intoxicated.

lost causes Pretext for drinking.

lost memory Cheap wine.

low-bottom drunk One who has reached the lowest limit of alcoholic degradation.

lush A drunk, a lover of whisky; also, whisky itself. ON A LUSH = on an extended drinking bout. LUSHED UP = intoxicated.

lush it To drink, usually excessively and in a group.

lush-roller Same as *jackroller*. See *roll*.

make a jug Obtain alcohol, usually through *panhandling*.

make a score Obtain one's goal; e.g., the price of a drink or a *flop*. Also MAKE IT.

make a strike To *roll* a drunk.

make the run Go to the liquor store to buy a bottle for a group of men who have contributed toward the purchase.

marked Plainly identified by police officers, leading to immediate arrest whether the person marked has been drinking or not.

Martini alcoholic Any alcoholic of high status, low visibility, and, hence, less social punishment.

medicine Alcohol in any form, used to alleviate a hangover.

merchandise Alcoholic beverages.

merchant Man in search of free drinks.

mission A rehabilitation center for homeless men, usually religiously oriented. Also called RESCUE MISSION. MISSION BUM, MISSION STIFF = one who frequently uses or exploits the facilities of a mission.

mocus Intoxicated. Sometimes refers to the stupor that wine drinkers are supposed to attain. Perhaps most characteristic of *plateau drinkers*. Also HALF-MOCUS; MO-MO.

monkey juice Cheap wine or *Sneaky Pete*.

monkey off the back See *get the monkey* . . .

moonshine Bootleg whisky.

moxie Courage, usually obtained after a number of drinks.

mug's game A useless, continually painful endeavor; e.g., alcoholism.

mulled up Intoxicated. Also, HALF-MULLED UP. WELL-MULLED = pleasant state of intoxication.

muskabooby Muscatel wine. Also MUSKADOO. MUSKADOODLE, MUSKY, MUSKYDOODLE, MUSKY PETE, MUSTN'T TELL.

needle Fortify any drink with additional alcohol.

nibble To sample small quantities of alcohol in a furtive manner.

nip *n* A small drink, *v* Same as *nibble*.

nipper A man who buys a half-pint of whisky early in the morning and *nips* secretly from the bottle, throughout the day at work.

nursemaid Alcoholism counselor.

nursing off Gradual withdrawal of alcohol; cf. *cold turkey*.

nut, on the On Skid Row.

off a drunk Just completed a drinking bout. Also OFF THE HUMMER.

off it Staying abstinent.

off the wagon Currently drinking, after a period of abstinence.

Old Sneak Another term for *Sneaky Pete*.

old soak Aged inebriate.

on it Currently drinking.

on pills Using pills (commonly barbiturates) regularly, usually as a substitute for alcohol.

one of the boys A member of the drinking fraternity.

opener Short for *eye-opener*.

ossified Intoxicated, usually in an unconscious state.

panhandle Beg for money, usually for drinks.

pantry drinker A clandestine drinker.

paper-hanger One who writes worthless checks in order to pay for his drinks.

parade Same as the *line-up*.

paraldy Short for paraldehyde, a sedative used in the treatment of postalcoholic states.

paralyzed Intoxicated.

pay the freight Pay one's own way; cf. *free-loader*.

perform To behave indiscreetly after a few drinks so as to cause arrest.

performer A person who becomes assaultive when intoxicated and draws police attention.

periodic One who gets inebriated at spaced intervals. Also PERIODICAL, PERIODICAL DRINKER.

Pete Short for *Sneaky Pete*.

pheno Short for phenobarbital.

pick-me-up A reviving drink.

piece off To give money to former drinking companions.

pill addict Barbiturate addict. Also PILLHEAD.

pill baby A woman who relies heavily on barbiturates.

pill-crazy (1) Intoxicated, usually on barbiturates. The state is sometimes induced by physicians. (2) A lover of pills.

pillman One who mixes his drinks with barbiturates.

Pink Lady Same as the *squeeze*. So called because of its reddish color.

pitching curves Devious ways of getting results. See *scheming*.

plastered Intoxicated.

plateau drinkers Those who maintain a more or less steady state of mild inebriation for lengthy time periods.

play To seduce a person; e.g., a drunk goes into a homosexual bar and intimates that he may be a homosexual in order to obtain free drinks.

pledge The abstinence vow.

ploxed Intoxicated.

plumber's helper Same as a *ball and a half*.

policeman Disulfiram (Antabuse).

price, the Short for the "price of a drink." "Have you got the price?" (of a drink, a bottle, a jug) is the drunk's common entreaty. Or, "Are you carrying anything?"

prime To prepare another person for an illicit move, to remove the inhibitions of an intended victim; e.g., using alcohol for sexual seduction.

promote To employ any strategy which if successful results in either drink or money for drink.

promoter An expert at raising funds for a group bottle.

prowl, on the In search of drinking money and companions; living by one's wits.

pt (pronounced *pee tee*) Pint, from its abbreviation.

put the make on To solicit money for drink; to *panhandle*.

put the squeeze on Make the drink known as the *squeeze*.

putting it on Simulating a condition which entitles one to assistance. For example, men sometimes simulate tremors to obtain alcohol or paraldehyde while in jails or hospitals.

queer joint A homosexual bar.

radiator fluid A source of alcohol when in dire need.

rams Alcoholic convulsions. See also *all rammed up*.

rat race, the Alcoholism.

reaches Same as *dry heaves*.

red-eye Wine.

reformed bum A person who has given up drinking, is unhappy and miserable over his sacrifice, and manages to make all other people equally unhappy; in general, an unpleasant symbol of abstinence. According to drunk culture, this person was much happier when drinking. Now sober, he proselytizes constantly on behalf of abstinence. Also REFORMED DRUNK.

religion Abstinence, as in *get religion*.

rescue mission See *mission*.

revved up Mildly intoxicated.

rim-rams Same as the *rams*.

robbin' the robbers Stealing from thieves; ingroup theft, rolling one's fellow drunks.

rocking chair money See *drunk money*.

roll (1) *v* To rob drunks of their money usually while they are asleep. (2) *n* Money.

rot gut Inferior, inexpensive whisky.

round A sequence of drinks shared by a group.

rubberneck A tourist, particularly those who visit Skid Row to see the sights.

rubby-dub Rubbing alcohol. Also RUBBY-DUBBY.

rum fit Delirium tremens or alcoholic convulsions.

rum-dumb In a drunken stupor.

rumhead Alcoholic or heavy drinker. Also RUM HOUND.

rummed up Intoxicated.

rummer An extended drinking bout.

rummy An alcoholic.

rummynose A term describing the red nose characteristic of heavy drinkers. Sometimes used to describe any heavy drinker. Also RUM NOSE.

rum-pot Inebriate.

rum-sick Experiencing a hangover.

runner The man who is sent to *make the run;* in general, an alcoholic.

Sally The Salvation Army.

Sally stiff A Salvation Army worker.

Santa Fe Express A half-pint of wine fortified with two codeine tablets. Usually consumed in the lavatory of a bar.

scheming The kind of thinking and acting required to obtain, maintain and protect a supply of liquor.

scratched Removal of one's name from a bartender's or package-store owner's credit list, because of failure to pay.

set 'em up To buy drinks for a group, to purchase a *round*.

shakes Tremors in alcohol withdrawal.

shake-up Another term for *smoke*. Sometimes refers to *canned heat* mixed with water, or rubbing alcohol mixed with water.

shaky Experiencing a hangover.

shim-shams Alcoholic convulsions.

shitfaced Intoxicated. Also SHIT HOUSE, SHITTED UP.

shitter A drinking bout.

shooting angles The practice of obtaining drinks or money for drinks by devious ways.

short beer A 4-oz mug of beer.

shot (1) A 2-oz measure of whisky; or, any small amount of alcohol. (2) Medicine.

shot and a beer Same as a *ball and a half*.

shot-and-beer joint Unobtrusive bar; simple tastes.

shut it off Stop or control drinking at will.

shut off To refuse service at a bar for some violation of house rules. Can be generalized to the denial of contact with nonalcoholic liquids or other humans, under appropriate conditions.

sick Experiencing a hangover.

silk-stocking Usually refers to A.A. groups composed of more socially acceptable alcoholics; alcoholics of the higher social classes.

single-o Same as *lone eagle*.

Skid Row Either the place or state of mind where one goes on the *bum*.

Skid Row bum Man who lives on Skid Row. Also SKID ROWER.

skids See *hit the skids*.

slip A.A. term for an interruption of abstinence.

slopped up Intoxicated.

sloud Intoxicated.

smoke Industrial alcohol mixed with water. Sometimes paint thinner mixed with water.

Snake Pit Any bar of ill repute.

snap To arrest, usually for public intoxication.

sneak bottle (1) A bottle of *Sneaky Pete*. (2) A bottle from which a person drinks surreptitiously. Or both (1) and (2).

sneak drinker One who drinks in private, not indulging to excess in public. Also *closet drinker*.

Sneaky Pete Inexpensive fortified wine. The term usually refers to muscatel, but can be extended to the entire class of wines. Also SNEAK-DOODLE, SNEAKY.

Sneaky Pete pounder Headache and hangover following a wine-drinking bout.

Sneaky Peter A man who drinks Sneaky Pete.

snifter A drink.

snort A small drink.

solo *adj, adv* To travel alone. Also *lone eagle*.

source of supply Person or agency upon whom one depends for alcohol.

soused Intoxicated.

south See *go south*.

sparrow Inferior liquor.

speakeasy Illegal drinking place during Prohibition. Also shortened to SPEAK.

spike To add alcohol to any beverage.

splash An extended drinking bout. SPLASHED = intoxicated.

split a few seals Share drinks from the same bottle.

spring *v* To obtain a release from jail prior to serving the full sentence.

squashed Intoxicated.

squeeze *Canned heat* wrung through a sock or handkerchief and then added to Coca-Cola or water. SQUEEZE IT OUT = manufacture the squeeze, play the *chemist*.

squirrel-cage Alcoholism.

stand To order a round of drinks for one's associates.

start, the The first drink in the morning.

starter (1) A small amount of money toward the purchase of a bottle. (2) The first drink in the morning.

stealin' the drunks Ingroup predation; when one drunk *rolls* another.

stem To panhandle. Also STEM IT.

Sterno See *canned heat*.

stewbum Any drunk in a poor condition—dirty, poorly clothed, unshaven.

stewed Intoxicated. Also STEWED TO THE EARS, STEWED TO THE GILLS.

stick (1) That part of a mixed drink which is alcoholic in content. (2) The bar. BEHIND THE STICK = working as a bartender.

stick 'em up To stand drinks at a bar for a drinking companion.

stiff *n* A drunk. *adj* Intoxicated.

stinking Intoxicated. Also STINKING DRUNK, STINKO.

stoned Intoxicated.

story Explanation given the judge for being in court on a public drunkenness charge.

straight Abstinent.

straighten out To become sober after an extended drinking bout.

straightener The first drink in the morning.

stuff, the Alcohol.

stumble-bum Any drunk.

suffer it out Experience withdrawal symptoms.

sure pinch Person, behavior or situation which generally leads to an arrest by the police. Individuals with reputations for bizarre actions when drinking, attention-getting actions while drinking in public, or crowd formation around a bottle are examples of all three. See *jail bait*, *performer*.

sweat it out Experience withdrawal symptoms without any aid; *cold turkey*.

sweats Discomfort endured during detoxication.

Sweet Lucy Port wine.

swill To drink heavily.

tab Same as *tick*.

take a pull Take a drink, usually from a bottle. Also TAKE A SWIG.

take a walk Same as *go south*.

take care of Provide for; usually funds for alcohol, food or shelter.

tanked up Intoxicated.

taper down To decrease slowly the amount one has been drinking. Also TAPER OFF.

tarpolian muster The *Frisco circle*; a corruption of seamen's term "tarpaulin muster."

tear (1) Final drops which remain in a bottle. (2) An extended drinking bout.

tick One's bill at a liquor store.

tie a good one on To get drunk.

tip To drink; e.g., "I tipped too many last night."

Tokay blanket Effects of Tokay wine; West Coast term.

too sick to stop Unable to terminate a bout, usually for fear of withdrawal symptoms.

took the fall Resumed drinking after a period of abstinence. Also TOOK A FLIP.

toot A drinking bout.

tough Description of one suffering a hangover; e.g., "He looks tough" or "in tough shape."

towline Spontaneous group emerging at the sight of a *live one*, following him wherever he goes in order to help him share his good fortune. Term originated in merchant seamen culture.

town bum Same as *homeguard*.

turkey See *cold turkey*.

twister A drinking bout.

under the table Place set aside for persons who lose consciousness in drinking bouts; intoxicated.

under the weather Suffering the effects of excessive drinking.

wagon, the (1) Abstinence; e.g., "On (or off) the wagon." (2) Police wagon.

waiter Man who waits for a person to leave the liquor store so he can ask him for a drink.

well-mulled Pleasant state of intoxication.

went Dixie Same as *go south*.

wet Intoxicated.
wet brain Severe neurological consequences of alcoholism.
whammy Delirium tremens.
what are you holding? Phrase used when soliciting contributions toward a group bottle.
whisky habit Alcohol addiction; e.g., "I have to support my whisky habit."
wine shits Diarrhea experienced by a *wino*.
wine-cooler Port wine and ginger ale.
wined up Intoxicated, presumably on wine.
winehead A wine drunk. See *wino*.
wine-nose A nose marked by rosacea.
wing-ding A drinking bout.
wino A habitual excessive drinker of fortified inexpensive wine. By extension, any Skid Row alcoholic.

REFERENCES

1. Berrey, L. V., and Van den Bark, M. *The American Thesaurus of Slang*. New York: Crowell, 1942.
2. Wentworth, H., and Flexner, S. B. *Dictionary of American Slang*. New York: Crowell, 1960.
3. Rubington, E. "The Bottle Gang." *Quart J. Stud. Alc.* 29 (1968), pp. 943–955.
4. Bloomfield, L. Language. New York; Holt; 1933.
5. Rubington, E. Grady "Breaks Out": A Case Study of an Alcoholic's Relapse. *Social Probl.*, 11 (1964), pp. 372–380.
6. Rubington, E. "Organizational Strains and Key Roles." *Admin. Sci. Quart.*, 9 (1965), pp. 350–369.
7. Rubington, E. "Referral, Past Treatment Contacts and Length of Stay in a Halfway House: Notes on Consistency of Societal Reactions to Chronic Drunkenness Offenders." *Quart. J. Stud. Alc.*, 31 (1970), pp. 659–668.
8. Anderson, N. *The Hobo*, Chicago: University of Chicago Press, 1923.
9. Wallace, S. E. *Skid Row as a Way of Life*. Totowa, N. J.: Bedminster Press, 1965.

In Praise of Gossip

by
Patricia Meyer Spacks

"DON'T GOSSIP," MY mother used to say. Or alternately: "If you can't say something good about a person, don't say anything at all."

The two injunctions implied one another. Gossip, back in my childhood, meant malice; it dabbled in the forbidden. Everyone else's mother said the same things. Some mothers gossiped themselves, while warning their daughters away; others abstained. Women tell of their mothers' lengthy, inaudible telephone conversations with female friends, of satisfied smiles in the aftermath. "What did you talk about?" a girl might ask. "Oh, nothing, really . . .": a non-answer epitomizing the mystery of adulthood. Holiday gatherings, in those mythical times, felt rich in their shared detail about the absent: family gossip. Yet we all knew and know: we're not supposed to do it, even—or especially—if we enjoy it.

But perhaps we enjoy it for good reasons. Some people have thought so (I certainly do); it is worth ruminating about why, about how gossip has been perceived, and how it feels, and what purposes it serves. "I don't call it gossip," says a character in a 1978 novel by Laurie Colwin. "I call it 'emotional speculation.' " Such re-naming attempts to evade negative associations clustering around the word, a word with a vexed history. Definitions of gossip often illuminate the definer more than the object of consideration.

In its original meaning, *gossip* implied no gender; it meant "godparent," of either sex. Its increasingly degraded connotations follow its intensifying association with women. By the mid-eighteenth century, Dr. Johnson could offer three definitions:

Reprinted by permission from *The Hudson Review*, vol. XXXV, no. 1. (Spring 1982), pp. 19–38. Copyright © 1982 by Patricia Meyer Spacks.

1. One who answers for the child in baptism.
2. A tippling companion.
3. One who runs about tattling like women at a lying-in.

The third meaning foretells the future, with its faintly resentful tone about female mysteries, its emphasis on the trivial, on secrecy (from men specifically, those beings excluded from the ceremony of lying-in), and on feminine bonding.

The definition also suggests ways in which men have defended themselves from the dangers they imagine in female talk: by denial and contempt, contempt conveyed in the dismissive verbs, denial in the refusal to grant significance. The hidden life of women, rarely onstage, always whispering in the wings, can frighten those who do not share it. What secrets do they tell one another, what power do they conceal?

Those who would rescue the idea of gossip have often tried to redefine it. A rapid survey of apologists may map ground to stand on. Such apologists insistently exclude malice: an early nineteenth-century periodical defiantly or defensively called *The Gossip*, for example, insists that malice marks slander, not gossip. They may emphasize the value of the data which gossip preserves. Julia Byrne, in a work published in 1892, argues that "*all* gossip is not necessarily frivolous, nor need it be malicious"—a comment which of course reflects her awareness of deprecating common assumption. She continues, however, to offer a more powerful justification. "History owes most of what little truth it contains, to the gossip of diarists and annotators as well as to the intimate confidences of friendly correspondence, and notwithstanding the necessarily trifling details of these private effusions and the *banalités* with which they often abound, the sidelights of such records have become invaluable to the groping student of past times, and of departed humanity; nor can we possess too many such chronicles." The writer implicitly assumes that the truth of history resides in particularity: a debatable proposition. A male defender writing at about the same time, Henry Morley, describes and defines gossip in ways which claim its attractiveness as well as its importance. "Gossip is in its tone familiar, in its matter very often personal, and always quick in passing from one subject to another. At the root of it, say etymologists, there lies an honest Saxon meaning—'God's sib'—'of one kindred under God.' " This somewhat disingenuous argument prefaces a miscellaneous collection of essays called *Gossip*, essays unified only by their personal interest to the writer; for him too, gossip evidently links itself with the concerns of the individual.

We need not feel surprised that defenses sound defensive. These, however, strike a special note—a response to the devious nature of the implied opposition. Gossip's connection with malice, trivia, lack of seriousness belongs to the realm of assumption for practitioners of the mode as well as for critics, even when they declare the falsity of the linkage. Practitioners and critics, indeed, are often the same. Few gossip without guilt, few defend without ambivalence.

Yet gossip has value, both social and individual. Sociologists and anthropologists have specified purposes it serves in various kinds of society. Thus the anthropologist Robert Paine, in an essay entitled "What Is Gossip About?," claims to have "no *a priori* assumption that gossip of itself either avoids conflict or exacerbates it, that it brings people together or pushes them into opposing factions. . . . On the other hand, I think it can be demonstrated that gossip is a catalyst of social process. . . . In this sense, it may be held that gossip serves to pattern issues which were but vaguely or confusedly perceived by a local population." Although an occasional social scientist argues the importance of gossip for the individual participant, such thinkers more typically insist on social meaning. "What an individual gossips about and how in that gossiping he gratifies his emotions or serves his self-interest, cannot be explained solely by reference to him."

This emphasis on the social, characteristic of most printed discussion of gossip, directs attention to a paradox implicit in efforts to explore the subject. Gossip itself eschews the general. Efforts to explain it necessarily generalize. The incongruity between the language of the genre and that in which it must be explicated weakens cases made for it. To explain what's rewarding in gossip, like efforts to elucidate what's funny in a joke, risks destroying what the explanation purports to clarify.

Nonetheless, I propose to join the company of explainers.

To begin with the obvious: men as well as women gossip. Both sexes acknowledge this fact, men with an air of large concession ("even we sometimes indulge in this foolish female activity"), women with defensive or aggressive energy ("men do it too, it can't be so bad"). But the fact of male participation does not weaken the tenacious link between the female and this conversational mode. The term "male gossip," as a designation of a person, sounds contemptuous, just short of an unfriendly accusation of homosexuality. The term "female gossip" hardly exists: the noun now assumes gender—not only because women gossip, but, more importantly, because gossip is the *sort* of thing women do.

Male philosophers shed light on this matter, although they do not explicitly associate gossip with women. For both Kierkegaard and Heidegger, gossip typifies inauthentic discourse. Kierkegaard's account belongs to a series of observations on the evils of the present age, an historical epoch of diminished spiritual substance. His description of gossip carries a heavy weight of negative judgment:

> Mere gossip anticipates, real talk. . . . When people's attention is no longer turned inwards, when they are no longer satisfied with their own inner religious lives, but turn to others and to things outside themselves, . . . when nothing important ever happens to gather the threads of life together with the finality of a catastrophe: that is the time for talkativeness. . . . People who are talkative certainly chatter away about something and, indeed, their one wish is to have an excuse for more gossip, but the subject is non-existent from the ideal point of view. It always consists of some trivial fact such as that Mr. Marsden is engaged and has given his fiancée a Persian shawl. . . . If we could suppose for a moment that there was a law which did not forbid people talking, but simply ordered that everything that was spoken about should be treated as though it had happened fifty years ago, the gossips would be done for, they would be in despair. On the other hand, it would not really interfere with anyone who could really talk.

"From the ideal point of view," gossip can provide few justifications for itself. Heidegger says essentially the same thing, although he begins by claiming no " 'disparaging' signification" for the term (*Gerede*) translated as "gossip" or "idle talk." His elaboration does not support this assertion. "The groundlessness of idle talk is no obstacle to its becoming public, instead it encourages this. Idle talk is the possibility of understanding everything without previously making the thing one's own. . . . Idle talk is something which anyone can rake up; it not only releases one from the task of genuinely understanding, but develops an undifferentiated kind of intelligibility, for which nothing is closed off any longer." Gossip occurs in writing as well as speech, Heidegger says, and the average reader will have difficulty discriminating it from more meaningful forms of assertion.

"The average understanding of the reader will *never be able* to decide what has been drawn from primordial sources with a struggle and how much is just gossip." Discourse "is the way in which we articulate 'significantly' the intelligibility of Being-in-the-world," but gossip perverts this function by ignoring its crucial terms: gossip concerns neither true "intelligibility" nor true "Being-in-the-world."

Between them the two philosophers articulate at a high level traditional ground for disparagement of gossip, neglecting only the matter of malice. Gossip, as they describe it, opposes "real talk," concerns the superficial and external, involves trivia, implies no struggle for understanding. Anyone can do it. It represents an obstacle rather than a means to communication.

One may agree that the world needs modes of talk besides gossip, yet still question the grounds of judgment in these accounts. I think of Freud's famous summary of the difference between the male and female superego. For reasons which he specifies, the male superego develops, he says, to a higher degree. Consequently, men and women conduct their moral lives in different ways; women prove far less capable of impersonal and abstract considerations, more vulnerable to the claims of the individual situation. If one penetrates beneath the value-laden terminology, Freud's description delineates with considerable accuracy two opposed modes of dealing with problems of moral judgment. Only by privileging the abstract, general, and theoretical over the concrete, specific, and personal does male superiority become self-evident. Just so with Kierkegaard and Heidegger. Both assume the high value of generalizable truth (the conclusions that can be drawn from what happened more than fifty years ago) and the low value of specific detail. From their assumptions stem their conclusions: gossip emerges from minds not seriously engaged, from inferior states of culture.

How necessary are the assumptions? Perhaps gossip shouldn't be considered a mode of "discourse" at all. People discourse *to* one another; they gossip *with*. Communication, Heidegger suggests, constitutes an end or purpose of discourse; it provides the means of gossip. One discourses from a height, gossips around the kitchen table. Why value platforms to the exclusion of rocking chairs? We need not reject discourse in its concern with large truth, but we might acknowledge also—as the philosophers do not—the revelatory power of the small, shared truth.

Catherine Morland, in *Northanger Abbey*, confesses to her lover-mentor her distaste for history. "I read it a little as a duty," she says, "but it tells me nothing that does not either vex or weary me. The quarrels of popes and kings, with wars or pestilences, in every page; the men all so good for nothing, and hardly any women at all—it is very tiresome." Henry Tilney, of course, rebukes and finally silences her, assuming rather than arguing the significance of historical narrative and asserting his own moral superiority in his comment that Catherine does not "altogether seem particularly friendly to very severe, very intense application." Catherine has no language, no concepts, to defend herself against the implicit charges of laziness and ignorance. The value system behind her key critical adjective, *tiresome*, remains unarticulated. Catherine believes that reading should provide pleasure, that ordinary people matter more than important people, that women count as much as men. Henry and the historians appear to believe the opposite. They believe, in other words, that the public matters more than the private; and the public realm belongs to men. (Symbolically if not literally, that statement remains as true of the late twentieth century as of the eighteenth-century world of *Northanger Abbey*. Women inhabit the public realm on male terms.) If the affairs of that realm prove "tiresome," the charge means little to those inhabiting it, who seldom measure the worth of occupations by enjoyment. To imply such a measure convicts Catherine of frivolity; but it also suggests her respect for the life of feeling. Gossip, seldom tiresome to informed participants, might satisfy some of her needs.

In making such a statement, I rest on my own assumptions about what gossip may involve—assumptions which I hope soon to clarify. Jane Austen helps toward clarification with an interchange from *Persuasion*. Anne Elliot, the protagonist, has befriended a poor, sick widow, Mrs. Smith, who indicates her moral stature by remaining cheerful in adversity. During one of Anne's visits, Mrs. Smith speaks of her sustaining contacts with Nurse Rooke, who brings reports from the outside world. "Call it gossip if you will; but when nurse Rooke has half an hour's leisure to bestow on me, she is sure to have something to relate that is entertaining and profitable, something that makes one know one's species better." Anne, in her sympathy for her friend, enthusiastically remarks that such women have the opportunity of seeing "all the conflicts and all the sacrifices that ennoble us most," the best of human nature. Mrs. Smith reacts doubtingly. "Here and there, human nature may be great in times of trial, but generally speaking it is its weakness and not its strength that appears in a sick chamber; it is selfishness and impatience rather than generosity and fortitude, that one hears of." The pleasure of Nurse Rooke's gossip, in other words, derives from its recitals of base rather than noble manifestations.

Despite its slightly apologetic tone, Mrs. Smith's defense of gossip articulates important issues. Unlike the sociologist's description of gossip's functions, it emphasizes pleasure as the activity's primary value. It also links pleasure with profit ("entertaining and profitable") in a fashion reminiscent of classic defenses of poetry: literature too unites the sweet and the useful. The usefulness of gossip, like that of literature, in traditional views, depends on its revelations about human motive and action. Gossip, like poetry and fiction, penetrates to the truth of things, reporting not fantasies of human greatness but realities of human pettiness.

For Mrs. Smith, gossip enlarges the world. For women in less confined situations, it does the same thing. A psychoanalyst friend of mine defines it: Gossip is healing talk. Yet Mrs. Smith's tone adumbrates the guilt which almost every participant feels—and not only from fear of social disapproval. Whence the pleasure, the profit, the guilt? The answers to all three questions, I suspect, are much the same, and they chart complex paths of psyche and socialization.

The notion of gossip as healing talk involves radical reimagining of the familiar. It posits, by implication, a wound or a sickness: in our time the sickness repeatedly described as characteristic of society—*anomie*, impersonality, rootlessness. It excludes destructiveness as an aspect of gossip, or suggests that even gossip's cruelty has positive functions. It insists on an aim beyond immediate pleasure, and on the importance of that aim. And it suits my purposes far better than social scientists' definitions which delineate the phenomenon in ways which are easy to accept, yet which always somehow miss the point. Thus Robert Heilman, examining the functions of gossip in the social life of an urban synagogue, describes the mode as "a social construction of reality which may or may not be grounded in indubitable fact." More specifically: "It is information about the personal affairs of others, identifies these others by name or in some other unmistakable way, is socially significant only to a specified group of others, and stimulates further gossip." Well, yes. But also no, because the emphasis on the social, the public, obscures another set of possibilities.

The word *gossip* designates two quite different kinds of activity; my immediate interest focuses on only one of them. One sort of gossip has nothing to do with healing talk. It takes place often in a more or less public realm—at upper middle class dinner parties, say, and academic conventions, to say nothing of lunch breaks in factories. Who has been considering what job, who is sleeping with whom, who has just revealed his utter untrustworthiness? Such gossip exists to be circulated. It uses private material for public ends; it confirms Heidegger's point about how "groundlessness" provides no obstacle but rather an encouragement to promulgation. Often malicious, often idly destructive, self-aggrandizing, not infrequently resting on false assertions, gossip of this sort expresses individual envy and aggression and serves purposes of social solidarity as well as transmits often useful information. Most people indulge in it at least occasionally, and they often have reason to feel guilty about it, recognizing the self-serving, frivolous, and potentially destructive aspects of such talk. One would not feel inclined to praise this gossip.

The other kind, the healing kind, may use the same raw materials—who is sleeping with whom and the like—but for different purposes. I think of it as "good gossip"; it consists simply of intimate conversation about other people, people not present. Such gossip flourishes only in groups of two or at most three. It takes place in a special tone, a tone defined partly by motives of discovery and expression; it concerns itself with facts or pseudo-facts for the sake of eliciting belief. This is the variety of gossip that women keep secret. Mostly they can't describe it; but also, perhaps, they won't. It is in a sense too important.

The "bad" kind of gossip, the kind most people mean when they use the term casually, presents problems well worth talking about. Novelists have explored them, as have psychologists; moralists have commented on them. Awareness of Peyton Place, however, may obscure the more benign side of gossip. Let us inquire how and why it heals, postponing detailed inquiry into how and why it can hurt.

What does Nurse Rooke really do for Mrs. Smith in *Persuasion*? She hardly alleviates the invalid's physical maladies, but she modifies the confined woman's psychic malaise. We may readily imagine the kind of story she tells. She might, for example, report the unexpected pregnancy of a patient, perhaps with commentary on the husband's reaction to it. Such a report, even including the commentary, only begins the process of gossip. Its substance involves the talker's reactions to nuggets of raw material. Nurse Rooke and Mrs. Smith might discuss, more or less explicitly, the feelings associated with pregnancy at various times of life, the implications of family size, the effect of childbearing on marriage. In their twentieth-century avatars, they could reflect about contraception, child-care, abortion, the possibilities open to women outside the domestic sphere. They would use details of someone else's experience, in other words, to stimulate expression of responses and beliefs through that process Laurie Colwin calls "emotional speculation." And the beliefs they articulated would not necessarily correspond to those they revealed to their husbands, if they had any.

I can offer no evidence for this assertion except personal experience, about which I don't care to be too specific. Private gossip supplies little data for the researcher. Yet it provides a way of *saying* often vital to its participants, a way to express what they care about and how.

Such talk requires time, a reason sometimes alleged for the relative infrequency of intimate gossip among men. Busy women I know make time for it, thus often bewildering husbands and lovers who fail to comprehend its necessity. Those who take the time, make the time, for gossip declare allegiance to small personal facts and to the knowledge gained by contemplation of such facts. People and their concerns matter to gossipers, it goes without saying, but the special way in which they matter evolves from belief in small particulars. Gossip defends this belief, always. The other beliefs it embodies and supports differ according to the participants. By talking about the concerns of other people's lives, the talkers grow to understand their own more fully. That shawl Mr. Marsden gave his fiancée, a subject of conversation for which Kierkegaard has only contempt, may yield material for profound speculation. As the linguist Thomas Pavel has pointed out, gossip involves a rudimentary hermeneutic act: interpretation is its essence. The hermeneutic force of gossip—on occasion far beyond the rudimentary—derives from its capacity to move from small to large, from particular to general—and back again. Gossip involves a special mode of knowing, as well as of saying.

Another value always implicit in intimate gossip, and another function it serves, involves the affirmation of alliance. A Rumanian man told me that in his country men gossip a lot, they sit over coffee and discuss in minute detail the happenings of other people's lives. In America, he believes, men do not gossip in the true sense. They are too competitive, he says, they don't understand the healing power of such talk.

Gossip directs competitive feelings outward, toward the absent other, the subject of discussion. For the two or three discussers, it supports comradeship, connection; it enables them to distance, even to deny, their own competitive impulses. They declare their closeness by sharing their secrets, and by investing those secrets with meaning. The sharing involves more than exchange of information. It implies self-revelation as well as exposure of other people's affairs because responses to news matter more than news itself in intimate gossip. By gossiping people know one another.

Or one might say with equal accuracy that they gossip *because* they know one another. Women who move away from a familiar community often report suffering from lack of gossip in their new environment. They don't know what there is to talk about, they lack the context of knowledge and acquaintance which situates new information and points its meaning. But they also lack people to talk with. To various degrees, but always a good deal, gossip depends upon and derives from trust. Although one knows (sometimes relies upon) the likelihood that information transmitted in one intimate situation will pass to new hearers in another such situation, the exchange assumes the fundamental fidelity of its participants. They can trust one another to allow room for moral speculation; they can expose to one another their deep beliefs. The patterns of gossip reflect patterns of intimacy. Tomorrow I may gossip with the woman I have just gossiped about, but I will not gossip about my closest friend with someone to whom I feel less firmly attached.

But the account I have just offered suggests also the problematic aspect of even "good" gossip. Such conversation posits and depends upon fidelity and intimacy among its participants, yet in its nature it encourages instability of alliance. Gossip generates immediate temptations. The pleasure and profit of intimate talk may lead the talkers insensibly to betrayal of other alliances, to revealing secrets that should remain untold, to exposing other people's vulnerabilities—not from malice, necessarily; perhaps from excessive involvement in the moment. Gossip's potential for moral insight, which depends on the active participation of its practitioners, implies its moral danger. One risks harm to others, not only to oneself. I will return to this indigestible problem; the negative potential of gossip can only be properly assessed, I believe, in the context of its understood positive power.

That power derives partly from the ways—often harmless— gossip makes use of other people. Such verbal exchange locates its subjects temporarily at a firm distance. Talk about our children, our spouses, even, in most cases, our *ex*-spouses, rarely falls into gossip's modes, although it may share the healing power and some of the pleasure. But gossip does not deal directly with the gossiper's personal problems. If I'm worried because my son appears to be rather too emotionally involved with an unsuitable young woman, my talk about the entanglement has a kind of psychic utility too immediate and straightforward for gossip. Talk about my neighbor's son's similar entanglement, on the other hand, which allows consideration of the issues with less anxiety about the outcome, may qualify as gossip. The borderlands are murky. It's a certain atmosphere, most of all, that makes gossip recognizable: of intimacy, of gusto, often of surprise and revelation. The atmosphere both marks and encourages friendship.

By its context of freedom and friendship, its opportunity to articulate and to transmit values, its affirmation of alliance and its effective distancing of competitive feelings, gossip generates pleasure. As the atmosphere of secrecy intensifies intimacy, it simultaneously engenders the aura of power: another source of pleasure. "I know something you don't know," children chant, declaring their dominance in their knowledge. Adults too increase their stature by knowledge which excludes others. To know, to tell, to be told: these actions assert dominance.

Of course gossip involves not only facts, but interpretations; not just facts, but facts organized into stories; not just stories, but stories located in private history. Catherine Morland would approve of such history: a record of interpretations preserved mainly by oral tradition, concerning domestic affairs, small events, childbirth rather than war and pestilence, women as much as men. Communities of gossip share these private histories. History—this special kind of oral history—provides the fundamental context for further interpretation. The power of gossipers in a community derives partly from the sense in which they control history.

From the narrower perspective which interests me more, possession of the history provides another form of power in the immediate personal control implicit in it. Knowledge is power, knowledge about other people is power over them, knowledge of the past provides an illusion of predictive possibility and an air of interpretive authority. The interpretations gossip offers inhere in the stories it tells. The organizer of a narrative controls its meaning, thus takes partial possession of other people's lives.

Alliance, secrecy, shared values never proclaimed aloud: these foster collective as well as individual force. Social condemnation of the female activity of lengthy, trivial conversation may reflect anxiety about the dimensions of this power. Dr. Johnson's definition about women at a lying-in stems from the same male nervousness (what's really going on there?) reflected in the common instant association, for most men, between gossip and malice. Women tend to associate gossip first with pleasure (although sometimes also with prohibition); men, more often with danger, catty destructive women, schools for scandal. The sense of danger acknowledges the power—power never claimed out loud, never charted. Women only talk, in an ancient stereotype; men *do*. But what possibilities lurk in private talk?

Nonparticipants both perceive and imagine gossip's power, but those who exercise it also feel it. One probably understands it most clearly in its absence: deprivation of pleasure and vague loss of strength when change of scene or some other circumstance eliminates established conversational networks. The complaint, ''I have no one to gossip with,'' speaks of an experience of diminishment, both in the loss of collectivity and the loss of opportunity for self-discovery which reveals to the self its own potency. Gossip's power, as experienced by gossipers, is less sinister but no less strong than that fantasized by outsiders.

Power, values, alliance—to claim such issues as integral to gossip sounds rather too portentous. It ignores the sheer *fun* which for most gossipers explains their involvement: the simple pleasure of companionship, the joy of verbal play, the freedom to exercise and explore the possibilities of wit, to take risks with limited danger. The self-exposures of gossip carry the forbidden joy of exhibitionism; the concern with other people's erotic life provides the thrill of voyeurism. And always gossip supplies the exhilaration of story. As a literary critic I take story very seriously; I also take it seriously as a gossip. By stories, as I have already suggested, we attribute meaning; by stories we declare the sense made by other people's experience and by our own. The organizing activity of gossip has far-reaching implications; it also provides immediate and solid satisfaction. At least at the domestic level we can assert that the things that happen have meaning, form patterns, yield to analysis, and that we have the right to take pleasure in the small concerns of life: even they provide narrative substance.

Every effort to say what it is distances us from the immediate experience of pleasure inherent in gossip as activity. To make large claims for it contradicts gossip's commitment to the small. Praising gossip begins to sound rather like praising folly: there must be some irony here somewhere; in the best of all possible worlds surely we wouldn't need gossip. (A novelist friend of mine, on the other hand, argues that in the best of all possible worlds we would need nothing but gossip. Lots of gossip, no wars and pestilence.)

Gossip is healing talk. The sources of pleasure in gossip duplicate the forces of healing. Both large and small claims for this form of verbal action reiterate its capacity to affirm the self. As one discovers one's values, and skill at verbal play, and ability to take risks, and pleasure in sharing, and potential power, one discovers one's self. The healing comes both from what the gossiper does and from what she learns. In the doing, the talking, the story-telling, she encounters her own capacities and experiences her own pleasures. She also learns and relearns what she shares with the rest of humanity. Gossip's obsessive concern with the minute reflects the assumption that most lines compose themselves mainly of minutiae. The more we learn of other lives, the more we learn of our own: another truism from traditional defenses of literature. We have come back again to Mrs. Smith and her delight in encountering vicariously even (or especially) the base aspects of human nature. Gossip heals by allowing us to express who we are, to know the others with whom we talk, to imagine richly those we talk about.

As a social phenomenon, gossip often appears to blunt moral discrimination. I think once more of Jane Austen: *Pride and Prejudice*, where the voice of the community articulates all Elizabeth's mistaken judgments. *Everyone* says that Darcy is proud, Wickham charming, Bingley agreeable. Elizabeth does not derive her own opinions from the utterance of "everyone," but the communality of gossip helps protect her from the necessity of examining her own convictions until circumstances directly challenge them. Moreover, the social reality of gossip hints its sinister side in the community's eagerness to believe the worst of Wickham, once his flaws begin to show, and to anticipate a dreadful fate for Lydia. As the narrator of *Emma* comments, any young person who marries or dies is sure to be well spoken of: an observation suggesting the blurring effect of communal judgment, communal talk.

For the sensitive individual who participates, on the other hand, gossip develops the capacity for moral discrimination. Think of the talk about other people in Henry James (to say nothing of Proust): by endless discussion of how others behave, normative characters develop their own subtle perceptions. As an activity in the world, sustained gossip demands fine discrimination: otherwise, one runs out of things to talk about. The simple facts can hardly sustain interest long. To distinguish between the ways in which two different women conduct their love affairs, on the other hand, to establish distinctions where none appear to exist—such mental and moral exercise refines the palate and strengthens the mind.

Except in my choice of pronouns, I seem to have abandoned the subject of women as intimately connected with that of gossip. All that I have said, however, applies with particular force to the experience of a class largely deprived of social power and filling limited functions in the public world. Those with grander public roles have other ways of forming alliances and exercising power. The nation's leaders proclaim their values from the platform; they need not discover them to one another over the telephone or around the kitchen table. Competition largely governs male lives, in the traditional patterns: no need to direct it toward the absent. Men, stereotypical men, have other outlets for the impulse toward verbal play; they need not interest themselves in the small because they have direct power over the large.

I am, of course, describing a parody version of male experience, but a parody based on common assumptions and established mythology. And the mythic versions of male and female lives are most relevant here. Reality shifts, but history and mythology remain powerful: a history and a mythology, for women, of confined opportunity, narrow physical scope, private rather than public outlets. The values, the pleasures, the rewards of gossip all conform to these stereotypes. Indeed, if one tried to invent a female pastime to provide the greatest possible expressive possibility while remaining bound by rigid social actuality, such a pastime would closely resemble gossip. It can be interpreted as the resource of a deprived class, with its ethos of secrecy, its concealed power, its surreptitious alliances. And its ways of working reiterate ways women typically function.

Gossip proceeds by a rhetoric of inquiry rather than of authority. "Have you heard . . . ?" the gossiper says. "Don't you think . . . ?" "Do you suppose . . . ?" I recall a conversation about a woman whose love affair with a married man had endured for almost a decade. Why didn't she break with him, we wondered, or demand that he choose between the women in his life? Perhaps, my companion suggested, the unconventional arrangement solved problems otherwise impossible for the career woman. After all, she didn't have to cook dinner for him every evening, she had more control over her time than those with orthodox commitments. . . . Our interchange turned into an exploration of the tensions women experience between work and love.

Exploration, indeed, is gossip's mode. It furthers a variety of moral investigation perhaps also typical of women. Inquiries into women's use of language in their writing have begun to suggest that a style based on the tentative and conditional characterizes many female writers—not a style of weakness, but one of peculiarly feminine strength. I heard recently a brilliant paper by Myra Jehlen comparing the first paragraphs of Henry James's *Portrait of a Lady* and Edith Wharton's *House of Mirth*. It demonstrated how all James's doubling back on himself, his parentheses and qualifications, generated authoritative assertions, whereas Wharton's more straightforward manner in fact established an atmosphere of pervasive doubt. The need to question the given which emerges in Wharton's prose appears also in the dialectic of gossip.

The moral investigation supported by gossip's inquiries proceeds by means of the emphases Freud declared characteristic of women, stress on the personal, particular, and contextual. Recent studies by Carol Gilligan, a psychologist at Harvard, have confirmed the notion that women typically make more contextual ethical decisions than men and that they think first of their responsibilities to others rather than of such abstract principles as justice. Gossip elevates contextuality to a central position and makes other people its subject. It allows women to think about what they appear to value most; it supports the development of fine discriminations growing from concentration on the particular.

Yet the fact remains: to gossip generates guilt. If it encourages subtle thought about other people, it paradoxically involves violation of the cardinal tenet of female morality: care for others. It issues from interest in the multifariousness of experience and of human possibility; but it can imply reification of its subject. The pleasures and the profits of gossip, as I have discussed them, all support and affirm and discover the self—but sometimes at cost to others.

Each source of pleasure implies a specific cause for guilt. Secrecy, for example, an essential aspect of gossip's every mode—the secrecy of shared confidences, the secrecy of gossip's pleasure, power, and alliances—secrecy, obviously, implies something to hide. An activity which involves only two or three, which cannot take place in the light of day: such activity must have something wrong about it. Most particularly, the sense of secret power in gossip's interchange often disturbs participants. Whether or not one feels uncomfortable with the idea of power, something distasteful clings about the power which cannot declare itself.

Healing talk for the talker, enlargement of experience; but talk dependent on the manipulation of another by secret use of language. As the conclusions of such talk circulate, they may damage reputations and generate pain. Only by focusing steadily on special aspects of gossip can one celebrate it.

Gossip's alliances also sometimes bear guilt because they reflect hierarchies of intimacy. By choices of whom one will gossip about, whom one will gossip with, one registers often uncomfortable discriminations among people. Gossip says that we like some people better than others, we take some more seriously than others. Even the declaration of values in gossip can generate discomfort, for we may discover in intimate interchange the divergence between what we profess and what we believe. Gossip's self-revelations are often disturbing. We turn out both more harsh and more tolerant than we had anticipated. And many gossipers worry about the apparent trivia that concern them. If we spend so much time talking about unimportant matters, can we really be serious people? Aren't our mothers right?

I no longer sound as though I'm praising gossip. I am, instead, expressing the anxiety most gossipers feel. Part of the anxiety and guilt reflect uncertainty about the validity of the assumptions and values underlying gossip, those values of intimacy and particularity and curiosity about small details. Female values, one might call them—not because males don't sometimes share them, but because they have been insistently associated with women, and insistently deprecated. Many who hold them have trouble taking them seriously.

But some of the anxiety stems from what I earlier called the indigestible problem of the real harm gossip may cause. One cannot simply discount this possibility. The fact that gossip may damage others, both by threatening reputations and by converting people into fictions—that fact must be seriously acknowledged. There is nothing to be done about it. Each gossiper must perform her own precarious balancing act between the possibility of harm—harm even when the talkers feel quite free of malice—and the probability of personal enrichment for the gossipers. The trouble is that no clear line divides what I've called "good" gossip from what I've called "bad": they inhabit a continuum. One can slide from one to the other, and then slide back again. To gossip involves a risk to personal integrity as well as to the subjects of the talk. What justifies the risk is the promise of insight, comprehension, and enlargement through an imaginative and judicious activity.

Let me conclude by telling a story. A youngish man—I'll call him Baxter—sets out to spend a summer on Martha's Vineyard. On the ferry to the island he meets a beautiful young woman (Clarissa, let's say), the recently-acquired daughter-in-law of an aggressive middle-aged woman whom he knows well and rather dislikes. Clarissa's husband, it develops, is away on business; her mother-in-law soon leaves. Twice divorced, at loose ends, captivated by Clarissa's unfamiliar beauty, Baxter sets out to seduce the bride. She proves resistant, committed to marital fidelity, suspicious of men, apparently too stupid to find Baxter captivating. Finally, however, he succeeds: he discovers and exploits Clarissa's longing that someone should believe her intelligent, although in fact her incapacity for lucid thought is staggering.

A rather ugly piece of gossip, distanced yet farther by my summary? An elaborated male chauvinist joke? In fact, a short story by John Cheever, "The Chaste Clarissa."

Mary McCarthy and others have noted before the analogies between the material of the novel and that of gossip. I want to push the analogy farther, to inquire why realistic fiction seems so much more respectable than gossip. It goes without saying that fiction supplies aesthetic satisfactions seldom available in gossip—but why does reading it not raise comparable moral questions? The Cheever story relies on precisely the kind of substance that makes one feel guilty about gossiping. It deals in the erotic, it uncovers base aspects of human nature, it examines trivia. Its tone partakes of malicious speculation. "From the look on Clarissa's face when he gave her the box of candy, Baxter judged that she liked to get presents. An inexpensive gold bracelet or even a bunch of flowers might do it, he knew, but Baxter was an extremely stingy man, and while he saw the usefulness of a present, he could not bring himself to buy one." While purporting to enter Baxter's mind, these observations convey the narrator's judgment and interpretation. Why doesn't Baxter ply Clarissa with gifts? Because he's so stingy: a gossiper's conclusion, and an ungenerous gossiper at that. The story avoids profound analysis of motive and feeling in favor of interpretation at this rather superficial level. Its charm derives from its resolute preservation of a slightly distant, slightly amused perspective, one which refuses to acknowledge the potential for tragedy in the banal sexual situation.

A critic might condemn this story on literary grounds, as slight, easy, and superficial. But neither critic nor ordinary reader will feel conscious guilt in reading it, any more than John Cheever presumably felt guilt writing it. A good gossiper would probably perceive more meaning in the narrative than does the teller of the written story. Unlike Cheever's narrator, the gossip would understand Clarissa too as a center of consciousness, a woman with feelings and problems despite her apparent lack of intelligence. But to imagine the gossip's reaction implies imagining Baxter and Clarissa as real people. And they aren't: they're only fictions.

A good deal of fiction derives more or less directly from actuality. Clarissa and Baxter may well have existed, under different names; the seduction may have taken place. No matter: the conventions of fiction protect us from guilt by removing us from avowed connection with the real world. " 'Er gossip is so fascinatin', you wish you knew who she was on about," observes that profound philosopher Andy Capp in the comic strip. He too can partake of the pure pleasure of narrative, without the guilt of personality, although he acknowledges the potential enrichment of specificity. Mrs. Capp's accounts and John Cheever's in their fictionality share the purification toward which Kierkegaard aspired when he wished that talk about events and people should deal only with matters treated as though they happened more than fifty years ago. Specificity and immediacy contribute to guilt. If the story has nothing to do with anyone real—under such circumstances, we can enjoy it with no culpability. Yet the immediacy and reality of gossip's material often generate deeper humanity, more penetrating analysis than one finds in any but the best fiction: the moral risks of gossip accompany real moral possibility.

Perhaps, too, the guiltlessness of reading fiction bears some relation to the lack of human interchange in the transaction. Gossip takes place between people; reading occurs in solitude. The act of reading involves two people, reader and writer, but their connection has been made bloodless. The possibilities for challenge and revision remain limited. No one looks in anyone else's eyes.

"Poetry makes nothing happen": a debatable proposition. Those of us who spend our professional lives thinking about poetry believe that it makes a great deal happen in the mind and heart—where gossip also makes things happen. But the rhetorical claim that poetry has no effect in the world privileges it and protects it from culpability. Gossip can arrogate no such privilege, no such protection: we who engage in it fear its possible consequences beyond ourselves. On the other hand, the opprobrium attached to even the most intimate and fulfilling gossip bears little proportion to the actual harm caused. Does gossip embody female magic? I suspect it does (I mean something good by that), and I suspect men think it does (meaning something bad). Yet it can be argued that it embodies, more importantly, the distinctively human. A final excerpt from the 1821 essay in *The Gossip* makes the point. "We are all gossips by nature. Why do men associate? Some say it is owing to our weakness, and our wants, but it would be more correct to attribute it to the delights afforded us by the sound of the human voice. . . . Those only who amuse, amend, and instruct others, are really wise and pious." Gossips look in each other's eyes, listen to each other's voices, amuse, amend, and instruct each other. Their magic is wise and pious: worthy of non-ironic praise.

IV

SEX AND SEX ROLES

How do porcupines make love? *Very* carefully.

Anonymous

There is only one way for women to reach full human potential—by participating in the mainstream of society, by exercising their own voice in all decisions shaping that society.

Betty Friedan

SEX IS A two-edged sword: a sharp and lustful side called pleasure, a dull but deadly side called politics. As pleasure, sex is an outlet for fantasy, experimentation, and light conflict. The conflict is here between the proper and the possible. Humans are often intrigued by the possible even when it is defined as improper. At times, therefore, the male-female conflict is forgotten as both sexes join together to "fight" against social norms of propriety. For example, recently the Iranian parliament put a ban on kissing, punishable by a hundred lashes. Predictably, Iranians interested in continuing this germ-transmitting encounter will find ways to avoiding lashes while receiving kisses.[1]

For modern Americans almost anything which is possible and pleasurable is considered proper, at least in some circles. Modern attempts to do whatever contradicts the "Protestant ethic" lead many into sexual experimentation. Since America has also become a "read-how-to-do-it" society, much has been published to aid those personally dedicated to the experimental method.[2]

The upper limits of fascination with variety are provided by Alfred Kinsey's and Wardell Pomeroy's discussion of the sex life of a college graduate:

> We had heard of a man who had kept an accurate record of a lifetime of sexual behavior. . . This man had homosexual

[1]Those who find the kiss intellectually stimulating will want to read E. Royston Pike, "The Natural History of a Kiss," in *The World's Strangest Customs* (London: Odhams Books, 1966, pp. 11–19).

[2]Dennis Brissett and Lionel S. Lewis "The Big Toe, Armpits and Natural Perfume: Notes on the Production of Sexual Ecstasy, *Society*, vol. 16, no. 2 (January/February 1979), pp. 63–73.

relations with 600 preadolescent males, heterosexual relations with 200 preadolescent females, and intercourse with countless adults of both sexes and animals of many species; he also used elaborate techniques of masturbation . . . his grandmother introduced him to heterosexual intercourse, and his first homosexual experience was with his father. If that sounds like *God's Little Acre*, I will add that he was a college graduate who held a responsible government job.[3]

Human sexuality, an odd mixture of pure lust and lust for power, has obvious links to politics. From a Freudian perspective politics could be considered a subsystem of sexual life. Such a categorization—dubbing sex as the mother of politics—gives new meaning to an old counter-culture slogan: "Make love not war!"

Sexual politics divides communities into two camps which maintain a measure of peaceful coexistence. Generally, the costs of peace are higher for women than for men. In the ongoing struggle for supremacy a major weapon is language. In English, for example, many endearing and hostile words communicate the same message. Men are strong, women are weak: the weak woman is childlike ("baby"), a "cute" little thing identifiable with a female toy ("doll"). Like the real child, the "little woman" brings sweetness into social life ("honey," "sweetheart"). Some men are ever ready to take advantage of her unprotected charms ("wolves"). Others ("tigers" and "teddy bears")—perhaps descended from chivalrous knights—protect this weak but cuddly "pussycat."

The myth of the helpless woman runs into trouble in the real, empirical world. But words are ever available to protect the myth by manipulating events. The woman who (somehow) outsmarts a man is dubbed a "foxy lady"—clever in a sly, inhuman sort of way. Should foxiness, or anything else, lead to an exchange of insults, the foxy lady becomes a "cunt." Here, as Germaine Greer reminds us in her book *The Female Eunuch*, the woman is identified with an organ which is most satisfying when it is small and unobtrusive. The foxy lady may fight back by referring to her verbal assailant as a "prick." Parrying in this manner still leaves the woman on the defensive: a prick is an organ which is most satisfying (it is rumored) when it is large and obtrusive.

In the sex-power game the male organ is more than just an instrument for pleasure and reproduction. Symbolically, it may

[3]"Alfred C. Kinsey: Man and Method" by Wardell B. Pomeroy, *Psychology Today*, March 1972, volume 5, no. 10.

be seen as a gun. As Greer tells us, in British slang "women cry when they want their mate to ejaculate: 'Shoot me! Shoot me!' " In Trinidad, as Lewis Coser and I show, this shooting is part of a game with two names. From the male perspective this is a "sex-fame game" in which he who shoots the most becomes known as a "famous man." From the female perspective it is a "secret sex game." Women who are often shot at must hide their role as "targets." Women's attempts to appear as nonplayers are generally unsuccessful. Male eloquence almost invariably falsifies female denials. This Trinidadian system, like many others in various parts of the world, is one in which men exploit women.

How does one explain the exploitation of women? Men, Ernestine Friedl writes ("Society and Sex Roles") generally control the distribution of valued goods and services. It is this control which provides the power to transform women into second-class members of society. This control gives men their superior position and status. Women in modern society, Friedl believes, can raise their status by competing successfully for positions with power. I would add that successful competition for power requires a change of image. A "pussycat" label is hardly appropriate for a manager, executive, or company president. The new image must counter the old view that women should not work. D. H. Lawrence, though often sensitive to human issues, once wrote in his novel *Sons and Lovers* (1913): "I suppose work can be almost anything to a man. But a woman only works with part of herself. The real and vital parts are covered up." Views such as these should have received an indecent burial as soon as Margaret Mead had published her early studies.[4] Unfortunately, outmoded ideas of woman's biology and social role still abound.

The power-transfer problem cannot be fully discussed here. A suggested solution points to cultural change and deserves brief comment. Ann Tolstoi Wallach believes that power transfer can be harnessed to a bed. Sex, in short, can become a fast elevator to high social status. While her views are expressed in terms of pleasure ("The ideal corporate affair is a combination of professional motivation and fun"), her focus is serious ("Try to stay away from married men—if not for moral considerations, then for practical ones"). Wallach's ideas, neither novel nor useful, have been given a public platform (*Harper's Bazaar*, October

---

[4]Margaret Mead, *Sex and Temperament in Three Primitive Societies.* New York: Morrow, 1963 (originally published 1935).

1981). This foxy-lady strategy twists an old peace slogan into a war cry: "Make love *as* war!"

The male-female conflict is muted and linguistically managed in the service of the sick. The general public and the doctor (generally a male in Western societies) believe that the doctor knows best. Empirically, the doctor often knows second-best, especially after the first few visits. At that time the nurse (generally a female) may know better. The nurse must communicate this knowledge to the doctor while seemingly supporting his omniscient image. The con game played by doctor and nurse—described in "The Doctor-Nurse Game" by Leonard I. Stein—is *almost* victimless. The doctor maintains an image which gives him power and esteem. The patient profits by the faith provided that the healing process is in (almost) supernatural hands. And the nurse gets a superior working relationship with the doctor. In keeping the system in a kind of balance the nurse is a partial victim; she sacrifices the recognition of her actual contribution to patient welfare.

REFERENCES

Friedan, Betty, *The Feminine Mystique*. New York: Dell, 1975.

Greer, Germaine, *The Female Eunuch*. London: Paladin Books, 1971.

Lawrence, D. H., *Sons and Lovers*. Baltimore: Penguin Books, 1971 (originally published 1913).

Reiter, Rayna, ed. *Toward an Anthropology of Women*. New York: Monthly Review Press, 1975.

Schlegel, Alice, ed. *Sexual Stratification: A Cross-Cultural View*. New York: Columbia University Press, 1977.

Structured Imbalances in Caribbean Mating

by
Morris Freilich and Lewis A. Coser

A DESCRIPTION AND analysis of the sex life of Negro peasants in a community of Eastern Trinidad will reveal how a social system that is based on complementarity between sexual partners nevertheless presents such asymmetry that its equilibrium is extremely precarious. Marx remains the most powerful analyst of asymmetrical relationships. He shows why, when resources or power positions are unequal, the resultant relationship between actors is likely to be unbalanced, unilateral rather than multilateral. Marx's analytical focus is on institutionalized exploitation, "the right to something for nothing," to use Veblen's telling phrase.[1]

Marx's insights have been further developed in two seminal papers by Alvin Gouldner which have not yet been given the attention they deserve.[2] Gouldner argues in particular that reciprocity is indeed a pervasive feature of social interaction in all social systems but that the norm of symmetrical reciprocity can be infringed upon when power relations between two parties are such that one of them is in a position to coerce the other. Such unequal exchanges based on unequal power may be said to be exploitative in that they are based on asymmetri-

Adapted from "Structured Imbalances of Gratification: The Case of the Caribbean Mating System," *British Journal of Sociology*, vol. 23, no. 1 (March 1972), pp. 1–19, by permission of the authors and Routledge and Kegan Paul Ltd.

[1] Cf. Lewis A Coser, *Continuities in the Study of Social Conflict* (New York: Free Press, 1968), pp. 147ff.

[2] Alvin Gouldner, "Reciprocity and Autonomy in Functional Theory," in Llewellyn Gross, ed., *Symposium on Sociological Theory* (Evanston, Ill.: Row and Peterson, 1959); and Alvin Gouldner, "The Norm of Reciprocity: A Preliminary Statement," *Amer. Sociol. Rev.*, vol. 25, no. 2 (April 1960), pp. 161–78.

cal dependence. "Power arrangements may serve to compel continuances of services for which there is little functional reciprocity."[3] Peter Blau puts the matter well: "A person upon whom others are dependent for vital benefits has the power to enforce his demands. A person who commands services others need, and who is independent of any at their command, attains power over others by making the satisfaction of their need contingent upon their compliance."[4]

The notion of exploitation is, of course, central to the Marxist critique of capitalist relations of production, but as Gouldner points out, it may also serve us well in other areas. In particular it has upon occasion been used in the sociological analysis of sexual relations as when males of higher status are said to use their position of superiority to take advantage of women of lower status, or, more generally, when one partner in a sexual relationship takes advantage of the attachment and dependence of the other in order to extract favours and advantages without adequate compensatory acts of his own.

A detailed analysis of sexual life in a small peasant community in Trinidad will show that complementarity of expectations between the sexes does not preclude a serious imbalance in the reward system for males and females.

LIFE IN ANAMAT, EASTERN TRINIDAD

Anamat is a dispersed settlement community, spread over six or so square miles of land at an elevation of approximately five thousand feet. For the Anamatians the relative isolation of their community—due to poor roads, a lack of direct public transportation to larger towns, and the derogatory label of "the bush country"—helps them to live "cool, cool" away from "uncivilized" town living. For the townsfolk only a savage or someone with a deranged mind would spend a lifetime in "the bush," doing without such basic comforts as electricity, gas, running water, indoor latrines and telephones.

The peasants of Anamat farm holdings ranging from ten to thirty acres of land, with cocoa as the major cash crop and coffee and citrus fruits as subsidiary cash crops. Most of the peasants have full title to all the land they work. The land not

[3]Gouldner, "Reciprocity," op. cit. p. 250.
[4]Peter Blau, *Exchange and Power in Social Life* (New York: Wiley, 1964), p. 22.

owned is rented to make kitchen gardens which provide a regular supply of food for the table. At the time of the study,[5] Anamat had a population of 651 men, women, and children made up of two major and conflicting groups: East Indians (whose ancestors had been brought to Trinidad from India, as indentured servants) and Negroes (whose ancestors had been brought to Trinidad as slaves).

Since this paper focuses on the sexual life of Negro peasants little more will be said about the Indians, and the hate which exists between Negro and Indian. In passing it should be noted, however, that sexual relations do occur between Negroes and Indians and the form it most frequently takes is between an Indian male and a Negro woman. These kinds of relationships are greatly frowned upon by almost all Anamatians, and almost invariably Negro-Indian love affairs are of short duration, and are kept far more secret than sexual affairs between two Negroes.

The sexual life of the Negro peasant must be understood within the context of his socio-economic standing and within the framework of his mating system. It is necessary therefore to comment briefly on these two areas of social living.

RANK, MATING, AND SEX

As Trinidadians, the Anamatian peasants consider themselves as the cream of Caribbean society. As Anamatians they discuss the superiority of their community over other places in Trinidad. And as peasants they constantly refer to their personal good fortune in not having to work for anyone, and being independent enough to work when, and if, they please. The concept of "independence" provides a major prestige-giving criteria in Anamat. Those who are economically independent of the whim of another man. Hence, the peasant farmers are seen, and see themselves as the upper-class members of their community: a status they share with the *school*

[5] The data collected are part of a larger anthropological field study conducted by Morris Freilich from July 1957 through July 1958. For further details, cf. Morris Freilich, "Serial Polygyny, Negro Peasants and Model Analysis," *Amer. Anthropologist*, vol. 63, no. 5 (Oct. 1961), pp. 958–75, and Morris Freilich, "Mohawk Heroes and Trinidadian Peasants," in M. Freilich, ed., *Marginal Natives at Work* (Cambridge, Mass.: Schenkman, 1977).

teachers and *government overseers* of local projects. Below
them, forming a kind of middle class, were the *semi-peasants*
(those who owned some land, but who had to work for others
part of the year) and the *shopkeepers*. And, on the bottom of
this three-class system were those who always worked for
others and were therefore completely non-independent: the
labourers on nearby estates and those who did *road-work* for
the government.

Other things being equal, the more independent the Anamatian
the more he could afford many love affairs, and the more he
actually had them. His freedom to pursue women, however, is
also a function of his marital status. Other things being equal,
men currently unmarried had more time and more opportunities for sexual involvement and this fact contributed to the
"divorce" rate: in local, operational terms, to the frequency
with which a given man left a given spouse. To some extent
therefore sex functions as a marriage breaker; but this whole
matter must be understood within its cultural context.

The terms used in Anamat to describe the sex act are:
"breed" and "brush." The term "breed" seems to designate
several phenomena: first, it refers to a situation where the male
has some sexual right over a woman; second, it points to his
ability to exercise such rights because of frequency of contact
under the same roof; and third, it emphasizes the offspring.
The term "breed" is most frequently used to refer to the
relationship of a given man and his spouse. It is, however, at
times extended to refer to an implied right of a man to sexual
intercourse with any female living in his house, with whom
such intercourse would not constitute incest.[6]

Prestige from a "breeding" situation is obtained, not by the
sexual act itself, since the man gets only that which is already
his, but at such times when children are born.

A "brush" is a sex act where the male has no right over a
given woman, and he must therefore approach her as a suppliant.
The term used for this kind of approach is "beg." A man
telling another of a recent conquest will frequently use the
following sentence: "I begged and begged for a brush . . . and
she couldn't refuse me." This kind of "stooping to conquer"

---

[6] Only two cases of incest were discovered. One was a single incident
between a brother and his full sister and the other was a long-term
relationship which led the girl to bear two children sired by her father. In
the latter case, the girl and her father, and indeed everyone living in that
household, were ostracized by the rest of the community.

180 SEX AND SEX ROLES

carries prestige. A man who has many love affairs becomes known as a "hot boy," a prestigeful status denoting a *real man*.[7]

Entering a "breeding" situation, which usually means taking a wife, is part of the following sequence. First, a lot of "begging" is done while still under the parental roof. On leaving school, whether a job is obtained within the village or outside the village, a man rarely stays very long in his parents' house if the father is still alive. The young adult male leaves home and gets an apartment for himself. At this time he is in a position to take a spouse. He has a place to put the spouse, and he is earning money. The forces that usually spur a man to take a wife are several: (1) he needs someone to cook, clean the house, wash his clothes; (2) his "begging" may have produced a child; (3) entering a "breeding" situation does not put him out of the "begging" market, so why not get the best of both worlds?

In local terminology, when a man takes a spouse he "gets married," and local terminology, while not always consistent with the language used by Trinidadian church officials, is congruent with Murdock's views of marriage: "Marriage is a complex of customs centering upon the relationship between a sexually associating pair of adults . . . [it] defines the manner of establishing and terminating such a relationship, the normative behaviour and recipient obligations within it and the locally accepted restrictions upon its personnel."[8]

A marriage is established in Anamat by a man bringing a woman into a house and living with her. The woman then has the status of wife. In some cases a religious service precedes the woman's entrance into the status of wife. Irrespective of the presence or the absence of the religious sanction, a woman who goes to live with (say) Mr. Jones, is referred to directly and indirectly as "Ma Jones," that is, the wife of Jones. A marriage is terminated by one of the parties leaving the household. No third party is brought into such a "divorce," whether or not the marriage was religiously sanctioned. For Anamat (and we suspect for many of the Negro villages in the Caribbean) generally, there is little purpose in differentiating between legal marriage, common-law marriage, etc. In terms

[7]"Hot boy" is a term used to define a *real man*, in contrast to a "sissie boy," who has no or very few sexual relations with women.
[8]George Peter Murdock, *Social Structure* (New York: Macmillan, 1949), p. 1.

of most problems which are meaningful to Trinidadian peasants, these terms are all structurally and functionally the same.

In Anamat, according to many informants, marriage is a highly formalized procedure. A man is supposed to write "a demand" for a girl, stating that he wished to frequent the house with intentions to marry at a future specified date. Actually this rarely happens. Young adults usually meet informally and a female decides that she will go and live with a male. Three factors are usually involved here: (1) The male must have a place to put the female, ideally this should be his own house; (2) he must be able to support her; and (3) her consent is necessary. In the final analysis, there is freedom of movement based on individual choice.

Once set up in a household, the couple is recognized as man and wife. "Mr. Brown" has the usual obligations of economic support, while his wife, "Ma Brown," is expected by the community to provide the husband with meals, sexual services, and a clean house.

A given marriage is expected to last only as long as a couple can "cooperate together." Each party to the union is understood to be quite capable of judging when and if cooperation exists. At the break-up of a union the wife usually leaves the house in which she has been living (unless she owned the house) and goes with her children, either to her mother's house or to the house of a new husband. In some rare occasions, she may rent a room somewhere in the village. The male may live alone for a while in his house or may have another woman ready to move in with him.

A given household is thus a temporary dwelling for a woman and her children, paralleled by the fact that a given marriage is a temporary union for a given couple. Although many of the peasants will probably change their spouses again at least once before they die, and one young peasant had not yet taken a wife, the average Anamatian peasant has lived with three spouses; and 45 per cent of the group have lived with three or more spouses (see Table I).

Even when a peasant has lived with a given spouse for many years, he still does not consider this a union for life. Marriage according to the Anamatian Negroes is a "now-for-now affair"; and any given union is therefore considered a temporary one.

When a man has frequent sexual relations with a woman who is not his wife he is said to be "in a love affair." Most of the Creole adults of Anamat are involved in such "love affairs,"

TABLE I. Number of Spouses of Peasant Household Heads in Anamat

Number of heads of households	Number of spouses lived with
1	0
6	1
10	2
6	3
4	4
1	5
1	6
2	9

and we would but present a few ethnographic examples: (1) On most evenings Mr. Barg[9] brings his bull to graze near Mr. Fisher's house. While the animal is grazing outside, Mr. Barg is inside Mr. Fisher's house with Mrs. Fisher. (2) Mr. Fisher is very frequently away from home evenings; he is a great friend of the Smith family, and spends most of his evenings at the Smith house. (3) Mr. Smith is often out at night on some kind of "business" that no one knows about. (4) While Mr. Little is out seeing a girl friend (who his wife openly discusses as such) Mr. Paul's bicycle is usually parked outside the Littles' house. (5) Mr. Jones frequently spends the night away from home. At such times, Mr. Jack generally keeps Mrs. Jones company. (6) Mr. Fred, one of the more wealthy peasant farmers of Anamat, may be found most evenings at the house of Mrs. Bryan, an attractive middle-aged widow.

A pattern may be charted from these examples: A given male leaves his house on an evening to have a little fête, either with some of the boys or with a girl friend. His wife, now alone, can be visited by one of her admirers. This second male, by leaving his own house, provides a place for a third man and so forth.

Additional evidence which shows that outside love affairs are common with Anamat Creoles is indicated by the following: A statement commonly made by the Creoles of Anamat is that where a man is alone for five minutes with a woman who is

---

[9]For obvious reasons these names are fictitious but they refer to real people and to real events.

not his spouse, they are talking about sex. It is reasonable to assume that repeated nightly meetings, alone, for several hours involve love making. For, from the standpoint of a Creole male: "It is glory for a man to fool a woman [dupe a woman into having sexual intercourse with him]. If you can't fool a woman, you are not a famous man." And "Married men and bachelors both have the same sight and the same lust, so both must have many women. Some women want to limit the man to one woman; but you don't limit the bull . . . the priest say, 'Stay with one woman, you know canon law.' I say, 'I am no lawyer, but I know that is not common sense!' "

Further, in a number of cases, husbands have beaten their wives while accusing them of unfaithfulness. Several women spoke freely to the interviewer about their husband's outside sexual activity; and what seemed to annoy them most was the fact that money was spent on these other women. Informants were generally agreed as to the existence of specific love affairs, and no contradictory data were given about any one love affair.

The following quotes from female informants will indicate the sexual situation as considered from their viewpoint:

> Girls run around with married men on the promise that the man will divorce his wife. . . . A woman who is not shy will know how to do things so she can fool people good, and go with other men. And those who are shy . . . others will know when they speak to a man what is going on.

It is very likely that the husbands, too, know what is "going on," but will only make a row when they feel their reputations are suffering. Actually it is convenient for them that their wives are "occupied" on the evenings they have made plans to be with another woman. In this way, the wife does not ask too many questions, nor does she insist too strongly that the husband stay at home.

In return for sexual favors received from the paramour, a man is supposed to provide goods and services. A richer peasant can thus afford to have more outside women than a poorer peasant. Many peasants frequently made envious and sarcastic remarks about the many outside affairs of one of the oldest and richest peasants in the community. The economic aspect of outside affairs is further indicated by the following. One Creole peasant showed little sympathy when a shapely Anamatian woman complained about her economic situation. After staring at her body for several minutes the peasant finally said: "You have lots of ways to make money, but you don't make enough use of what you have."

That similar "outside affairs" occur in other Creole communities in the Caribbean area is evident from R. T. Smith's writings. For example: "Within the household these [sexual services] are provided only between spouses in non-incestuous unions, but they may be provided across the boundaries of household groups between persons who will be referred to as 'lovers.' "[10]

From a male viewpoint sexual involvements are for fun and fame. Unlike what appears to be the case in "Puritan ethic" countries, in Trinidad love affairs carry no attachment of guilt, which automatically gets transferred to the "players." Hence sexual involvements are here simple, and purely pleasurable. In addition broadcasts of conquests carry "fame" for the virile and eloquent male. Understandably, the sex game in Trinidad, like the money game in America, keeps the players constantly and passionately interested. Men whose sexual needs are almost insatiable are referred to as "hot boys," "sweet men," and "wild men."

The critical factors which appear to account for who plays in the sex-fame game and why some play more often than others are (1) beliefs of males; (2) beliefs of females; and (3) a set of operational rules—rules which help actors predict the probable outcome of given actions. Men believe that all women—single or married—may be begged for sex, and that all men may play the role of sexual beggar.

Two general exceptions exist to these beliefs: first a given male believes that his sister—if single—is not approachable for sex, and—if married—is only approachable by her husband. Second, a given male believes that his wife is approachable by none but himself for sexual favours. In sum, men believe that they and the husbands of their sisters have monopolistic sexual privilege with their wives, but other men have only preferential sexual privileges. Other husbands thus only have first call (so to speak) for their wives' sexual services; they themselves have the only call.

Women's beliefs in the area of sexual relations are strongly associated with a more fundamental female belief; that men and woman are social equals and that therefore social rules apply equally to males and females. Since their husbands never give up

---

[10]Raymond T. Smith, *The Negro Family in British Guiana* (London: Routledge and Kegan Paul, 1956), p. 67.

the sex-fame game after marriage, and since other men continue to approach them for sex, sooner or later most women come to believe that outside sex is permissible, as long as such affairs are kept secret. These beliefs, almost invariably, are of the "general" kind, translatable here as "it's all right if *other* husbands have lovers as long as they keep things secret." However, most wives of Negro peasants are annoyed by the sexual exploits of their husbands. Thus a goal of Anamatian females—rarely attained—is to have a husband who does not "run all about." However, the emotional reaction of women to the sexual exploits of their husbands is not uniform; some women get more upset than others, and some express their annoyance more violently than others. Some of the women, temperamentally, are more jealous than others, and very jealous wives will at times make embarrassing scenes and do their utmost to break up an outside affair. Generally, the wives of the community, even the jealous ones, find such confrontations extremely distasteful. A crisis in family relations is always created when the lover initiates a confrontation with the wife and publicly proclaims that she is "the outside woman." Such a broadcast usually includes verbal attacks on the wife's ability to fulfill her sexual role. The reactions of the wife to the taunts of the lover are always extreme. The wife always becomes very angry and frequently either threatens the lover with bodily harm or attacks her then and there.

Wives who "do not jealous their husbands" pride themselves on the control they maintain over their feelings, and describe their reactions as "cool, cool."

No matter how little a woman "jealouses her husband" and how "cool, cool" she is, the money spent on outside women is frequently a major source of conflict between husbands and wives. What many wives find particularly annoying is the fact that they help their husbands economically by "working in the cocoa," and then income that they helped create is spent on other women. Other things being equal, the amount of concern a woman shows appears to be inversely related to her age: the older the wife the less the emotional reaction to her husband's exploits.

Women translate their beliefs and sexual experiences into a set of operational rules which guides their behaviour in the sex-fame game. These operational rules for sexual involvements—information which the women of Anamat share with each other—include data as to (1) how well given men keep their conquests secret; (2) the spending abilities (economic standing) and the spending habits (economic "personality") of various "hot boys";

(3) the marital position of the males (legally married, common-law married, "promised" or engaged, free and loose); and (4) men's reputation as lovers. The richer the male, other things being equal, the more economically rewarding the love affair will be. The man who is legally married must work harder to be believed, when he promises his lover that he intends to marry her. Legally married wives are harder to dispose of than common law wives.[11]

Some men have reputations for great power and artistic ability in bed, and such great lovers have far less trouble getting into sexual involvements than old Mister F. The latter, although rich and "always good to his friends," will on rare occasions be denied. It is well known that Mr. F., a hard worker with honorable intentions, often "just can't get it up."

Irrespective of the reputation given males have for keeping secrets, men regularly—and quite often eloquently—broadcast their sexual escapades. They obviously have to, since their fame depends on (1) their sex activities, (2) their abilities to distribute personal sex information, and (3) their abilities to make such information appear credible.

The men, just like the women, have a set of operational rules which guides their behavior in the sex-fame game. Men know that the probability of successful "begging" is higher (1) with women who are currently husbandless than with women currently living with a man; (2) with lower-class women than with the wives of peasants, (3) with women whose husbands stray frequently than with those whose husbands are relatively faithful, (4) with women who need the goods and services they receive in exchange for sexual favours, than with women for whom such goods and services are but extra luxury items. The men also know that some of the peasants' wives firmly believe that marriage puts an end to past affairs and to any possible future ones. Women with such beliefs will rarely be approached for sexual favours. How much begging a woman receives is also a function of her attractiveness. Younger women, generally, are considered

[11]In actual fact legally married wives are not harder to "dispose of." The wife who is *legal*, who is a "mistress" of the house, is left as quickly and as easily as the common-law wife. However, the female lover *believes* that husbands are more strongly tied to legal wives. The enigma is solved, we believe, as follows: "divorce," operationally speaking, meant physical leaving, for the Anamatians. Such *physical leaving* never included court proceedings in the past in this village; but it could. The fear of possible legal repercussions seems to lie at the base of female beliefs here.

more attractive than older women; and virginity is considered a most attractive feature. As one Negro peasant put it, mimicking British understatement, "Some men have preference for a virgin, but to achieve that is hard."

The men spend considerable time and energy discussing their own sexual exploits and such conversations always include statements concerning "fooling." A "great man" is able to fool any woman into believing all of his promises. In begging for sex there is nothing which is considered wrong, as long as physical force is not used. A woman is supposed to succumb to a man's attractiveness and eloquence, not his brute force. And the eloquent beggar is given great verbal latitude. One peasant boasting of his own superior abilities as a woman-fooler said:

> Some of the fellows here don't know how to fool a woman. They don't know how to speak to a woman properly; they can't tell her, "I love you." After I get a woman alone for a while and talk to her, I begin to beg for a brush. I beg and beg and she can't refuse me.

The information of a given broadcaster is generally evaluated rather critically. Both his message and the analysis of it then get communicated through informal community channels. Since the siring of an outside child is proof positive of a conquest, a strategy used by some men to achieve greater fame is to claim paternity over children whose parentage is in doubt. Anamatians generally achieve a consensus as to who sired a given child; and males other than the agreed-on father, who continue to claim paternity, are referred to as "trying to give themselves fame." A more subtle strategy used by a few is to deny paternity in situations where there is general agreement that the child is theirs. The latter situation generates much talk involving the "denying father" who thereby increases his "fame." Thus, and to put it conservatively, for males there is little reason to worry about contraceptive measures. In the words of one informant:

> If I had an outside child I would try to keep it. I would offer it first to my mother and then to my sister. My mother would not be vexed [in this kind of situation]. The son becomes a hero, like a fellow goes to war and returns with medals. The women can't push this boy around; he pushes them around.

An outside child, while a sign of fame for a man, is a source of trouble for the woman. As one woman said: "For a girl to bring an outside child home is to disgrace the family. They will take you in, but you will see much trouble." For the married woman, any extra child is more work and more restrictions on her freedom of movement. As one woman put it: "The children hold the Creole women back so they don't want many; with many they can't go to dances as they like, nor to wakes. Nor can they get about the way they like to."

Attempts to guard against pregnancy are common; and generally they require the woman to do something. The contraceptive devices used most frequently include: gynomin tablets, "withdrawal," Epsom salts placed inside the vagina prior to intercourse, drinking quicksilver and rum, and eating young pineapples. Since most of the adult males have sired some outside children—uncertainty existed on exactly how many a given male had sired—clearly these contraceptive devices are frequently ineffective.

THE SYSTEM

The data presented can be described as a system by (1) isolating the critical elements involved, and (2) showing how these elements have functional interconnections. This can be done as in Table II.

The system, *qua* system, has tendencies making both for states of equilibrium and states of disequilibrium. The former can be described as follows:

Sexual encounters have a dualistic quality for women; sexual experiences, while intrinsically pleasurable, have a possible unfortunate consequence: pregnancy. For men, sexual encounters are intrinsically enjoyable and are avenues to social applause. Since men and women are equals in a sexual encounter, its rewards are equalized by defining women as giving and men taking sex. The "takers" must beg and reciprocate for favors received. By keeping their sex "expenses" low, men have "funds" for many affairs and they receive extra fame for their fooling power. Such fooling tends to cut short given affairs. Short duration affairs with one woman are congruent with men's desires for variety in sexual experiences and for fame—partly a function of the number of women with whom involvements exist.

The richer the peasant the more he can afford sexual affairs, the more his promises are believed and the more affairs he

Table II. The Sex-Fame Game

I.	Players	Men	Women
II.	Beliefs	1. Sex is good	Sex is good
		2. Real men want sex often, with many women	"Hot boys" are exciting
		3. Women give sex	Women give sex
		4. Men give valued objects for sex	Men must pay for sex
		5. Clever men "pay" far less than they promise	Beware of men who are good at fooling
		6. Sexual affairs must be broadcast discreetly	Sexual affairs are secret
		7. The successful beggar is a "famous man"	The "cool cool" wife is a wise woman
III.	Goals	8. To be famous as a "hot boy"	To have their love affairs kept secret
		9. To get prestige as a great fooler	To have promises kept
		10. To avoid confrontation with irate husbands	To avoid confrontation with "outside" women
		11. To have wives who do not have lovers	To have a husband who rarely takes an outside woman
IV.	Strategies	12. To broadcast real and fictional involvements eloquently and convincingly.	To act as if their home life is perfect
		13. To exaggerate promises to minimize sexual "payments"	To take lovers with reputations of honesty
		14. To keep watch on the behavior of the wife	Not to marry "hot boys"
		15. To get women pregnant; to claim fatherhood of children of doubtful parentage and to deny fatherhood in cases where everyone knows the "denier" is really the father	To avoid pregnancy in a love affair; and to deny fatherhood claims of outside men
V.	Sentiments associated with sexual affairs	16. Excitement, freedom and pleasure	Excitement, freedom and pleasure

actually has. The poorer his lover the more often she will accept lovers. The sex-fame game is thus a mechanism for the distribution of surplus goods within the community. Marriage is considered by the peasant as a "now-for-now" affair; and the sex-fame game helps to lead a peasant from wife to wife—that is, facilitates serial polygamy—by providing him with relationships with many women, each of which can be evaluated as a possible future wife. The disruptive elements of the sex-fame game on marital relations weakens the nuclear family and (consequently) strengthens the matrifocal family: a membership unit peasants consider of prime importance in their lives. The children produced by outside affairs create pseudo-kin ties between males, females, and their offspring. Community bonds are enhanced by these pseudo-kin links which also act as mechanisms for the distribution of surplus goods.

Viewed as a system in a general state of equilibrium, the sex-fame game has a major flaw; male and female players have diametrically opposite goals. Indeed our label for this game, though well fitting the man's viewpoint, does little justice to that of the woman's. The secret-sex game is a more appropriate title for her views of these encounters. Since it is the male's goals which are generally met (see Table III), the sex-fame game remains an appropriate label for this system. Most community members know the "secret" sex life of most community members: women's attempts to avoid pregnancy are not always successful; promises made are rarely kept in their entirety; conjugal relations are rarely lasting and husbands have many, not few, outside women.

TABLE III. Contrasting Male and Female Goals

Sex-fame (male)	Secret-sex (female)
1. Maximal movement of sexual information (loud broadcasts)	1. Minimal movement of sexual information (secrecy)
2. To get lovers pregnant for greater fame	2. To avoid pregnancy to maintain secrecy
3. To keep few promises, for the broadcast of "fooling-power"	3. To have promises kept to maintain "social equality"
4. To have many outside women for greater fame	4. To have a husband who does not spend money on *any* outside women

Given the system's apparent preference for male goals, what options are available to the women? The women can elect to avoid the sex-fame game; or, they can play cautiously—selecting partners who are comparatively honorable; or, they can play "normally" and create crises when partners do them wrong. Avoidance means giving up the positive consequences of active involvement—companionship, pleasure, goods and services, and presentation-of-self as an equal of the males. Playing cautiously helps little, for in order to achieve their goal of fame men must fool and they must broadcast their conquests. Playing and creating crises is the only realistic option left; it is the option generally taken, and is not totally satisfying.

The angry, tearful, and upset wife loses community prestige and sees her husband rarely. The wife who accosts her husband's lover loses even more prestige and creates considerable problems for herself (see below). The lover, who, because of broken promises, acts like an angry wife, quickly loses her lover. Should she accost his wife, the lover gets to be known as "a shameless woman" from whom married men stay away. Men are blamed as much as their "shameless" lovers when a wife is accosted by their "sweethearts." As one wife put it: "Every man has a girl friend and that is all right if kept secret. But many men allow the girl to give the wife words: that is unmoral. These things make the woman at home feel bad."

The socio-cultural system described is not adequately presented as being in a state of equilibrium. From a systems viewpoint, two factions exist with many contradictory goals. From the viewpoint of individuals in interaction, this is a *man against woman situation*: fame versus secrecy, fooling against promise-keeping.

Yet, the system contains mechanisms which allow it to minimize undue threats to its stability. Among these, perhaps the most important, is secrecy concerning the operation of the sex-fame game. Secrecy serves to allow the operation of the game while partially neutralizing its potentially destructive impact.

SECRECY AND ITS FUNCTIONS

Why should a woman approaching the wife of her lover be considered shameless? Why are they "unmoral" if they don't do this? If it is "all right that every man has a girl friend," why should it be kept secret? And, since such "secrets" are well known in the community, why does "the woman at home" feel bad when confronted by the husband's lover?

The women of Anamat know that all men have outside women most of the time. However, frequently they do not have positive proof of the existence of a specific love affair, at a specific point in time, involving their husband. The wise, "cool, cool" wife, generally, is well aware when "something is going on" but she acts *as if* it is not. Such behavior is most functional both for the wife and for the system. The wife gets approval from the community when she acts maturely. In exchange for her mature actions the community pays in its most cherished currency: prestige. Moreover, she gets the benefits of a "self-fulfilling prophecy." By acting as if the husband had no outside woman, her conjugal relationship can and does improve; and the husband may (if only temporarily) put off outside affairs. At very worst, the "cool, cool" wife sees more of her husband and has a better relationship with him than do angry and upset wives. The wife who acts as if all was well at home gets more than approval in the form of prestige or esteem from the community for such behavior: she gets practical support. People will not talk openly about her husband's affairs. These escapades become, so to speak, classified material, which can only be transmitted to close friends as "secrets." The wife keeps her own suspicions and information secret and other community members do the same, helping her maintain the fiction that all is well in her house, thus to save face. By each Anamatian providing this service to all wives, the women of the community do not lose face by their husbands' activities; and the men can continue their sexual life with but minimal troubles from their wives. In brief, on the personal level the "secret" sex life of Anamatians helps everyone live better in the community, with minimal loss of face and embarrassment.

On the system level of analysis, the treatment of sexual matters as classified data provides a compromise solution to the conflict which lies at the heart of this system. The males' sex-fame game requires *maximal communication of sexual encounters:* the females' secret-sex game requires *maximal secrecy for sexual encounters*. A compromise solution is to move sexual-encounter information *quietly* (as to speak) through underground channels. Those who are able to tap these channels—sooner or later most of the community—must act publicly as if they really do not know: as if such channels and their information do not exist.

A woman approaching the wife of her lover makes the wife feel bad by providing positive proof of her husband's outside sex life. The wife's immediate reaction of anger, and, at times, physical violence, is a function of being made to look an unhappy truth in the face. The encounter has yet more serious consequences: the wife can no longer publicly present herself as an adequate role-player. Outside women when confronting a wife usually make sure that an audience is present. The wife-lover encounter thus includes a public broadcast of classified information. Such a broadcast temporarily breaks the convention of "secrecy" for this particular affair. The wife (at least temporarily) is put "on stage" as an *inadequate wife*.

Since every Anamatian peasant has outside women, every wife in the community is vulnerable to similar "on-stage" placement: every wife can be labeled "inadequate wife." Since such labeling temporarily breaks the convention of secrecy, it is always possible that the sexual life of all the community can be transferred out of the "classified file."

If the sexual life of system members were made public, the compromise solution (the fiction of secrecy) would be shattered and the contradictory goals of the two major factions would stand out brilliantly in stark opposition. The system attempts to "protect itself" from structural change by providing supports for its compromise solution. Actors who break the fiction of secrecy are defined as "shameless" and "unmoral"; those who support it are called "good," "responsible" and "cool, cool."

The system's "efforts" at maintaining a state of equilibrium frequently fall short of desired goals. Actors find it difficult to live in terms of the compromise solution. As the tensions of individuals increase, acts eroding the fiction of secrecy pile up: broadcasts to get fame are made too openly; sexual information is distributed too publicly; wives chastise lovers and lovers confront wives. At those times actors accept the negative sanctions of the system, for the personal rewards they receive. Open broadcasts of sexual conquests—although considered bad form by some of the listeners—have valuable feed-back effect: weakening egos are invigorated. Confrontations with wives or lovers function as problem-airing and problem-sharing devices. Tensions are temporarily reduced by a direct confrontation with an assumed cause of one's problems—a husband's lover, a wife. Sufferings are lessened by distributing them into the realm of men's lives—by quarrels with husbands or with lovers.

Secrecy helps contain the potential conflict between males and females, thus preventing disruptive consequences for the community. Secrecy helps to keep expression of hostilities within bounds. It is system-maintaining not only in the sense that social life can run more smoothly than if secrecy would not obtain, but in the sense that it helps maintain the respective power positions of the actors.

Yet, while serving as a lightning rod, so to speak, it cannot prevent a recurrent gathering of the clouds, it cannot prevent repeated accumulation of tensions.[12] The basic structural asymmetries between men and women cannot be hidden, nor can they be compensated for through secrecy.

One could argue that continued secrecy between people who engage in frequent and intensive interaction, such as wives, husbands, and lovers in a small community where everybody knows everyone, is in itself tension-producing. It requires much energy on everybody's part to keep the game going. While each one of the partners knows that he is engaged in a game of "make-believe," they all have to cooperate in spite of the fact that all of them have antagonistic interests in regard to each other.

Hence, it is at the expense of much tension that secrecy keeps the system going. Moreover, secrecy does not alter the fact that the system as a whole primarily benefits the men. We have here an almost classical case of exploitation, of asymmetrical types of relations, where benefits received by no means equal benefits conferred. Given the superior power positions of males, they manage to utilize their resources so as to shore up their positions *vis-à-vis* the women. The system does not bestow equal rewards to both sides in the sexual equation; the game is rigged in favor of the males.

The sex-fame game is positively functional for the male members of the community since it allows them the maximum of sexual gratification with a minimum of responsibility. Moreover, it allows them to attain secure bases for invidious status appraisal in a society where other means of attaining such status are unavailable. Matters are fundamentally different for females. From their point of view, dysfunctional elements seem to loom at least as large as functional ones. They gain some advantages, to be sure, especially if the game is played within the bounds of secrecy. Non-cooperation would yield even fewer rewards than the sparse ones they can attain now.

Yet the women are basically but the objects, or counters, in a game in which the males are the sole autonomous players. It would be an exaggeration to say that the males receive some-

---

[12]Cf. Lewis A. Coser, *The Functions of Social Conflict* (New York: Free Press, 1956), p. 35ff.

thing for nothing in this game, but they get much in return for comparatively little. The terms of exchange are unequal, so that what prevails is exploitation rather than reciprocity.

In view of their minimal rewards, women will gladly turn to alternatives if such should present themselves. They will have much to gain from modernization which would offer them some means for reducing their dependency on their sexual partners. When forces of industrialization or urbanization begin seriously to impinge on the system, the male-female relationship will emerge as one of the weakest links in the structure. Here, as elsewhere, exploitative relationships will be resisted, and strains toward complete reciprocity will emerge in full force once traditional impediments to equalization have begun to crumble.[13]

---

[13]The implied question here, "How will these anticipated changes enter the system?" can be briefly answered with: "Through the institutionalization of new *operational rules*." Cf. Morris Freilich, *The Meaning of Culture* (Cambridge, Mass: Schenkman, 1982) p. 290ff.

Society and Sex Roles

by
Ernestine Friedl

"WOMEN MUST RESPOND quickly to the demands of their husbands,"
says anthropologist Napoleon Chagnon describing the horticultural Yanomamo Indians of Venezuela. When a man returns
from a hunting trip, "the woman, no matter what she is doing,
hurries home and quietly but rapidly prepares a meal for her
husband. Should the wife be slow in doing this, the husband is
within his rights to beat her. Most reprimands . . . take the form
of blows with the hand or with a piece of firewood. . . . Some of
them chop their wives with the sharp edge of a machete or axe,
or shoot them with a barbed arrow in some nonvital area, such as
the buttocks or leg."

Among the Semai agriculturalists of central Malaya, when one
person refuses the request of another, the offended party suffers
punan, a mixture of emotional pain and frustration. "Enduring
punan is commonest when a girl has refused the victim her
sexual favors," reports Robert Dentan. "The jilted man's 'heart
becomes sad.' He loses his energy and his appetite. Much of the
time he sleeps, dreaming of his lost love. In this state, he is in
fact very likely to injure himself 'accidentally.' " The Semai are
afraid of violence; a man would never strike a woman.

The social relationship between men and women has emerged
as one of the principal disputes occupying the attention of scholars and the public in recent years. Although the discord is
sharpest in the United States, the controversy has spread throughout the world. Numerous national and international conferences,
including one in Mexico sponsored by the United Nations, have
drawn together delegates from all walks of life to discuss such
questions as the social and political rights of each sex, and even
the basic nature of males and females.

Reprinted from *Human Nature*, April 1978 by permission of *Human
Nature*.

Whatever their position, partisans often invoke examples from other cultures to support their ideas about the proper role of each sex. Because women are clearly subservient to men in many societies, like the Yanomamo, some experts conclude that the natural pattern is for men to dominate. But among the Semai no one has the right to command others, and in West Africa women are often chiefs. The place of women in these societies supports the argument of those who believe that sex roles are not fixed, that if there is a natural order, it allows for many different arrangements.

The argument will never be settled as long as the opposing sides toss examples from the world's cultures at each other like intellectual stones. But the effect of biological differences on male and female behavior can be clarified by looking at known examples of the earliest forms of human society and examining the relationship between technology, social organization, environment, and sex roles. The problem is to determine the conditions in which different degrees of male dominance are found, to try to discover the social and cultural arrangements that give rise to equality or inequality between the sexes, and to attempt to apply this knowledge to our understanding of the changes taking place in modern industrial society.

As Western history and the anthropological record have told us, equality between the sexes is rare; in most known societies females are subordinate. Male dominance is so widespread that it is virtually a human universal; societies in which women are consistently dominant do not exist and have never existed.

Evidence of a society in which women control all strategic resources like food and water, and in which women's activities are the most prestigious, has never been found. The Iroquois of North America and the Lovedu of Africa came closest. Among the Iroquois, women raised food, controlled its distribution, and helped to choose male political leaders. Lovedu women ruled as queens, exchanged valuable cattle, led ceremonies, and controlled their own sex lives. But among both the Iroquois and the Lovedu, men owned the land and held other positions of power and prestige. Women were equal to men; they did not have ultimate authority over them. Neither culture was a true matriarchy.

Patriarchies are prevalent, and they appear to be strongest in societies in which men control significant goods that are exchanged with people outside the family. Regardless of who produces food, the person who gives it to others creates the obligations and alliances that are at the center of all political relations. The greater the male monopoly on the distribution of scarce items, the stronger their control of women seems to be. This is most obvious in relatively simple hunter-gatherer societies.

Hunter-gatherers, or foragers, subsist on wild plants, small land animals, and small river or sea creatures gathered by hand; large land animals and sea mammals hunted with spears, bows and arrows, and blow guns; and fish caught with hooks and nets. The 300,000 hunter-gatherers alive in the world today include the Eskimos, the Australian aborigines, and the Pygmies of Central Africa.

Foraging has endured for two million years and was replaced by farming and animal husbandry only ten thousand years ago; it covers more than 99 percent of human history. Our foraging ancestry is not far behind us and provides a clue to our understanding of the human condition.

Hunter-gatherers are people whose ways of life are technologically simple and socially and politically egalitarian. They live in small groups of fifty to two hundred and have neither kings, nor priests, nor social classes. These conditions permit anthropologists to observe the essential bases for inequalities between the sexes without the distortions induced by the complexities of contemporary industrial society.

The source of male power among hunter-gatherers lies in their control of a scarce, hard to acquire, but necessary nutrient—animal protein. When men in a hunter-gatherer society return to camp with game, they divide the meat in some customary way. Among the Kung San of Africa, certain parts of the animal are given to the owner of the arrow that killed the beast, to the first hunter to sight the game, to the one who threw the first spear and to all men in the hunting party. After the meat has been divided, each hunter distributes his share to his blood relatives and his in-laws, who in turn share it with others. If an animal is large enough, every member of the band will receive some meat.

Vegetable foods, in contrast, are not distributed beyond the immediate household. Women give food to their children, to their husbands, to other members of the household, and rarely, to the occasional visitor. No one outside the family regularly eats any of the wild fruits and vegetables that are gathered by the women.

The meat distributed by the men is a public gift. Its source is widely known, and the donor expects a reciprocal gift when other men return from a successful hunt. He gains honor as a supplier of a scarce item and simultaneously obligates others to him.

These obligations constitute a form of power or control over others, both men and women. The opinions of hunters play an important part in decisions to move the village; good hunters attract the most desirable women; people in other groups join camps with good hunters; and hunters, because they already participate in an internal system of exchange, control exchange with other groups for flint, salt, and steel axes. The male monopoly on hunting unites men in a system of exchange and gives them power; gathering vegetable food does not give women equal power even among foragers who live in the tropics, where the food collected by women provides more than half the hunter-gatherer diet.

If dominance arises from a monopoly on big-game hunting, why has the male monopoly remained unchallenged? Some women are strong enough to participate in the hunt and their endurance is certainly equal to that of men. Dobe San women of the Kalahari Desert in Africa walk an average of ten miles a day carrying from fifteen to thirty-three pounds of food plus a baby.

Women do not hunt, I believe, because of four interrelated factors: variability in the supply of game; the different skills required for hunting and gathering; the incompatibility between carrying burdens and hunting; and the small size of seminomadic foraging populations.

Because the meat supply is unstable, foragers must make frequent expeditions to provide the band with gathered food. Environmental factors such as seasonal and annual variation in rainfall often affect the size of the wildlife population. Hunters cannot always find game, and when they do encounter animals, they are not always successful in killing their prey. In northern latitudes, where meat is the primary food, periods of starvation are known in every generation. The irregularity of the game supply leads hunter-gatherers in areas where plant foods are available to depend on these predictable foods a good part of the time. Someone must gather the fruits, nuts, and roots and carry them back to camp to feed unsuccessful hunters, children, the elderly, and anyone who might not have gone foraging that day.

Foraging falls to the women because hunting and gathering cannot be combined on the same expedition. Although gatherers sometimes notice signs of game as they work, the skills required to track game are not the same as those required to find edible roots or plants. Hunters scan the horizon and the land for traces of large game; gatherers keep their eyes to the ground, studying the distribution of plants and the texture of the soil for hidden roots and animal holes. Even if a woman who was collecting plants came across the track of an antelope, she could not follow it; it is impossible to carry a load and hunt at the same time.

Running with a heavy load is difficult, and should the animal be sighted, the hunter would be off balance and could neither shoot an arrow nor throw a spear accurately.

Pregnancy and child care would also present difficulties for a hunter. An unborn child affects a woman's body balance, as does a child in her arms, on her back, or slung at her side. Until they are two years old, many hunter-gatherer children are carried at all times, and until they are four, they are carried some of the time.

An observer might wonder why young women do not hunt until they become pregnant, or why mature women and men do not hunt and gather on alternate days, with some women staying in camp to act as wet nurses for the young. Apart from the effects hunting might have on a mother's milk production, there are two reasons. First, young girls begin to bear children as soon as they are physically mature and strong enough to hunt, and second, hunter-gatherer bands are so small that there are unlikely to be enough lactating women to serve as wet nurses. No hunter-gatherer group could afford to maintain a specialized female hunting force.

Because game is not always available, because hunting and gathering are specialized skills, because women carrying heavy loads cannot hunt, and because women in hunter-gatherer societies are usually either pregnant or caring for young children, for most of the last two million years of human history men have hunted and women have gathered.

If male dominance depends on controlling the supply of meat, then the degree of male dominance in a society should vary with the amount of meat available and the amount supplied by the men. Some regions, like the East African grasslands and the North American woodlands, abounded with species of large mammals; other zones, like tropical forests and semi-deserts, are thinly populated with prey. Many elements affected the supply of game, but theoretically, the less meat provided exclusively by the men, the more egalitarian the society.

All known hunter-gatherer societies fit into four basic types; those in which men and women work together in communal hunts and as teams gathering edible plants, as did the Washo Indians of North America; those in which men and women each collect their own plant foods although the men supply some meat to the group, as do the Hadza of Tanzania; those in which male hunters and female gatherers work apart but return to camp each evening to share their acquisitions, as do the Tiwi of North Australia; and those in which the men provide all the food by hunting large game, as do the Eskimo. In each case the extent of male dominance increases directly with the proportion of meat supplied by individual men and small hunting parties.

Among the most egalitarian of hunter-gatherer societies are the Washo Indians, who inhabited the valleys of the Sierra Nevada in what is now southern California and Nevada. In the spring they moved north to Lake Tahoe for the large fish runs of sucker and native trout. Everyone—men, women, and children—participated in the fishing. Women spent the summer gathering edible berries and seeds while the men continued to fish. In the fall some men hunted deer but the most important source of animal protein was the jack rabbit, which was captured in communal hunts. Men and women together drove the rabbits into nets tied end to end. To provide food for the winter, husbands and wives worked as teams in the late fall to collect pine nuts.

Since everyone participated in most food-gathering activities, there were no individual distributors of food and relatively little difference in male and female rights. Men and women were not segregated from each other in daily activities; both were free to take lovers after marriage; both had the right to separate whenever they chose; menstruating women were not isolated from the rest of the group; and one of the two major Washo rituals celebrated hunting while the other celebrated gathering. Men were accorded more prestige if they had killed a deer, and men directed decisions about the seasonal movement of the group. But if no male leader stepped forward, women were permitted to lead. The distinctive feature of groups such as the Washo is the relative equality of the sexes.

The sexes are also relatively equal among the Hadza of Tanzania but this near-equality arises because men and women tend to work alone to feed themselves. They exchange little food. The Hadza lead a leisurely life in the seemingly barren environment of the East African Rift Gorge that is, in fact, rich in edible berries, roots, and small game. As a result of this abundance, from the time they are ten years old, Hadza men and women gather much of their own food. Women take their young children with them into the bush, eating as they forage, and collect only enough food for a light family meal in the evening. The men eat berries and roots as they hunt for small game, and should they bring down a rabbit or a hyrax, they eat the meat on the spot. Meat is carried back to the camp and shared with the rest of the group only on those rare occasions when a poisoned arrow brings down a large animal—an impala, a zebra, an eland, or a giraffe.

Because Hadza men distribute little meat, their status is only slightly higher than that of the women. People flock to the camp of a good hunter and the camp might take on his name because of his popularity, but he is in no sense a leader of the group. A Hadza man and a woman have an equal right to divorce and each can repudiate a marriage simply by living apart for a few weeks. Couples tend to live in the same camp as the wife's mother but they sometimes make long visits to the camp of the husband's mother. Although a man may take more than one wife, most Hadza males cannot afford to indulge in this luxury. In order to maintain a marriage, a man must supply both his wife and his mother-in-law with some meat and trade goods, such as beads and cloth, and the Hadza economy gives few men the wealth to provide for more than one wife and mother-in-law. Washo equality is based on cooperation; Hadza equality is based on independence.

In contrast to both these groups, among the Tiwi of Melville and Bathurst Islands off the northern coast of Australia, male hunters dominate female gatherers. The Tiwi are representative of the most common form of foraging society, in which the men supply large quantities of meat, although less than half the food consumed by the group. Each morning Tiwi women, most with babies on their backs, scatter in different directions in search of vegetables, grubs, worms, and small game such as bandicoots, lizards, and opossums. To track the game, they use hunting dogs. On most days women return to camp with some meat and with baskets full of *korka*, the nut of a native palm, which is soaked and mashed to make a porridge-like dish. The Tiwi men do not hunt small game and do not hunt every day, but when they do they often return with kangaroo, large lizards, fish, and game birds.

The porridge is cooked separately by each household and rarely shared outside the family, but the meat is prepared by a volunteer cook, who can be male or female. After the cook takes one of the parts of the animal traditionally reserved for him or her, the animal's "boss," the one who caught it, distributes the rest to all near kin and then to all others residing with the band. Although the small game supplied by the women is distributed in the same way as the big game supplied by the men, Tiwi men are dominant because the game they kill provides most of the meat.

The power of the Tiwi men is clearest in their betrothal practices. Among the Tiwi, a woman must always be married. To ensure this, female infants are betrothed at birth and widows are remarried at the gravesides of their late husbands. Men form alliances by exchanging daughters, sisters, and mothers in marriage and some collect as many as 25 wives. Tiwi men value the quantity and quality of the food many wives can collect and the many children they can produce.

The dominance of the men is offset somewhat by the influence of adult women in selecting their next husbands. Many women are active strategists in the political careers of their male relatives, but to the exasperation of some sons attempting to promote their own futures, widowed mothers sometimes insist on selecting their own partners. Women also influence the marriages of their daughters and granddaughters, especially when the selected husband dies before the bestowed child moves to his camp.

Among the Eskimo, representative of the rarest type of forager society, inequality between the sexes is matched by inequality in supplying the group with food. Inland Eskimo men hunt caribou throughout the year to provision the entire society, and maritime Eskimo men depend on whaling, fishing, and some hunting to feed their extended families. The women process the carcasses, cut and sew skins to make clothing, cook, and care for the young; but they collect no food of their own and depend on the men to supply all the raw materials for their work. Since men provide all the meat, they also control the trade in hides, whale oil, seal oil, and other items that move between the maritime and inland Eskimos.

Eskimo women are treated almost exclusively as objects to be used, abused, and traded by men. After puberty all Eskimo girls are fair game for any interested male. A man shows his intentions by grabbing the belt of a woman and if she protests, he cuts off her trousers and forces himself upon her. These encounters are considered unimportant by the rest of the group. Men offer their wives' sexual services to establish alliances with trading partners and members of hunting and whaling parties.

Despite the consistent pattern of some degree of male dominance among foragers, most of these societies are egalitarian compared with agricultural and industrial societies. No forager has any significant opportunity for political leadership. Foragers, as a rule, do not like to give or take orders, and assume leadership only with reluctance. Shamans (those who are thought to be possessed by spirits) may be either male or female. Public rituals conducted by women in order to celebrate the first menstruation of girls are common, and the symbolism in these rituals is similar to that in the ceremonies that follow a boy's first kill.

In any society, status goes to those who control the distribution of valued goods and services outside the family. Equality arises when both sexes work side by side in food production, as do the Washo, and the products are simply distributed among the workers. In such circumstances, no person or sex has greater access to valued items than do others. But when women make no contribution to the food supply, as in the case of the Eskimo, they are completely subordinate.

When we attempt to apply these generalizations to contemporary industrial society, we can predict that as long as women spend their discretionary income from jobs on domestic needs, they will gain little social recognition and power. To be an effective source of power, money must be exchanged in ways that require returns and create obligations. In other words, it must be invested.

Jobs that do not give women control over valued resources will do little to advance their general status. Only as managers, executives, and professionals are women in a position to trade goods and services, to do others favors, and therefore to obligate others to them. Only as controllers of valued resources can women achieve prestige, power, and equality.

Within the household, women who bring in income from jobs are able to function on a more nearly equal basis with their husbands. Women who contribute services to their husbands and children without pay, as do some middle-class Western housewives, are especially vulnerable to dominance. Like Eskimo women, as long as their services are limited to domestic distribution they have little power relative to their husbands and none with respect to the outside world.

As for the limits imposed on women by their procreative functions in hunter-gatherer societies, child-bearing and child care are organized around work as much as work is organized around reproduction. Some foraging groups space their children three to four years apart and have an average of only four to six children, far fewer than many women in other cultures. Hunter-gatherers nurse their infants for extended periods, sometimes for as long as four years. This custom suppresses ovulation and limits the size of their families. Sometimes, although rarely, they practice infanticide. By limiting reproduction, a woman who is gathering food has only one child to carry.

Different societies can and do adjust the frequency of birth and the care of children to accommodate whatever productive activities women customarily engage in. In horticultural societies, where women work long hours in gardens that may be far from home, infants get food to supplement their mothers' milk, older children take care of younger children, and pregnancies are widely spaced. Throughout the world, if a society requires a woman's labor, it finds ways to care for her children.

In the United States, as in some other industrial societies, the accelerated entry of women with preschool children into the labor force has resulted in the development of a variety of child-care arrangements. Individual women have called on friends, relatives, and neighbors. Public and private child-care centers are growing. We should realize that the declining birth rate, the increasing acceptance of childless or single-child families, and a de-emphasis on motherhood are adaptations to a sexual division of labor reminiscent of the system of production found in hunter-gatherer societies.

In many countries where women no longer devote most of their productive years to childbearing, they are beginning to demand a change in the social relationship of the sexes. As women gain access to positions that control the exchange of resources, male dominance may become archaic, and industrial societies may one day become as egalitarian as the Washo.

REFERENCES

Friedl, Ernestine. *Women and Men: An Anthropologist's View*. New York: Holt, Rinehart and Winston, 1975.

Martin, M. Kay, and Barbara Voorhies, eds. *Female of the Species*. New York: Columbia University Press, 1977.

Murphy, Yolanda, and Robert Murphy. *Women of the Forest*. New York: Columbia University Press, 1974.

Reiter, Rayna, ed. *Toward an Anthropology of Women*. New York: Monthly Review Press, 1975.

Rosaldo, M.Z., and Louise Lamphere, eds. *Women, Culture, and Society*. Stanford, Calif.: Stanford University Press, 1974.

Schlegel, Alice, ed. *Sexual Stratification; A Cross-Cultural View*. New York: Columbia University Press, 1977.

Strathern, Marilyn. *Women in Between: Female Roles in a Male World*. New York: Academic Press, 1972.

The Doctor-Nurse Game

by
Leonard I. Stein

THE RELATIONSHIP BETWEEN the doctor and the nurse is a very special one. There are few professions where the degree of mutual respect and cooperation between co-workers is as intense as that between the doctor and nurse. Superficially, the stereotype of this relationship has been dramatized in many novels and television serials. When, however, it is observed carefully in an interactional framework, the relationship takes on a new dimension and has a special quality which fits a game model. The underlying attitudes which demand that this game be played are unfortunate. These attitudes create serious obstacles in the path of meaningful communications between physicians and nonmedical professional groups.

The physician traditionally and appropriately has total responsibility for making the decisions regarding the management of his patients' treatment. To guide his decisions he considers data gleaned from several sources. He acquires a complete medical history, performs a thorough physical examination, interprets laboratory findings, and at times, obtains recommendations from physician-consultants. Another important factor in his decision-making is the recommendations he receives from the nurse. The interaction between doctor and nurse through which these recommendations are communicated and received is unique and interesting.

THE GAME

One rarely hears a nurse say, "Doctor, I would recommend that you order a retention enema for Mrs. Brown." A physician,

Reprinted from *Archives of General Psychiatry*, 16 (June 1967), pp. 699–703. Copyright 1967, American Medical Association. Reprinted by permission of the author and the publisher.

upon hearing a recommendation of that nature, would gape in amazement at the effrontery of the nurse. The nurse, upon hearing the statement, would look over her shoulder to see who said it, hardly believing the words actually came from her own mouth. Nevertheless, if one observes closely, nurses make recommendations of more import every hour and physicians willingly and respectfully consider them. If the nurse is to make a suggestion without appearing insolent and the doctor is to seriously consider that suggestion, their interaction must not violate the rules of the game.

Object of the game. The object of the game is as follows: the nurse is to be bold, have initiative, and be responsible for making significant recommendations, while at the same time she must appear passive. This must be done in such a manner so as to make her recommendations appear to be initiated by the physician.

Both participants must be acutely sensitive to each other's nonverbal and cryptic verbal communications. A slight lowering of the head, a minor shifting of position in the chair, or a seemingly nonrelevant comment concerning an event which occurred eight months ago must be interpreted as a powerful message. The game requires the nimbleness of a high wire acrobat, and if either participant slips the game can be shattered; the penalties for frequent failure are apt to be severe.

Rules of the game. The cardinal rule of the game is that open disagreement between the players must be avoided at all costs. Thus, the nurse must communicate her recommendations without appearing to be making a recommendation statement. The physician, in requesting a recommendation from a nurse, must do so without appearing to be asking for it. Utilization of this technique keeps anyone from committing themselves to a position before a sub rosa agreement on that position has already been established. In that way open disagreement is avoided. The greater the significance of the recommendation, the more subtly the game must be played.

To convey a subtle example of the game with all its nuances would require the talents of a literary artist. Lacking these talents, let me give you the following example which is unsubtle, but happens frequently. The medical resident on hospital call is awakened by telephone at 1:00 A.M. because a patient on a ward, not his own, has not been able to fall asleep. Dr. Jones answers the telephone and the dialogue goes like this:

This is Dr. Jones.

[An open and direct communication.]

Dr. Jones, this is Miss Smith on 2W—Mrs. Brown, who learned today of her father's death, is unable to fall asleep.

[This message has two levels. Openly, it describes a set of circumstances, a woman who is unable to sleep and who that morning received word of her father's death. Less openly, but just as directly, it is a diagnostic and recommendation statement; i.e., Mrs. Brown is unable to sleep because of her grief, and she should be given a sedative. Dr. Jones, accepting the diagnostic statement and replying to the recommendation statement, answers.]

What sleeping medication has been helpful to Mrs. Brown in the past?

[Dr. Jones, not knowing the patient, is asking for a recommendation from the nurse, who does know the patient, about what sleeping medication should be prescribed. Note, however, his question does not appear to be asking for a recommendation. Miss Smith replies.]

Pentobarbital mg 100 was quite effective night before last.

[A disguised recommendation statement. Dr. Jones replies with a note of authority in his voice.]

Pentobarbital mg 100 before bedtime as needed for sleep; got it?

[Miss Smith ends the conversation with the tone of a grateful supplicant.]

Yes, I have, and thank you very much, doctor.

The above is an example of a successfully played doctor-nurse game. The nurse made appropriate recommendations which were accepted by the physician and were helpful to the patient. The game was successful because the cardinal rule was not violated. The nurse was able to make her recommendation without appearing to, and the physician was able to ask for recommendations without conspicuously asking for them.

The scoring system. Inherent in any game are penalties and rewards for the players. In game theory, the doctor-nurse game fits the nonzero sum game model. It is not like chess, where the players compete with each other and whatever one player loses the other wins. Rather, it is the kind of game in which the rewards and punishments are shared by both players. If they play the game successfully they both win rewards, and if they are unskilled and the game is played badly, they both suffer the penalty.

The most obvious reward from the well-played game is a

doctor-nurse team that operates efficiently. The physician is able to utilize the nurse as a valuable consultant, and the nurse gains self-esteem and professional satisfaction from her job. The less obvious rewards are no less important. A successful game creates a doctor-nurse alliance; through this alliance the physician gains the respect and admiration of the nursing service. He can be confident that his nursing staff will smooth the path for getting his work done. His charts will be organized and waiting for him when he arrives, the ruffled feathers of patients and relatives will have been smoothed down, and his pet routines will be happily followed, and he will be helped in a thousand and one other ways.

The doctor-nurse alliance sheds its light on the nurse as well. She gains a reputation for being a "damn good nurse." She is respected by everyone and appropriately enjoys her position. When physicians discuss the nursing staff it would not be unusual for her name to be mentioned with respect and admiration. Their esteem for a good nurse is no less than their esteem for a good doctor.

The penalties for a game failure, on the other hand, can be severe. The physician who is an unskilled gamesman and fails to recognize the nurses' subtle recommendation messages is tolerated as a "clod." If, however, he interprets these messages as insolence and strongly indicates he does not wish to tolerate suggestions from nurses, he creates a rocky path for his travels. The old truism "If the nurse is your ally you've got it made, and if she has it in for you, be prepared for misery" takes on life-sized proportions. He receives three times as many phone calls after midnight as his colleagues. Nurses will not accept his telephone orders because "telephone orders are against the rules." Somehow, this rule gets suspended for the skilled players. Soon he becomes like Joe Bfstplk in the "Li'l Abner" comic strip. No matter where he goes, a black cloud constantly hovers over his head.

The unskilled gamesman nurse also pays heavily. The nurse who does not view her role as that of consultant, and therefore does not attempt to communicate recommendations, is perceived as a dullard and is mercifully allowed to fade into the woodwork.

The nurse who does see herself as a consultant but refuses to follow the rules of the game in making her recommendations has hell to pay. The outspoken nurse is labeled a "bitch" by the surgeon. The psychiatrist describes her as unconsciously suffering from penis envy and her behavior as the acting out of her hostility towards men. Loosely translated, the psychiatrist is saying she is a bitch. The employment of the unbright outspoken nurse is soon terminated. The outspoken bright nurse whose recommendations are worthwhile remains employed. She is, however, constantly reminded in a hundred ways that she is not loved.

GENESIS OF THE GAME

To understand how the game evolved, we must comprehend the nature of the doctors' and nurses' training which shaped the attitudes necessary for the game.

Medical student training. The medical student in his freshman year studies as if possessed. In the anatomy class he learns every groove and prominence on the bones of the skeleton as if life depended on it. As a matter of fact, he literally believes just that. He not infrequently says, "I've got to learn it exactly; a life may depend on me knowing that." A consequence of this attitude, which is carefully nurtured throughout medical school, is the development of a phobia: the over-determined fear of making a mistake. The development of this fear is quite understandable. The burden the physician must carry is at times almost unbearable. He feels responsible in a very personal way for the lives of his patients. When a man dies leaving young children and a widow, the doctor carries some of her grief and despair inside himself; and when a child dies, some of him dies too. He sees himself as a warrior against death and disease. When he loses a battle, through no fault of his own, he nevertheless feels pangs of guilt, and he relentlessly searches himself to see if there might have been a way to alter the outcome. For the physician a mistake leading to a serious consequence is intolerable, and any mistake reminds him of his vulnerability. There is little wonder that he becomes phobic. The classical way in which phobias are managed is to avoid the source of the fear. Since it is impossible to avoid making some mistakes in an active practice of medicine, a substitute defensive maneuver is employed. The physician develops the belief that he is omnipotent and omniscient, and therefore incapable of making mistakes. This belief allows the phobic physician to actively engage in his practice rather than avoid it. The fear of committing an error in a critical field like medicine is unavoidable and appropriately realistic. The physician, however, must learn to live with the fear rather than handle it defensively through a posture of omnipotence. This defense markedly interferes with his interpersonal professional relationships.

Physicians, of course, deny feelings of omnipotence. The evidence, however, renders their denials to whispers in the wind. The slightest mistake inflicts a large narcissistic wound. Depending on his underlying personality structure the physician may be obsessed for days about it, rationalize it away, or deny it. The guilt produced is unusually exaggerated and the incident is handled defensively. The ways in which physicians enhance and support each other's defenses when an error is made could be the topic of another paper. The feeling of omnipotence becomes generalized to other areas of his life. A report of the Federal Aviation Agency (FAA), as quoted in *Time* magazine (August 5, 1966), states that in 1964 and 1965 physicians had a fatal-accident rate four times as high as the average for all other private pilots. Major causes of the high death rate were risk-taking attitudes and judgments. Almost all of the accidents occurred on pleasure trips, and were therefore not necessary risks to get to a patient needing emergency care. The trouble, suggested an FAA official, is that too many doctors fly with "the feeling that they are omnipotent." Thus, the extremes to which the physician may go in preserving his self-concept of omnipotence may threaten his own life. This overdetermined preservation of omnipotence is indicative of its brittleness and its underlying foundation of fear of failure.

The physician finds himself trapped in a paradox. He fervently wants to give his patient the best possible medical care, and being open to the nurses' recommendations helps him accomplish this. On the other hand, accepting advice from nonphysicians is highly threatening to his omnipotence. The solution for the paradox is to receive sub rosa recommendations and make them appear to be initiated by himself. In short, he must learn to play the doctor-nurse game.

Some physicians never learn to play the game. Most learn in their internship, and a perceptive few learn during their clerkships in medical school. Medical students frequently complain that the nursing staff treats them as if they had just completed a junior Red Cross first-aid class instead of two years of intensive medical training. Interviewing nurses in a training hospital sheds considerable light on this phenomenon. In their words they said,

A few students just seem to be with it, they are able to understand what you are trying to tell them, and they are a pleasure to work with; most, however, pretend to know everything and refuse to listen to anything we have to say and I guess we do give them a rough time.

In essence, they are saying that those students who quickly learn the game are rewarded, and those that do not are punished.

Most physicians learn to play the game after they have weathered a few experiences like the one described below. On the first day of his internship, the physician and nurse were making rounds. They stopped at the bed of a fifty-two-year-old woman who, after complimenting the young doctor on his appearance, complained to him of her problem with constipation. After several minutes of listening to her detailed description of peculiar diets, family home remedies, and special exercises that have helped her constipation in the past, the nurse politely interrupted the patient. She told her the doctor would take care of the problem and that he had to move on because there were other patients waiting to see him. The young doctor gave the nurse a stern look, turned toward the patient, and kindly told her he would order an enema for her that very afternoon. As they left the bedside, the nurse told him the patient has had a normal bowel movement every day for the past week and that in the twenty-three days the patient has been in the hospital she has never once passed up an opportunity to complain of her constipation. She quickly added that *if* the doctor wanted to order an enema, the patient would certainly receive one. After hearing this report the intern's mouth fell open and the wheels began turning in his head. He remembered the nurse's comment to the patient that "the doctor had to move on," and it occurred to him that perhaps she was really giving him a message. The experience and a few more like it, and the young doctor learns to listen for the subtle recommendations the nurses make.

Nursing student training. Unlike the medical student who usually learns to play the game after he finishes medical school, the nursing student begins to learn it early in her training. Throughout her education she is trained to play the doctor-nurse game.

Student nurses are taught how to relate to physicians. They are told he has infinitely more knowledge than they, and thus he should be shown the utmost respect. In addition, it was not many years ago when nurses were instructed to stand whenever a physician entered a room. When he would come in for a conference the nurse was expected to offer him her chair, and when both entered a room the nurse would open the door for him and allow him to enter first. Although these practices are no longer rigidly adhered to, the premise upon which they were based is still promulgated. One nurse described that premise as, "He's God almighty and your job is to wait on him."

To inculcate subservience and inhibit deviancy, nursing schools, for the most part, are tightly run, disciplined institutions. Certainly there is great variation among nursing schools, and there is little question that the trend is toward giving students more autonomy. However, in too many schools this trend has not gone far enough, and the climate remains restrictive. The student's schedule is firmly controlled and there is very little free time. Classroom hours, study hours, mealtime, and bedtime with lights out are rigidly enforced. In some schools meaningless chores are assigned, such as cleaning bedsprings with cotton applicators. The relationship between student and instructor continues this military flavor. Often their relationship is more like that between recruit and drill sergeant than between student and teacher. Open dialogue is inhibited by attitudes of strict black and white, with few, if any, shades of gray. Straying from the rigidly outlined path is sure to result in disciplinary action.

The inevitable result of these practices is to instill in the student nurse a fear of independent action. This inhibition of independent action is most marked when relating to physicians. One of the students' greatest fears is making a blunder while assisting a physician and being publicly ridiculed by him. This is really more a reflection of the nature of their training than the prevalence of abusive physicians. The fear of being humiliated for a blunder while assisting in a procedure is generalized to the fear of humiliation for making any independent act in relating to a physician, especially the act of making a direct recommendation. Every nurse interviewed felt that making a suggestion to a physician was equivalent to insulting and belittling him. It was tantamount to questioning his medical knowledge and insinuating he did not know his business. In light of her image of the physician as an omniscient and punitive figure, the questioning of his knowledge would be unthinkable.

The student, however, is also given messages quite contrary to the ones described above. She is continually told that she is an invaluable aid to the physician in the treatment of the patient. She is told that she must help him in every way possible, and she is imbued with a strong sense of responsibility for the care of her patient. Thus she, like the physician, is caught in a paradox. The first set of messages implies that the physician is omniscient and that any recommendation she might make would be insulting to him and leave her open to ridicule. The second set of messages implies that she is an important asset to him, has much to contribute, and is duty-bound to make those contributions. Thus, when her good sense tells her a recommendation would be helpful to him she is not allowed to communicate it directly, nor is she allowed not to communicate it. The way out of the bind is to use the doctor-nurse game and communicate the recommendation without appearing to do so.

FORCES PRESERVING THE GAME

Upon observing the indirect interactional system which is the heart of the doctor-nurse game, one must ask the question, "Why does this inefficient mode of communication continue to exist?" The forces mitigating against change are powerful.

Rewards and punishments. The doctor-nurse game has a powerful innate self-perpetuating force—its system of rewards and punishments. One potent method of shaping behavior is to reward one set of behavioral patterns and to punish patterns which deviate from it. As described earlier, the rewards given for a well-played game and the punishments meted out to unskilled players are impressive. This system alone would be sufficient to keep the game flourishing. The game, however, has additional forces.

The strength of the set. It is well recognized that sets are hard to break. A powerful attitudinal set is the nurse's perception that making a suggestion to a physician is equivalent to insulting and belittling him. An example of where attempts are regularly made to break this set is seen on psychiatric treatment wards operating on a therapeutic community model. This model requires open and direct communication between members of the team. Psychiatrists working in these settings expend a great deal of energy in urging for and rewarding openness before direct patterns of communication become established. The rigidity of the resistance to break this set is impressive. If the physician himself is a prisoner of a set and therefore does not actively try to destroy it, change is near impossible.

The need for leadership. Lack of leadership and structure in any organization produces anxiety in its members. As the importance of the organization's mission increases, the demand by its members for leadership commensurately increases. In our culture human life is near the top of our hierarchy of values, and organizations which deal with human lives, such as law and medicine, are very rigidly structured. Certainly some of this is necessary for the systematic management of the task. The excessive degree of rigidity, however, is demanded by its members for their own psychic comfort rather than for its utility in efficiently carrying out its mission. The game lends support to this thesis. Indirect communication is an inefficient mode of transmitting information. However, it effectively supports and protects a rigid organizational structure with the physician in clear authority. Maintaining an omnipotent leader provides the other members with a great sense of security.

Sexual roles. Another influence perpetuating the doctor-nurse game is the sexual identity of the players. Doctors are predominately men and nurses are almost exclusively women. There are elements of the game which reinforce the stereotyped roles of male dominance and female passivity. Some nursing instructors explicitly tell their students that their femininity is an important asset to be used when relating to physicians.

THE COMMUNITY

The doctor and nurse have a shared history and thus have been able to work out their game so that it operates more efficiently than one would expect in an indirect system. Major difficulty arises, however, when the physician works closely with other disciplines which are not normally considered part of the medical sphere. With expanding medical horizons encompassing cooperation with sociologists, engineers, anthropologists, computer analysts, etc., continued expectation of a doctor-nurselike interaction by the physician is disastrous. The sociologist, for example, is not willing to play that kind of game. When his direct communications are rebuffed the relationship breaks down.

The major disadvantage of a doctor-nurselike game is its inhibitory effect on open dialogue which is stifling and anti-intellectual. The game is basically a transactional neurosis, and both professions would enhance themselves by taking steps to change the attitudes which breed the game.

V

UNDERSTANDING "CULTURE"

He who sleeps on the floor will not fall out of bed.

Turkish proverb

Man alone is able to go beyond himself as an organism
and to transform . . . everything (himself included) into
an object of knowledge.

Max Scheler

"CULTURE" IS BOTH the key to and the integrating concept of anthropology. To better understand culture we dig up the past, study the present, and make projections about the future. For over one hundred years professional anthropologists have irritated and intrigued colleagues in other fields with stories of "strange" customs which are just as "civilized" as the British "tea-time." Cultural evolution, cultural ecology, cultural diffusion, culture core: these and many other important concepts in anthropology get their basic meaning from "culture." Yet paradoxically, were you to ask ten anthropologists: "What do you mean by 'culture'?" you would probably receive ten different answers.

"Culture" for anthropology is like "life" for biology: a rich, fuzzy, productive, and necessary concept too full of meaning for easy intellectual digestion. Probing for the meaning of culture is a rewarding process even if no agreed-upon answer is ever found. As we poke, pull apart, argue, and research this concept it becomes apparent (at least to me) that "culture" is a modern word for "fate." Moreover, while "fate" is a tragic word presenting our lives as preordained, "culture" is essentially a happy word. Culture is learned, taught, and controllable. Culture, when well understood, can make us masters of our fate.

In pursuit of the meaning of culture, Kluckhohn and Kelly describe a make-believe discussion group. Here each of a variety of professionals demands a definition which has relevance for his work. Each discussant, moreover, wants to understand culture by using words with which he is familiar. Some agreement is reached that culture is a *design for living*—what I have referred to as a *guidance system* (see Introduction). In modern American culture, much human interaction involves the exchange of money. Money, for us, talks. Its speech is so powerful that it can provide anything we desire. None need ask: "Is this for sale?" Rather, the proper question is: "How much?" Our money is "carried" to places where it can do its talking. But in some societies money walks on its own four legs. The money used by the Vanuata consists of well-tusked pigs. Elsewhere, money just sits. Among the Yap, money consists of *fei*—large, wheel-like stones.[1]

The Western image of money talking—telling people what to do, where to go, and whom to obey—leads us to misrepresent some situations. For example, many Mohawk Indians do dangerous construction work high on the narrow ledges of buildings and bridges. They are well paid for this work. Using talking-money logic we might reasonably assume that Mohawks do structural-steel work *because* the price is right. Such American-cultural reasoning misrepresents Mohawk culture. Mohawk "warriors" have their own special reasons for doing structural-steel work that demonstrate the persistence of the culture through, essentially, the continuation of the male warrior role.[2]

Lauriston Sharp's analysis of Yir Yoront life ("Steel Axes for Stone-Age Australians") highlights culture change. The stone axe was very important in the subsistence economy of the aboriginal and in interpersonal relations. The introduction of steel axes changed almost every aspect of traditional life. As Sharp puts it, "The steel axe, shifting hopelessly between one clan and the other, is not only replacing the stone axe physically, but is hacking at the supports of the entire cultural system."

Sharp's essay on the Yir Yoront describes a whole culture—a system consisting of many interconnected elements. It is also useful to pick one activity and analyze its functions, meanings, and consequences. Yngve Georg Lithman, in "Feeling Good and Getting Smashed," asks why anyone wants to "get smashed." He has observed that when people get smashed they act inappropriately and people make excuses for them. His hypothesis, while perhaps startling at first sight, makes good sense. He believes that people get smashed *in order to* behave inappropriately. The proper way of behaving is often restrictive: things we want to do, perhaps *need* to do, are not allowed. There are things we want to tell people but are not allowed to because the message is

[1]Gary Turbak, "Money's Many Faces." *The Rotarian*, vol. 138, no. 4 (April 1981), pp. 39–40.
[2]Morris Freilich, "Cultural Persistence Among the Modern Iroquois." *Anthropos*, vol. 53 (1958), pp. 473–483.

too personal, too critical, interfering, or likely to be misunderstood. There are actions we wish to take that do not fit the status we hold or the roles we play. We may want to fight, cry, kiss someone, or throw something. By getting smashed we pick up energy, courage, and excuses.

There is more to getting smashed than meets the eye; similarly, C. Paul Dredge believes, there is more to smoking than meets the throat. Dredge's ideas were tested in Korea, but his general conclusion fits any society: any cultural complex, such as smoking, has many causes. Tell a Korean to quit smoking and he will tell you a story: A man once made up his mind to stop this wasteful activity. He quite smoking and used the money so saved to buy an ox. But a tiger carried off the ox and ate it! For Koreans, the message instructs us, those who give up smoking lose much and gain nothing. Tobacco is a means of conspicuous consumption (the rich smoke expensive brands to prove they are rich); tobacco is a useful exchange commodity; and tobacco is a means of expressing adulthood.

Humans like peacocks, tend to show off their best feature. So, while pride in one's culture is very human, its exaggeration provides a perfect target for a profound and witty scholar, Ralph Linton ("One Hundred Per Cent American").

REFERENCES

Freilich, Morris. "The Smart and the Proper: Rethinking Culture." In *Cultures*. Paris: UNESCO, in press.

Freilich, Morris, ed. *The Meaning of Culture*. Cambridge, Mass.: Schenkman, 1982.

Geertz, Clifford. *The Interpretation of Culture*. New York: Basic Books, 1973.

Goodenough, Ward. *Culture, Language and Society*. Menlo Park, Calif.: Benjamin/Cummings, 1981.

Pulliam, H. Ronald, and Christopher Dunford. *Programmed to Learn: An Essay on the Evolution of Culture*. New York: Columbia University Press, 1980.

The Concept of Culture

by
Clyde Kluckhohn and
William H. Kelly

THE LAWYER: At the last meeting of this little discussion group of ours, we got into quite an argument about "culture" as a technical term in anthropology—exactly what anthropologists mean by it and whether it is any use or not. The big dictionaries and even the anthropological books here in the club library didn't help us out very much. We did gather that the anthropological conception, like all the other scientific and popular usages, carries with it an implication of human interference, of something being added to, or altered from, a state of nature. But we found ourselves wishing that we could ask questions which might clear up points which were sidestepped or simply not discussed by these formal statements. We therefore prevailed upon you gentlemen to come here and let us put you on the spot.

THE HISTORIAN: Was I right in insisting last time that the anthropologist's conception of culture is much more inclusive than the historian's?

FIRST ANTHROPOLOGIST: Yes, to anthropologists a humble cooking pot is as much a cultural product as is a Beethoven sonata.

THE BUSINESSMAN: I am relieved to hear that. For my wife a person who has culture is a person who can talk about Debussy, T. S. Eliot, Picasso, and those people.

THE LAWYER: Do anthropologists apply the term "culture" to our civilization? Isn't there a difference between "culture" and "civilization"?

SECOND ANTHROPOLOGIST: To most anthropologists, a civilization is simply a special type of culture, namely, a complex or "high" culture. More specifically, a civilization is—as the deri-

Reprinted from *The Science of Man in the World of Crisis*, ed. Ralph Linton. New York: Columbia University Press, 1945, pp. 187–201, by permission of the publisher.

vation of the word itself suggests—the culture of a people who live in cities. People who have lived in cities have invariably possessed a somewhat complex way of life, and have almost always had a written language.

THIRD ANTHROPOLOGIST: Perhaps it would also be well to state for the record that anthropologists have never followed another distinction which certain sociologists have made between culture and civilization. This usage discriminates between "civilization" as comprising the sum total of human "means" and "culture" as constituting the collectivity of human "ends."

FIRST ANTHROPOLOGIST: Many educated people seem to have the notion that "culture" applies only to exotic ways of life or to societies where relative simplicity and relative homogeneity prevail. Some sophisticated missionaries, for example, will use the anthropological conception in discussing the special modes of living of South Sea Islanders, but seem amazed at the idea that it could be applied equally to the inhabitants of New York City. And social workers in New York City will talk about the "culture" of a colorful and well-knit immigrant group, but boggle at utilizing the concept toward understanding the behavior of staff members in the social service agency itself.

THE ECONOMIST: A moment ago you used the term "society." This brings me to a point which I have found confusing in certain recent more or less popular writings of anthropologists. Sometimes the terms "culture" and "society" seem to have been used almost as synonyms.

FIRST ANTHROPOLOGIST: There would be fairly general agreement in our profession that this is undesirable. The usage which has attained almost complete acceptance among us can be put simply, though not altogether precisely, as follows: A "society" refers to a group of people who have learned to work together; a "culture" refers to the distinctive ways of life of such a group of people.

THE PHILOSOPHER: In my language, then, "a culture" is an abstraction, whereas "a society" is not?

THIRD ANTHROPOLOGIST: That is certainly correct in the sense that you can see the individuals who make up a society, while you never see "culture." However, the statement must not be made to imply that the processes of inference and abstraction are not involved in many of the specific problems of deciding where one society leaves off and another begins. Some anthropologists assert that such problems can always be resolved by sufficiently detailed observation of the frequencies with which human beings in a defined territory interact. This is doubtless a valid operation by which to decide what individuals constitute "a society," but we should be deluding ourselves if we pretended that reasoning were not as necessary as observation to the delimitation of a society.

SECOND ANTHROPOLOGIST: I can't agree with your first statement that culture is never observed directly. What does an anthropologist actually do when he is working in the field? Yes, he sees the human organisms who make up a society. He sees not only them, but also their behavior. He likewise sees the objects they have made and all of the alterations which they produced in their natural environment. What the anthropologist does is to record the distinctive ways of behaving which he sees and those results of behavior which are also characteristic. These constitute the culture of the group.

THIRD ANTHROPOLOGIST: There is no doubt that you have rightly described what anthropologists actually do in the field. But those recordings which you have mentioned I would prefer to consider as the anthropologist's raw data. Both "society" and "culture" are conceptual constructs. In each case, although in importantly different ways, the anthropologist has added to or subtracted from what he actually saw. Both the society and the culture which he portrays are conceptual models—not firsthand recordings of all he observed.

THE PSYCHOLOGIST: Let me see if I can translate into my own lingo. Culture means the totality of social habits.

FIRST ANTHROPOLOGIST: "Habit" is too neutral a term. It would be more exact to say "socially valued habits," for a group is never affectively indifferent to its culture.

THE PSYCHOLOGIST: I suppose that branch of psychology which is most intimately related to "culture" is what we today call "learning theory." Wouldn't you agree that the transmission of culture can be understood only in so far as learning and teaching are understood?

FIRST ANTHROPOLOGIST: Yes, inasmuch as all human beings of whatever "races" seem to have about the same nervous systems and biological equipment generally, we would anticipate that the basic processes of learning are very similar if not identical among all groups. We therefore look to the psychologist to inform us about the laws of learning. On the other hand, we can show that *what* is learned, from whom learning takes place, and when the learning of certain skills usually occurs, varies according to culture. Also, I should like to point out that there is one danger in speaking of culture as being "taught." "Teaching" is not limited, as in the popular sense, to conscious instruction.

Individuals learn—"absorb" more nearly suggests, in nontechnical language, the process—much of their culture through imitation of both the "matched-dependent" and "copying" types. Take, for example, those gestures and expressive movements ("motor habits") which are observed as characteristic of certain groups. Every anthropologist regards these as cultural phenomena, and yet only in dancing schools, armies, and the like is explicit instruction as to posture, and so forth, given.

THE PSYCHOLOGIST: If I am not mistaken, C. S. Ford has defined culture as consisting of "traditional ways of solving problems" or "learned problem solutions."

THIRD ANTHROPOLOGIST: It is true that any culture is, among other things, a set of techniques for adjusting both to the external environment and to other men. In so far as Ford's statement points to this fact, it is helpful, but it will not do as a synoptic definition. For cultures create problems as well as solving them. If the lore of a people states that frogs are dangerous creatures, or that it is not safe to go about at night because of were-animals or ghosts, threats are posed which do not arise out of the inexorable facts of the external world. This is why all "functional" definitions of culture tend to be unsatisfactory: they disregard the fact that cultures create needs as well as provide a means of fulfilling them.

THE PSYCHIATRIST: In fact, my profession has always tended to think of culture as something which was repressive to the "natural" nature of man, as something which produced needless neuroses by demands and thwartings during the process of molding individuals into shapes uncongenial to their native temperament.

THIRD ANTHROPOLOGIST: This seems to us to be another half-truth. Culture is *both* fulfilling and frustrating.

FOURTH ANTHROPOLOGIST: I have held my peace, but at this point I really must protest. Where is this "culture" which you talk about as doing this and that? If anthropology is to become a natural science, it must deal only in empirical and observable entities. In spite of the fact that most archeologists, ethnologists, and social anthropologists still feel that "culture" is their master concept, I maintain we would get further if we stuck to human interaction with other humans and with the natural environment. You can see those things, but has any of you ever seen "culture"?

FIRST ANTHROPOLOGIST: I freely admit that to say "culture" does something in an inexact or metaphorical way of speaking. But this is merely a convenient shorthand expression in place of the longwinded though admittedly more precise "the human representatives of the group which share this culture do thus and so." As for "seeing": your admired natural scientists have never seen "gravity" or "evolution." And yet they find the introduction of these concepts indispensable for making the facts intelligible and for predicting them. "Culture" is an abstract generalizing concept, as essential to the understanding and prediction of events in the human world as is gravity to the understanding and prediction of events in the physical world.

SECOND ANTHROPOLOGIST: I accept and use the concept "culture," but I shy away from these high abstractions. I think it is better to stick to a more traditional definition, such as: "Culture is that complex whole which includes artifacts, beliefs, art, all the other habits acquired by man as a member of society, and all products of human activity as determined by these habits."

FIRST ANTHROPOLOGIST: That is all right as a descriptive statement of what students of culture investigate. But as a definition I find it awkward. The enumeration is incomplete, and experience shows that in definitions by enumeration those elements which are not explicitly stated tend to be forgotten even though they be implied. You, for example, have not even mentioned language.

THIRD ANTHROPOLOGIST: I would file two other objections. First, the definition is too intellectualistic. One gets no hint that people are other than affectively neutral toward their culture. This is just a list of culture content. Except, possibly, for the single word "whole," there is no indication that culture has organization as well as content.

THE ECONOMIST: How about "social heredity" as a brief abstract definition of culture?

THIRD ANTHROPOLOGIST: This definition has been widely current and has been of much utility in drawing attention to the fact that human beings have a social as well as a biological heritage. The principal drawbacks to this conception of culture are that it implies too great stability of culture and too passive a role on the part of man. It suggests that man gets his culture as he gets his genes—without effort and without resistance. It tends too much to make us think of the human being as what Dollard has called "the passive porter of a cultural tradition." Men are, as Simmons has recently reminded us, not only the carriers and the creatures of culture—they are also creators and manipulators of culture. "Social heredity" suggests too much of the dead weight tradition.

THE PSYCHIATRIST: Yes, culture is not merely a "given." Really, in a strictly literal sense, it is not a "given" at all—it is only available. Indeed, Ortega y Gasset has defined culture as "that which is sought." The phrase "social legacy" perhaps avoids some of these difficulties, but even this is hardly satisfactory. One wants a definition which points to the fact that the irreducible datum of the social scientist is the individual and his behavior. From the angle of individual psychology, no definition to culture is adequate which does not make us aware of the active role of the individual as regards his culture and of the fact that he has an impulse life.

THE BUSINESSMAN: Much of what has been said was mildly diverting as an exhibition in logical adroitness, but frankly I still don't altogether see why anybody bothers about "culture" at all.

FIRST ANTHROPOLOGIST: Well, one of the interesting things about human beings is that they try to understand themselves and their own behavior. While this has been particularly true of Europeans in recent times, there is no group which has not developed a scheme or schemes to explain man's actions. I would claim that the concept of culture is essential to such understanding.

SECOND ANTHROPOLOGIST: I would phrase the case a little differently. Science is concerned with all observable phenomena, including man himself and his behavior. "Culture" is a convenient descriptive category for organizing our objective reports on human behavior.

THE PHILOSOPHER: It strikes me that the last two statements contain the key to much of our apparent disagreement. For some anthropologists "culture" is primarily a descriptive concept; for others it is primarily an explanatory concept. So-called definitions are always constructed from a point of view—which is all too often left unstated. Not all definitions are substantive (that is, "descriptive"). Nor is "explanatory" the only other alternative. Some of the definitions which have been partially stated or implied have been "functional"; others may be characterized as epistemological—that is, they have been intended to point toward the type of phenomena from which we gain our knowledge of "culture." There is also the point that some definitions look toward the actions of the individual as the starting point of all assertions, whereas others, while perhaps admitting these as ultimate referents, depart from abstractions attributable to groups. However, the distinction between "explanatory" and "descriptive" seems to be most central.

"CULTURE" AS AN EXPLANATORY CONCEPT

THIRD ANTHROPOLOGIST: *By "culture" we mean those historically created selective processes which channel men's reactions both to internal and to external stimuli.*

SECOND ANTHROPOLOGIST: That is certainly an "analytical abstraction" all right.

THIRD ANTHROPOLOGIST: That is precisely the idea: that with this concept certain aspects of the concrete phenomena may be analyzed out, and thus whole events may be better "explained" and predicted.

FIRST ANTHROPOLOGIST: Very neat. And it seems to me to cover the ground. It avoids the difficulty lurking in those many definitions of culture which employ the phrase "acquired by man as a member of society." That phrase seems to suggest that "culture" as an explanatory concept refers *only* to dimensions of the behavior of individuals resultant upon their membership in a particular society (either through birth or through later affiliation). But "culture" also helps us to understand such processes as "diffusion," "culture contract," "acculturation."

THIRD ANTHROPOLOGIST: Yes, culture as an explanatory concept is useful alike in analyzing actions of individuals (whether treated as individuals or as groups) and in elucidating geographical distributions of artifacts or forms of behavior and historical sequences.

FIRST ANTHROPOLOGIST: One could perhaps rephrase your definition along substantive lines by saying that by culture we mean those historically created definitions of the situation which individuals tend to acquire by virtue of participation in or contact with groups which tend to share ways of life which are in some respects distinctive.

FOURTH ANTHROPOLOGIST: Even I find some merit in the explanatory definition proposed. You at least make some concession to a behavioristic approach when you speak of "reactions" and "stimuli."

THIRD ANTHROPOLOGIST: Naturally I would agree that any concept or proposition in social science must be ultimately referable back to human behavior. Even when we deal with distribution of "culture traits," we must not forget that we are dealing with products of human hands, with traces left by human activity.

FOURTH ANTHROPOLOGIST: But why did you find it necessary to include "*internal* stimuli"?

THIRD ANTHROPOLOGIST: When a man eats, he is reacting to an internal "drive," namely, hunger contractions consequent upon the lowering of blood sugar and so forth, but his precise reaction to these internal stimuli cannot be predicted by physiological knowledge alone. Whether a healthy adult tends to "feel hungry" twice, three times, or four times a day and the hours at which these "feelings" tend to recur is a question of culture. *What* he eats is of course limited by sheer objective availability, but is also partly regulated by culture. It is a biological fact that some types of berries are poisonous, but it is a cultural fact that, a few generations ago, most Americans considered tomatoes to be poisonous and refused to eat them. On the other hand, milk, which we regard as a healthful and pleasing food, is regarded by certain peoples of the earth as either dangerous or disgusting. Such selective, discriminative use of the environment is characteristically cultural. In a still more general sense, too, the process of eating is channeled by culture. Whether a man eats to live, lives to eat, or eats and lives is partly individual idiosyncrasy, but there are also marked correlations of individual tendencies along these lines with cultural groups.

SECOND ANTHROPOLOGIST: Why do you use the word "reaction" instead of more straightforward "action"?

THIRD ANTHROPOLOGIST: Because "reaction" comes nearer to conveying the feeling tone which is associated with all selective designs for living.

FOURTH ANTHROPOLOGIST: I am partially convinced, but I must once more come back to my question: Why did you introduce this unseen "culture"?

THIRD ANTHROPOLOGIST: There is no human being, if he be even a few weeks old, who reacts completely freshly to any stimulus situation. Very few human responses indeed can be explained entirely through even the most complete knowledge of the individual biological equipment, private experience up to that point, and the objective facts of the given situation.

FOURTH ANTHROPOLOGIST: But where does "culture" come from? You seem to invoke it as a kind of *deus ex machina*.

THIRD ANTHROPOLOGIST: Culture is, as it were, the precipitate of history. It includes those aspects of the past which, usually in altered form, live on in the present. In more than one sense "history is a sieve."

BIOLOGIST: Do you mean that culture consists of those ways of meeting situations which prove to have survival value?

THIRD ANTHROPOLOGIST: This is a large and important part of the truth. The process of culture may well be regarded as something added to man's innate biological capacities; it provides instruments which enlarge or may even substitute for biological functions and which to a limited degree compensate for biological limitations—as in insuring that the biological fact of death does not always mean that what the dead individual has learned is lost to humanity.

Nevertheless, I believe this to be a dangerously misleading formulation unless it is properly explained and qualified. In the first place, as Linton and others have documented, it is an observed fact that most groups elaborate certain aspects of their culture far beyond maximal relative utility or survival value. In other words, not all culture is adaptive—in the sense of promoting sheer physical survival. At times indeed it does exactly the opposite. We must bring in the concept of adjustment (that is, lowering of tension) as well as that of adaptation. In the second place, aspects of culture which once directly promoted survival may persist even after they have ceased to have survival value. An analysis of contemporary Navaho culture will disclose many features which cannot possibly be construed as adaptations to the total environment in which Navahos now find themselves. However, it is altogether likely that these represent survivals, with modifications which have occurred during the centuries, of cultural forms which were adaptive in one or another environment in which certain ancestors of the contemporary Navaho lived prior to entering the Southwest.

FIRST ANTHROPOLOGIST: In other words, you are saying that no way of reacting is taken over by the group unless it has direct adaptive or adjustive value for individuals as such (or as constituting a group) at the time the design for living becomes cultural.

THIRD ANTHROPOLOGIST: Right. The main point is that, as Boas so often insisted, we cannot account for complex historical changes by any simple formula. While many patterned ways of reacting unquestionably represent almost inevitable responses to an external environment in which the group lives or once lived, there are certainly also many cases where the inexorable conditions of action merely limit the possibility of response rather than eventually compelling one and only one mode of adaptation. These "choices" are probably themselves determined—if we make our theoretical system wide enough to encompass all possible types of factors. But, within the more usual frame of reference, they are the "accidents of history."

Let me give an example or two. In a society where the chief really has great power, one particular chief happens to be born with an endocrine imbalance which brings about certain (to that group) unusual idiosyncrasies in personality. By virtue of his position, he is able to bring about certain modifications in the way of life of his group (say, in religion) which are congenial to his "temperament." It may be argued, and it may be true, that no amount of authority could insure the persistence of such alterations unless they somehow had adjustive or adaptive value for more than a single individual. I do not believe that the empirical evidence bearing on this problem has been sufficiently analyzed to permit a definite answer to the question. But what is certain is that such a circumstance has been known to be followed by relatively temporary or relatively enduring changes in group designs for living—sometimes primarily in the form of strong "reaction formations." The fact of the chief's position and all that was consequent upon it is not an accident from the point of view of the theoretical systems usually employed in analyzing such steps. The unusual temperament is, however, due to an "accident of the genetic process."

Or, suppose that in the same group a chief dies as a relatively young man, leaving an infant as his heir. This has been observed to result in a marked crystallization of two factions around two rival older relatives, each of whom has about an equally valid claim to act as "regent." Through these circumstances a complete and lasting splitting off of two groups has been observed to take place. Each group thereafter has pursued its own separate destiny, and the end result is the formation of two distinguishable variants of what was at one time a more or less homogeneous culture. Now, to be sure, it is likely that the original factional lines had their bases in "economic," demographic, or other "external" conditions. Yet, had it not been for the "accidental" death of the one chief in his early maturity, the society might have indefinitely continued intact as an equilibrium of opposed tendencies. In short, the form and the mesh of the "sieve which is history" must be seen and shaped not only by the total "environment" at any given point in time but also by individual "psychological" and "accidental" factors.

FIRST ANTHROPOLOGIST: Could we then say that culture includes all those ways of feeling, thinking, and acting which are not inevitable as a result of human biological equipment and process and (or) objective external situations?

THIRD ANTHROPOLOGIST: My objection to that definition would be: first, that this defines culture as a "residual category"—which is logically undesirable; second, I believe it is better to mention explicitly the time dimension as indicated by the phrase "historically created."

FIRST ANTHROPOLOGIST: This suggests also the cumulative nature of culture.

THIRD ANTHROPOLOGIST: Yes, provided we remember that in another sense culture is not exactly "cumulative." Culture at any given time-point has likewise the property of uniqueness. That is why it is absolutely essential to include the word "selective" in any definition.

THE LAWYER: I can see that there has been a selection of possible modes of behavior and that these selections then may become established in a group, but aren't you overemphasizing this aspect? It seems to me that in common sense terms if we understand human nature, and if we then make our interpretation in the light of the concrete situation at hand, we get along very well.

FIRST ANTHROPOLOGIST: No, if you will look beyond the records of our own time and place you will find that the matter is not so simple. There are certain recurrent and inevitable human problems, and the ways in which man can meet them are limited by his biological equipment and by certain facts of the external world. Anthropologists have perhaps in recent years been too much preoccupied with the diversity found upon the earth and have neglected the basic similarities. But apart from these important but very general resemblances, the conception of the one single, unchanging "human nature" is a reassuring fiction of folklore. When it comes to details, there are "human natures." For example, old age is a situation to which all human beings who live long enough must adjust. But we find that in some human societies the old, regardless of their particular achievements, are entitled to respect and even to authority. In other societies, we find that the old, again regardless of individual differences, are ordinarily treated with relative indifference or active contempt. In still other societies, whether or not an aged person is treated with deference or with neglect seems to depend on his own past history rather than upon his period of life. Thus we see that though age is a biological fact it is always culturally defined. This fact of the plasticity of "human nature" is the widest and the most certain induction which anthropologists can derive from the cross-cultural record.

The precise *forms* which biological and social processes take are myriad, and these *forms* are cultural. Let us take an instance where, as so often, biological and social facts are intertwined. In many human groups which have been described, the physically weak have been, almost without qualification, at a disadvantage.

In some groups, however, it has been observed that there have been effective deterrents against the strong taking advantage of the weak. Bullying has been punished by social disapproval and hence has actually been relatively rare. In a few societies, there is a tendency to give privileged positions to the physically weak or to certain types of the physically weak.

Just as sociobiological situations or purely social situations can be stylized, so also some purely biological situations may be stylized. Take vomiting, for example. Vomiting is a biological event and it can be produced by causes which are solely biological. But in other cases, although individual differences in neurological equipment and in previous experience play their part, the event sequence which would lead up to vomiting could never be predicted purely on the basis of biological knowledge. For instance, Americans who have eaten rattlesnake have been known to vomit upon being told what they had been fed. Since rattlesnake meat is perfectly nutritious, the vomiting is produced by some extrabiological factor.

Similar illustrations could be given for other biological processes, such as weeping and fainting. These biological processes are also caught in a cultural web, as it were. Here is a particularly telling example. The newborn infant excretes whenever tensions in bladder and colon reach a certain level of intensity. Before long, however, biological rhythms have surrendered to superimposed designs which are not directly derived from the facts of biology. Most adult human beings in normal health defecate only once or at most twice during a day. This tends to occur within rather fixed hours and, in many human groups, only at certain designated places and under defined conditions as to who else may (should) or may (should) not be present. So interesting and so vital is the interrelation of the biological and the cultural dimensions of human behavior that some anthropologists feel the study of these connections to be the differential feature of anthropology.

THE PSYCHOLOGIST: Isn't this just a kind of "conditioning"?

THE BIOLOGIST: Yes, couldn't we call it simply "environmental conditioning"?

FIRST ANTHROPOLOGIST: A very special sort of conditioning. No group deliberately sets out to train its children to vomit under certain circumstances. This result, rather, is a kind of incidental by-product of a style of life or of some aspect of such a style of life.

THIRD ANTHROPOLOGIST: The naïve—and very powerful—view is that we have individual organisms (they can be seen) and that they exist in an external world (which can also be seen and described). This is the view which "common sense" takes, and it is very hard to shake oneself out of this apparently sensible formula. But it simply won't cover the facts, the awareness of the external environment is too highly selective for that. Put down various groups of adults who have been trained in different social traditions in the same desert island. What they see in their surroundings will not be identical at all. Nor will, of course, the techniques by which they endeavor to adjust themselves to the surroundings. Between culturalized men and their environment there exists, as it were, a screen which is intangible and invisible but none the less real. This screen is "culture."

THE PSYCHOLOGIST: In trying to understand a single concrete act on the part of an individual I have found it helpful to ask these questions:

1. What are the innate endowments and limitations of the individual?

2. What has his total experience been prior to the act we are studying?

3. What is his immediate situation?

FIRST ANTHROPOLOGIST: No one of these variables can be elucidated in a completely satisfactory manner without introducing the concept "culture."

1. Except in the case of newborn babies and of individuals born with clear-cut structural or functional abnormalities we can observe "innate endowments" only as modified by cultural training. In a hospital in New Mexico where Zuni Indian, Navaho Indian, and white American babies are born it is possible to classify the newly arrived infants as hyperactive, average, and hypoactive. Some babies from each "racial" group will fall into each category, though a higher proportion of the white babies will fall into the hyperactive class. But if a Navaho baby, a Zuni baby, and a white baby—all classified as about equally hyperactive at birth—are again observed at the age of two years, the Zuni baby—*as compared with the white child*—will no longer seem given to quick and restless activity, though he may seem so as compared with other Zunis of the same age. The Navaho child is likely to fall in between as contrasted with the Zuni and the white though he will probably still seem hyperactive if seen against the standard of a series of Navaho youngsters.

2. The sheer factual description of the individual's experience doesn't get us very far. His interpretation of these events is indispensable, and this will be made, at least in part, in terms of

norms current in his group. Losing a mother tends to mean one thing in one society, quite a different thing in another society.

3. Naturally, the immediate situation as well as past experience is reacted to, not in purely rational objective fashion but in terms of the situation as meaningfully defined by the participant. Almost no human situations are viewed in ways which are altogether a consequence of the individual's experience. Culture is—among other things—a set of ready-made definitions of the situation which each participant only slightly retailors in his own idiomatic way.

THE BIOLOGIST: May we get back to some examples?

THIRD ANTHROPOLOGIST: If we are to begin at the beginning we start off, I suppose, with the basic observation of the diversity of human behavior.

A few years ago a young man of American parentage who had been reared in a Chinese family from infancy on paid his first visit to America. Reporters commented not only upon his apparently complete bewilderment in the American way of life, but also upon the fact that his walk, arm and hand movements, and facial expression were "Chinese—not American." They insisted that one had to fix one's attention upon his blond hair and blue eyes to convince oneself that he was of white stock at all. Here the point is that an individual's acts and attitudes not only failed to resemble those of his own close relatives in this country but that they resembled those of all members of an alien physical group and contrasted with those of all members of his own physical group.

To take a less dramatic but better-known illustration, a third generation Italian, unless he has been reared in the Italian colony of a large American city, shows "social habits" which resemble those of "Old Americans" much more closely than they do those of residents of Italy. The influence of the various domestic and geographical environments in which these Italian-Americans grew up was not so powerful but that we can recognize common tendencies in all of them which ally them to other "Americans."

The variations and similarities which obtain between groups of human beings must also both be clarified. Groups of the same strain of physical heredity show great differences in behavioral norms and groups of unquestionably different strains show great similarities. It has been remarked by many observers in the Japanese relocation centers that Japanese who have been born and brought up in this country, especially those who were reared apart from any large colony of Japanese, resemble their white neighbors in all behavioral characteristics much more closely than they do their own Japanese relatives who had been educated in Japan and then immigrated to this country.

THE PSYCHOLOGIST: This proves that human beings can learn from each other—and we knew that already. What proof is there that if all white Americans were wiped out the Japanese-American wouldn't eventually revert to designs for living highly similar to those characteristics of the Japanese of Japan?

THIRD ANTHROPOLOGIST: Obviously, there can be no certain answer to such a hypothetical question. But note carefully that the concept of culture as I have phrased it in no way denies the possible importance of innate factors. It does not assert the patent absurdity that the behavior of all Japanese (of Japan) or the behavior of all white Americans is minutely identical. It says merely that the behavior of each group though showing much individual variation still shows certain common tendencies within the one group which contrast sharply with those within the other group. Since the common tendencies of the American group are also to a perceptible degree exhibited by large numbers of individuals of Japanese racial stock—although it is not claimed that their behavior shows precisely the same modalities as the white Americans—it is argued that these shared trends may be attributed to the presence and influence of communicable designs for living.

THE ECONOMIST: Perhaps if Japan were depopulated and colonized by white Americans these would, within a certain number of generations, develop social definitions of the situation which would hardly be distinguishable from those characteristic of the Japanese today.

THIRD ANTHROPOLOGIST: The natural environments of the United States are various, and yet the Americans of the arid Southwest and of rainy Oregon still behave in ways which are easily distinguishable from inhabitants of the Australian desert on the one hand and from those of verdant England on the other.

Tribes like the Pueblo Navaho, living in substantially identical natural and biological environments, still manifest very different ways of life. The English who live in the Hudson Bay region and those who live in British Somaliland still share common designs for living. It is true, of course, that the different natural environments are responsible for observable alterations. But the striking fact is that, in spite of the tremendous environmental differences, shared designs for living still persist.

The inhabitants of two not widely separated villages in New

Mexico, Ramah and Fence Lake, are both of the so-called "Old American" physical stock. Almost certainly a physical anthropologist would say they represented random samples from the same physical population. The rocky tablelands, the annual rainfall and its distribution, the flora and fauna surrounding the two villages hardly show perceptible variations. The density of population and the distance from a main highway is almost exactly the same in the two cases. Nevertheless, even the casual visitor immediately notices distinctions. There are characteristic differences in dress; the style of the houses is different; there is a saloon in one town and not in the other. A completion of this catalog would conclusively demonstrate that very different patterns of life prevail in the two settlements. Why? Primarily because the two villages represent variants of the general Anglo-American social traditions. They have slightly different cultures.

THE PHILOSOPHER: There are two questions upon which I must pin you down. The first is: where is the locus of culture—in society or in the individual?

THIRD ANTHROPOLOGIST: Asking the question that way poses a false dilemma. Remember that "culture" is an abstraction. Hence culture as a concrete, observable entity does not exist anywhere—unless you wish to say that it exists in the "minds" of the men who make the abstractions. The objects and events from which we make our abstractions do have an observable existence. But culture is like a map. Just as a map isn't the territory but an abstract representation of the territory so also a culture is an abstract description of trends toward uniformity in the words, acts, and artifacts of human groups. The data, then, from which we come to know culture are not derived from an abstraction such as "society" but from direct observable behavior and behavioral products. Note, however, that "culture" may be said to be "supraindividual" in at least two nonmystical, perfectly empirical senses:

1. Objects as well as individuals manifest culture.

2. The continuity of culture never depends upon the continued existence of any particular individuals.

THE PHILOSOPHER: Very good. Now my second question: Can "culture" ever be said to be the cause of anything?

THIRD ANTHROPOLOGIST: Not in any very strict or exact way of speaking. In the first place, I would always question the advisability of using the term "cause" in any social science theory. Too much of a unidirectional force is implied. Rather I should use "determinant" with its connotation of interdependence of the relevant forces. But even to say "culture determines" is a very inexact and elliptical way of speaking, justified perhaps in certain circumstances by the convenience of brevity. Inexact, however, it is, because no concrete phenomenon is ever completely and solely determined by culture. Sometimes, to be sure, culture may be the "strategic factor"—that is, the crucial element that determines that a given act tends to be differently carried out in one group than in another or that the fact is somehow not what we would anticipate from a knowledge of the physical and biological forces operative. But "cultural determinism" in any simple or literal sense is as objectionable as any other class of unilateral determinism such as "geographical determinism" or "economic determinism."

Although, in the concrete, the influence of culture is always mediated by men or artifacts, one is nevertheless justified in speaking of culture as *a* determinant of events when a discussion is being carried on at a high level of abstraction—provided the degree of abstraction is not lost sight of. The point may become clearer from an analogy—though all analogies (including this one!) are dangerous. Suppose a man who has a plague which is thought to be due to a postulated but unseen virus enters a city and infects the population. What "causes" the epidemic—the man or the virus? Clearly, either answer is equally correct depending upon the conceptual system within which one is working. We should be too close to reifying an abstraction if we said that, in similar fashion, either men or things can become "hosts" to culture. Also, this metaphor, like the definition of culture as "social heredity" implies too passive a relationship between men and culture—as if culture were a bacteria acquired entirely casually and unknowingly by contact. And yet the simile remains tantalizing. One may even point out that it is less misleading than "social heredity," for genes are acquired in fixed and immutable form—once and for all—at birth, whereas bacteria change with the host and in time, though a given species remains recognizable in spite of this variation according to different hosts.

THE PHILOSOPHER: Could you relate what you have just said to the arguments over the proposition of Spengler, Sorokin, and others that cultures have their own independent laws of growth and decay?

THIRD ANTHROPOLOGIST: If what I have said is correct, anthropologists have probably been too hasty in their rejections of these theories. The theories you mention have, to greater or lesser degree, been phrased unfortunately so that condemnations of them as "mystical" or "metaphysical" can be given superficial plausibility. But an anthropologist who really wishes to understand these interpretations can "translate" them into his own conceptual scheme so that, if the levels of abstraction be kept straight, they seem to merit partial acceptance or at least careful re-examination.

For, while no culture is "superorganic" in the sense that it would continue to "exist" after all the human beings who shared it had died and all the nonhuman manifestations of that culture had been destroyed, still a culture that is a going concern has properties which exhibit some independence from the forces with which the culture is in interaction. One of the diagnostic features of a culture is its selectivity. Most specific needs can be satisfied in a wide variety of ways but "the culture selects" only one or a very few of the organically and physically possible modes. "The culture selects" is, to be sure, a metaphorical way of speaking. The *original* choice was necessarily made by an individual and then followed by other individuals (or it wouldn't have become culture). But from the angle of those individuals who later learn this bit of culture the existence of this element in a design for living has the *effect* of a selection which was not made by these human beings as a reaction to their own particular situation but was rather a choice made by individuals long gone but which still tends to bind our contemporary actors.

Such a selective awareness of the natural environment, such a stereotyped interpretation of man's place in the world is not merely inclusive; by implication it also excludes other possible alternatives. Because of the "strain toward consistency" in cultures such inclusions and exclusions are meaningful far beyond the specific activity which is overtly involved. Just as the "choice" of an individual at a crucial epoch commits him in certain directions for the rest of his life, so the original bents, trends, "interests" which become established in the designs for living of a newly formed society tend to channel a culture in some directions as opposed to others. Subsequent variations in the culture—both those which arise internally and those which are a response to contact with other cultures or to changes in the natural environment—are not random. In some sense, at least, there is probably "cultural orthogenesis" as well as biological orthogenesis.

THE LAWYER: Now I only wonder how you are going to make the transition from "culture" to "a culture." No physicist speaks of "a gravity."

FIRST ANTHROPOLOGIST: Surely when the physicist "explains" the falling of certain concrete bodies at a given time and place he must—if he is to be precise as to details—get beyond the general principle of "gravity." He must describe the particular field of gravity which affected those bodies at just that time. Similarly "a culture" is just a convenient short expression for "a special field of that force known as culture."

"CULTURE" AS A DESCRIPTIVE CONCEPT

THE PHYSICIAN: Can we say that culture in general as a descriptive concept means the accumulated treasury of human creation: books, paintings, buildings, and the like; the knowledge of ways of adjusting to our surroundings, both human and physical; language, customs, and systems of etiquette, ethics, religion, and morals that have been built up through the ages?

FIRST ANTHROPOLOGIST: In referring to culture as "a storehouse of adjustive responses" and as a human creation you strike notes upon which we would all now agree. But the objections to an enumerative definition and to a definition which lists, in part, concrete phenomena are serious.

SECOND ANTHROPOLOGIST: Yes, I also now fully share the view that, even at a descriptive level, culture must be considered as an abstraction. Even a "culture trait" is, in a sense, an "ideal type." Take, for instance, the alarm clock. No two are ever exactly alike: some are large, some are small; some work perfectly and others don't; some are shiny and some are painted in soft colors. If we examine minutely enough several which have just been produced by the same factory, we should find that even these show small differences.

THE BUSINESSMAN: Let me take this idea a little further. A bank is a general term applying to all the specific institutions that conduct certain types of financial transactions. Doesn't culture, then, as a descriptive concept mean the sum of all such generalizations?

FIRST ANTHROPOLOGIST: I would prefer to say "a summation of all the ideas for standardized types of behavior."

THIRD ANTHROPOLOGIST: The notion of defining culture, in a descriptive sense, as a set of blueprints for action in the widest sense (including feeling, of course) is very attractive. And it is probably perfectly sound, provided that it is clearly realized that such a statement is made from the standpoint of the observer, the student of culture, rather than from that of the participant in culture. For the participant much of culture is unverbalized and probably in a still wider sense implicit.

THE PSYCHIATRIST: I agree. I have always protested against such statements as "culture consists of ideas" because we know well from comparative psychiatry that there is also such a thing as "culturally standardized unreason."

FIRST ANTHROPOLOGIST: Yes, while a great deal of culture is cognitive and is cognitively transmitted, the place of feeling bulks enormously.

THE ECONOMIST: Perhaps we need three categories: rational, irrational, and nonrational.

THIRD ANTHROPOLOGIST: Quite. In Pareto's jargon, some of culture is "logical," some is "illogical," but probably the highest proportion is "non-logical."

FOURTH ANTHROPOLOGIST: May we then give the following substantive definition: *By culture we mean all those historically created designs for living, explicit and implicit, rational, irrational, and nonrational, which exist at any given time as potential guides for the behavior of men.*

THE LAWYER: I have only one question: Why is it necessary to say "at any given time"?

FOURTH ANTHROPOLOGIST: Because culture is constantly being created and lost. No definition must suggest that culture is static or completely stable.

SECOND ANTHROPOLOGIST: Does "designs for living" mean that you intend the concept to include only "theory"—that is, the ways in which things ought to be done or felt?

FOURTH ANTHROPOLOGIST: No, "design" denotes both "theory" and "practice." In our own professional jargon "design" is meant to designate both "behavioral patterns" and "ideal patterns." Remember that culture is always a conceptual construct. The anthropologist not only observes that people say (or otherwise indicate) that they have certain standards for behavior, violations of which are punished by great or small sanctions; he equally notes that even disapproved behavior systems tend to fall into certain modalities. From the observer's standpoint it is as if people were unconsciously adhering to certain "blueprints" or "designs" also for conduct which is prohibited or indifferent from the standpoint of shared "moral" norms.

THE LAWYER: May we have a definition of "a culture," in the descriptive sense?

FIRST ANTHROPOLOGIST: *A culture is a historically derived system of explicit and implicit designs for living, which tends to be shared by all or specially designated members of a group.*

THIRD ANTHROPOLOGIST: That satisfies me. The word "system" does a lot of work in that definition. It suggests abstraction. It directly implies that a culture is organized, that it is selective.

THE PSYCHOLOGIST: I like the word "tends." Some of us have in the past felt cheated because we have been assured that studying a culture would give us the common ground against which various personality figures emerged. Our own investigations along this line seem to indicate that it was misleading to depict any single background as being in any literal sense "common" to all members of any group.

FIRST ANTHROPOLOGIST: Yes, just as "tends" reminds us that no individual thinks, feels, or acts precisely as the "design" indicates that he will or should, so also "specially designated" is a reminder that not all of the "blueprints" which constitute a culture are meant to apply to each and every individual. There are sex differentials, age differentials, class differentials, prestige differentials, and so on.

THIRD ANTHROPOLOGIST: It seems to me that you have enunciated two related but separate propositions. It is important that we should not mix them. First, there is the proposition that the sharing is tendency rather than fact. As L. K. Frank puts it, what we can actually observe is the "idiomatic version of each personality's utilization of cultural patterns." And he goes on to make a useful analogy something along these lines:

> We can abstract the regularities and uniformities and likewise observe the personality distortions and skewings, as we have learned to observe the statistical regularities of a gas but also recognize and acknowledge the irregular and non-conforming behavior of individual molecules of that gas.

Second, there is the proposition of the compartmentalization and segmentation of a culture. While each individual's utilization of pattern is idiomatic, some sets of patterns are always felt as appropriate for certain categories of individuals. A background of culture is to be regarded as approximately constant—not for every individual in all groups which have some continuity and functional wholeness, but rather for those who occupy the same set of statuses or perform about the same roles within the total group.

FIRST ANTHROPOLOGIST: Correct. But this important fact must not obscure another fact of equal or greater significance. At least in those groups which have some historical continuity and which are generally designated as "societies," all individuals tend to share common interpretations of the external world and man's place in it. To some degree every individual is affected by this common "view of life." A culture is made up of overt patterned ways of behaving, feeling, and reacting. But it also includes a characteristic set of unstated premises or hypotheses which vary greatly in different societies. Thus one group unconsciously assumes that every chain of actions has a goal and that when this goal is reached tension will be reduced or disappear. To another group, thinking based upon this assumption is meaningless: they see life not as a series of purposive sequences but as made up of experiences which are satisfying in and of themselves, rather than as means to ends.

THE PHILOSOPHER: Are you saying that each culture is integrated about certain dominant interests and in accord with certain postulates and assumptions?

THIRD ANTHROPOLOGIST: Probably very few cultures indeed can be regarded as completely integrated systems. Most cultures, like most personalities, can be regarded as equilibria of opposed tendencies. But even in cultures which do not approach complete integration one may detect certain recurrent themes in a variety of specific contexts.

THE PSYCHOLOGIST: Are you talking about what anthropologists have called the "absolute logics" of a people or about what others refer to as "the logic of the sentiments"?

THIRD ANTHROPOLOGIST: Both. Every people not only has a sentiment structure which is to some degree unique but also a more or less coherent body of distinctive presuppositions about the world. This last is really a borderland between reason and feeling. Perhaps in a certain ultimate sense the "logic" of all peoples is the same. But their premises are certainly different.

THE PHILOSOPHER: Do you mean the conscious, the stated premises—what a logician would call the "postulates"—or the unstated premises or "assumptions"?

THIRD ANTHROPOLOGIST: Both. Certainly some of the most critical premises of any culture are often unstated, even by the intellectuals of the group. Likewise the basic categories of "thinking" are implicit, save, perhaps, to a tiny minority in rationally sophisticated societies like our own.

FOURTH ANTHROPOLOGIST: If the premises and the system of categories are unconscious, how are they transmitted?

FIRST ANTHROPOLOGIST: Mainly, probably, through the language. Especially the morphology of a language preserves the unformulated philosophy of the group. For example, Dorothy Lee has shown that among the Trobriand Islanders "the sequence of events does not automatically fall into the mold of causal or telic relationship." Because of the mold which grammar imposes upon their "thinking" these people find certain types of communication with Europeans difficult since Europeans almost inevitably talk in causal terms.

The very morphology of language inevitably begs far-reaching questions of metaphysics and of values. A language is not merely an instrument for communication and for rousing the emotions. Every language is also a device for categorizing experience. The continuum of experience can be sliced very differently. We tend all too easily to assume that the distinctions which Indo-European languages (or our own particular language) force us to make are given by the world of nature. As a matter of fact, comparative linguistics shows very plainly that any speech demands unconscious conceptual selection on the part of its speaker. No human organism can respond to all the kaleidoscopic stimuli which impinge upon it from the external world. What we notice, what we talk about, what we feel as important is in some part a function of our linguistic patterns. Because these linguistic habits tend to remain as unquestioned "background phenomena," each people tends to take its fundamental categories, its unstated basic premises for granted. It is assumed that others will "think the same way," for "it's only human nature." When others face the same body of data but come to different conclusions, it is seldom thought that they might be proceeding from different premises. Rather, it is inferred that they are "stupid" or "illogical" or "obstinate."

FOURTH ANTHROPOLOGIST: How does it happen that different people have different systems of categories?

FIRST ANTHROPOLOGIST: A language is one aspect of a culture. Therefore, we must refer to the "accidents of history" and to all the other forces which we mentioned as producing the forms of culture. Each individual tends to classify his experiences along the lines laid down by the grammar to which he is habituated, but the grammar itself is a cultural product. Dorothy Lee has made this point very well:

True enough, the thought of the individual must run along its grooves; but these grooves, themselves, are a heritage from individuals who laid them down in an unconscious effort to express their attitudes toward the world. Grammar contains in crystalized form the accumulated and accumulating experience, the Weltanschauung of a people.

THIRD ANTHROPOLOGIST: There is perhaps also another angle to the perpetuation of cultural organization, particularly at the implicit level. This is the culturally prescribed system of child training. If all adults have been subjected to about the same deprivations and frustrations during socialization, they tend to see life in somewhat the same terms. Roheim says, "The dominant idea of a culture may be an addiction but it is always a system formation that can be explained on the basis of the infantile situation." Margaret Mead deals with the relation of "infantile traumas" to the one or more focal points in each culture under the conception of "plot in culture."

FOURTH ANTHROPOLOGIST: Although partially won over, I am still unhappy about this term "implicit culture."

THIRD ANTHROPOLOGIST: A conception of this order is made necessary by certain eminently practical considerations. It is well documented that programs of the British Colonial services or of our own Indian service which have been carefully thought through for their continuity with the cultural inventory and with the overt cultural patterns, nevertheless fail to work out. Intensive investigation also does not reveal any flaws in the set-up at the technological level. The program is sabotaged by resistance which must be imputed to the manner in which the members of the group have been conditioned by *implicit* designs for living to think and feel in ways which were unexpected to the administrator.

FIRST ANTHROPOLOGIST: Students of culture change are also agreed that the way in which a group accepts, rejects, or readapts borrowed elements cannot be fully understood in terms of direct and explicit functions. The process is also related to the cultural structure, including those portions of it which are implicit. Even after the content of the culture of a group of American Indians has become completely European, its way of life still somehow retains a distinctive flavor, as if the "container" remained "aboriginal."

THIRD ANTHROPOLOGIST: We would freely admit that conceptual instruments which are objective enough and precise enough to deal with the patterning of implicit culture are only beginning to be evolved. The importance of tacit cultural premises and categories is probably obvious enough. But the sheer statement of the presence and absence of these (and of all other features of culture, whether implicit or explicit) is not enough. The full significance of any single element in a cultural design will be seen only when that element is viewed in the total matrix of its relationship to other elements and indeed to other designs. Naturally, this includes accent or emphasis, as well as position. Accent is manifested sometimes through frequency, sometimes through intensity. The indispensable importance of these questions of arrangement and emphasis may be driven home by an analogy. Take a musical chord made up of three notes. If we are told that the three notes in question are A, B, and G, we receive information which is fundamental. But it alone will not enable us to predict the type of sensation which the playing of this chord is likely to evoke in us or in other specified visitors. We need many different sorts of relationship data. Are the notes to be played in that or some other order? What duration will each receive? How will the emphasis, if any, be distributed? We also need, of course, to know whether the cord will be played in the key of C or in the key of B-flat minor, and whether the instrument is to be a piano or an accordion.

THE UTILITY OF THE CONCEPT "CULTURE" IN ITS VARIOUS SENSES

THE BUSINESSMAN: I'd like to interject a practical question: What good is the concept so far as the contemporary world is concerned? What can you do with it?

FIRST ANTHROPOLOGIST: First and foremost I would insist that its use lies in the aid the concept gives to man's endless quest to understand himself and his own behavior. For example, this relatively new idea makes some of the questions which trouble one of the most learned and acute thinkers of our age, Reinhold Niebuhr, seem pseudo-problems. In his recent book *The Nature and Destiny of Man* he argues that the universally human sense of guilt or shame and man's capacity for self-judgment necessitates the assumption of supernatural forces. But these facts are susceptible of self-consistent and relatively simple "explanation" in purely naturalistic terms through the concept of culture. Social life among humans never occurs without a system of "conventional understandings" which are transmitted more or less intact from generation to generation. Any individual is familiar with some of these and they constitute a set of standards against which he judges himself. To the extent that he fails to conform he experiences discomfort, because the intimate conditioning of infancy and childhood put great pressure on him to internalize these norms, and his unconscious tendency is to associate withdrawal of love and protection or active punishment with deviation.

This and other issues which have puzzled philosophers and scientists for countless generations become fully or partially understandable by means of this fresh conceptual instrument. But if your interest is in action rather than thought, the principal claim which can be made for culture is that it helps us enormously toward predicting human behavior. One of the reasons that such prediction has not been very successful thus far has been that it has been carried out, for the most part, on the naïve assumption of a minutely homogenous "human nature." In the framework of this assumption all human thinking proceeds from the same premises; all human beings are motivated by the same needs and goals. But in the cultural framework we see that, while the ultimate logic of all peoples may be the same (and thus communication and understanding are possible), the thought processes depart from radically different premises—especially unconscious or unstated premises. But those who have the cultural outlook are more likely to look beneath the surface and bring the culturally determined premises to the light of day. This may well not bring about immediate agreement and harmony, but it will at least facilitate a more rational approach to the problem of "international understanding," and to diminish friction between groups within a nation.

The conception of culture also encourages paying attention to the more concrete aspects of ways of life other than our own. It suggests, for example, the usefulness of knowledge of alien "customs" if we wish to predict how a foreign people will behave in a certain situation and of respect for these same customs if we wish to get along with that foreign people.

A culture is not only a reticulum of patterned means for satisfying needs but equally a network of stylized goals for individual and group achievement. If we need to predict human action we must not assume that the effective motivations in all human groups are the same. Even the primary drives, like hunger and sex, though biological "givens," are subtly modified and channeled by culture. What kind of food, what type of sexual experience will be most striven after cannot be predicted through biological knowledge alone. There exists for every human group "secondary drives." Among us, for example, the "need" for cars or radios often goads individuals even harder than that for sexual satisfaction.

Every culture is also a structure of expectancies. If we know a culture, we know what various classes of individuals within it expect from each other—and from outsiders of various categories. We know what types of activity are held to be inherently gratifying.

SECOND ANTHROPOLOGIST: One great contribution is that of providing some persons with some detachment from the conscious and unconscious emotional values of their own culture. The phrase "some detachment" must be emphasized. An individual who viewed the designs for living of his group with complete detachment would almost certainly be disoriented and unhappy. But I can prefer (that is, feel affectively attached to) American manners while at the same time perceiving certain graces in English manners which are lacking or more grossly expressed in ours. Thus while unwilling to forget that I am an American and hence with no desire to ape English drawing room behaviors, I can still derive a lively pleasure from association with English people on "social" occasions. Whereas if I have no detachment, if I am utterly provincial, I am likely to regard English manners as utterly ridiculous, uncouth, perhaps even immoral. With that attitude I shall certainly not get on well with the English and I am likely to resent bitterly any modification of our manners in the English or any other direction. Such attitudes clearly do not make for international understanding, friendship, and cooperation. They equally make for a too rigid social structure. Anthropological documents and anthropological teachings are valuable, therefore, in that they tend to emancipate individuals from a too perfervid allegiance to every item in the cultural inventory. The person who has been exposed to the anthropological perspective by incongruity is more likely, on the one hand, to "live and let live" both within his own society and in his dealings with members of other societies; on the other hand, he will probably be more flexible in regard to needful changes in social organization to meet changed technological structure and changed economies.

THIRD ANTHROPOLOGIST: In a way, I would say that the most important implication of "culture" for action is the profound truth (so frequently overlooked by every sort of "social planners") that you can never start with a clean slate so far as human beings are concerned. No human being or group of human beings can ever freshly see the world in which they move. Every human is born into a world defined by already existing cultural patterns. Just as an individual who has lost his memory is no longer "normal," so the idea that at any point in its history a society can become completely emancipated from its past culture is inconceivable. This is the source of the tragic failure of the Weimar constitution in Germany. Seen in detached context, it was an admirable document. But it failed miserably in actual life, partly because it provided for no continuity with existent designs for acting, feeling, and thinking.

Finally, as the word "design" in our definitions implies, every culture has organization as well as content. This fact carries with it the highly practical warning to administrators and lawmakers that a "custom" which it is desired to abolish or modify cannot be isolated. Any change may have repercussions in areas of behavior where they are least expected.

Steel Axes for Stone-Age Australians

by
Lauriston Sharp

I

LIKE OTHER AUSTRALIAN aboriginals, the Yir Yoront group which lives at the mouth of the Coleman River on the west coast of Cape York Peninsula originally had no knowledge of metals. Technologically their culture was of the old stone age or paleolithic type. They supported themselves by hunting and fishing, and obtained vegetables and other materials from the bush by simple gathering techniques. Their only domesticated animal was the dog; they had no cultivated plants of any kind. Unlike some other aboriginal groups, however, the Yir Yoront did have polished stone axes hafted in short handles which were most important in their economy.

Towards the end of the nineteenth century metal tools and other European artifacts began to filter into the Yir Yoront territory. The flow increased with the gradual expansion of the white frontier outward from southern and eastern Queensland. Of all the items of western technology thus made available, the hatchet, or short handled steel axe, was the most acceptable to and the most highly valued by all aboriginals.

In the mid 1930's an American anthropologist lived alone in the bush among the Yir Yoront for thirteen months without seeing another white man. The Yir Yoront were thus still relatively isolated and continued to live an essentially independent economic existence, supporting themselves entirely by means of their old stone age techniques. Yet their polished stone axes were disappearing fast and being replaced by steel axes which came to

From *Human Organization*. 11 (1952), pp. 17–22. Reprinted by permission of the Society for Applied Anthropology.

them in considerable numbers, directly or indirectly, from various European sources to the south.

What changes in the life of the Yir Yoront still living under aboriginal conditions in the Australian bush could be expected as a result of their increasing possession and use of the steel axe?

II. THE COURSE OF EVENTS

Events leading up to the introduction of the steel axe among the Yir Yoront begin with the advent of the second known group of Europeans to reach the shores of the Australian continent. In 1623 a Dutch expedition landed on the coast where the Yir Yoront now live.[1] In 1935 the Yir Yoront were still using the few cultural items recorded in the Dutch log for the aboriginals they encountered. To this cultural inventory the Dutch added beads and pieces of iron which they offered in an effort to attract the frightened "Indians." Among these natives metal and beads have disappeared, together with any memory of this first encounter with whites.

The next recorded contact in this area was in 1864. Here there is more positive assurance that the natives concerned were the immediate ancestors of the Yir Yoront community. These aboriginals had the temerity to attack a party of cattle men who were driving a small herd from southern Queensland through the length of the then unknown Cape York Peninsula to a newly established government station at the northern tip.[2] Known as the "Battle of the Mitchell River," this was one of the rare instances in which Australian aboriginals stood up to European gunfire for any length of time. A diary kept by the cattle men records that: ". . . ten carbines poured volley after volley into them from all directions, killing and wounding with every shot with very little return, nearly all their spears having already been expended. . . . About thirty being killed, the leader thought it prudent to hold his hand, and let the rest escape. Many more must have been wounded and probably drowned, for fifty-nine rounds were counted as discharged." The European party was in the Yir Yoront area for three days; they then disappeared over the horizon to the north and never returned. In the almost three-year-long anthropological investigation conducted some seventy years later—in all

---

[1] An account of this expedition from Amboina is given in R. Logan Jack, *Northmost Australia*, 2 vols. (London, 1921), vol. 1, pp. 18–57.

[2] R. Logan Jack, op. cit. pp. 298–335.

the material of hundreds of free association interviews, in texts of hundreds of dreams and myths, in genealogies, and eventually in hundreds of answers to direct and indirect questioning on just this particular matter—there was nothing that could be interpreted as a reference to this shocking contact with Europeans.

The aboriginal accounts of their first remembered contact with whites begin in about 1900 with references to persons known to have had sporadic but lethal encounters with them. From that time on whites continued to remain on the southern periphery of Yir Yoront territory. With the establishment of cattle stations (ranches) to the south, cattle men made occasional excursions among the "wild black-fellows" in order to inspect the country and abduct natives to be trained as cattle boys and "house girls." At least one such expedition reached the Coleman River where a number of Yir Yoront men and women were shot for no apparent reason.

About this time the government was persuaded to sponsor the establishment of three mission stations along the seven-hundred-mile western coast of the Peninsula in an attempt to help regulate the treatment of natives. To further this purpose a strip of coastal territory was set aside as an aboriginal reserve and closed to further white settlement.

In 1915, an Anglican mission station was established near the mouth of the Mitchell River, about a three-day march from the heart of the Yir Yoront country. Some Yir Yoront refused to have anything to do with the mission, others visited it occasionally, while only a few eventually settled more or less permanently in one of the three "villages" established at the mission.

Thus the majority of the Yir Yoront continued to live their old self-supporting life in the bush, protected until 1942 by the government reserve and the intervening mission from the cruder realities of the encroaching new order from the south. To the east was poor, uninhabited country. To the north were other bush tribes extending on along the coast to the distant Archer River Presbyterian mission with which the Yir Yoront had no contact. Westward was the shallow Gulf of Carpentaria on which the natives saw only a mission lugger making its infrequent dry season trips to the Mitchell River. In this protected environment for over a generation the Yir Yoront were able to recuperate from shocks received at the hands of civilized society. During the 1930's their raiding and fighting, their trading and stealing of women, their evisceration and two- or three-year care of their dead, and their totemic ceremonies continued, apparently uninhibited by western influence. In 1931 they killed a European who wandered into their territory from the east, but the investigating police never approached the group whose members were responsible for the act.

As a direct result of the work of the Mitchell River mission, all Yir Yoront received a great many more western artifacts of all kinds than ever before. As part of their plan for raising native living standards, the missionaries made it possible for aboriginals living at the mission to earn some western goods, many of which were then given or traded to natives still living under bush conditions; they also handed out certain useful articles gratis to both mission and bush aboriginals. They prevented guns, liquor, and damaging narcotics, as well as decimating diseases, from reaching the tribes of this area, while encouraging the introduction of goods they considered "improving." As has been noted, no item of western technology available, with the possible exception of trade tobacco, was in greater demand among all groups of aboriginals than the short handled steel axe. The mission always kept a good supply of these axes in stock; at Christmas parties or other mission festivals they were given away to mission or visiting aboriginals indiscriminately and in considerable numbers. In addition, some steel axes as well as other European goods were still traded in to the Yir Yoront by natives in contact with cattle stations in the south. Indeed, steel axes had probably come to the Yir Yoront through established lines of aboriginal trade long before any regular contact with whites had occurred.

III. RELEVANT FACTORS

If we concentrate our attention on Yir Yoront behavior centering about the original stone axe (rather than on the axe—the object—itself) as a cultural trait or item of cultural equipment, we should get some conception of the role this implement played in aboriginal culture. This, in turn, should enable us to foresee with considerable accuracy some of the results stemming from the displacement of the stone axe by the steel axe.

The production of a stone axe required a number of simple technological skills. With the various details of the axe well in mind, adult men could set about producing it (a task not considered appropriate for women or children). First of all a man had to know the location and properties of several natural resources found in his immediate environment: pliable wood for a handle, which could be doubled or bent over the axe head and bound tightly; bark, which could be rolled into cord for the binding; and gum, to fix the stonehead in the haft. These materials had to be correctly gathered, stored, prepared, cut to size and applied or manipulated. They were in plentiful supply, and could be taken from anyone's property without special permission. Postponing consideration of stone head, the axe could be made by any normal man who had a simple knowledge of nature and of the technological skills involved, together with fire (for heating the gum), and a few simple cutting tools—perhaps the sharp shells of plentiful bivalves.

The use of the stone axe as a piece of capital equipment used in producing other goods indicates its very great importance to the subsistence economy of the aboriginal. Anyone—man, woman, or child—could use the axe; indeed, it was used primarily by women, for their's was the task of obtaining sufficient wood to keep the family campfire burning all day, for cooking or other purposes, and all night against mosquitoes and cold (for in July, winter temperature might drop below 40 degrees). In a normal lifetime a woman would use the axe to cut or knock down literally tons of firewood. The axe was also used to make other tools or weapons, and a variety of material equipment required by the aboriginal in his daily life. The stone axe was essential in the construction of the wet season domed huts which keep out some rain and some insects; of platforms which provide dry storage; of shelters which give shade in the dry summer when days are bright and hot. In hunting and fishing and in gathering vegetable or animal food the axe was also a necessary tool, and in this tropical culture, where preservatives or other means of storage are lacking, the natives spend more time obtaining food than in any other occupation—except sleeping. In only two instances was the use of the stone axe strictly limited to adult men: for gathering wild honey, the most prized food known to the Yir Yoront; and for making the secret paraphernalia for ceremonies. From this brief listing of some of the activities involving the use of the axe, it is easy to understand why there was at least one stone axe in every camp, in every hunting or fighting party, and in every group out on a "walk-about" in the bush.

The stone axe was also prominent in interpersonal relations. Yir Yoront men were dependent upon interpersonal relations for their stone axe heads, since the flat, geologically-recent, alluvial country over which they range provides no suitable stone for this purpose. The stone they used came from quarries four hundred miles to the south, reaching the Yir Yoront through long lines of male trading partners. Some of these chains terminated with the Yir Yoront men, others extended on farther north to other groups, using Yir Yoront men as links. Almost every older adult man had one or more regular trading partners, some to the north and some to the south. He provided his partner or partners in the south with surplus spears, particularly fighting spears tipped with the barbed spines of sting ray which snap into vicious fragments when they penetrate human flesh. For a dozen such spears, some of which he may have obtained from a partner to the north, he would receive one stone axe head. Studies have shown that the sting ray barb spears increased in value as they move south and farther from the sea. One hundred and fifty miles south of Yir Yoront one such spear may be exchanged for one stone axe head. Although actual investigations could not be made, it was presumed that farther south, nearer the quarries, one sting ray barb spear would bring several stone axe heads. Apparently people who acted as links in the middle of the chain and who made neither spears nor axe heads would receive a certain number of each as a middleman's profit.

Thus trading relations, which may extend the individual's personal relationships beyond that of his own group, were associated with spears and axes, two of the most important items in a man's equipment. Finally most of the exchanges took place during the dry season, at the time of the great aboriginal celebrations centering about initiation rites or other totemic ceremonials which attracted hundreds and were the occasion for much exciting activity in addition to trading.

Returning to the Yir Yoront, we find that adult men kept their axes in camp with their other equipment, or carried them when travelling. Thus a woman or child who wanted to use an axe—as might frequently happen during the day—had to get one from a man, use it promptly, and return it in good condition. While a man might speak of "my axe," a woman or child could not.

This necessary and constant borrowing of axes from older men by women and children was in accordance with regular patterns of kinship behavior. A woman would expect to use her husband's axe unless he himself was using it; if unmarried, or if her husband was absent, a woman would go first to her older brother or to her father. Only in extraordinary circumstances would she seek a stone axe from other male kin. A girl, a boy, or a young man would look to a father or an older brother to provide an axe for their use. Older men, too, would follow similar rules if they had to borrow an axe.

It will be noted that all of these social relationships in which the stone axe had a place are pair relationships and that the use of the axe helped to define and maintain their character and the roles of the two individual participants. Every active relationship among the Yir Yoront involved a definite and accepted status of superordination or subordination. A person could have no dealings with another on exactly equal terms. The nearest approach to equality was between brothers, although the older was always superordinate to the younger. Since the exchange of goods in a trading relationship involved a mutual reciprocity, trading partners usually stood in a brotherly type of relationship, although one was always classified as older than the other and would have some advantage in case of dispute. It can be seen that repeated and widespread conduct centering around the use of the axe helped to generalize and standardize these sex, age, and kinship roles both in their normal benevolent and exceptional malevolent aspects.

The status of any individual Yir Yoront was determined not only by sex, age, and extended kin relationships, but also by membership in one of two dozen patrilineal totemic clans into which the entire community was divided.[3] Each clan had literally hundreds of totems, from one or two of which the clan derived its name, and the clan members their personal names. These totems included natural species or phenomena such as the sun, stars, and daybreak, as well as cultural "species": imagined ghosts, rainbow serpents, heroic ancestors; such eternal cultural verities as fires, spears, huts; and such human activities, conditions, or attributes as eating, vomiting, swimming, fighting, babies and corpses, milk and blood, lips and loins. While individual members of such totemic classes or species might disappear or be destroyed, the class itself was obviously ever-present and indestructible. The totems, therefore, lent a permanence and stability to the clans, to the groupings of human individuals who generation after generation were each associated with a set of totems which distinguished one clan from another.

The stone axe was one of the most important of the many totems of the Sunlit Cloud Iguana clan. The names of many members of this clan referred to the axe itself, to activities in which the axe played a vital part, or to the clan's mythical ancestors with whom the axe was prominently associated. When it was necessary to represent the stone axe in totemic ceremonies, only men of this clan exhibited it or pantomimed its use. In secular life, the axe could be made by any man and used by all; but in the sacred realm of the totems it belonged exclusively to the Sunlit Cloud Iguana people.

[3] R. Lauriston Sharp, "Tribes and Totemism in Northeast Australia," *Oceania*, vol. 8 (1939), pp. 254–275, 439–461 (esp. 268–275).

Supporting those aspects of cultural behavior which we have called technology and conduct, is a third area of culture which includes ideas, sentiments, and values. These are most difficult to deal with, for they are latent and covert, and even unconscious, and must be deduced from overt actions and language or other communicating behavior. In this aspect of the culture lies the significance of the stone axe to the Yir Yoront and to their cultural way of life.

The stone axe was an important symbol of masculinity among the Yir Yoront (just as pants, or pipes are to us). By a complicated set of ideas the axe was defined as "belonging" to males, and everyone in the society (except untrained infants) accepted these ideas. Similarly spears, spear throwers, and fire-making sticks were owned only by men and were also symbols of masculinity. But the masculine values represented by the stone axe were constantly being impressed on all members of society by the fact that females borrowed axes but not other masculine artifacts. Thus the axe stood for an important theme of Yir Yoront culture: the superiority and rightful dominance of the male, and the greater value of his concerns and of all things associated with him. As the axe also had to be borrowed by the younger people it represented the prestige of age, another important theme running through Yir Yoront behavior.

To understand the Yir Yoront culture it is necessary to be aware of a system of ideas which may be called their totemic ideology. A fundamental belief of the aboriginal divided time into two great epochs: (1) a distant and sacred period at the beginning of the world when the earth was peopled by mildly marvelous ancestral beings or culture heroes who are in a special sense the forebears of the clans; and (2) a period when the old was succeeded by a new order which includes the present. Originally there was no anticipation of another era supplanting the present. The future would simply be an eternal continuation and reproduction of the present which itself had remained unchanged since the epochal revolution of ancestral times.

The important thing to note is that the aboriginal believed that the present world, as a natural and cultural environment, was and should be simply a detailed reproduction of the world of the ancestors. He believed that the entire universe "is now as it was in the beginning" when it was established and left by the ancestors. The ordinary cultural life of the ancestors became the daily life of the Yir Yoront camps, and the extraordinary life of the ancestors remained extant in the recurring symbolic pantomimes and paraphernalia found only in the most sacred atmosphere of the totemic rites.

Such beliefs, accordingly, opened the way for ideas of what *should be* (because it supposedly *was*) to influence or help determine what actually *is*. A man called Dog-chases-iguana-up-a-tree-and-barks-at-him-all-night had that and other names because he believed his ancestral alter ego had also had them; he was a member of the Sunlit Cloud Iguana clan because his ancestor was; he was associated with particular countries and totems of this same ancestor; during an initiation he played the role of a dog and symbolically attacked and killed certain members of other clans because his ancestor (conveniently either anthropomorphic or kynomorphic) really did the same to the ancestral alter egos of these men; and he would avoid his mother-in-law, joke with a mother's distant brother, and make spears in a certain way because his and other people's ancestors did these things. His behavior in these specific ways was outlined, and to that extent determined for him, by a set of ideas concerning the past and the relation of the present to the past.

But when we are informed that Dog-chases-etc. had two wives from the Spear Black Duck clan and one from the Native Companion clan, one of them being blind, that he had four children with such and such names, that he had a broken wrist and was left handed, all because his ancestor had exactly these same attributes, then we know (though he apparently didn't) that the present has influenced the past, that the mythical world has been somewhat adjusted to meet the exigencies and accidents of the inescapably real present.

There was thus in Yir Yoront ideology a nice balance in which the mythical was adjusted in part to the real world, the real world in part to the ideal pre-existing mythical world, the adjustments occurring to maintain a fundamental tenet of native faith that the present must be a mirror of the past. Thus the stone axe in all its aspects, uses, and associations was integrated into the context of Yir Yoront technology and conduct because a myth, a set of ideas, had put it there.

IV. THE OUTCOME

The introduction of the steel axe indiscriminately and in large numbers into the Yir Yoront technology occurred simultaneously with many other changes. It is therefore impossible to separate all the results of this single innovation. Nevertheless, a number of specific effects of the change from stone to steel axes may be noted, and the steel axe may be used as an epitome of the increasing quantity of European goods and implements received by the aboriginals and of their general influence on the native culture. The use of the steel axe to illustrate such influences would seem to be justified. It was one of the first European artifacts to be adopted for regular use by the Yir Yoront, and whether made of stone or steel, the axe was clearly one of the most important items of cultural equipment they possessed.

The shift from stone to steel axes provided no major technological difficulties. While the aboriginals themselves could not manufacture steel axe heads, a steady supply from outside continued; broken wooden handles could easily be replaced from bush timbers with aboriginal tools. Among the Yir Yoront the new axe was never used to the extent it was on mission or cattle stations (for carpentry work, pounding tent pegs, as a hammer, and so on); indeed, it had so few more uses than the stone axe that its practical effect on the native standard of living was negligible. It did some jobs better, and could be used longer without breakage. These factors were sufficient to make it of value to the native. The white man believed that a shift from steel to stone axe on his part would be a definite regression. He was convinced that his axe was much more efficient, that its use would save time, and that it therefore represented technical "progress" towards goals which he had set up for the native. But this assumption was hardly born out in aboriginal practice. Any leisure time the Yir Yoront might gain by using steel axes or other western tools was not invested in "improving the conditions of life," nor, certainly, in developing aesthetic activities, but in sleep—an art they had mastered thoroughly.

Previously, a man in need of an axe would acquire a stone axe head through regular trading partners from whom he knew what to expect, and was then dependent solely upon a known and adequate natural environment, and his own skills or easily acquired techniques. A man wanting a steel axe, however, was in no such self-reliant position. If he attended a mission festival when steel axes were handed out as gifts, he might receive one either by chance or by happening to impress upon the mission staff that he was one of the "better" bush aboriginals (the missionaries definition of "better" being quite different from that of his bush fellows). Or, again almost by pure chance, he might get some brief job in connection with the mission which would enable him to earn a steel axe. In either case, for older men a preference for the steel axe helped change the situation from one of self-reliance to one of dependence, and a shift in behavior from well-structured or defined situations in technology or conduct to ill-defined situations in conduct alone. Among the men, the older ones whose earlier experience or knowledge of the white man's harshness made them suspicious were particularly careful to avoid having relations with the mission, and thus excluded themselves from acquiring steel axes from that source.

In other aspects of conduct or social relations, the steel axe was even more significantly at the root of psychological stress among the Yir Yoront. This was the result of new factors which the missionary considered beneficial: the simple numerical increase in axes per capita as a result of mission distribution, and distribution directly to younger men, women, and even children. By winning the favor of the mission staff, a woman might be given a steel axe which was clearly intended to be hers, thus creating a situation quite different from the previous custom which necessitated her borrowing an axe from a male relative. As a result a woman would refer to the axe as "mine," a possessive form she was never able to use of the stone axe. In the same fashion, young men or even boys also obtained steel axes directly from the mission, with the result that older men no longer had a complete monopoly of all the axes in the bush community. All this led to a revolutionary confusion of sex, age, and kinship roles, with a major gain in independence and loss of subordination on the part of those who now owned steel axes when they had previously been unable to possess stone axes.

The trading partner relationship was also affected by the new situation. A Yir Yoront might have a trading partner in a tribe to the south whom he defined as a younger brother and over whom he would therefore have some authority. But if the partner were in contact with the mission or had other access to steel axes, his subordination obviously decreased. Among other things, this took some of the excitement away from the dry season fiesta-like tribal gatherings centering around initiations. These had traditionally been the climactic annual occasions for exchanges between trading partners, when a man might seek to acquire a whole year's supply of stone axe heads. Now he might find himself prostituting his wife to almost total strangers in return for steel axes or other white man's goods. With trading partnerships weakened, there was less reason to attend the ceremonies, and less fun for those who did.

Not only did an increase in steel axes and their distribution to women change the character of the relations between individuals (the paired relationships that have been noted), but a previously rare type of relationship was created in the Yir Yoront's conduct toward whites. In the aboriginal society there were few occasions outside of the immediate family when an individual would initiate action to several other people at once. In any average group, in accordance with the kinship system, while a person might be superordinate to several people to whom he could suggest or command action, he was also subordinate to several others with whom such behavior would be tabu. There was thus no overall chieftanship or authoritarian leadership of any kind. Such complicated operations as grass-burning animal drives or totemic ceremonies could be carried out smoothly because each person was aware of his role.

On both mission and cattle stations, however, the whites imposed their conception of leadership roles upon the aboriginals, consisting of one person in a controlling relationship with a subordinate group. Aboriginals called together to receive gifts, including axes, at a mission Christmas party found themselves facing one or two whites who sought to control their behavior for the occasion, who disregarded the age, sex, and kinship variables of which the aboriginals were so conscious, and who considered them all at one subordinate level. The white also sought to impose similar patterns on work parties. (However, if he placed an aboriginal in charge of a mixed group of post-hole diggers, for example, half of the group, those subordinate to the "boss," would work while the other half, who were superordinate to him, would sleep.) For the aboriginal, the steel axe and other European goods came to symbolize this new and uncomfortable form of social organization, the leader-group relationship.

The most disturbing effects of the steel axe, operating in conjunction with other elements also being introduced from the white man's several sub-cultures, developed in the realm of traditional ideas, sentiments, and values. These were undermined at a rapidly mounting rate, with no new conceptions being defined to replace them. The result was the erection of a mental and moral void which foreshadowed the collapse and destruction of all Yir Yoront culture, if not, indeed, the extinction of the biological group itself.

From what has been said it should be clear how changes in overt behavior, in technology and conduct, weakened the values inherent in a reliance on nature, in the prestige of masculinity and of age, and in the various kinship relations. A scene was set in which a wife, or a young son whose initiation may not yet have been completed, need no longer defer to the husband or father who, in turn, became confused and insecure as he was forced to borrow a steel axe from them. For the woman and boy the steel axe helped establish a new degree of freedom which they accepted readily as an escape from the unconscious stress of the old patterns—but they, too, were left confused and insecure. Ownership became less well defined with the result that stealing and trespassing were introduced into technology and conduct. Some of the excitement surrounding the great ceremonies evaporated and they lost their previous gaiety and interest. Indeed, life itself became less interesting, although this did not lead the Yir Yoront to discover suicide, a concept foreign to them.

The whole process may be most specifically illustrated in terms of totemic system, which also illustrates the significant role played by a system of ideas, in this case a totemic ideology, in the breakdown of a culture.

In the first place, under pre-European aboriginal conditions where the native culture has become adjusted to a relatively stable environment, few, if any, unheard of or catastrophic crises can occur. It is clear, therefore, that the totemic system serves very effectively in inhibiting radical cultural changes. The closed system of totemic ideas, explaining and categorizing a well-known universe as it was fixed at the beginning of time, presents a considerable obstacle to the adoption of new or the dropping of old culture traits. The obstacle is not insurmountable and the system allows for the minor variations which occur in the norms of daily life. But the inception of major changes cannot easily take place.

Among the bush Yir Yoront the only means of water transport is a light wood log to which they cling in their constant swimming of rivers, salt creeks, and tidal inlets. These natives know that tribes 45 miles further north have a bark canoe. They know these northern tribes can thus fish from midstream or out at sea, instead of clinging to the river banks and beaches, that they can cross coastal waters infested with crocodiles, sharks, sting rays, and Portuguese men-of-war without danger. They know the materials of which the canoe is made exist in their own environment. But they also know, as they say, that they do not have canoes because their own mythical ancestors did not have them. They assume that the canoe was part of the ancestral universe of the northern tribes. For them, then, the adoption of the canoe would not be simply a matter of learning a number of new behavioral skills for its manufacture and use. The adoption would require a much more difficult procedure; the acceptance by the entire society of a myth, either locally developed or borrowed, to explain the presence of the canoe, to associate it with some one or more of the several hundred mythical ancestors (and how decide which?), and thus establish it as an accepted totem of one of the clans ready to be used by the whole community. The Yir Yoront have not made this adjustment, and in this case we can only say that for the time being at least, ideas have won out over very real pressures for technological change. In the elaborateness and explicitness of the totemic ideologies we seem to have one explanation for the notorious stability of Australian cultures under aboriginal conditions, an explanation which gives due weight to the importance of ideas in determining human behavior.

At a later stage of the contact situation, as has been indicated, phenomena unaccounted for by the totemic ideological system begin to appear with regularity and frequency and remain within the range of native experience. Accordingly, they cannot be ignored (as the "Battle of the Mitchell" was apparently ignored), and there is an attempt to assimilate them and account for them along the lines of principles inherent in the ideology. The bush Yir Yoront of the mid-thirties represent this stage of the acculturation process. Still trying to maintain their aboriginal definition of the situation, they accept European artifacts and behavior patterns, but fit them into their totemic system, assigning them to various clans on a par with original totems. There is an attempt to have the myth-making process keep up with these cultural changes so that the idea system can continue to support the rest of the culture. But analysis of overt behavior, of dreams, and of some of the new myths indicates that this arrangement is not entirely satisfactory, that the native clings to his totemic system with intellectual loyalty (lacking any substitute ideology), but that associated sentiments and values are weakened. His attitudes towards his own and towards European culture are found to be highly ambivalent.

All ghosts are totems of the Head-to-the-East Corpse clan, are thought of as white, and are of course closely associated with death. The white man, too, is closely associated with death, and he and all things pertaining to him are naturally assigned to the Corpse clan as totems. The steel axe, as a totem, was thus associated with the Corpse clan. But as an "axe," clearly linked with the stone axe, it is a totem of the Sunlit Cloud Iguana clan. Moreover, the steel axe, like most European goods, has no distinctive origin myth, nor are mythical ancestors associated with it. Can anyone, sitting in the shade of a *ti* tree one afternoon, create a myth to resolve this confusion? No one has, and the horrid suspicion arises as to the authenticity of the origin myths, which failed to take into account this vast new universe of the white man. The steel axe, shifting hopelessly between one clan and the other, is not only replacing the stone axe physically, but is hacking at the supports of the entire cultural system.

The aboriginals to the south of the Yir Yoront have clearly passed beyond this stage. They are engulfed by European culture, either by the mission or cattle station sub-cultures or, for some natives, by a baffling, paradoxical combination of both incongruent varieties. The totemic ideology can no longer support the inrushing mass of foreign culture traits, and the myth-making process in its native form breaks down completely. Both intellectually and emotionally a saturation point is reached so that the myriad new traits which can neither be ignored nor any longer assimilated simply force the aboriginal to abandon his totemic system. With the collapse of this system of ideas, which is so closely related to so many other aspects of the native culture, there follows an appallingly sudden and complete cultural disintegration, and a demoralization of the individual such as has seldom been recorded elsewhere. Without the support of a system of ideas well devised to provide cultural stability in a stable environment, but admittedly too rigid for the new realities pressing in from outside, native behavior and native sentiments and values are simply dead. Apathy reigns. The aboriginal has passed beyond the realm of any outsider who might wish to do him well or ill.

Returning from the broken natives huddled on cattle stations or on the fringes of frontier towns to the ambivalent but still lively aboriginals settled on the Mitchell River mission, we note one further devious result of the introduction of European artifacts. During a wet season stay at the mission, the anthropologist discovered that his supply of toothpaste was being depleted at an alarming rate. Investigation showed that it was being taken by old men for use in a new tooth paste cult. Old materials of magic having failed, new materials were being tried out in a malevolent magic directed towards the mission staff and some of the younger aboriginal men. Old males, largely ignored by the missionaries, were seeking to regain some of their lost power and prestige. This mild aggression proved hardly effective, but perhaps only because confidence in any kind of magic on the mission was by this time at a low ebb.

For the Yir Yoront still in the bush, a time could be predicted when personal deprivation and frustration in a confused culture would produce an overload of anxiety. The mythical past of the totemic ancestors would disappear as a guarantee of a present of which the future was supposed to be a stable continuation.

Without the past, the present could be meaningless and the future unstructured and uncertain. Insecurities would be inevitable. Reaction to this stress might be some form of symbolic aggression, or withdrawal and apathy, or some more realistic approach. In such a situation the missionary with understanding of the processes going on about him would find his opportunity to introduce his forms of religion and to help create a new cultural universe.

Feeling Good and Getting Smashed

by
Yngve Georg Lithman

THEORETICAL PROPOSITIONS

UNTIL FAIRLY RECENTLY, the effects of alcohol were thought to be founded primarily in its effects on the human brain. Impaired vision and motoric inabilities are obvious consequences of alcohol consumption. So, it was thought, were effects such as "lessening of inhibitions," impairment of judgment and loss of self-control. That alcohol has these latter effects has been effectively denied by MacAndrew and Edgerton (1969). Against the background of the multitude of data they present, they argue that the presence of alcohol in the human body does not produce any of these effects. Not only is there no positive proof of them, but there is ample evidence that people have a very discriminatory sense of what inhibitions one is allowed to "lose" during drunkenness, and how and in what areas of social life one is allowed to act when lacking in judgment and self-control.[1] Instead of the physiological explanation for these aspects of drunken behavior, MacAndrew and Edgerton argued that people in the course of their socialization learn what their society "knows" about drunkenness, and by accepting and acting in accordance with this knowledge, they become living confirmations of their society's teachings. Furthermore, they argue, because of its effects on motoric ability, alcohol in a number of societies has become a symbol for what might be called "time out," i.e.

Adapted from "Feeling Good and Getting Smashed: On the Symbolism of Alcohol and Drunkenness Among Canadian Indians," *Ethnos*, vol. 44, 1–II (1979), pp. 119–133.

[1]The empirical material to be presented comes from a Canadian Indian community with a province-wide reputation for hard and incessant drinking.

occasions when a society's ordinary rules and norms are situation-ally lifted. When discussing why societies have time out, however, MacAndrew and Edgerton rely on a fundamentally psychological explanation, that the time out gives people the chance to get pent-up frustrations etc. "out of their system with a minimum of negative consequences" (1969:169). I think it is possible to substitute this psychological approach for one that is more firmly entrenched in an analysis of social relations.

In analysing the role of alcohol and drunken comportment in the context of social relations, I will rely on my own discussion of certain Indian actions against Whites as the expression of an "opposition ideology" (Lithman 1978). A fundamental property of an opposition ideology, which is likely to be found in a majority-exploited minority-exploited relationship, is that it artic-ulates the difference between two ethnic groups. I will also make implicit use of my own discussion of inter-ethnic interaction (Lithman 1978). However, in the presentation of four fairly common types of drinking situations below, only one involves directly Indians as well as Whites, while the other three have only Indian participants.

TYPES OF DRINKING EVENTS

When going through notes on the various drinking situations I encountered during a prolonged residence in an Indian reserve community, I have found that they can be sorted into two main types, one in which the presence of alcohol is only incidental to the activity, and one in which alcohol serves to symbolize to the participants that a specific chain of events is likely to unravel unless some unexpected obstacle materializes.

The first of these two types is by far the most common, and also the least spectacular. The specific event might be a hunting trip at night, when a few young men set out at dusk and are gone for a couple of hours. If going by car, they might bring a few beers for each of the participants, and while waiting or changing location, the hunters are likely to have a beer. Nobody gets drunk, nobody loses control, nobody seems in any way affected by alcohol. Before the hunting trip is over, the small supply is likely to have been exhausted, but nobody is likely to complain about it or make any suggestions that they should take the time to replenish the supply.

Similar events, in the sense that the presence of alcohol is incidental to the joint act being performed, might be e.g. a more formally structured wedding dinner in the school gymnasium. The guests are invited by card, the tables are formally arranged, and the activities include a welcome toast, a three-course dinner, and a dance to taped music. Although alcohol might be present all through the evening, this is not noted in an ostentatious manner, and if someone starts to show signs of inebriation, he or she is likely to be reprimanded not to spoil the fun for the newlyweds. If this does not produce the desired effect, some of the guests might well take the inebriated "for a walk" in order to "sober him (or her) up."

In these instances, it is certainly clear that the structure of the events determines the use of alcohol. The consumption is usually fairly modest, and signs of drunkenness are likely to be scoffed upon. Nobody likes a drunk person with a loaded 30–30 rifle as a hunting companion, nor to have a formal wedding reception, arranged at great expense and much work, spoiled by rowdy or unseemly behavior.

Such drinking situations are obviously not the ones which have given the Indians a well-established reputation for heavy alcoholism, prompted a substantial amount of research into "Indian drinking" and produced statements such as that "the major structural pressure to drink experienced by Indians in . . . society derives from their marginal economic position" (Graves 1970:32) and that to the Indians, "alcohol is the simplest and quickest way to kill one's consciousness and to forget one's sense of inability (to cope with modern society)" (Dozier 1966:14). In what situations, then, do Indians drink alcohol and get drunk? And why?

WHEN ALCOHOL MATTERS

I will give examples of three different kinds of drinking situations where the presence of alcohol is likely to be a significant item in the interaction, and drunken behavior is likely to be exhibited. They differ with respect to the recruitment of parties to the interaction, and with respect to the chain of events that develops. The first instance might be labeled "peer group drinking," where Indian men drink together, the second "the drinking party," where both Indian men and women participate, and the third "the ethnic brawl," where Indians, primarily men, when drunk, engage in scraps with non-Indians (Whites). Each of these types of drinking acts can be seen performed as self-contained entities, but due to situational factors such as acciden-

tal change in the recruitment to the act, they might also change
over from one type to another. I also believe that there is one
more type of drinking situation where alcohol matters but which
is not treated here, the female equivalent of male peer group
drinking. For obvious reasons, my data here are hearsay, scant
and inconclusive.

MALE PEER GROUP DRINKING

One night I came over to Bob's, and found that he had several
guests, all male. His wife and a couple of the children were busy
in the kitchen. His guests were all a part of Bob's usual crowd, a
couple of his political associates, a couple of his close friends,
and a neighbor. They had a couple of cases of beer, which were
leisurely consumed as the night wore on. The others already
seemed a bit drunk when I arrived. The discussion centered on
Bob's political fortunes, or rather, present misfortunes. Bob had
recently been caught in an act which was highly discrediting to
his involvement in the Indian political movement, and the possible implications of this, as well as what to think of the Indian
political movement itself, were discussed with a frankness which
I had never heard before. Although the participants' comportment revealed drunkenness (occasionally loud voices, some staggering when going out on the yard to relieve oneself, some
surprising bluntness when discussing each others' and absent
persons' actions and political ideas), the discussion was perfectly
coherent. Slightly after midnight, most of us left to go home. We
all declared that we had had "a good time," and that to
have a few beers and "talk away" was a good way to spend an
evening. A couple of days later, I tried to engage Bob in a
discussion of some of the themes during that evening, especially
those he had expressed himself with a candor about sensitive
topics which I had never heard from him before. He looked at
me, smiled and replied "Did I say that? That's just drunken talk.
You talk too damn much when you're drinking."

Several similar examples of virtually identical drinking situations could be given. The participants are virtually all male,
either friends, political cronies, neighbors, relations or members
of the same sports team. The topic of conversation in the example above was fairly well-defined, but might well circle around
several items, such as marital problems, women, or reserve
community politics. Often these events start as a couple of
persons accidentally engage in conversation, e.g. as a result of

visiting. A supply of beer is picked up at one of the vendors' in the nearby white communities and will usually last for the night unless additional persons appear. If they don't bring their own beer, they might be asked to go and pick some up if the original supply is depleted.

The real significance of these events, however, lies in the ways that the presence of alcohol defines the conversation. When drinking, you are not responsible for your statements. Accordingly, the male peer group drinking provides an opportunity for "time out" in the sense that one can be far more outspoken on a number of subjects than would be the case if one was not "drinking." Drinking, also talked about as "fooling around" (which is also used about sexual exploits), provides an opportunity for reserve community politicians to test out ideas, sound out the possibilities of successfully attacking somebody else, for people to hear possible gossip about their wives and to have discussions with others in which what was said will later be considered "drunken talk."

The male peer group situation thus provides an opportunity of exchange of information and ideas where the restraints imposed upon the participants in ordinary life are situationally relaxed. And the symbol for "time out" is the presence of alcohol and drunken behavior.

THE DRINKING PARTY

Jimmy's party started fairly late at night. In fact, there was no particular point in time when it started; it came about rather as a happening. In the afternoon there had been a softball game, and it seemed as if Jimmy and his wife had invited some persons over to their house after the game. After supper, they had gone to the beach for a swim, and on their way home picked up a few cases of beer. While at the vendor's, they had met some friends outside the pub, and they had also been invited to Jimmy's later in the evening. When a couple of cars had assembled outside Jimmy's house, and one could hear their voices, everybody who passed by would guess that there was a party in progress. If someone was uncertain whether there really was a party at Jimmy's, he or she could ask some kid in the neighborhood, and be told that "they are drinking at Jimmy's."

There are several men and women present in Jimmy's house. The women tend to gather in one of the bedrooms or in the kitchen, while the men occupy the living room. The segregation, however, is not very pronounced, as people mingle with each other. Also, some people arrive, usually bringing a case of beer, while others leave. Occasionally, some of the men, or the women, get into an argument. On this occasion, there is no fighting, although this would not be exceptional at a party like this.

As the evening goes on, the participants get increasingly drunk. Some women leave temporarily, excusing themselves by pointing out that they have to check on their kids, and that they will return. Some men go off to relieve themselves, or to pick up some more beer. The party seemingly disintegrates. Some men start to wonder where their women are, and some women where their men are. In one instance, a man is on the verge of starting to hit his wife, who has been gone from the party for some time, accusing her of "fucking around." The woman teases him that that would be "damn right of me to do, you're no damn good, that's for sure." A couple of other participants interfere, and prevent what would obviously have become a fisticuffs.

Several times during the night, husbands and wives accuse each other, women complaining that their men are drunks, impotent, etc., and the men complaining that their women are "old rags," or "don't know how to handle a family."

Rather than having an end, the party peters out. A couple of persons have passed out, and one of them stays to sleep it off on Jimmy's couch, while some others are helped into cars. Some persons wonder where their wives or husbands are, but will seldom receive any positive answers.

The interaction during the party was very much characterized by the dichotomy between the sexes, and by the fact that husbands and wives were likely to display some measure of hostility against each other.

The next day, and later on, virtually no one who participated would admit to remembering very much of what took place. "At Jimmy's? Gee, did I ever get smashed. I must have passed out. I don't think I remember a damned thing."

I think it is possible to pinpoint some fundamental principles underpinning the drinking party event. When doing this, however, it is important to caution the reader that I do not claim to give a "complete analysis." Too neat and detailed an analysis of the drinking party would probably do injustice to the variety that this kind of activity might exhibit. Still, Jimmy's party was in many ways a typical drinking party.

The recruitment to the drinking party is fairly haphazard. The core group of guests, however, will be made up of friends, neighbors, and relatives. The person who knows that he doesn't get along with the host is unlikely to appear. If he does, he is likely to be made uncomfortable through the other participants' choice of conversation topics. On the whole, however, there is largely an open door to these parties, especially if the newcomers contribute to the supplies.

The drinking party is also characterized by a very marked emphasis on an often ostentatious display of drunken comportment. People talk loudly, occasionally they act aggressively, reel, and show all the signs of considerable inebriation.

The topics of conversation might range over a large number of issues, but are likely to include standard topics such as reserve politics, local lore about important persons and events, but also, of particular interest in this article, family relations, gossip about extra-marital affairs, boasting about manliness, teasing about lack of manliness from female participants, and a whole range of similar topics dealing with relations between men and women.

The question of how men and women relate to each other during the party is of fundamental importance, and requires a complex answer. Men and women observe some measure of interactive separateness. Occasionally, this might develop into a pronounced spatial segregation, even resulting in some men or women leaving the party together. At Jimmy's party, three women left together. They had all some arguments with their husbands at the party, whereupon they had been talking in the kitchen. When they left the party, they managed to secure a ride to the provincial capital some hundred miles away. One of the women reappeared in the community the next day, another a couple of days later, having phoned her husband the night after the party to let him know that she was staying with her sister. The third woman made her way to Toronto, several thousands of miles away, was not seen in the area for several months, and never resettled in the community. She and her husband are now divorced.

The hostility between husband and wife, and the occasional infidelity that might occur in connection with the drinking party must be analyzed against the background of ordinary family life in the community. The husbands and wives in this impoverished community often lack resources to live up to each other's expectations. Few men are able to perform the breadwinner role, which is an ideal. Few men can provide a "good life" for their families. Women rarely have the resources at hand, in the form of knowledge, authority and time, to provide a determining input into their children's education. Nor are men and women very pleased with their capabilities of displaying themselves as models for their children.

The very difficult conditions under which most families exist make the relation between the parties in many marriages, and between parents and children, very fragile. In many cases, the parties in a family are so dissatisfied with each other's performance in a variety of matters of ordinary family concern that it is very difficult to communicate about family matters generally. Instead, the communication is usually restricted to very practical matters of immediate concern. A more broadly inclusive discussion would in many cases release a violent argument about personal shortcomings. A consequence of this would often be a separation between the parties. Many couples, also where the parties are dissatisfied with each other, would shun separation, not only for reasons of fundamental affection but also for many times imperative material reasons.

In this situation, the drinking party becomes the arena for blunt communication between many married couples. The presence of alcohol and the fact that everybody is drunk defines the situation as "time out." You are not responsible for your actions, you are "smashed." A married couple are now able to communicate to each other that they are mutually dissatisfied with each other's behavior in everyday life. At the same time, it is possible for men and women to discuss for example marital problems collectively. Occasionally, such discussions might lead some of the women or some of the men to leave the party collectively, in some instances even eventually leading to a separation or divorce.

The day after a drinking party, the participants will claim that they "don't remember anything," because they were "smashed." Thus, the discussions and the actions at the drinking party might not have to be dealt with verbally, and everybody's "hangover" clearly manifests that the participants were "stoned out of their mind." Still, the drinking party has its obvious impact and is part of some married couples' way of seriously communicating with each other about the shortcomings they see in each other, and about the problems of their marriage. And if this was not done in a time-out situation, such communication would have consequences which the parties would not usually be willing to face.

THE ETHNIC BRAWL

It was rice picking time when Peter and his friends got into trouble. Wild rice picking is important for the community members, both for financial and symbolic reasons—it is now virtually the only Indian activity which can be linked to traditional pursuits. Peter and three of his friends and myself got together late in the afternoon, and one of the participants had brought beer. We started to drink and talked about a variety of topics. Eventually, however, the conversation focused on Indian-White relations, and how these were reflected in the changes that had taken place in wild rice harvesting, such as machine picking and the use of artificial paddies and improved seeds. As the evening and the darkness approached, the participants became more and more agitated. Particularly, a power dam in a nearby river was resented, as it was supposed to have had a very adverse effect on the wild rice crops ever since its construction. "It should be blown up," suggested one of the participants. While this discussion went on, the participants played music of the country and western style, moody, sad, and often despairing.

As the beer supply was exhausted, the participants decided to go to a beer parlor in a nearby town. "We're off to the war," the host declared to his wife as they parted. After less than an hour in the beer parlor, where Peter and his friends behaved in a way that demonstrated to everybody that they had "put a few under the belt," the trouble started. Peter felt that one of his friends had been slighted by one of the waiters, and an argument developed. Some lugging and tugging began, and another of Peter's friends intervened. In a matter of seconds, a full-fledged bar-room fight was under way. Chairs started to fly, people broke out in fighting in several places, the mirror over the bar was smashed, and the whole scene almost looked as if taken from a western movie. The police arrived, presumably summoned by the proprietor. After a little while, order was restored, and Peter and his friends were taken to the police station, together with some others of the participants.

This incident has become part of the local community lore. The time when Peter and his friends went to town to raise hell is now the subject of much amusement, and the story has also been elaborated with details about the fight, the cowardliness of the bartender (hiding, in classical fashion, behind the counter), the ferocity of one of Peter's friends (when the fight started, he is presumed to have punched one White "right out with one blow"), and so forth.

The recruitment to the initial event, the drinking at Peter's house, was not directly related to what took place later. Instead, the four participants were all good friends, who often met. That they later ended up in a bar-room brawl can be understood not solely because they had emptied their beer supply and wanted to go on. Instead, in their conversation they had reached a consensus that the Indians were being cheated by the white men, and that nothing could really be done about it. One way of protest, however, is to demonstrate to white men that the Indians do not accept the rules of the game, that white men have no sanctions they can apply to Indians which the Indians care about. Put differently, to demonstrate that Indians are Indians, and white men are white men, and that Indians are not subjugating themselves to the Whites' values. This is what happened in the bar room.

In several ways, Peter and his friends behaved in most outrageous ways to Whites. They showed up at the tavern drunk. The drunken Indian image is firmly entrenched in white minds as a symbol of the no good Indian. By starting the fight, they literally added injury to insult.

As a demonstration of ethnic difference, it is also easy to see why the incident has become part of the local lore. Here is, to the community residents, another example of Indians who don't care about White sanctions. As such, Peter and his friends become local heroes in the ever-present conflict between Indians and Whites. And nobody in the community, of course, would claim that they didn't know what they were doing. And they themselves remember every bit of the scrap in the tavern. In fact, the very next morning they discussed last night's events in the greatest detail while having pop on Peter's lawn. And the consensus was that they had had a "good time."

CONCLUSIONS

In this article, four different types of drinking situations have been described, one in which alcohol does not matter in the structure of the event (e.g. the hunting trip), and three in which it does—male peer group drinking, the drinking party and the ethnic brawl. In the hunting trip, the consumption is very limited, and there is no trace of intoxication among the participants. In the male peer group drinking and the drinking party, there is a heavy emphasis on the use of alcohol, and the participants exhibit clearly "drunken behavior." The next day, they will display signs of hangover, and claim that they do not remember what took place. And the whole community "knows" that one is not responsible for one's actions in these kinds of drinking situations. In the ethnic brawl, however, the participants also display drunken behavior, but they will not claim any loss of memory, nor will anybody suggest that the participants are not responsible for their actions.

We are thus confronted here with a situation where alcohol and drunken comportment do not signify one, but many things. In the male peer group drinking and the drinking party, they symbolize time out and the fact that nobody can be held responsible for whatever is said or done. In the ethnic brawl, they symbolize that white men's sanctions against Indians are of no concern. In the former case, it makes possible communication between the parties which would otherwise be difficult to obtain. This is to some extent true also of the ethnic brawl, but the emphasis here is on the symbolization of the ethnic boundary.

The reified ideas about alcohol and drunken comportment prevalent in our own society hold that alcohol produces certain inescapable effects, such as impairment of judgment and loss of inhibitions. This folk model of alcohol use has for a long time also guided social scientists. To the extent that this article has demonstrated that alcohol and drunken comportment are part of elaborate symbolic systems, where their role might be different in different situations, it will be part of a process where a more sophisticated view of alcohol use will result.

REFERENCES

Dozier, E. P. "Problem Drinking among American Indians: The Role of Sociocultural Deprivation." *Quarterly Journal of Studies on Alcohol,* 27 (1966), pp. 72–87.

Feldman, H. "Ideological Supports to Becoming and Remaining a Heroin Addict." *Journal of Health and Social Behavior,* 9 (1968), pp. 131–39.

Field, P. B. "A New Cross-Cultural Study of Drunkenness." In D. J. Pittman and C. R. Snyder, *Society, Culture and Drinking Patterns.* New York: John Wiley, 1962.

Graves, T. "The Personal Adjustment of Navajo Indian Migrants to Denver, Colorado." *American Anthropologist,* 72 (1970), pp. 35–54.

Horton, D. J. "The Functions of Alcohol in Primitive Society: A Cross-Cultural Study." *Quarterly Journal of Studies on Alcohol,* 4 (1943), pp. 199–320.

Lithman, Y. G. *The Community Apart: A Case Study of a Canadian Indian Reserve Community*. Stockholm: Stockholm Studies in Social Anthropology, no. 6 (1978).

MacAndrew, C., and R. B. Edgerton. *Drunken Comportment*. Chicago: Aldine, 1969.

Robertson, H. *Reservations Are for Indians*. Toronto: James Lewis and Samuel, 1970.

Smoking In Korea

by
C. Paul Dredge

He quit smoking and drinking to buy an ox but a tiger
carried it off and ate it.

Korean proverb

Yi Sŭng-hun, a leader of the Korean political and social
reform movement of the 1890's, once shocked a group with whom
he was meeting by taking an older gentleman's long pipe and
cutting the stem to only about one quarter of its original length,
replacing the bowl and mouthpiece, and giving it back to its owner
with an admonition to the group to smoke shorter pipes.

Kim Sŏ-bang, a farmer who has lived in the same Chŏlla
province village all his life, has recently begun to cultivate
tobacco in some of his fields. As he and his brother-in-law and
the women and children of both families weave the stem of each
leaf into the strands of rice-straw rope for hanging in a vinyl
drying house (where the sun will cure them), they are careful to
collect into a basket all the leaves which are damaged or de-
formed too badly to be strung up to cure. These rejected portions
of the crop will be sold as lowest grade tobacco to the government tobacco monopoly, where they will be burned in a furnace.
The government incurs this expense to discourage the illegal
practice of farmers smoking their own home-grown tobacco.

Pak Ae-yŏn, a young businessman in Naju, walked by three
of the little tobacco shops on the street before he approached the
fourth and asked for two packs of Turtle Ship brand cigarettes.
He joked with the girl in the booth for a moment, paid his
six-hundred won, and walked across the street to his regular tea
room to meet a client.

Adapted from *Korea Journal* v. 20, no. 4 (April 1980), pp. 25–36, ©
copyright by the Korean National Commission for UNESCO.

The three cases above are intended to provoke specific questions which relate to broader issues concerning smoking in Korea. What was shocking about Yi's behavior, and why did he choose to teach a lesson with a pipe? Why does the government choose to monopolize the tobacco industry; and what is it about tobacco that makes it so valuable, and the demand for it so inelastic, in spite of the fact that it is not, strictly speaking, an absolute necessity? Why does Pak bypass closer shops and why does he buy only Turtle Ship brand cigarettes? The process of finding answers to these questions will involve an inquiry into historical, symbolic, and social aspects of smoking in Korea. The goal of the inquiry is to come to a deeper understanding of the meaning that tobacco and smoking have in Korean culture and of the ways people actually use tobacco in everyday social interaction. Information for this study comes both from written sources and from material gathered incidentally during eighteen months of field research, mostly in rural Chŏlla province, on a socio-linguistic topic.

The proverb which introduces this paper is a good place to begin the analysis. While the proverb refers to both smoking and drinking, and indeed the two go together in many contexts, the focus here will be on smoking alone. Although it is not immediately apparent, this old saying designates tobacco as a special kind of necessity in Korean life: more than a physical necessity, tobacco is a means of symbolic expression and an aid in social interaction. Tobacco has, of course, physical effects and uses, and is often thought of by Koreans in terms of its properties as a drug. In this sense it has a kind of practical, if not survival, value, or at least a material/physical function. But there is much more to the use of tobacco in Korea (or anywhere else, I suspect) than its physical effects. The most basic interpretation of the proverb is that to sacrifice the smoking of tobacco to get ahead financially is sure to be a net loss of value in the long run. The apparent implication is that the pleasures of smoking are more important than the unreliable chance of a small increase in other facets of one's living standard. This aspect of the proverb pertains most obviously to the physical effects of smoking. The more fundamental reasons for the emergence of such a proverb in the first place, however, are to be found in the function of tobacco in gift exchange, where offering and accepting smoking materials is a symbol of friendship or alliance. A man who doesn't even have tobacco to share is seen to be either miserly and antisocial or poverty-stricken. Getting an ox is fraught with risk anyway; why risk losing an important social tool and jeopardizing friendship or reputation over such a thing? In Korea, tobacco is the poor man's luxury and the poor man's gift—the one consumer good beyond absolute necessity which all but the most destitute can afford. The proverb tells Koreans that to give up even such a minimal luxury, especially if it is the only one a person's poverty allows, is to sink from living into mere subsistence.

To view tobacco as both a simple luxury and a simple gift is to address a larger issue: the symbolic nature of gifts and gift exchange. To see the exchange of cigarettes and other tobacco in Korea from this wider perspective is useful in understanding the meaning and social functions of tobacco in Korean life.

Even the most material things may have their non-material essence or meaning. Such meanings are established through association of material objects with a cultural and social context in which they are used in a consistent, significant way. In most societies clothing, though material, carries innumerable associations with social class, taste, style, and appropriateness for occasion. Certain articles of clothing can be gifts of great import to which associated memories are forever attached. Lévi-Strauss speaks of the reluctance French people have toward eating certain foods such as large roasts of beef or turkeys or hams without inviting someone to share in the bounty they symbolize (Lévi-Strauss, 1969). In the U.S., flowers of various colors and kinds convey messages of widely differing significance—particular floral arrangements are deemed appropriate for specific kinds of occasions. Household goods presented as wedding gifts can be highly symbolic. Kitchen knives are very practical for newly wedded couples, but people who share the understanding in American culture of the negative symbolic message of knives as wedding gifts do not give knives. In all these cases, a material object has come to have an associated message to communicate and has become much more than "goods."

The less practical an object is in terms of mere subsistence, the more power it has to convey symbolic meaning (Mauss, 1954; Lévi-Strauss, 1969). The merchandise sold in gift shops tends to be highly impractical, and although few customers think consciously of such subliminal motivations, the articles they buy at gift shops function more as symbols of the buyer's friendship than as items for the recipient's practical use. The very non-utilitarian nature of most gifts means that they can perform almost purely symbolic functions. On the other hand, highly useful items, especially living things, which are destroyed as a sacrifice for a god or as a proof of interpersonal commitment have substantial symbolic value because they could have been used and perhaps were even badly needed. With regard to use in gift exchange, an object which is non-utilitarian and highly symbolic, and which is also sacrificed, combines the significant features of both sacrificial objects and non-useful but highly symbolic objects. Such objects may be the most powerful gifts of all. This combination of non-utility *and* sacrifice may account for the traditional preference in the U.S. for cut roses over flowering potted plants as expressions of love. Neither cut roses nor flowering houseplants are truly utilitarian; the higher romantic value assigned to cut roses in comparison to potted plants lies precisely in the fact that the roses cannot survive, and are therefore sacrificed, squandered, for the loved one.

Once a firm symbolic association has been established in an object, its remaining utilitarian value may become quite irrelevant to either its "real" value or its market price. The object may in that case become valuable almost exclusively as a symbol—and the use of the object as a symbol, while not a necessity of survival, can become a necessity of life. In Korea, tobacco has become such a necessity, beyond whatever physical needs it may satisfy. To offer a cigarette is to offer a gift which is beyond practical use, and which has powerful historical and cultural symbolic meanings. In spite of the high symbolic value of a cigarette, its economic value is relatively low; cigarettes have the advantage of being relatively inexpensive and very convenient to have on hand. The combination of symbolic power with convenience and economy makes tobacco an unparalleled social tool. It is of course because of this fact that the tobacco industry is a most reliable source of government revenue and a logical choice for a regulated monopoly industry.

HISTORY OF KOREAN SMOKING

One expression Koreans use to indicate "a long time ago" or "once upon a time" is "when tigers smoked tobacco." The literal Korean actually means "to eat" rather than "to smoke," and both the implied ancientness and the expression "to eat" raise interesting questions with regard to the history and cultural position of Korean smoking. It is already clear from historical sources that tobacco did not enter the country until the 1600's. The saying, however, conjures up an olden time when animals did human things, a motif found in much of mythology. To say that tigers smoked tobacco is to impute the same venerableness to the practice of smoking as is attributed to anthropomorphic tigers. This tie to ancient tradition appears to be a measure of the great importance, general acceptability, and necessity of smoking. To "eat" tobacco, an expression often used even in modern conversation, could indicate the completeness of the incorporation of smoking into the Korean way of life—i.e. it approaches edibles in its importance as a necessity of life.

Tobacco was unknown to Korea through the end of the sixteenth century. Portuguese trading expeditions to Japan led to the introduction of smoking into Korea during the beginning of the seventeenth century, where it spread rapidly. It is said that the first real devotee of tobacco in the nation was Chang Yu (1587–1638), one of the famous four masters of Chinese herbal medicine in Korea at that time. The Korean word for tobacco, *tambae*, is a corruption of the Japanese version of the Portuguese, which was still another derivative of the West Indian native term *tabaco*, from the Taino language of the Antilles. Other Korean terms, mostly regional dialect variations, are closer to the original *tobaco*, such as *tombago* or *tambagui*—like the Korean *ipsagui*, for "leaf," which has connotations of nurturance for an immature plant and of the "ears" (*kui*) of a plant—i.e. the leaves. Some other terms no longer in general use, all Chinese derivatives, were *sinda* (new tea), *namch'o* (southern grass), and *namryŏngch'o* (southern spirit grass).

It was in the earliest period of tobacco use that the Kwanghaegun (fifteenth king of the Chosŏn dynasty) forbade smoking in his presence, ostensibly because it made the breath of his officials and courtiers smell unpleasant. The Encyclopedia of Korean Studies (*Hangukhak Taepaekkwasajŏn*) cites this as the original precedent for the rule that social inferiors must not smoke in front of their superiors, and indicates that the king's preference soon found its way into all superior-inferior relationships. Although there is considerable change taking place presently, superior-inferior relationships have traditionally been defined by such variables as age (older is superior), generation of descent from a common patrilineal ancestor (earlier generation is superior), socioeconomic class (landed gentry superior to tenants and servants), bureaucratic and military position (higher office or rank is superior), sex (men superior to women of equal age, with a general formality in interaction between male and female adults of *any* status), and educational level (learned are superior to unlearned).

The encyclopedia's explanation of the Taewŏngun's smoking

rule fails to examine deeper implications of smoking when it tacitly assumes that no superiors smoked or that all were offended by the breath of smokers. The Kwanghaegun story is in fact less an explanation than a rationalization or a mythical foundation for a modern social practice. The attempted explanation does not get to the real reasons why such social conventions developed, reasons that lie below the surface of such folk interpretations or supposed historical causes. At least two things about smoking likely made it seem inappropriate in the presence of superiors from its very beginnings in Korea. They are that 1) smoking is a form of physical pleasure and that 2) smoking changes the nature of social space independently of the wishes of anyone but the smoker himself. To enjoy oneself or even to be comfortable physically is behavior which has traditionally been inappropriate in Korean social situations where superiors are present. The superior has some authority over the inferior, and expresses this symbolically in his control of the physical comfort of his inferior. Assuming to control social space—in the case of smoking it is by putting one's own smoke into someone else's space—is also an infringement on the prerogative of the superior. Authority over interpersonal space in Korea is comparable to the situation of a U.S. Marine commanding officer and a private in the same military organization. The commander can draw to within two inches of a private's face and yell reprimands at him, whereas the private must salute at a distance of six feet and keep at least arm's length when speaking to his commander. The Korean superior can fill the air with his smoke, but the inferior may not make a similar intrusion into their common space.

A good analogy between smoking and another form of social interaction in Korea can be made by comparing traditional attitudes about how people sit in a room together with attitudes about smoking. When a man sits on the floor of a room with a superior, he must sit in the formal, uncomfortable kneeling position until given permission by the superior to sit comfortably with his legs crossed. He must also refrain, after having been asked to sit in this more comfortable, but space-inefficient (and therefore imposing) way, from making further incursions into the superior's space. This is done by keeping the legs crossed and the torso erect, as though to confine the inferior's space to the necessary minimum. By contrast, the superior may, if he desires, sit in complete cross-legged comfort. He may even extend one of his legs forward, although this is rather impolite behavior even for a superior. He also will sit on the warmest, most comfortable part of the heated floor, the place of honor where either the male head of the household or a special guest is usually seated. In this setting, as in others which are similarly marked by inequality of social status, the superior may smoke at will, while the inferior will not smoke at all. Hence the privilege of smoking correlates with the privilege of relative comfort in sitting.

The proper behavior of women with regard to smoking is also comparable to the traditional protocol for sitting in a room. In polite society women do not sit cross-legged in the presence of a superior and are not invited to do so; they also maintain the kneeling posture as a sign of formality when men outside the immediate family are present. They remain in the more uncomfortable and perhaps more ladylike kneeling position for as long as they are sitting with a superior or stranger. Again drawing the analogy between sitting and smoking, it is not acceptable for women to smoke at all until they are widows or grandmothers (some would say as a substitute for sexual pleasure), and even then only the most wizened of old women smoke publicly in the presence of males. Old women have few superiors in terms of the status hierarchy, and they are also beyond many of the restrictions on female behavior which promote the feminine image. They tend to sit cross-legged in most situations and smoke in a wide range of less formal situations. Adherence to such traditional attitudes and practices is still quite strong in much of rural Korea today, especially in villages and towns where people are particularly concerned with questions of social class and ''good breeding'' in the context of former gentry vs. commoner distinctions. As might be suspected, cities provide a much more relaxed environment with regard to smoking by women; women of all ages can be seen smoking in public.

These descriptions of conventional behavior indicate that the superior/inferior or sex status restrictions which apply to sitting in the presence of people of superior social status or opposite sex are very similar to those which apply to smoking. The similar restrictions on these two different categories of behavior support the idea that it was not just the smell of smoke which caused the Taewŏngun to ban smoking in his court, but more fundamental cultural principles regarding social stratification and propriety. The control of personal space and the control of personal comfort, both involved in sitting and in smoking, are most clearly at issue, as are understandings concerning the relationship between the sexes, notions of proper feminine behavior, power relationships between males and females, questions of social class, and urban-rural differences. Smoking was, from its beginnings in

Korea, a highly symbolic form of social behavior, and that significance persists in modern Korea as well.

Historically, tobacco was smoked in a pipe with a bowl and mouthpiece made of metal of varying quality, depending on the wealth of the smoker. The two pieces were connected by a two-to-three-foot-long stem of hollowed bamboo. These pipes were originally used by *yangban* (gentry/ruling class) gentlemen who could afford both the tobacco and the time to sit and smoke in a leisurely manner, and became symbols of *yangban* power, as portrayed in pictures painted by the artist Kim Hong-do in the eighteenth century. Later, pipe smoking became popular among the common people, but the impractically long pipe remained a symbol of the leisurely class who first took up smoking and had no reason to design a pipe of a more practical shape. One author notes that some of the very wealthy had pipes so long that they had to be lit by servants (Moose, 1911). The long pipe also became associated with older people and their authority in society generally and more specifically in the individual family. It still has connotations of elderly crotchetiness and the power of older people over younger, for it was with the long stem of the pipe that children were often disciplined by their elders, or boys were punished in the schools by their teachers. Hence when Yi Sŭng-hun shortened the pipe belonging to an older gentleman he was assaulting a long-standing symbol of venerableness and the power of the elders. He was also professing a new ethic of utility and pragmatism, in direct challenge to the old values most dearly held by gentlemen like the one whose pipe he so audaciously modified. Traditional, tedious, inefficient, formal, and lengthy ways of doing things were symbolized by the long pipe; thus to shorten it was an eloquent symbolic statement.

Only a few very old and usually poor country folk use long-stemmed pipes today; many of them have found their way to the antique shops of Seoul to be sold as curiosities. Cigarettes are relatively new to Korea, but whether manufactured or rolled at home they are now the main smoking material of the nation. Cigars or varieties of scented pipe tobacco are not commonly smoked, although they are available. Imported cigars and pipe tobacco are available as novelty items from the U.S. Army PX-supplied black market.

Interestingly, there is no place for tobacco in Korean ancestral rites. Wine, fruit, and many kinds of cooked foods, including a bowl of rice and a bowl of soup, are placed on the offering table, but tobacco is never seen there. This is probably a result of the fact that the proper forms for ancestral offerings, i.e. arrangement of food on the offering table, were well established at least a century before tobacco became available in Korea. However, a person's pipe is sometimes placed in his coffin when he dies, or included in the articles symbolically sent along on his journey to the spirit world by virtue of their inclusion in a "spirit house" which precedes the coffin in some funeral processions.

Koreans today still view smoking as a pleasure, but in light of recent medical research in the U.S. and other countries they also regard it as a potentially unhealthy habit. An insightful cartoon focuses in on the dilemma of the smoker, who knows he is doing something unhealthy, debating with himself and saying: "Is it better to stop smoking or to get lung cancer?" He ends up asking the tobacconist for "a pack of lung cancer," and obviously goes on smoking, just like his father and grandfather before him.

SOCIAL CONVENTIONS WITH REGARD TO SMOKING

As the Taewŏngun story indicates, smoking must take place in the proper social context. In most cases this means that it must be done with people of relatively equal social status, defined in terms of age, sex, and freedom from asymmetrical power positions in kinship, bureaucratic, or other hierarchical structures. This is particularly true of people who live in the countryside, in closely knit communities which often consist largely of kinsmen. Among rural villagers in Chŏlla province, the men smoke with others of the category they call *pŏt*, defined as men within ten years of the same age as themselves whom they know well as long-term neighbors, but who are not close kinsmen. Members of such groups also drink liquor together on some occasions, participate in joking (including jokes about sexual matters) and use a rather informal and non-deferential speech form which is deemed appropriate among the members of such groups. One can hear old men call each other by first names in these groups, social settings which allow the otherwise staid Confucian gentlemen to "let down their hair" and enjoy themselves. Attitudes with regard to a breach of such restrictions on interpersonal relations are not as strictly negative as with some other aspects of social behavior, and there is some flexibility. Two brothers, both in their fifties, may spend time together with mutual friends in the evening and smoke together, even though convention would dictate that the younger should not smoke openly in front of the elder. When public meetings are held and men of widely divergent kinship or other statuses meet together the younger men will still smoke, but in doing so will turn their backs to the elders, hold their cigarettes cupped out of sight in their hands, lean out the door, and use other methods to avoid being seen smoking. The elders, for their part, pretend not to notice, because they understand the difficulty which necessary considerations of social distance and respect can create when such considerations would prohibit smoking for extended periods of time. Still, the resulting behavior is rather amusing to see, since the act of "covering up" is so obvious and so self-conscious on the part of the younger smokers that it amounts to the statement: "I'm smoking, but please don't notice."

The right to smoke is also restricted by absolute age. Relative age is one variable in the assessment of social superiority/inferiority, but absolute age is another independently important variable. For instance, a young man must be nearing adulthood to smoke in public, even when he is smoking only in the presence of his friends. Hence beginning to smoke in public is a kind of informal rite of passage which marks transition into adulthood for young men, and it carries with it the same connotations of manliness and maturity that it has sometimes held for young men in American society. As might be expected, today's Korean youth often learn to smoke and enjoy it long before they are allowed to do so in public. While a few are against smoking because of health or religious considerations, others who are merely reluctant to assert themselves as adults are subject to strong social pressures to begin smoking publicly if they have not done so by the time their friends have begun to smoke (usually by age twenty or in the first year of college for students). One scholarly acquaintance recounted how during college a girl he was dating encouraged him to smoke so that he would appear to be more masculine and mature. He began smoking to please her, to prove his manhood, and then retained his new habit even though the relationship cooled. He is at this point such an enthusiastic smoker that his students know him as the professor who smokes while lecturing, a highly unusual practice which only an *aeyŏnga* (literally, "one who loves smoke") would adopt. Still, as the professor it is his privilege to smoke in class, while the students must wait until the lecture is over.

In small groups or pairs of men who are smoking, individuals seldom smoke cigarettes from their own packs alone. Two men will normally alternate, smoking cigarettes first from one man's pack and then the other's, and groups will often share the same pack. The prevalence of exchange and sharing is an important feature of Korean social interaction in other spheres as well, such as when one goes to a restaurant with a friend and the bill must be paid. Koreans invariably have a bit of an argument over the bill and then one person pays for it. This sets up future obligations and implies a continuing relationship in which such generalized exchange can take place on a reciprocal basis over time. Accepting and offering cigarettes are forms of this same exchange structure. Even though cigarettes are purchased with money, their value as trade goods is beyond purely monetary considerations. Cigarettes offered to and accepted from others become the most inexpensive but a nonetheless very substantial part of a system of exchange in which bus, train, and taxi fares, fruit, meat, honey and candy, liquor, and tea, coffee, and herbal medicines are most often purchased for other people and consumed only as gifts, however informal or impromptu the occasion of the gift and its acceptance. The numerous small shops where such items are purchased, which dot the cities and towns of Korea, are a testament to the fact that the exchange of gifts is vital to the continuous building and maintenance of social relationships. Such a pervasive system of reciprocal exchange leads to household budgets which are designed to buy such things for others with the expectation that they will return in kind as gifts at some later time. Because of the mutual obligations and social ties involved, it could be said that a Korean housewife budgets money for buying gifts in order to maximize not just economic but social benefits. The amount budgeted for a husband's cigarettes is thus partially incorporated into the gift and reciprocity portion of family expenses; the cigarettes he buys and smokes himself are of course considered part of personal consumption.

When feasts are held on the occasion of a wedding, funeral, birthday, or other important time of social transition, cigarettes are passed out as part of the meal, to be smoked at the end. The usual number in the rural area around Naju is three per guest. At large gatherings where the hosts cannot personally serve everyone a helper will pass the cigarettes out, breaking open pack after pack until each guest has the determined number of cigarettes at his place at the table. In smaller gatherings, the host will place a pack of cigarettes on the table and guests will help themselves. It is possible, although probably not verifiable, that when three cigarettes for each guest are distributed there is a hidden message as to how long the guests should stay. Historical sources on Korean smoking indicate that time was often marked in former days by keeping track of the number of pipes that had been smoked and that work was planned by calculating the number of pipes likely to be smoked while the work was being done. Hence there were three pipe jobs, ten pipe jobs, etc. Perhaps hosts who pass out three cigarettes per guest are saying: "Remain and visit for a three-cigarette stay." It would be, at any rate, a rather shameful thing for the host if his guests had to smoke their own cigarettes.

Smoking is regarded most explicitly as something to do when relaxing—while socializing in the evening or while taking a break on the job. The after-dinner cigarette is also a well-established custom in Korea, one which is so prevalent that it is almost bad etiquette to suggest leaving a restaurant or returning to work after a lunch break at home until after time has been taken to smoke. Conversation of any length calls for smoking to accompany it, and the visitor routinely assumes, usually without asking, that his host won't mind if he smokes. If he sees no ashtray he asks for one *after* he lights up and needs to use it. One also comes quickly to understand that a visitor will not leave before he has smoked his entire cigarette. My own experience with unwelcome or overstayed guests is that they will *never* leave with a lighted cigarette. A guest who hints at leaving, and is subtly but not impolitely encouraged to do so, can effectively prolong his visit by lighting up again. Smoking a cigarette seems to fit into a highly regular routine for the Korean smoker, one which helps to structure his daily life and lend an element of consistency to it, and it is impolite for anyone to ask him to alter that routine.

FUNCTIONS AND SYMBOLIC MEANINGS OF SMOKING

In Korea smoking is functional—it accomplishes or aids in the accomplishment of important goals in the context of social life. Some of the functions and meanings of smoking found in Korea have already been explained in the context of the introductory and historical sections of this paper. Additional social functions of smoking beyond those already outlined will now be described in detail, and then some further symbolic meanings associated with tobacco will be discussed.

Interpersonal relationships in Korea are often conceived of in terms of formality and distance vs. intimacy and closeness. Like human relationships everywhere, a particular relationship in Korea can change over time from mutual suspicion on the part of two individuals to mutual trust, from extreme formality and discomfort to total informality and comfort. Because of the rigidity of age, sex, class, and kinship categories and the restrictions they place on possible interpersonal relationships or kinds of relationships in Korea, much social behavior between Koreans is undeviatingly and unchangeably formal or polite, no matter how well or how long the individuals have known each other. The superior in such relationships tends to fall into the category of those with whom the inferior cannot smoke. Many people, however, are potential associates, if not friends, with whom closer relationships can be developed. One way to maximize the potential of a relationship is to enter into the round of reciprocal gift exchange which has already been alluded to. Unlike market transactions, where any future obligation is eliminated through immediate money payment, gift exchange implies mutual commitment and a long-term relationship. As has already been explained, cigarettes are particularly useful in Korea as very modest gifts. They are light and easy to carry, inexpensive yet not "cheap," almost universally acceptable, and they double as items for personal consumption when one is alone. Offering a cigarette implies at least a desire to pause and visit and perhaps more. Because of their convenience and low cost cigarettes are unrivalled tools for "breaking the ice" and making new friends or for helping to convert initially formal, distant relationships into informal and more intimate ones.

When a Korean farmer asks his neighbor to help him on a project and feels obligated for the friend's time, he will often buy cigarettes and present them as a token of appreciation. An attempt to pay for the labor with money would be refused by the neighbor, but the gift can be gracefully accepted and the scales of mutual obligation kept at a better balance. A farm hand hired to work for a day will be paid not only in cash but will also receive lunch and dinner, both served with *makkŏli* (rice beer) and/or *soju* (a distilled, clear liquor), and a pack of cigarettes. The wages and food are payment, while the cigarettes and liquor can be seen as something extra to express appreciation to make the arrangement more sociable and personal.

Most business at local government administrative offices is transacted after an advance expression of appreciation in the form of a pack of cigarettes. Western observers have ethnocentrically regarded such gifts as bribes, but that is an overstated description of what the cigarettes do. The gift is an attempt to convert the recipient from a stranger to a friend, to enable bureaucratic business to proceed along the same friendly lines as business between merchants or employees of service industries and their customers. (It should be noted, however, that while most service industry employees have traditionally been seen as serving their customers and hence in an inferior position, bureaucrats are still seen more as people to be beseeched than as real public "servants.") A pack of cigarettes is not enough to prejudice a civil servant *for* anything in particular, and is thus not really a bribe. On the other hand, the custom has become widely enough practiced, perhaps because of a previous tradition of very low salaries for such public employees, that the omission of the cigarettes can prejudice the bureaucrat *against* acting with any dispatch. Many lower-level bureaucrats assume they will never have to spend money on cigarettes, even though they are confident of having plenty to offer their friends.

With neighbors, farm hands, and bureaucrats, and in other transactions as well, cigarettes provide compensation for that which cannot be purchased with money—they elicit, or it is hoped that they elicit, personal attention and more than usual commitment, and they definitely pave the way for continued cordial relationships. In all three of the cases cited here, and in others as well, tobacco serves as a kind of social grease to smooth the mechanisms of interpersonal relationships and transactions.

The symbolic functions of tobacco in cementing alliances, building friendships, and extending informal hospitality in Korea have at this point been entensively analyzed, but other symbolic aspects of tobacco use remain to be discussed. Prime among them is the price and quality hierarchy in cigarette brands and the socio-economic class distinctions which correlate with smoking them. In the U.S., cigarette prices differ only 10 percent or so among domestic brands. The Korean tobacco monopoly, on the other hand, has successfully designed a line of products which ranges in price from/W50 ($.10) to/W300/($.60) for a pack of cigarettes. This wide range of prices is sometimes attributed to the practice of introducing a new, more expensive brand each time inflation drives up the price of tobacco, leaving a built-in hedge against inflation for smokers whose income cannot keep pace and a new status symbol for the upwardly mobile. Each new brand, however, has usually represented a quality improvement as well. The package design, quality and mildness of tobacco, quality of cigarette paper, length of cigarette, and presence and quality of the filter all differ from brand to brand.

The armed forces distribute a daily ration of cigarettes to the troops free of charge (which surely is an illustration of the idea of tobacco as a basic necessity). The brand is *Hwarangdo* ("Way of the Warrior," a military code of conduct of the ancient Silla dynasty), and is of reasonably good quality. The poor and the old, especially old people who wish to smoke but who also wish to minimize their financial demands on sons who support them, often buy loose pack tobacco in cans, and if they prefer cigarettes to pipe smoking they buy paper for making their own cigarettes. This kind of tobacco is the lowest quality of all, but like the cheaper brands of cigarettes it provides a comparatively large concentration of nicotine, and is seen by some people to be preferable to more expensive tobacco because of its potency. It is called, rather ironically, *P'ungnyŏnch'o* ("Bumper Crop Grass").

The least expensive brand of cigarettes is filterless, wrapped in cheap paper, short, and the tobacco is strong, with a rough taste and aroma. The most expensive brand has three gold bands around the filter, is wrapped in the best quality paper, is made of extremely mild, blended tobacco (including Turkish and American imports), is "king-sized," and is packaged in a very attractively designed wrapper. Most of the various price levels of cigarettes include more than one brand, and in each such case there is a clearly preferred brand even though the price is the same. As with *Hwarangdo*, the brand names are associated with something in Korean history or tradition which make the names significant for more than their association with tobacco. The least expensive cigarette brand was renamed *Saemaŭl*, after the program of rural development which has been in effect for the past eight years, and now when a farmer asks for a pack of cigarettes he also recites a slogan and is reminded of the government program, much as the soldiers are supposed to be reminded of military ideals when they smoke *Hwarangdo*. The various brands, with their prices, are listed below:

Hwarangdo		free for service personnel
P'ungnyŏnch'o	W30	(loose tobacco)
Saemaŭl	W50	("New Community")
Chindallae	W80	("Azalea Blossom")
P'agoda	W100	(after Pagoda park, where the March 1st Independence Movement began)
Paekyang	W120	
Ch'ŏngja	W150	("Celadon Vase")
Arirang	W150	(famous folk song)
Saem	W150	("Water well")
Hansando	W220	(an island)
Eŭnhasu	W220	("Milky way")
Kŏbuksŏn	W300	("Turtle Ship" after first iron-clad warship)
T'aeyang	W300	("Sun" the only brand with the English translation on the back side of the pack)

Korean families, especially in the countryside, tend to live on very strict budgets. The brand of cigarette smoked by the man of the house can, over the long run, have a considerable financial impact, so a man normally chooses a standard of smoking he can afford and then consistently smokes that brand. Hence the relative socio-economic standing of a person is often symbolized by the brand he smokes. His friends tend to be those who smoke the same brand, since exchanging cigarettes of asymmetrical value cannot continue over a long period (not to mention the more obvious fact that friendships tend to form within, not across, class lines). Mr. Pak, in the case cited at the beginning, took his two packs of Turtle Ship brand with him to meet a client. There the brand he smoked would help him establish himself as a prosperous businessman among others of the same status. Thus beyond the cut of a man's coat, his haircut, and general demeanor, the pack of cigarettes in his pocket will indicate to one who observes him either his actual socio-economic status or in some cases the standard which he is willing to make sacrifices in order to appear to maintain. Men in rural villages whose social circle includes numerous people outside their local communities will sometimes smoke two brands—one for use in the home community and one for outside. My friend the village head smoked the W150 brand at home and the W220 brand on trips to the district office. He explained that outside the village he associated with other village and district leaders, and their status or pretentions to it required all of them to keep up certain standards. The one school teacher who lived in the village, a young married man with one infant child, carried Kŏbuksŏn, the most expensive brand, which he deemed appropriate for his social status. Even though teachers' salaries are not very high, people have traditionally expected, and still do expect, a teacher to maintain the life style of an upper-class gentleman, at least to the best of his financial ability. The marital and parental status of this particular teacher are mentioned because another, older man in the village, a school principal, smoked a lesser brand. He was willing to make a sacrifice for the benefit of his teenaged and adult children by smoking something less than his place in life should call for. He also had less interest in creating a good impression or in social climbing than most younger men, including the young school teacher, who are still on their way up the social ladder.

Distribution of the various brands tends to leave cities with the greatest supply of more expensive brands and the countryside with the less expensive ones, thus reflecting in terms of supply and demand for cigarettes the difference between rural and urban living standards. *Kŏbuksŏn* brand cigarettes are not sold in villages at all and comparatively few are for sale in district and county administrative centers or market towns. Higher level bureaucrats, teachers, police and military officials, and wealthy businessmen in such places generally establish a regular customer relationship with a tobacco retailer so that they can buy this most prestigious brand. This is of course why Mr. Pak passed three tobacco shops before making his purchase—he knew that "his" shop would have saved some *Kŏbuksŏn* for him. People in Seoul, in contrast to those in the countryside, can seldom find Saemaŭi brand cigarettes even if they want them. Observers' impressions of city slickers and country bumpkins are often confirmed by the brands of cigarettes seen in shirt pockets.

CONCLUSION

Although it is not an indigenous plant, tobacco has become very thoroughly integrated into Korean life. It symbolizes the traditional power and prominence of elders, as it did in the case of the shortened pipe. It serves the government as a commodity which, because of the stable, inelastic demand for it, can be controlled and taxed without having to weigh the politically and morally complex issues involved in producing or taxing a survival staple. It serves as a symbol of socio-economic status, as it was intended to do in the case of Mr. Pak on his way to the tea room. The social situations which either allow or prohibit smoking are clearly indicative of hierarchical structures in Korean society and of various forms of interpersonal relationships. The giving and receiving of cigarettes is a quintessential example of the importance and pervasiveness of reciprocal exchange in Korean social life. While some may risk the danger of tigers and ostracism by giving up tobacco, it is likely that most Koreans will continue to use it, for its smoke says more than words and its influence extends far beyond its aroma.

REFERENCES

Dredge, C. Paul. "Speech Variation and Social Organization in a Korean Village." Unpublished Ph.D. dissertation. Harvard University, 1977.

Lévi-Strauss, Claude. *The Elementary Structures of Kinship*. Boston: Beacon Press, 1969 (French original published in 1949).

Mauss, Marcel. *The Gift*. Boston: Beacon Press, 1954. (French original published in 1929).

Moose, J. Robert. *Village Life in Korea*. Nashville: Publishing House of the Methodist Episcopal Church, South, 1911 (reference from HRAF files).

One Hundred Per Cent American

by
Ralph Linton

THERE CAN BE no question about the average American's Americanism or his desire to preserve this precious heritage at all costs. Nevertheless, some insidious foreign ideas have already wormed their way into his civilization without his realizing what was going on. Thus dawn finds the unsuspecting patriot garbed in pajamas, a garment of East Indian origin; and lying in a bed built on a pattern which originated in either Persia or Asia Minor. He is muffled to the ears in un-American materials: cotton, first domesticated in India; linen, domesticated in the Near East; wool from an animal native to Asia Minor; or silk, whose uses were first discovered by the Chinese. All these substances have been transformed into cloth by methods invented in Southwestern Asia. If the weather is cold enough he may even be sleeping under an eiderdown quilt invented in Scandinavia.

On awakening he glances at the clock, a medieval European invention, uses one potent Latin word in abbreviated form, rises in haste, and goes to the bathroom. Here, if he stops to think about it, he must feel himself in the presence of a great American institution; he will have heard stories of both the quality and frequency of foreign plumbing and will know that in no other country does the average man perform his ablutions in the midst of such splendor. But the insidious foreign influence pursues him even here. Glass was invented by the ancient Egyptians, the use of glazed tiles for floors and walls in the Near East, porcelain in China, and the art of enameling on metal by Mediterranean artisans of the Bronze Age. Even his bathtub and toilet are but slightly modified copies of Roman originals. The only

Reprinted from *The American Mercury*, vol. 40 (1937), pp. 427–429.

purely American contribution to the ensemble is the steam radiator, against which our patriot very briefly and unintentionally places his posterior.

In this bathroom the American washes with soap invented by the ancient Gauls. Next he cleans his teeth, a subversive European practice which did not invade America until the latter part of the eighteenth century. He then shaves, a masochistic rite first developed by the heathen priests of ancient Egypt and Sumer. The process is made less of a penance by the fact that his razor is of steel, an iron-carbon alloy discovered in either India or Turkestan. Lastly, he dries himself on a Turkish towel.

Returning to the bedroom, the unconscious victim of un-American practices removes his clothes from a chair, invented in the Near East, and proceeds to dress. He puts on close-fitting tailored garments whose form derives from the skin clothing of the ancient nomads of the Asiatic steppes and fastens them with buttons whose prototypes appeared in Europe at the close of the Stone Age. This costume is appropriate enough for outdoor exercise in a cold climate, but is quite unsuited to American summers, steam-heated houses, and Pullmans. Nevertheless, foreign ideas and habits hold the unfortunate man in thrall even when common sense tells him that the authentically American costume of gee string and moccasins would be far more comfortable. He puts on his feet stiff coverings made from hide prepared by a process invented in ancient Egypt and cut to a pattern which can be traced back to ancient Greece, and makes sure that they are properly polished, also a Greek idea. Lastly, he ties about his neck a strip of bright-colored cloth which is a vestigial survival of the shoulder shawls worn by seventeenth-century Croats. He gives himself a final appraisal in the mirror, an old Mediterranean invention, and goes downstairs to breakfast.

Here a whole new series of foreign things confronts him. His food and drink are placed before him in pottery vessels, the popular name of which—china—is sufficient evidence of their origin. His fork is a medieval Italian invention and his spoon a copy of a Roman original. He will usually begin the meal with coffee, an Abyssinian plant first discovered by the Arabs. The American is quite likely to need it to dispel the morning-after effects of overindulgence in fermented drinks, invented in the Near East; or distilled ones, invented by the alchemists of medieval Europe. Whereas the Arabs took their coffee straight, he will probably sweeten it with sugar, discovered in India; and dilute it with cream, both the domestication of cattle and the technique of milking having originated in Asia Minor.

If our patriot is old-fashioned enough to adhere to the so-called American breakfast, his coffee will be accompanied by an orange, domesticated in the Mediterranean region, a cantaloupe domesticated in Persia, or grapes domesticated in Asia Minor. He will follow this with a bowl of cereal made from grain domesticated in the Near East and prepared by methods also invented there. From this he will go on to waffles, a Scandinavian invention, with plenty of butter, originally a Near-Eastern cosmetic. As a side dish he may have the egg of a bird domesticated in Southeastern Asia or strips of the flesh of an animal domesticated in the same region, which have been salted and smoked by a process invented in Northern Europe.

Breakfast over, he places upon his head a molded piece of felt, invented by the nomads of Eastern Asia, and, if it looks like rain, puts on outer shoes of rubber, discovered by the ancient Mexicans, and takes an umbrella, invented in India. He then sprints for his train—the train, not sprinting, being an English invention. At the station he pauses for a moment to buy a newspaper, paying for it with coins invented in ancient Lydia. Once on board he settles back to inhale the fumes of a cigarette invented in Mexico, or a cigar, invented in Brazil. Meanwhile, he reads the news of the day, imprinted in characters invented by the ancient Semites by a process invented in Germany upon a material invented in China. As he scans the latest editorial pointing out the dire results to our institutions of accepting foreign ideas, he will not fail to thank a Hebrew God in an Indo-European language that he is a one hundred percent (decimal system invented by the Greeks) American (from Americus Vespucci, Italian geographer).

VI

MARRIAGE AND KINSHIP

If women are to effect a significant amelioration in their
condition . . . they must refuse to marry. No worker
can be required to sign for life: if he did his employer
could disregard all his attempts to gain better working
conditions.

Germaine Greer

MODERN DISENCHANTMENT WITH marriage is a phenomenon not limited to women. Men frequently refer to marriage as servitude, hiding their serious concerns in jest. "When my wife says jump," an eloquent "slave" remarked, "I ask 'How high?' and 'Where shall I land?' " Such attitudes explain a jump in the divorce rate of 250 percent in the past twenty years in the United States. What remains unexplained is the high remarriage rate. In the United States about 80 percent of those who were previously married remarry. Data such as these present modern social scientists with many fascinating problems. For example: If many men and women equate marriage with servitude, why is remarriage so popular? Are second marriages generally "happier" than first ones, and if so, what makes them superior forms of union? What happens to kinship ties in systems with high divorce rates? Questions such as these show that marriage and kinship studies are both interesting and relevant.

Modern life is not, in any obvious way, more dismal than life in "the good old days." It seems implausible, therefore, to argue that high divorce and remarriage rates are a worrisome phenomenon.[1] Rather, I believe, these data illustrate yet again how creative and adaptable is the human animal. Human social and cultural life includes many different sets of rules, and each set seems adequate (at the very least) for its purposes.

Human creativity, when associated with environmental variety, produces many different types of kinship systems. Family, Meyer

[1]This position is supported by Lionel Tiger ("Omnigamy: The New Kinship System," *Psychology Today*, July 1978). High divorce and remarriage rates, according to Tiger, create a functional system with extensive kinship links.

300

Fortes reminds us in "Primitive Kinship," is based on marriage and parentage. In "primitive" society, parentage (or descent line) is the major principle for assigning people into social roles. Most often one line is selected as dominant: the paternal (producing "patrilineal" descent) or the maternal (producing "matrilineal" descent). A. R. Radcliffe-Brown, according to Fortes, has provided three general principles which seem to explain the essentials of "primitive" kinship relationships. Principle 1, *the generational principle*, explains the gap created between people of different generations. Principle 2, *the sibling rule of unity*, is the other side of the coin. Here, those who belong to the same generation are shown as having an intimacy lacking between the generations.[2] Principle 3, *the rule of affiliation*, identifies a curious lumping of people of the same descent group.

The rule of affiliation is discussed by Radcliffe-Brown himself in a paper now considered a classic, "The Mother's Brother in South Africa." This paper is an attempt to steer anthropologists away from speculative history (that is, making historical inferences when historical data are sparse or missing). In the absence of "good" history we must focus on structural analysis. Radcliffe-Brown's paper demonstrates that this structural focus provides us with the power to solve basic cultural problems.

BaThonga boys expect and receive care and indulgence from their mothers. They also expect and receive similar treatment from their mothers' brothers. Why should mother and brother be "equated" among the BaThonga, that is, why are they lumped together under one set of role expectations? This phenomenon, according to Radcliffe-Brown, is explained by the rule of affiliation. The mother and her brother belong to the same descent group. At times it becomes reasonable for a group to "equate" people purely on the basis of descent. Among the BaThonga and in many other tribes in South Africa, intimate ties exist between a boy and his mother's brother. And such intimacy acts as a counterbalance to the more authoritarian relationships which exist between boys and their fathers. Radcliffe-Brownian structuralism, clearly, seeks to identify the "structure" of a system by examining actual relationships and attempting to discover how they form a pattern. The pattern consists of relationships which are considered "equivalent" (e.g., *mother* to *sons* = *boy* to

---

[2] The label "sibling" usually refers to both "brother" and "sister" (that is, "child of my parents"). As used to describe principle 2, "sibling" is extended to refer to all the members of a given generation.

mother's brother) and relationships which create some kind of system "balance" (e.g., *boy* to *mother's brother* versus *boy* to *father*).[3]

I assume that modern readers almost invariably will have the question of relevance on their minds. In this context the question is: What use is kinship analysis—of whatever structural tradition—particularly when the data concern tribes whose lives are quite different from our own? Moreover, these very tribes are currently undergoing much culture change. Why discuss a kinship system which probably no longer exists? In "The Therapeutic Triad" Rose Laub Coser demonstrates that kinship studies are most relevant to modern issues.

The therapeutic triad is based on a model developed by means of a structural analysis of "primitive" kinship relationships. The model, in the hands of a brilliant analyst like Rose Coser, isolates fundamental conflicts which exist in the treatment of hospitalized mental patients. There is a double aspect to the psychiatric role, "the control of patient's behavior and their psychotherapy." As a controller the psychiatrist is a boss to be obeyed and (at times) feared. This "high-status authority" has the right to make decisions which profoundly affect a patient's life. How can this person be given the psychotherapy role and be expected to perform adequately? A psychotherapist is a friend. Helpful psychotherapy is based on a "therapeutic alliance" between patient and psychiatrist. How can this relationship of mutual trust be developed and maintained if the psychiatrist is also charged with the control of patients? In the language of the model, how can a psychiatrist be both "high status authority" and "high-status friend"?

At O'Brien—a fictitious name for a real psychiatric facility—a division of labor has been created among the psychiatric staff. The ward psychiatrist, or high-status authority, does not do

[3]The reader should note that the term "uncle," while meaningful to those living in many Western societies, is confusing when applied to tribes such as the BaThonga. There, the role "mother's brother" has quite different requirements from the role "father's brother." It should also be noted that the structuralism here being discussed (that of Radcliffe-Brown) is quite different from the structuralism discussed in section II of this book, "Fieldwork." There (see the headnote and the article by Mary Douglas) structuralism follows an approach developed by Claude Lévi-Strauss. Those who find themselves intrigued by structural analysis are invited to consider a novel approach to the Adam and Eve story as stimulated by structural analysis: see Morris Freilich, "Myth, Method and Madness," *Current Anthropology*, vol. 16 (1976), pp. 207–226.

psychotherapy, and the psychotherapist does not act as a bossy controller. This seemingly Solomon-like solution is not as perfect as it may appear. As Coser writes, "The split of the administrative and therapeutic tasks has brought about an intricate social structure, which is the source of the stability of the system at the same time that it brings in its wake a new set of ambiguities for both patients and practitioners."

Data and concepts, problems and solutions which yet create new problems—all are elegantly and insightfully interwoven in "The Therapeutic Triad."

REFERENCES

Coser, Rose Laub. *Training in Ambiguity: Learning Through Doing in a Mental Hospital*. New York: Free Press, 1981.

Fox, Robin. *Kinship and Marriage: An Anthropological Perspective*. Baltimore: Penguin Books, 1967.

Freilich, Morris. "The Natural Triad in Kinship and Complex Systems." *American Sociological Review*, vol. 29, no. 4 (1964).

Greer, Germaine. *The Female Eunuch*. London: Paladin Books, 1971.

Henry, Jules. *Pathways to Madness*. New York: Random House, 1973.

Schneider, David. *American Kinship: A Cultural Account*. Englewood Cliffs, N.J.: Prentice-Hall, 1968.

Primitive Kinship

by
Meyer Fortes

MINISTERS, POLITICAL ORATORS and editorial writers are apt to tell us that the family is the keystone of society. From the biological point of view it would indeed seem to be the ultimate social institution. The conjugal family—husband and wife and their children—gives social expression to the function of human reproduction. Early travelers from our civilization were sometimes shocked because they could find no obvious counterpart of our family among primitive peoples. When they found large communal households, inhabited by men, women, and children having the most bizarre and sometimes downright indecent relationships to one another (in the terminology of our family), they took this as conclusive evidence that these cultures were barbaric.

We have come to know primitive peoples at closer range in recent years. What they have taught us has radically altered our judgment of their family organizations and given us an humbler understanding of our own. Primitive family types vary in their constitution, but they are always precisely structured institutions, embracing the primary loyalty and life activity of their large membership and enduring from generation to generation. The exact prescription of relationships among members gives each individual a significantly defined connection to a wide circle of his kin. To the individual member, the family's property is the source of livelihood, its ancestors are his gods, its elders his government, and its young men his defense and his support in old age. In simpler cultures (e.g., the Australian aborigines) family and society are actually coterminous: all men are either kinsmen or potential enemies.

We, in contrast, are primarily citizens, not kinsmen. The

Reprinted from *Scientific American*, 200 (June 1959), pp. 147–158 by permission of W. H. Freeman and Company. Copyright © 1959 by *Scientific American*, Inc.

family is organized anew with each marriage. It must share our allegiance with the many competing claims of our society: the loyalties we owe to the institutions that employ us, to our professional organizations, to political parties, to community and nation. A family of such reduced status and scope is, as a matter of fact, distinctly out of the ordinary as families go. The Hebrew families of the Bible and the Roman *gens* more closely resemble the extended family systems of contemporary primitive cultures than they do our own. Of all the primitive societies I know, the one that most closely resembles ours in isolating the conjugal family as the basic social unit is the Iban, a tribe of headhunters in North Borneo. The vocabulary we employ to describe our kin—our uncles, aunts and cousins—beyond the immediate conjugal family fails to suggest the compelling ties that bind the kinship of peoples other than those of modern European and American civilization. Students of primitive kinship systems have found that they employ a terminology wholly unlike our own: the "classificatory" system, which groups relatives by status rather than sorting out their genetic interrelationships. It appears that all kinship systems obey certain universal principles governing the separation, inner unity, and orderly sequence of generations. Viewed from the vantage point of such understanding, our family appears to be the much-curtailed form of a once far more elaborate and comprehensive organization.

Two "facts of life" necessarily provide the basis of every family: the fact of sexual intercourse is institutionalized in marriage; the fact of parturition is institutionalized in parenthood. Societies differ greatly, however, in which of these institutions they select as the more important. Our society selects marriage: the result is the conjugal family, centered upon a single marital relationship and the children it produces. Most human societies, however, rate parenthood above marriage. This results in the consanguineal family, centered upon a single line of descent.

Biologically our lineal inheritance derives equally from both sides of the family according to Mendelian law. Societies that prize lineage, however, restrict social inheritance either to the maternal or the paternal line. The social heritage—that is, property, citizenship, office, rank—passes either through the father or through the mother. "Patrilineal" descent (father to son) was the rule in ancient Rome, China and Israel, and occurs in many primitive societies. "Matrilineal" descent (mother's brother to sister's son) is common in Asia, Africa, Oceania, and aboriginal America.

One matrilineal society that flourishes today is the ancient, wealthy and artistic kingdom of Ashanti in Ghana, West Africa. While European mores have made some inroads among the Ashanti, back-country Ashanti villages still keep to their strictly matrilineal ways. Let us consider how such a society works.

First of all, let us note that a matrilineal society is not a matriarchal society: it is not ruled by women. So far as I know there is not, nor has there ever been, such a thing as a genuine matriarchal government. In every preliterate society men, not women, hold the political, legal and economic power; the women usually remain legal minors all their lives, subject to the authority of their menfolk. Primitive peoples usually understand quite well why men, not women, must be the rulers. The women, they say, are incapacitated for warfare and the affairs of state by the necessity of bearing and rearing children. Many peoples, including the Ashanti, believe that women are magically dangerous to men during menstruation and after childbirth.

In describing the Ashanti kinship system I am going to use common English terms (like "aunt" and "cousin") rather than attempt to translate the native terminology. The typical Ashanti household consists of an old woman, her daughters, their children, and one or two of her sons. The old woman, the daughters, and the sons are all married, but where are their spouses? We can suppose that all of these people are on good terms with their husbands and wives; nevertheless they do not form part of the same household with them, because they do not belong to the same clan. The spouses all live nearby, in households belonging to their own clans. The legal head of the household is one of the old woman's sons; he inherited his role from his mother's brother, not his father; he will pass it on to his sister's son, not his own.

Among the Ashanti marriage is governed by strict moral, legal and religious rules. Yet it is clear that the Ashanti find the fact of descent much more important than the fact of marriage. That is why the households are formed by mothers and children rather than by husbands and wives. The lineage group to which the old woman and her children belong is united by the bond of common descent from an ancestress of perhaps the tenth generation before that of the youngest members. Through this ancestress the group traces its descent from an even more remote mythological ancestress: the progenitor of their clan, one of the eight clans into which the Ashanti people is divided.

It is considered a sin and a crime for members of the same Ashanti lineage to have sexual relations; by this token they must look for spouses of independent descent, that is, of a different clan. Since husband and wife commonly reside in separate households, they must live near each other if they are to have a normal marital relationship. More than 80 percent of all marriages occur within the village community. Usually, therefore, one or two lineages of each of the eight clans is found in a village of average size.

The Ashanti rule of matrilineal descent has implications that reach far beyond the domestic household. Every Ashanti is by birth a citizen of the chiefdom to which his maternal lineage belongs. A man or woman can build a house freely on any vacant site in this chiefdom, and can farm any piece of unclaimed soil in the lands that it owns. An individual has no such rights in any other chiefdom. By the rule of matrilineal descent, a man can will no property to his own children; they belong to another household and another clan: his wife's. A man's heirs and successors are his sisters' sons. On his death his property and any position of hereditary rank he may hold pass automatically to his oldest nephew. If he wishes his own sons and daughters to benefit from his property, he must be content to make them gifts during his lifetime. They can accept his gifts only with the consent of his matrilineal heirs and of the elders in his lineage group. In the Ashanti tradition the individual comes under the authority of the mother's brother, not the father. It is the mother's brother whose consent is legally essential for a girl or boy to marry; he is also responsible for any costs that arise from divorce or other suits against them.

How do marriage and parenthood work out in such a system of kinship rules? It is undeniable that the Ashanti have delicate problems of marital adjustment. Both husband and wife must reach a compromise between their primary loyalties to matrilineal kin and their attachment to each other and to their children. When a man marries, he acquires legal rights to his wife's marital fidelity and to domestic services such as the regular provision of his meals. If a wife commits adultery, her husband can claim damages from the other man and apologies and a gift of placation from the wife, even if, as often happens, he does not divorce her. He can and will insist on divorce if his wife neglects her household duties or refuses to sleep with him. The husband is in turn obliged to provide food, clothing, and general care for his wife and children. If he fails in these duties, his wife can divorce him. In fact, divorce is very common among the Ashanti. Usually it is free of acrimony, for it does not involve the splitting of a household.

What an Ashanti man does not acquire by marriage is rights

over his wife's reproductive powers, that is, over the children she bears him. These belong to her lineage, as opposed to his. An Ashanti man cannot demand help from his sons, for example in farming or in the payment of a debt, as he can from his sisters' sons. He can punish his nephew, but not his sons. He can order his nieces to marry a man of his choice, but not his daughters.

At the opposite extreme from the Ashanti are the Tallensi, who live nearby in Ghana's remote northern uplands. The Tallensi kinship and marriage system is the mirror image of that of the Ashanti. The Tallensi household is not matrilineal but patrilineal; it consists of a group of men, usually a man and his sons and grandsons, together with their wives and unmarried daughters. The men of this household and others in the immediate neighborhood all share the same patrilineal descent, which they can trace back in the male line to a single male ancestor. Tallensi men share their land, are equally eligible for family offices and join in the worship of ancestral spirits. Like the Ashanti, the Tallensi are "exogamous"; their children must marry members of clans other than their own. Among the Tallensi, however, a woman joins her husband's household on marriage, because he has rights not only to her domestic services and marital fidelity, but also to her children. This is the crucial distinction between matrilineal and patrilineal systems.

Our Western way of reckoning kinship is neither matrilineal nor patrilineal. Rather, it is "bilateral." That is, we consider our mothers' kin to be as closely related to us as our fathers'. Nowadays we follow the same etiquette with both maternal and paternal relatives. Our terminology distinctly reflects the equality of our conjugal family system. Since we rate the conjugal (husband-wife) over the lineal (parent-child) bond, the paternal or maternal orientation of the lineage becomes a matter of indifference. In naming our spouses' relatives we assimilate them to our own: a mother-in-law is a kind of mother, a brother-in-law is a kind of brother, and we treat them accordingly.

Our kinship terminology, like that of the Eskimos and a few other peoples, follows the so-called descriptive system. We have separate labels for each category of our kin, according to their generation, their sex and their linkage to us by descent or marriage. We distinguish our parents ("father" and "mother") from their male siblings ("uncles") and their female siblings ("aunts"). We have different appellations for our own siblings ("brother," "sister") and for our aunts' and uncles' children ("cousins").

Most primitive peoples use the entirely different labels of the classificatory system. This system often strikes Westerners as odd, although it is widespread among the peoples of mankind. Its principle is that in each generation all relatives of the same sex are addressed in the same way, no matter how remote the relationship. A sister and a female first- or second-cousin are all called "sister"; a father, an uncle and more distant male collaterals of their generation are called "father." A woman addresses her nieces and nephews, as well as her own offspring, as "my children." The nieces and nephews, as well as her own children, call her "mother." The Tallensi, the Swazi of South Africa, and many other societies even use words for "father" with a feminine suffix added, to designate the sisters of all the men they address as "father." A Swazi calls his mother's brother a "male mother."

This terminology was recognized for the first time nearly a century ago by a great U.S. anthropologist, Lewis H. Morgan. His *Systems of Consanguinity and Affinity of the Human Family*, published in 1871, founded the modern study of kinship systems. Morgan and his followers believed that classificatory terminology had survived from an extremely primitive stage of social organization, in which a group of sisters would mate promiscuously with a group of brothers and would rear the offspring in common.

By now Morgan's theory of "group marriage" has been completely discredited. Modern anthropology has discovered far more cogent reasons for the existence of classificatory terminology. If a man calls all the male relatives of his generation "brother," it is not because at some remote period the promiscuity of the elder generation made it impossible to tell one's brother from one's cousin. The reason is that such generalized terminology expresses the deep sense of corporate unity in the extended family. A child in such a family knows very well which of the women of the household is his physiological mother. Like children anywhere in the world, he will love his real mother as he loves none of her sisters or female cousins. Yet in the joint family those sisters and cousins share his mother's duties to him, and he must observe the same code of politeness with each of them. If his real mother should die, another of the women he calls "mother" will replace her. The classificatory terminology binds together groups that share status and responsibilities. To people like the Ashanti and Tallensi the word "mother" has a social rather than a biological significance: it defines ones rank in a complex family system.

The need to define relationship is crucial in every society, and all kinship systems have evolved in response to this need. We are indebted to A. R. Radcliffe-Brown, the distinguished British anthropologist, for the most satisfactory statement of the underlying principles. The first of these establishes a clear demarcation between successive generations. The elders are not only physiological progenitors of their young; they also protect and nurture them throughout childhood and provide their first training in the crafts, customs, and morals of the tribe. This all-important relationship requires not only love on the part of the parents but also respect on the part of the children. Parental authority is incompatible with complete intimacy. Most societies banish everything sexual from the parent-and-child relationship; the universal taboo on incest between parent and child epitomizes the cleavage between elder and younger generations. Many societies enforce certain "avoidances" that help to maintain social distance between generations. The Tallensi, for example, forbid an eldest son to eat from his father's dish. Some central African tribes carry avoidance to extremes. One tribe, the Nyakyusa, requires fathers and children to live in separate villages. In the matrilineal Ashanti society, on the other hand, it is the uncle to whom children show respect (or at least resentful submission). Ashanti fathers are not figures of authority to their children and need not keep aloof from them. Indeed, the father's lack of authority over his children is compensated for by warm bonds of trust and affection.

Radcliffe-Brown's second principle is the so-called sibling rule of unity and loyalty among the members of a single generation. The unity among siblings (meaning cousins as well as brothers and sisters) is the converse of the first principle of separation between each generation of siblings and the next. Internally, of course, each generation is differentiated by sex and order of birth. Yet the rule generally prevails that siblings share all things on equal terms. Frequently the sibling principle is generalized to include all tribesmen of the same generation. In East and West Africa this is institutionalized in the so-called age-grade system. The pastoral Masai, for example, initiate youths into their lowest "grade" of junior warriors every seven years, two successive grades forming a "generation set." Members of a set are classificatory brothers to each other and are classificatory fathers to the next set. Cattle-keeping and warfare are the tasks of the junior sets, while government is the prerogative of the senior sets.

The third principle of kinship, according to Radcliffe-Brown's scheme, accounts for the orderly succession of the distinct sibling groups in time: this is the rule of "filiation." Most societies, as we have seen, stress this rule more strongly than we do. Filiation is usually traced on strictly matrilineal or patrilineal lines. Occasionally the two modes are combined. In some African tribes the individual inherits land and political offices from his father, and livestock and religious-cult memberships from his mother. The bond of common filiation forms social groups that reach beyond the single household in time as well as space. These groups are often called clans. Frequently they are exogamous; as among the Ashanti and Tallensi, their members may not marry one another but must seek mates from other clans. This establishes "affinal" (in-law) relationships between clans and binds them into a still larger unit: the tribe.

What happens to kinship-based societies when industry, a money economy and Western education impinge on them? Recent investigation shows an increasing breakdown of both patrilineal and matrilineal family systems under such conditions. In their place bilateral systems similar to our own become established. The reasons are obvious. Industry and commerce require the individual to earn wages and to enter legal contracts not as a member of a family but on his own. Western law and education emphasize the responsibilities of individual citizenship and parenthood, as opposed to group citizenship and collective responsibility of kinfolk to children. In his legal and economic roles the individual separates from his kin group. The family constituted by marriage becomes his primary concern. In Africa and elsewhere, as people become industrialized, we are witnessing processes of social evolution analogous to those that shaped the much more limited institution that we call the family.

The Mother's Brother in South Africa

by
A. R. Radcliffe-Brown

AMONGST PRIMITIVE PEOPLES in many parts of the world a good deal of importance is attached to the relationship of mother's brother and sister's son. Mr. Junod in his book on the BaThonga people of Portuguese East Africa (*The Life of a South African Tribe*) provides the following information (pages 225–255):

1. The uterine nephew all through his career is the object of special care on the part of his uncle.

2. When the nephew is sick the mother's brother sacrifices on his behalf.

3. The nephew is permitted to take many liberties with his mother's brother; for example, he may go to his uncle's home and eat up the food that has been prepared for the latter's meal.

4. The nephew claims some of the property of his mother's brother when the latter dies, and may sometimes claim one of the widows.

5. When the mother's brother offers a sacrifice to his ancestors, the sister's son steals and consumes the portion of meat or beer offered to the gods.

It must not be supposed that these customs are peculiar to the BaThonga. There is evidence that similar customs might be found amongst other South African tribes if they were looked for. And we know of the existence of similar customs amongst other peoples in various parts of the world. In South Africa itself customs of this kind have been found by Mrs. Hoernlé amongst the Nama Hottentots. The sister's son may behave with great freedom towards his mother's brother, and may take any particularly fine beast from his herd of cattle, or any particularly fine

Adapted from *South African Journal of Science*, vol. 21 (1924), by permission of the publisher.

object that he may possess. On the contrary, the mother's brother may take from his nephew's herd any beast that is malformed or decrepit, and may take any old and worn-out object that he may possess.

What is particularly interesting to me is that in the part of Polynesia that I know best, that is, in the Friendly Islands (Tonga) and in Fiji, we find customs that show a very close resemblance to those of the BaThonga. There, also, the sister's son is permitted to take many liberties with his mother's brother, and to take any of his uncle's possessions that he may desire. And there also we find the custom that, when the uncle makes a sacrifice, the sister's son takes away the sacred portion offered to the gods, and may eat it. I shall, therefore, make occasional references to the Tongan customs.

These three peoples, the BaThonga, the Nama, and the Tongans, have patrilineal or patriarchal institutions. That is, the children belong to the social group of the father, not to that of the mother; and property is inherited in the male line, passing normally from a father to his sons. The view that I am opposing is that the customs relating to the mother's brother can only be explained by supposing that, at some past time, these peoples had matrilineal institutions, such as are found today amongst other primitive peoples, with whom the children belong to the social group of the mother, and property is inherited in the female line, passing from a man to his brothers and to his sister's sons.

It is a mistake to suppose that we can understand the institutions of society by studying them in isolation, without regard to other institutions with which they coexist and with which they may be correlated. And I wish to call attention to a correlation that seems to exist between customs relating to the mother's brother and customs relating to the father's sister. So far as present information goes, where we find the mother's brother important we also find that the father's sister is equally important, though in a different way. The custom of allowing the sister's son to take liberties with his mother's brother seems to be generally accompanied with an obligation of particular respect and obedience to the father's sister.

Junod says little about the father's sister amongst the BaThonga. Speaking of a man's behaviour to this relative (his *rarana*) he says simply: "He shows her great respect. However she is not in any way a mother (*mamana*)."

About the Nama Hottentots we have better information, and there the father's sister is the object of the very greatest respect on the part of her brother's child. In Tonga this custom is very clearly defined. A man's father's sister is the one relative above all others whom he must respect and obey. If she selects a wife for him he must marry her without even venturing to demur or to voice any objection; and so throughout his life. His father's sister is sacred to him; her word is his law; and one of the greatest offenses of which he could be guilty would be to show himself lacking in respect to her.

Now this correlation (which is not confined, of course, to the three instances I have mentioned, but seems, as I have said, to be general) must be taken into account in any explanation of the customs relating to the mother's brother, for the correlated customs are, if I am right, not independent institutions, but part of one system; and no explanation of one part of the system is satisfactory unless it fits in with an explanation of the system as a whole.

In most primitive societies the social relations of individuals are very largely regulated on the basis of kinship. This is brought about by the formation of fixed and more or less definite patterns of behaviour for each of the recognised kinds of relationship. There is a special pattern of behaviour, for example, for a son towards his father, and another for a younger brother towards his elder brother. The particular patterns vary from one society to another; but there are certain fundamental principles or tendencies which appear in all societies, or in all those of a certain type. It is these general tendencies that it is the special task of social anthropology to discover and explain.

Once we start tracing out relationship to any considerable distance the number of different kinds of relatives that it is logically possible to distinguish is very large. This difficulty is avoided in primitive society by a system of classification, by which relatives of what might logically be held to be of different kinds are classified together into a limited number of kinds, very much as we classify together the relatives we call cousins. The principle of classification that is most commonly adopted in primitive society may be stated as that of the equivalence of brothers. In other words, if I stand in a particular relation to one man I regard myself as standing in the same general kind of relation to his brother; and similarly with a woman and her sister. In this way the father's brother comes to be regarded a sort of father, and his sons are, therefore, relatives of the same kind as brothers. Similarly, the mother's sister is regarded as another mother, and her children are therefore brothers and sisters. This system is the one to be found amongst the Bantu tribes of South Africa, and amongst the Nama Hottentots, and also in the Friendly Islands.

By means of this principle primitive societies are able to arrive at definite patterns of behaviour towards uncles and aunts and cousins of certain kinds. A man's behaviour towards his father's brother must be of the same general kind as his behaviour towards his own father, and he must behave to his mother's sister according to the same pattern as towards his mother. The children of the father's brother or of the mother's sister must be treated in very much the same way as brothers and sisters.

This principle, however, does not give us immediately any pattern for either the mother's brother or the father's sister. It would be possible, of course, to treat the former as being like a father and the latter as similar to a mother, and this course does seem to have been adopted in a few societies. A tendency in this direction is found in some parts of Africa and in some parts of Polynesia. But it is characteristic of societies in which the classificatory system of kinship is either not fully developed or has been partly effaced.

Where the classificatory system of kinship reaches a high degree of development or elaboration another tendency makes its appearance; the tendency to develop patterns for the mother's brother and the father's sister by regarding the former as a sort of male mother and the latter as a sort of female father. This tendency sometimes makes its appearance in language. Thus, in South Africa the common term for the mother's brother is *malume* or *umalume*, which is a compound formed from the stem for "mother"—*ma*—and a suffix meaning "male." Amongst the BaThonga the father's sister is called *rarana*, a term which Junod explains as meaning exactly "female father." In some South African languages there is no special term for the father's sister; thus, in Xosa, she is denoted by a descriptive term *udadc bo bawo*, literally "father's sister." In Zulu she may be referred to by a similar descriptive term, or she may be spoken of simply as *ubaba*, "father," just like the father's brothers. In the Friendly Islands the mother's brother may be denoted by a special term *tuasina*, or he may be called *fa'e tangata*, literally "male mother." This similarity between South Africa and Polynesia cannot, I think, be regarded as accidental; yet there is no possible connection between the Polynesian languages and the Bantu languages, and I find it very difficult to conceive that the two regions have adopted the custom of calling the mother's brother by a term meaning "male mother," either from one another or from one common source.

Now, let us see if we can deduce what ought to be the patterns of behaviour towards the mother's brother and the father's sister in a patrilineal society on the basis of the principle or tendency which I have suggested is present. To do this we must first know the patterns of the father and the mother respectively, and I think that it will, perhaps, be more reassuring if I go for the definition of these to Mr. Junod's work, as his observations will certainly not have been influenced by the hypothesis that I am trying to prove.

The relationship of father, he says, "implies respect and even fear. The father, though he does not take much trouble with his children, is, however, their instructor, the one who scolds and punishes. So do also the father's brothers." Of a man's own mother he says: "She is his true *mamana*, and the relation is very deep and tender, combining respect and love. Love, however, generally exceeds respect." Of the mother's relation to her children we read that "she is generally weak with them and is often accused by the father of spoiling them."

There is some danger in condensed formulae, but I think we shall not be far wrong in saying that in a strongly patriarchal society, such as we find in South Africa, the father is the one who must be respected and obeyed, and the mother is the one from whom may be expected tenderness and indulgence. I could show you, if it were necessary, that the same thing is true of the family life of the Friendly Islanders.

If, now, we apply the principle that I have suggested is at work in these peoples it will follow that the father's sister is one who must be obeyed and treated with respect, while from the mother's brother indulgence and care may be looked for. But the matter is complicated by another factor. If we consider the relation of a nephew to his uncle and aunt, the question of sex comes in. In primitive societies there is a marked difference in the behaviour of a man towards other men and that towards women. Risking once more a slight formula, we may say that any considerable degree of familiarity is only permitted in such a society as the BaThonga between persons of the same sex. A man must treat his female relatives with greater respect than his male relatives. Consequently, the nephew must treat his father's sister with even greater respect than he does his own father. (In just the same way, owing to the principle of respect for age or seniority, a man must treat his father's elder brother with more respect than his own father.) Inversely, a man may treat his mother's brother, who is of his own sex, with a degree of familiarity that would not be possible with any woman, even his own mother.

We have deduced from our assumed principle a certain pattern of behaviour for the father's sister and for the mother's brother. Now, these patterns are exactly what we find amongst the BaThonga, amongst the Hottentots, and in the Friendly Islands. The father's sister is above all relatives the one to be respected and obeyed. The mother's brother is the one relative above all from whom we may expect indulgence, with whom we may be familiar and take liberties.

The first and most obvious thing to do is to study in detail the behaviour of the sister's son and the mother's brother to one another in matriarchal societies. Unfortunately, there is practically no information on this subject relating to Africa, and very little for any other part of the world. Moreover, there are certain false ideas connected with this distinction of societies into matriarchal and patriarchal that it is necessary to remove before we attempt to go further.

In all societies, primitive or advanced, kinship is necessarily bilateral. The individual is related to certain persons through his father and to others through his mother, and the kinship system of the society lays down what shall be the character of his dealings with his paternal relatives and his maternal relatives respectively. But society tends to divide into segments (local groups, sibs, etc.), and when the hereditary principle is accepted, as it most frequently is, as the means of determining the membership of a segment, then it is necessary to choose between maternal and paternal descent. When a society is divided into groups with a rule that the children belong to the group of the father we have paternal descent, while if the children always belong to the group of the mother the descent is maternal or matrilineal.

There is, unfortunately, a great deal of looseness in the use of the terms matriarchal and patriarchal, and for that reason many anthropologists refuse to use them. If we are to use them at all, we must first give exact definitions. A society may be called patriarchal when descent is patrilineal (i.e., the children belong to the group of the father), marriage is patrilocal (i.e., the wife removes to the local group of the husband), inheritance (of property) and succession (to rank) are in the male line, and the family is patripotestal (i.e., the authority over the members of the family is in the hands of the father or his relatives). On the other hand, a society can be called matriarchal when descent, inheritance and succession are in the female line, marriage is matrilocal (the husband removing to the house of his wife), and when the authority over the children is wielded by the mother or her relatives.

If this definition of these opposing terms is accepted, it is at once obvious that the greater number of primitive societies are neither matriarchal nor patriarchal, though some may incline more to the one side, and others more to the other. Thus, if we examine the tribes of Eastern Australia, which are sometimes spoken of as matriarchal, we find that marriage is patrilocal, so that membership of the local group is inherited in the male line, the authority over the children is chiefly in the hands of the father and his brothers, property (what there is of it) is mostly inherited in the male line, while, as rank is not recognised, there is no question of succession. The only matriarchal institution is the descent of the totemic group, which is through the mother. So that these tribes, so far from being matriarchal, incline rather to the patriarchal side. Kinship amongst them is thoroughly bilateral, but for most social purposes kinship through the father is of more importance than kinship through the mother. There is some evidence, for example, that the obligation to avenge a death falls more strongly upon relatives in the male line than upon those in the female line.

It is now clear, I hope, that the distinction between matriarchal and patriarchal societies is not an absolute, but a relative one. Even in the most strongly patriarchal society some social importance is attached to kinship through the mother; and similarly in the most strongly matriarchal society the father and his kindred are always of some importance in the life of the individual.

In Africa we have in the South-East a group of tribes that incline rather strongly to patriarchy, so much so, in fact, that we may perhaps justifiably speak of them as patriarchal. Descent of the social group, inheritance of property, succession to chieftainship, are all in the male line; marriage is patrilocal, and authority in the family is strongly patripotestal. In the north of Africa, in Kenya and the surrounding countries, there is another group of strongly patriarchal peoples, some of them Bantu-speaking, while others are Nilotic or Hamitic. Between these two patriarchal regions there is a band of peoples stretching apparently right across Africa from east to west, on the level of Nyassaland and Northern Rhodesia, in which the tendency is towards matriarchal institutions. Descent of the social group, inheritance of property, and succession to the kingship of chieftainship are in the female line. In some of the tribes marriage seems to be matrilocal, at any rate temporarily if not permanently, i.e., a man on marriage has to go and live with his wife's people.

We have been considering the relation of the sister's son to his mother's brother; but, if we are to reach a really final explanation, we must study also the behaviour of a man to his other relatives on the mother's side, and to his mother's group as a whole. Now, in the Friendly Islands the peculiar relation between a sister's son and mother's brother exists also between a daughter's son and his mother's father. The daughter's son must be honoured by his grandfather. He is "a chief" to him. He may take his grandfather's property, and he may take away the offering that his grandfather makes to the gods at a kava ceremony. The mother's father and the mother's brother are the objects of very similar behaviour patterns, of which the outstanding feature is the indulgence on the one side and the liberty permitted on the other. Now, there is a hint of the same thing amongst the BaThonga, but again we lack the full information that we need. Mr. Junod writes that "a grandfather is more lenient to his grandson by his daughter than to his grandson by his son." In this connection the custom of calling the mother's brother *kokwana* (grandfather) is significant.

In primitive society there is a strongly marked tendency to merge the individual in the group to which he or she belongs. The result of this in relation to kinship is a tendency to extend to all the members of a group a certain type of behaviour which has its origin in a relationship to one particular member of the group. Thus, the tendency in the BaThonga tribe would seem to be to extend to all the members of the mother's group (family or sib) a certain pattern of behaviour which is derived from the special pattern that appears in the behaviour of a son towards his mother. Since it is from his mother that he expects care and indulgence, he looks for the same sort of treatment from the people of his mother's group, i.e., from all his maternal kin. On the other hand, it is to his paternal kin that he owes obedience and respect. The patterns that thus arise in relation to the father and the mother are generalised and extended to the whole kindred on the one side and on the other.

It will, perhaps, be of help if I give you a final brief statement of the hypothesis I am advancing, with the assumptions involved in it and some of its important implications.

(1) The characteristic of most of these societies that we call primitive is that the conduct of individuals to one another is very

largely regulated on the basis of kinship, this being brought about by the formation of fixed patterns of behaviour for each recognized kind of kinship relation.

(2) This is commonly associated with a segmentary organization of society, i.e., a condition in which the whole society is divided into a number of similar (and generally equal) segments (sibs, clans, etc.).

(3) While kinship is always and necessarily bilateral, the segmentary organization requires the adoption of the unilateral principle, and a choice has to be made between patrilineal and matrilineal institutions. In the same culture area some tribes may incline more to the matriarchal side, others to the patriarchal, under the influence, doubtless, of special local or historical factors.

(4) In patrilineal societies of a certain type, the special pattern of behaviour between the sister's son and the mother's brother is derived from the pattern of behaviour between the child and the mother, which is itself the product of the social life within the family in the narrow sense.

(5) This same kind of behaviour tends to be extended to all the maternal relatives, i.e., to the whole family or group to which the mother's brother belongs.

(6) In societies with patrilineal ancestor worship (such as the BaThonga and the Friendly Islanders) the same type of behaviour may also be extended to the gods of the mother's family.

(7) This special kind of behaviour to the maternal relatives (living and dead), or to the maternal group and its gods and sacra, is expressed in definite ritual customs, the function of ritual here, as elsewhere, being to fix and make permanent certain types of behaviour, with the obligations and sentiments involved therein.

The Therapeutic Triad

by
Rose Laub Coser

A BASIC CONTRADICTION in psychiatric hospital practice derives from the fact that the hospital has the mandate both to control the behavior of its patients and to treat them. As the mental hospital defines the mandate it has received from the public, and more specifically from patients' relatives, patients are entrusted to its care so that they will be prevented from violating basic taboos—killing or hurting themselves or others, engaging in sexually disapproved behavior, setting fires, etc.—and so that they can learn not to violate such taboos in the future. That is, the mental hospital has as a goal to control the behavior of its patients in such a way that their relatives and the community remain undisturbed, that the hospital can go about its business as the hospital defines it, and that all patients will be protected physically.

Whatever other responses the use of authority, and if need be coercion, calls forth, such as a sense of security and protection, for example, it always mobilizes some measure of hostility and distrust in those over whom it is exercised. This tends to impair the basic ingredient of the therapist-patient relationship, which is trust, and the basic aim, which is to help patients redefine their interpersonal relationships so that they can be relied upon not to violate social taboos.

Mutual trust is an important element of any professional-client relationship. Talcott Parsons has stated this well in an address to a group of lawyers:

> In situations of strain, there seems to be required scope for a certain permissiveness for expression of attitudes and senti-

Reprinted from Rose Laub Coser, *Training in Ambiguity: Learning Through Doing in a Mental Hospital* (New York: The Free Press, 1979), pp. 35–37, 46–57. Copyright © 1979 by The Free Press, a Division of Macmillan Publishing Co., Inc.

ments which, in ordinary circumstances, would not be acceptable. If this permissiveness is to operate effectively, it must be associated with relief from anxiety. In order to be capable psychologically of "getting things off his chest," a person must be assured that, within certain limits, otherwise ordinary or possible sanctions will not operate. In general, this implies a protected situation. The confidential character of the lawyer's relation to his client provides just such a situation.[1]

If such leeway in social sanctions is needed by any professional-client relationship, it is much more important in the encounter between psychotherapist and patient, especially in psychoanalytically oriented psychiatry. Patients are expected to reveal fantasies and wishes, illicit or not. To do this, they must be able to expect a large measure of immunity. In this way they will learn to integrate unconscious fantasies into the realm of rational thinking, so that the latter will inform their social behavior.

The psychoanalytically oriented technique of psychiatric treatment is especially well suited to grant patients the measure of immunity of which Parsons speaks because it is based on what psychotherapists call a "therapeutic alliance" between psychiatrist and patient; that is, on a relationship of mutual trust. Yet, the question remains how such "alliance" can be brought about and maintained under conditions of control and restrictions imposed by the hospital.

The double aspect of psychiatric practice—the control of patients' behavior and their psychotherapy—has given rise in some hospitals, including O'Brien, to a social arrangement in which both aspects are dealt with through a division of labor among the staff. Such division may take place informally. In some mental hospitals, such as O'Brien, psychiatric residents who are in charge of a service usually do not conduct psychotherapy with patients on their own service. In some other hospitals, experimenting with modern ideas of participation, the patients themselves are in charge of controlling one another, and the psychiatrist plays the role of a benevolent supervisor and "guide." In this case, the psychiatrist delegates the use of authority to patients' peers, thus remaining free to play a supportive role.

At O'Brien, the separation between ward psychiatry and psychotherapy has been made explicit. The split of the administrative and therapeutic tasks has brought about an intricate social structure, which is the source of the stability of the system at the same time that it brings in its wake a new set of ambiguities for both patients and practitioners. It provides emotional support to patients, granting them some permissiveness and leeway for learning, at the same time that it is suited for maintaining control over their everyday behavior. Yet, it also generates stresses in the relationships among the psychiatrists themselves.

The fact that a patient has two psychiatrists, one in charge of guiding everyday life in the hospital and another in charge of individual psychotherapy, means that the patient is part of a triadic relationship in which he or she is subordinate to two role partners who relate in different ways. An examination of the complex relationships that are part of such a triadic arrangement will make it possible to specify some of the functions it serves for patients, as well as some of the stresses and conflicts it has brought in its wake.

RELATIONS BETWEEN AUTHORITY HOLDERS

The relations between the two psychiatrists can best be explored according to the Simmel-related model of the "natural triad" developed by Morris Freilich on the basis of the kinship structure of patrilineal families, such as the Tikopia.[2] There, a growing young man has a supportive maternal uncle who counteracts the tension created by his father's exercise of authority. Freilich relates this triadic relationship of father, son, and maternal uncle to the Parsons-Bales dichotomy of instrumental and expressive leadership and calls attention to the fact that such triads exist in all sorts of social organizations in which a "high-status friend" like an uncle and a "high-status authority" like a father both relate to a "low-status subordinate" like a son. The fact that the image of the friendly uncle calls to mind such idiomatic expression as "he is the avuncular type," or "he is everybody's uncle," testifies to the broad application of Freilich's model.

The advantage of conceiving of a patient and his or her two role-partners as forming such a triad, in which the clinical administrator is the high-status authority and the psychotherapist the high-status friend of the patient, is that it directs attention not

[2]Morris Freilich, "The Natural Triad in Kinship and Complex Systems," *American Sociological Review*, 29 (August 1964), pp. 529–540.

only to the relation between the patient and each of two role-partners, as has been done so far, but also the relationship that must be upheld between the supportive and the instrumental leader. This brings us back to one of the most important points Merton makes in his theory of role-set.[3] He deduces from the fact that a person in a single role relates to several role-partners the structural circumstance that these role-partners have to enter into relation with each other by virtue of their common involvement with the same status occupant. For example, a teacher and the parent of one of the pupils will relate to each other for no other reason than that both are involved with the same child.

Similarly, in the hospital setting described here, two psychiatrists relate to each other by virtue of having a common patient. In order to analyze the relation between such supportive and instrumental leadership in their common involvement with the same subordinate, five propositions from Freilich's theory of the "natural triad" will be examined.

1. The high-status friend helps relieve the tension created by the high-status authority.
2. The high-status friend and the high-status authority provide benefits for each other.
3. The high-status friend is a check on the power of the high-status authority.
4. Conflict is endemic in the relationship between high-status friend and high-status authority.
5. In order to maintain the relationship, the high-status friend and the high-status authority must avoid each other to some extent.

1. *The psychotherapist helps relieve the tension* and antagonism created in the patient by the clinical administrator by helping the patient to re-evaluate the control imposed by the administrator. The psychotherapist helps strip the patient's hostile feelings of their distorting emotional content, as when countering complaints about life on the ward with the phrase: "There is really nothing I can do about ward policy; but let us explore the feelings you have about it."

The psychotherapist's refusal to alter the reality situation helps patients realize what the limitations are on changing the system. It encourages them to turn attention toward themselves and at the

[3]Robert K. Merton, *Social Theory and Social Structure*, rev. ed. (New York: The Free Press, 1957), pp. 368–380.

same time invites them to withdraw their antagonistic affect from the "high-status authority." A resident expressed this bluntly: "Frustration encountered by the patient in dealing with the administrator is taken care of in the therapeutic session." In this way, the psychotherapist helps cushion the system of ward psychiatry.

2. The patient's high-status *role-partners benefit from each other*. Not only does the administrator derive advantage from the tension-relieving activity of the psychotherapist, but also the latter gains assurance from not having to worry about the immediate consequences of supportive and permissive intervention. In the words of one supervisor of therapy, the administrator "relieves the [psychotherapist] of a certain burden." The psychotherapist feels that it is a good thing that "the other fellow" will take care of safety precautions, as when this same supervisor explains: "I am thinking of a very sick, severely schizophrenic boy who is homicidal and suicidal. . . . I feel that it is very helpful for [the psychotherapist] to have an administrator who is in continuous contact with the behavior of the patient." Because of the benefits that the psychotherapist and the clinical administrator derive from each other, they are interested in maintaining a balanced relationship.

3. As the patient's high-status friend, *the psychotherapist can exercise some subtle control over the administrator* even without having authority to interfere in ward policy. The psychotherapist can act as a conveyor of information between the patient and the hospital system, feeding into the system the information that comes from the patient about the management of the ward by letting the word go to the "right people" (the staff lunchroom being the preferred setting for this type of communication), and hence helping to protect the system from ignorance about an administrator's management of the ward. One hospital psychiatrist who holds a top position had this to say: "Dr. X comes to me to tell me what he hears from his therapy patient about the ward. Of course, he puts it in general terms, trying not to focus attention on his patient. He says, 'From what I hear, all is not going well there.' "

The psychotherapist does not actually have to pass on the precise information he receives. The mere knowledge on the part of the administrator that the psychotherapist can potentially do so serves as a deterrent and is therefore a means of social control.

4. *Conflicts are endemic* in the very mechanisms that assure the stability of the triad. For example, administrators who feel that a psychotherapist has pulled too strongly on the lever of

indirect control will conclude that the information channel has been misused for interference with their authority.

Another source of antagonism is the fact that both role-partners derive benefit from each other. The mutuality of expectations makes it possible for each to try to get more than is considered legitimate. That is, the very notion of reciprocity implies the danger of some asymmetry judged by the partners to be illegitimate, in that one of the partners may try to obtain a larger share of the benefit than entitled to. (The partner may also give *more* benefit than expected, thereby obligating the other beyond the measure required by the definition of the relationship.)

Indeed, psychotherapists often complain that some administrators' decisions about patients are too restrictive to be therapeutic, or not restrictive enough in view of their own permissive stance; and administrators often feel that some patients' misbehavior on the ward is the result of a psychotherapist's permissiveness and hence that "psychotherapy is not going well." The first complaint means that the administrator is said to create more tension than the psychotherapist wants to deal with or less safety than the therapist thinks he or she must be able to count on; the second implies that the administrator is relied upon too much to provide safety for a patient, which the psychotherapist can too easily ignore.

Since both high-status role-partners claim competence in the same field, each claims the right to judge the other's performance. Yet since they are interested in maintaining a balanced relationship from which they both can derive benefits, they will try to withhold negative judgment of each other as much as they feel is possible.

5. *The two high-status role-partners must avoid each other.* If they become too antagonistic, the psychotherapist can hardly remain a tension reliever, since the antagonism raises rather than lowers the tension level of the patient and, through the patient, often that of the whole ward.

Nor should the therapist be too friendly with the administrator, for a patient would sense this and would feel that the high-status friend could not be relied on because of his or her other seeming alliance with authority. This would threaten the therapeutic alliance which both high-status partners are interested in maintaining.

In order to remain the patient's high-status friend, the psychotherapist must be in some conflict with the administrator, but not too much. There are structural sources that press for or permit avoidance, both in order to prevent conflicts from coming to a head, and in order to prevent intensive interactions of any kind.

Interaction brings in its wake a strengthening of sentiments, either positive or negative, each of which threatens the smooth functioning of the triad. In other words, if in order to "cool out" the patient the therapist wants to remain a high-status friend, he or she must be able to remain "cool" in relation to the administrator.

There are various ways of resolving conflicts, some more disruptive of the balance of the triad than others. For example, if the administrator feels that the psychotherapist has interfered with his or her authority or if a therapist is annoyed by some action of the patient's administrator, the aggrieved party can resort to a diagnostic device, by which the patient is said to have "manipulated the psychiatrists." This means that equilibrium between the psychiatrists is being attained by displacing the conflict between themselves with a conflict between each of them and the patient. The view of one clinical administrator expresses a widely held opinion at O'Brien: "There are patients who are very manipulative and they immediately try to find ways to pit the administrator and the psychotherapist against each other. Now, this causes trouble."

A patient is said to have "manipulated his or her psychiatrists" when a conflict between them has occurred as a result of the patient's attempt to obtain the help of one psychiatrist to score gains with the other, as when the patient asks the administrator to help obtain a change in therapist, or asks the therapist to help the patient get discharged. It is no wonder that psychiatrists at O'Brien call such "manipulation" catastrophic, for it threatens the therapeutic triad both directly, through the patient's intention to remove one high-status role-partner, and through the psychiatrists' attempt at solution, which the incident calls forth. This is because the "solution" consists of an alliance by the two psychiatrists in their common accusation of "manipulation." While this alliance makes it easier for any one of them to conduct the conflict with the patient, it inhibits the psychotherapists' ability to support the patient and hence also the ability to cushion the system. This manner of displacing the conflict can take place only through interaction between the two high-status role-partners and tends to strengthen the bond between them through their realization of their common interest in not being "manipulated." It means at best a temporary weakening of the therapeutic triad and at worst, if the therapeutic alliance cannot be restored, the triad's dissolution. It is no wonder that an assessment of having been manipulated gets everybody concerned up in arms.

It should be noted in passing that the use of the mechanism by which a conflict is diverted neither contradicts nor confirms the correctness of the diagnosis itself. Correct or not, the diagnosis helps bring about a temporary alliance between partners who previously had some reason for mutual antagonism. A patient's possible "manipulation" of the two role-partners is part of the dynamics of any triad in which one member manages to become *tertius gaudens*—that is, the third party of a relationship who has benefited from conflict between the two other partners.

We recognize here the operation of a mechanism described by Merton by which the occupant of a status who is subjected to conflicting expectations "acts to make these contradictions manifest" and thereby attempts to "redirect the conflict so that it is one between members of the role-set, rather than, as was at first the case, between them and the occupant of the status." The patient who is said to "manipulate" his or her psychiatrists makes use of this mechanism, having managed to force them to confront each other. Thus a subtle interplay takes place in the triadic relationship in which conflicts arise, are displaced, and are used more or less profitably to establish temporary alliances by which a balance is threatened at the same time as it is obtained.

There are other ways than by displacement of the conflict to introduce a corrective into the working of the triad. If an administrator feels that a patient's misbehavior is the result of a psychotherapist's manner of treatment, he or she can withdraw from the triad through a legitimate procedure—that is, by transferring the patient to another ward that is said to provide more adequate physical and mental security for that patient. In this way the problem can be passed on to a colleague on another ward, who will now become the new high-status authority.

This is not to say, of course, that transfers of patients usually take place for reasons of maintaining equilibrium among the staff. From the point of view of the clinical management of patients as it is defined in the hospital, a patient who is "acting out" for whatever reasons is required to be provided with stronger "security." The point here is merely that whatever the administrator's motives, by having a patient transferred out of the ward the administrator removes himself or herself from this therapeutic triad.

The psychotherapist does not have similar organizational means for withdrawing from the triad. The main means available for introducing a corrective remains the indirect one provided by informal channels of communication. This is because the psychotherapist lacks the power of decision for changing the patient's program and also because the psychotherapeutic relationship is considered "sacred" in the normative system of the hospital in that it is defined as enduring and highly personal.

Both the administrator's withdrawal from the triad and the psychotherapist's indirect control can take place without any interaction between the patient's two high-status role-partners. There are, of course, other informal and formal ways of dealing with conflict through interaction. Informally, the two psychiatrists can stop each other in the hallway or talk over lunch. In this way, they make an attempt to be "nice" about something they in some measure feel antagonistic about. This informal handling of the relationship precludes the sustained interaction that would strengthen positive or negative sentiments and thereby threaten the triad.

In situations of extreme antagonism between the two high-status role-partners, a formal institutionalized procedure of consultation can be used. This is done only when the conflict cannot be solved within the triadic relationship itself. It is a measure of last resort not because it threatens the triad but because the conflict is so strong already that the dissolution of the triad is being envisaged. Consultation, which is a means for bringing such a change about, puts the relationship of all members of the triad into the field of visibility—that is, of social control within the hierarchy of the hospital. This situation both high-status role-partners are interested in avoiding.

One reason consultantship is usually needed to change a patient's psychotherapist is that in the value system of O'Brien the dyadic psychotherapeutic relationship is considered so important that it cannot easily be broken without being subject to social control emanating from a larger network than that of the involved triad. This raises the question of the extent to which the working of the "therapeutic triad" depends not only on its internal mechanisms, which have been explored so far, but on the normative structure of the organization.

THE NORMATIVE STRUCTURE OF AVOIDANCE AND CONFLICT

In order for the two role-partners to avoid each other to some extent within this limited setting, they must have an interest in doing so. Moreover, such an interest must be reinforced through the hospital's policy and through its value system.

The patient's two high-status partners have an interest in limiting contact with each other because this enables them better to perform their respective roles of "friend" and "authority," and thereby to benefit from each other's services. Yet, their interest in mutual avoidance is "skewed": each high-status role-partner is interested in preventing the other from influencing his or her own jurisdictional field but does not equally desire to be excluded from the other's jurisdictional field.

It is this unilateral interest in obtaining information "from the *other* guy" that accounts for a commonplace phrase in the hospital that "therapy goes best when there is good communication between therapist and administrator." That this notion is questioned by some other hospital psychiatrists, who call it an "empty cliché," explaining that they are "dubious of it on purely clinical grounds," is evidence of the coexistence of norms and counternorms. Indeed, there are forces at work within the hospital that press for both junction and disjunction between these two psychiatrists.

Interaction between the two psychiatrists is minimized by some purely physical arrangements that assure geographical separation and limit the time available for mutual briefing. Psychotherapists see patients in their offices, which usually are located in the central administration building, where patients go from their wards either by themselves or with an escort. This reduces the chance of casual meetings between a patient's administrator and the psychotherapist. Moreover, interaction between them is limited by the sheer pressure of work and the large number of psychiatrists who are active in this hospital. An administrator in charge of a ward of about twenty patients, of whom, say, ten are in psychotherapy would have to confer with as many as ten psychotherapists. For this, the pressure of work does not leave enough time.

Of course, if contacts between these two role-partners were highly valued in the hospital, the physical arrangements could be changed. For example, psychotherapists could be required to see their patients on the wards, where brief encounters with the ward psychiatrists would be possible. In fact, the norm is that the realm of psychotherapy be separated from ward life.

This directs our attention to the normative system. There are, first, inherently contradictory norms governing the relations between the two types of psychiatrists. Second, the practitioners face contradictory expectations from their various role-partners. Third, there is an unequal distribution of valued resources in the hospital's status and authority system.

Avoidance between the two high-status role-partners is formally provided through the policy of the training center, according to which ward management is not to be the psychotherapist's concern and, conversely, psychotherapy is to be insulated from observability. However, to what extent psychotherapy must also be insulated from knowledge by the psychiatrist who supervises the patient's management on the ward is not clearly defined.

As has been noted, the split between psychotherapy and ward management is based on the principle of freeing patients to reveal their inner dispositions without concern for any decisions that might be made about them regarding the regulation of daily life on the ward. Against this norm, however, there exists the norm that the provision of two psychiatrists for the same patient makes it possible for a second professional opinion to be "available," reached independently to some extent, and on the basis of important data. This implies (1) that there must be some contact between the psychotherapist and the administrator, in order to combine the two judgments, but (2) that the contact should not be so frequent as to impair "independence of judgment."

To be sure, it would be excessive to prevent all contact between the two psychiatrists. This would make for the coexistence of two different systems within the same hospital, with resulting lack of integration and polarization of perspectives and interests. Moreover, evaluation of patients' progress or readiness for discharge could never be arrived at through collective reasoning, which is the normative basis of work for any professional collectivity.

In spite of this need for communication, it is generally understood, although never clearly stated, that psychotherapists will refrain from giving details about the concrete content of a patient's hourly revelations. This is why it is possible for much of the psychotherapy at O'Brien to be conducted by "contract therapists," whose relations with the hospital staff are minimal. These outside psychotherapists usually do not partake of the hospital's organizational life; they do not participate in regular meetings, neither in the regular morning conferences, where reports about all the wards are exchanged, nor in the periodic staff meetings, where cases are being presented for discussion. They attend staff meetings only when their own patients are being evaluated, which may happen at intervals of several months. Their professional time, outside of the hours they are contracted for by the hospital, is their own, and hence they neither are present physically nor have the time for much interaction with the permanent hospital staff. If the patients' well-being in the hospital were thought of as requiring much communication between psychotherapists and clinical administrators, psychotherapy would not be conducted by outside psychiatrists.

As to residents, although they are at the hospital continuously, this is not solely by virtue of the psychotherapy they are conducting with patients but also by virtue of their total involvement in a learning situation. Yet, the mere fact of their availability and the fact of their lower professional and organizational status put them under more pressure to interact with their patients' clinical administrators than is the case with contract therapists. The problems this creates and the ways in which they are handled will be discussed in the next chapter.

The norms of avoidance and communication are difficult to deal with because of the ambiguous notion of confidentiality. Confidentiality is usually understood as having to be maintained against laymen, not between professionals who have a common interest in task performance. However, in the psychotherapeutic relationship, the patient is led to believe—whether deliberately told or not—that communications in therapy are confidential within the hospital, since this is one firm component of the "therapeutic alliance." It is unclear to everybody, not only to patients, how much information is or should be passed on between a psychotherapist and the ward administrator about their common patient, as is revealed by the following answer by a supervisor of therapy to a query on the issue: "Dr. A decided to keep strictly to the rule that he would keep everything confidential, that he wouldn't even tell the administrator. Dr. B was the administrator. When he heard this, he blew his top. How could he be administrator if A refused to tell him? I agreed with A, but didn't really know. . . ."

This little report is instructive on several counts. It seems that the administrator felt he had a right to "blow his top" at the therapist's insistence to live up to the contract with the patient. Also, the supervisor claims he "didn't really know" the rules of the game. And above all, it seems that the psychotherapist had to make an individual decision to "keep strictly to the rule." There seems to be some uncertainty, to say the least, about a rule that, if adhered to, arouses legitimately felt indignation.

In order to obtain some clarification on the subject, a senior psychiatrist who is a protagonist of the split between the two types of psychiatry was asked what he thought a therapist should communicate to an administrator. He said:

Quite a lot . . . I think it would be awfully nice if the psychotherapist gave the administrator practically an hour-by-hour account . . . of how things went, broadly. . . . That may be too much. . . . The therapist has to, I believe, constrain himself to the right to tell the administrator anything that amounts to serious danger of life and death. . . . [Beyond that an administrator] probably should not be told, if the patient doesn't want it.

In listing the whole range of possibilities, between informing an administrator hour by hour or only "broadly" or only in matters of "life and death," and otherwise letting the matter rest at the discretion of the patient, this psychiatrist is the spokesman for a whole variety of unclarified opinions among the staff. The confusion is not just a "weird phenomenon," nor is it due to ignorance or to personal whim. It results from contradictions embedded in the social structure.

Indeed, what both of the above responses reveal is that the norms are confused and contradictory and that the psychotherapist has to meet both the administrator's and the patient's expectations, although these are not always compatible.

Perhaps in extreme situations of "life and death" there would be no ambiguity about the need for communication. But many if not most issues are not so clearly definable. What if the therapist's woman patient has a sexual relationship? Here the administrator, who has to face responsibilities toward the family, may feel that these should be given priority rather than the patient's and the therapist's expectations of confidentiality.

There are also problems inherent in "doing a good job." It is commonly believed that decisions as well as treatment should be based on knowledge, and that the more knowledge is available, the better one can arrive at a sound judgment. As a generality, this view can hardly be disputed. But the question arises whether an administrator should consult with a therapist about the advisability of prescribing drugs or of transferring a patient to another ward. Or, conversely, whether a therapist should inform an administrator that the patient has this day revealed serious material concerning Oedipal fantasies which would make a planned weekend leave inadvisable. Each type of psychiatrist wants to obtain such pertinent information from the other, but each resists living up to the other's expectations. This is because such close cooperation between them would tend to restrict the administrator's autonomous authority and weaken the psychotherapist's therapeutic alliance.

Such matters are discussed usually *a posteriori* as individual "cases," when at some point one role-partner feels the need for information from the other, but they are hardly dealt with as issues that need normative guidance. There is a patterned and legitimate way of avoiding the need to define guidelines for behavior—namely, the use of the phrase, "it depends on the patient." The leeway for individual decisions that this phrase implies is, of course, part of the medical and professional ethic, according to which every practitioner follows his or her own best judgment. As a result of contradictory norms and expectations, however, there is confusion about the type of information a psychotherapist should convey to an administrator and in return how much information and consultation a psychotherapist can expect from an administrator. Such confusion threatens the balance of the therapeutic triad in that it harms the psychotherapist's therapeutic alliance with the patient at the same time that it blocks the administrator's instrumental wisdom.

These conditions lead to a questioning among the staff of the usefulness of the system of separation between the two spheres. Consequently, while the staunchest protagonists of the system—almost all the psychiatrists who occupy top rank in the hospital—continue to explain the clinical soundness of the split, a quiet (and sometimes not so quiet) battle goes on in the middle ranks, with expressions of dissatisfaction ranging from joking and shrugging of shoulders to raging controversies and open display of anger.

An argument that comes primarily from the contract therapists is that a psychotherapist cannot do good work with a patient without being consulted or even informed when major measures are taken, such as severe restrictions, a transfer to another ward, or the prescription of drugs. They, as well as some of the residents' supervisors of therapy, often invoke the professional norm that physicians have to be in authority over their patients. Another complaint, this one stemming primarily from administrators, is that psychotherapists have too little concern for the patients' behavior on the ward and that administrators have a right to know whether this behavior is a result of what goes on in therapy, although not all are so insistent as the one who said in an interview that he wanted to know "everything, from the coarse to the refined."

Administrators want to know more than psychotherapists are willing to reveal. And psychotherapists want to have more say about patients than administrators are willing to grant them. Underlying the administrators' wish to know is the conviction that psychotherapy is the *real* thing, where the important matters concerning the patients' health are being revealed. Underlying the psychotherapists' claim for more say is also the conviction that the psychotherapist *really* knows what is important for patients' health. Hence, underlying the conflict is a deeply entrenched consensus about the high value of psychotherapy for the health of patients. We have the paradoxical situation where a serious conflict results from the common adherence to strongly held values.

This is, of course, no paradox if we realize that a differentiated opportunity structure prevails at O'Brien. Some people have more access than others to a highly valued resource for the production of health: the revelation of the patients' inner dispositions. The situation is similar structurally to that prevailing in American society, where much conflict can be accounted for by the fact that the value of success tends to be shared by all, but access to the means for obtaining it is denied to many. Were this value not shared, the society would be much more stable; those who prefer not to seek success would be satisfied with the limited opportunities for obtaining it, and such limitations would hence not give rise to conflict. It is for this reason that those who glorify subcultures that allegedly do not share the American Dream are unwittingly advocating a stratified society in which all are neatly kept in place by their own inclinations so that the differentiated opportunity structure can remain stable.

Similarly, if in the hospital the values underlying the choice of treatment technique were legitimately divided between psychotherapy and milieu therapy, there would be more stability. But such a system would be mobility-blocked not only for staff but for patients as well. For them, it would mean that some would be given a high-status friend and others deprived of this privilege, and that the two types of patient would each have "their own" type of psychiatrist.

At the same time that it presses for conflict in the hospital system, the common value of psychotherapy is an integrative factor. Upon it depends the functioning of the natural triad, for it motivates the ward psychiatrist to support the patients' psychotherapy and makes it possible for the psychotherapist to exercise some measure of indirect control over the administrator. If it were not for this common value, there might be more "peace" in the hospital, but the whole hospital would be split into two noncomplementary systems, making it impossible for the psychotherapist to be an effective high-status friend, as defined in the therapeutic triad. The psychotherapist would be in the marginal role of a chaplain in a prison or in the military. The impact of such a completely split system on its patients, many of whom suffer from "split personality," can only be conjectured.

On the wards the commonly adhered-to psychoanalytic principle serves as a check against restrictiveness. Although decisions there are to be made on the basis of the reality situation, the staff, under the leadership of the ward psychiatrist and with the active participation of one or two residents, explore the "real meaning" of the patients' behavior. This introduces a measure of permissiveness. It also serves as a "cooling-out" process for an often legitimately angered and fearful staff, at the same time offering support through the affirmation of solidarity based on a common and highly valued perspective, that of depth psychology.

Yet, the high value placed on psychotherapy creates some problems in that everyone wants to have some share in it. The word "therapy" is imbued with magical attributes. The closer anyone comes to doing "therapy," the more important the role for the presentation of self. Hence, the person in charge of the gym is a "recreational therapist," the one in charge of crafts is an "occupational therapist." And the nurses see themselves as being part of the team to the extent that they understand the "deeper" implications of behavior and are prepared to sit and talk with patients.

At O'Brien, all concerned tend to have a share in the pie of the unconscious. Looked at from the point of view of the goal of the organization, the production of health, psychiatrists who make decisions about matters pertaining to health and illness—the administrators—are largely deprived of access to this highly valued raw material on the ward. And psychotherapists, who dispose of this highly valued resource, do not have access to the decision-making process. Hence, in both these activities, psychiatrists are alienated from important means of production and therefore to some extent from assessment of the product.

It has become fashionable to apply the term "alienation" to all sorts of frustrations and malaise. But here we have a case of alienation that approximates the core meaning of the concept as it was formulated by Marx, for whom alienation is rooted in the unequal distribution of rights and privileges.

VII

MAGIC AND RELIGION

God is subtle. He is not cruel.

Albert Einstein

Since the excitations in the cortex never cease . . . and since the structural elements are renewed at each instant, an enormous surplus of fantasy may be expected.

Max Scheler

MAGIC, MANY BELIEVE, is a primitive problem-solving strategy that modern people have discarded. This belief perpetuates a false dichotomy between "primitive" (savage, childlike, and mystical) and "civilized" (modern, mature and scientific). Magic, as Bronislaw Malinowski explained in *Magic, Science and Religion*, stems from a mixture of fear and hope. Since these sentiments exist among all humans, magic too can be expected everywhere.[1] Magic sits alongside two more respectable reality transformers: religion and science. According to Raymond Firth, the practice of magic usually includes three elements: (1) instruments or medicines, (2) rites, and (3) spells. Among its various functions magic helps in food production, in the protection of self and property, and in the destructive process. Being multifunctional, magic is difficult (if not impossible) to disprove. At the very least, its most general function always "works": magic tends to make for confidence in those who employ it.

Religion is not easily distinguishable from magic. Religion, like magic, "is founded on assumptions from beyond the sphere of reason, it uses manual rites and verbal formulae, and the condition of the performer is frequently held to be proper to the success of its appeal." For many scholars, therefore, magic and religion represent not two exclusive spheres, but a variety of a different combinations of similar elements (see Firth, table 2). Firth's discussion covers the basic concepts that anthropologists use to discuss magic and religion. He also provides interesting

[1] An interesting example of magic in a "scientific" society is described by George Gmelch in "Baseball Magic," *Transaction*, vol. 8, no. 8 (1971).

338

and informative examples of supernatural life among peoples that most Westerners have never heard of.

Magic and religion use *rituals* in their attempts to influence powerful forces to satisfy our desires. And a ritual, according to Victor W. Turner ("Symbols in African Ritual"), is a rigid or "stereotyped sequence of activities." Rituals may be *seasonal* (part of a temporal cycle), *contingent* (held in response to a crisis), *divinatory, political, professional* (held to initiate people into priesthoods, secret societies, etc.), or *sacrificial* (those associated with daily offerings to gods and ancestors). Turner digs deeply into the structure of ritual symbols, identifying their *multiple meanings*, and (among other things) their *condensation*— their ability to simultaneously represent many ideas and relationships. He relates ritual symbols to cultural themes and shows how some symbols (e.g., the mudyi tree of the Ndembu people of northwestern Zambia) are "dominant"—frequently found in many different types of rituals.

REFERENCES

Evans-Pritchard, E. E. *Theories of Primitive Religion*. Oxford: Clarendon Press, 1965.

Lévi-Bruhl, Lucien. *Primitive Mentality*. Boston: Beacon Press, 1966.

Mair, L. *Witchcraft*. New York: McGraw-Hill, 1969.

Malinowski, Bronislaw. *Magic, Science and Religion*. Boston: Beacon Press, 1948.

Turner, Victor W. *The Forest of Symbols*. Ithaca, N.Y.: Cornell University Press, 1967.

Magic and Religion

by
Raymond Firth

MAGIC

IT IS WELL known that in all the major aspects of primitive activity beliefs in the supernatural play a large part. If we follow a Polynesian canoe builder carefully we will find that side by side with his technical operations he performs other acts not dictated by purely technical principles. He believes that his canoe-working tool is controlled ultimately by a spirit being; he believes that through this being it has the power of killing borers in the timber; he dedicates the vessel to gods and ancestors whom he invokes to give it speed and seaworthiness, to send wind, or calm the rising waves, or bring fish. When we call this supernatural belief we do not mean that the things believed in are necessarily regarded by the natives as being "above" Nature, but that they do not form part of what our experience has led us to classify as *natural* forces. In action they are supplementary to ordinary human effort. Such beliefs in the supernatural—as taboos, or the power of ancestral spirits—can act as forces of social control. It is important to recognize that though the basis of a belief may be an illusion, the belief itself may have real and valuable effects. We might thus classify such types of belief and action as "irrational," not because they are illogical in their inference from certain premises, but because the premises themselves are not valid by our scientific analysis.

To base these beliefs on feelings of awe, mystery, or on a "religious thrill" is too simple an explanation. Their close integration with practical affairs, with economic wants, and with the critical periods of human life, cannot be accidental, and it seems, therefore, as if they have emerged in response to some fundamen-

Adapted from Raymond Firth, *Human Types*, (New York: New American Library, 1958), pp. 122–147.

tal human needs. But to say that they are primarily due to what the magician or priest makes out of them is too simple. An "exploitation" theory of magic or religion ignores the reality of the beliefs held by the practitioner himself, his own deep conformity to traditional values, and the pressure often put upon him by his community to carry out his spiritual ministrations.

Science and magic ordinarily represent the two poles of reason and unreason, but it is not easy to draw a rigid line between the rational and the irrational spheres of human activity. If, for instance, we take the question of the relation of technical knowledge to magic, we find a number of graded types of attitude and of activity in which elements of both are present. Some types of curative "magic" employ substances which do seem to produce a real effect. Others indulge in rational experiment. On the other hand, the practice of science itself is not entirely free from an irrational prejudice for certain theoretical views, from the refusal to give due weight to evidence which runs counter to a favourite assumption, and from the almost mystic reverence with which many people view a statement that is supposed to have the authority of "science" behind it.

But let us consider magic as commonly accepted, that is, a rite and verbal formula projecting man's desires into the external world on a theory of human control, to some practical end, but as far as we can see based on false premises. A broad classification of magic in terms of these practical ends, whether the promotion of human welfare, the protection of existing interests, or the destruction of individual well-being through malice or the desire for vengeance, is given in the following table (Table I).

This classification does not necessarily follow native linguistic distinctions between types of magic, which are often of a more concrete kind, with separate terms for the individual types mentioned. Sometimes, again, the productive magic may be described simply by the general word for "formula," while special words are used for protective and destructive magic.

Analysis of a magical act reveals several characteristic features. There is a definite practical aim to be achieved, and there is a human performer of the magic. This person, by the conditions of the magic itself, has frequently to be in an appropriate condition— he may have had to be abstinent from sexual intercourse, he may have refrained from eating certain foods, he may have to be in solitude, or to be clothed in a certain way. In the practice of the magic itself there are normally three elements: the things used; the things done; the things spoken. The first element is represented by the *instruments or medicines*; the second is the *rite*; the

Table I. Magic: Aim, Sphere, and Social Aspect

AIM AND SPHERE	SOCIAL ASPECT
A. *Productive*. Magic of hunting. Magic of fertility, planting, and harvest in agriculture. Magic of rain-making. Magic of securing a catch in fishing. Canoe and sailing magic. Magic for trading profit. Magic of love.	Performed either by private individuals for themselves, or by specialist magicians for others or the community as a whole. Socially approved. A stimulus to effort and a factor in organisation of economic activity.
B. *Protective*. Taboos to guard property. Magic to assist collection of debts. Magic to avert misfortune. Magic for the cure of sickness. Magic for safety in travelling.	Performed as above, and socially approved. A stimulus to effort and a force of social control.
Counter-magic to C.	*Sorcery*: performed as above, sometimes socially approved, sometimes disapproved. Often a force of social control.
C. *Destructive*. Magic to bring storms. Magic to destroy property. Magic to produce sickness. Magic to bring death.	*Witchcraft*: sometimes attempted, often doubtful if actually performed; and sometimes of imaginary occurrence. Classed as morally bad. Provides a native theory of failure, misfortune, and death.

third is the *spell*. Let us look at each of these in turn. The instruments used are often primarily of a technical kind. A canoe-builder who wishes to kill borers in the timber cuts gently with his adze on the wood and recites a form of words to destroy the insect. But sometimes the instrument is not of technical significance in craftsmanship. Such is the quartz crystal of the Australian curer of sickness, or the pointing-bone of the Central Australian death-dealing wizard. In Africa great use is made of "medicines," magical objects or compounds often fashioned or concocted from trees and plants. A list of medicines known among the Zande would probably number several thousand, though any individual knows and uses only a small fraction of these. The leaves of bulbs are eaten raw, or boiled in water with sesame and salt and eaten. Parasitic plants have whistles and charms manufactured from them. And from creepers are made medicines to enclose gardens and for winding around a man's wrist for protection. In many Bantu languages the word for "medicine" is the same as or akin to the word for "tree." It is alleged that some of these medicines have properties which do produce the desired physiological effect, but most of them appear to be inert. Medicines used in witchcraft, or believed to be so used, often contain exotic substances such as the brain of a crocodile, the flesh or the fat or the afterbirth of human beings. Usually special conditions have to be observed in the gathering of these medicines—just as for the materials of the witches' cauldron in Macbeth. Often these medicines are kept in special containers which themselves may have some magical virtue, or at least be an index to the kind of medicine they contain. Among the Bemba medicines are frequently contained in the horns of antelopes, in small gourds, or little cloth bags. In the gourds and bags magic of good luck, of popularity, or protection against illness are usually carried, and in the small *duiker* horns is carried hunting magic, but in the horns of bushbuck evil magic is usually placed. This animal has a bad reputation among the Bemba. It is believed to be an evil spirit, and is taboo as food to chiefs and pregnant women. With medicine in such a horn a wizard would be able to lay the spirit of his victim and send it back to the grave.

According to African native theory the power of magic is believed to reside in the medicine. In this it differs from most Oceanic magic, where the power is believed to lie in the spell.

The rite has almost an infinite variety, but in essence its function is to bring the magic and its object into contact. Sometimes the rite and the technical procedure are one, as when a Tikopia fisherman recites his formula to the fish as he lowers the line. He uses no medicines nor any act of a distinctively ritual kind. Sometimes, however, a specific act is performed with no practical value, as when a Trobriand canoe-builder sweeps the gunwale with a bundle of light grass as he recites the spell to give the canoe lightness and speed.

The verbal element in magic is extremely important—so much so that Malinowski* regards it as the fundamental constituent and the believed source of magical power. There are said to be a few magic rites when no spell is recited, but it is a question if the magician does not here at least express his formula in thought. In many communities such as the Maori, the Trobrianders, or the Dobuan, the form of words is thought to be fixed and invariable, so much so that a mistake in the recital may spoil the effects of the magic. In others, however, particularly in Africa, the form of words is variable, and consists rather in a conversational address to the medicine to perform its work, the magician modifying his phrases at his discretion. Where the form of words is fixed—the spell proper—then certain conventions usually obtain. The words are often alliterative and onomatopoeic, suggestive by their sound of the end desired. Again they convey analogies to what is wanted. When the red turmeric pigment is being manufactured in Tikopia some of the phrases used refer to the blood-red hue of the flowers of the coral tree and the ginger, to the bright red of fish, and to the red-fringed leaves of a plant. Figures of speech, and references to mythology are common, and again some of the words are cryptic in form and archaic, so that they have no meaning apart from their particular magical context. As Malinowski insists, they are not meant to convey information but to be a mode of action and an expression of human will. The formula is, then, a translation of the urge of human desire into words, and the rite and spell are the spur of the hand and voice to the forces of Nature.

One obvious question which must strike anyone who sees or reads of magical practices must be: Why do they exist when they rest upon principles which often run counter to those we know to be true? Long ago Edward Tylor pointed out four reasons for this. First, some of the results aimed at by magic do actually occur, though for other reasons, or because there may be some

---

*Bronislaw Malinowski (1884–1942), a major figure in British social anthropology, is one of the founders of *functionalism* in anthropology and social sciences. According to Malinowskian functionalism, all cultural systems satisfy the same basic needs in different ways. Malinowski's ideas (referred to by Firth) come from *Magic, Science and Religion and Other Essays* (Garden City, New York, Anchor Books, 1948).

real virtue in what is done or in the medicines used; secondly, in some cases trickery may be practised by the magician to deceive his fellows—though on the whole the magician believes as firmly in his magic as do others; thirdly, positive cases count for more than negative cases—even in our own experience we often ignore things which run counter to theories in which we believe; fourthly, there is the belief in the existence of counter-magic. If a rite fails to produce its end, then it is argued that the proper conditions have not been observed, or that someone else has magically conspired against it. A good example of the way in which the theory of magic puts up new bulwarks against an attack upon it out of its very own principles is seen in the case of the attempted resuscitation of a dog by some Papuan sorcerers in 1931. To the Europeans who saw it, the test failed; the sorcerers were shown to be pretentious liars. But the sorcerers themselves still believed in their powers; they argued, first, that the conditions in which the experiment was performed were not propitious; secondly, that the dog had been killed in a manner which gave them no opportunity of working on the remnant of vital essence, which it was essential for it to retain in order to be brought back to life. The impression of other natives present was that the experiment would have succeeded, and that the dog was actually coming back to life when over-zealous interference by a village constable spoilt the result, and again reduced the dog to a lifeless condition. From this it can be seen that the belief in magic and the practice of it cannot be simply put down to stupidity or credulity, but must be explained in terms of the acceptance of certain assumptions about the nature of things and logical argument from them. The strength of magic lies in the strength of the beliefs that these assumptions are valid. Why should they be so firmly held? To understand this it is necessary to see what is the rôle of magic in the social life.

Magical practices are not performed simply for their own sake; they have in each case a direct practical aim, and they are associated with other human activities of what we should call a rational kind; if we were to analyse in detail the relationships of productive magic to the enterprises with which it goes hand in hand, we should see that it normally performs certain functions in these enterprises. These have been admirably analysed by Malinowski. In the first place, productive magic often throws over the technical operation to which it is attached a cloak of sanctity, increasing the seriousness with which it is performed, and even threatening punishment if it is neglected. Again, productive magic often sets the pace for the actual work. According to the rules of the magical scheme, various stages of the work must be performed at due intervals to allow the magic itself to be carried out in proper sequence. Magic, then, can have a useful organizing power. A more general function which has been stressed by Malinowski is that magic tends to make for confidence in those who employ it. The sphere with which it purports to cope is essentially that of the unknown and the unpredictable—of rain and drought and insect pests in agriculture, of wind and storm and perils of the sea in sailing, of the desires and feelings of a trading partner, or the vagaries of the heart of one whom one loves. Productive magic asserts man's power over Nature, and allows him to go forward with his aims in the conviction that through his own efforts he can command success. From this point of view magic cannot be overthrown by any mere demonstration of its fallacy. It is too deeply interwined with the fundamental springs of human emotion.

This psychological theory of magic just mentioned must be taken as true only in a general sense in any given case. It may be impossible to demonstrate, and there are situations in which magic is not used though human knowledge cannot predict the issue. The Tikopia use no love magic; the Manus of the Admiralty Islands use no sailing magic, but rely upon their own skill and courage to face a rising storm; the Trobrianders, on the other hand, use both these kinds of magic to a high degree. Magic is, then, only one form of cultural response to situations of uncertainty. Other responses may be a reliance upon a beneficent God, a reliance upon the theory of probability—which is another name for science, or a simple fatalism which rejects both science and God. The reason for the different distribution of the magical and other responses in different types of society is something which as yet anthropology and psychology have not been able fully to explain. An answer commonly given, that it is due to historical processes, still leaves unsolved the problem of why the pattern of action took just this historical form.

Protective magic also has its obvious functions. Granted the belief in its efficacy, it serves to defend the rights of individuals, and though it may not produce any real effect upon offenders, it does serve to give sufferers a means of assuaging their feelings of outrage and their desire for vengeance. As Evans-Pritchard* has pointed out, for the Zande a belief that sorcery is an instrument of punishment, and can produce death in offenders, is a

---

*E. E. Evans-Pritchard, *Witchcraft, Oracles and Magic among the Azande.* (Oxford: Clarendon Press, 1937).

comparatively harmless method of enabling people to "let off steam." It causes less disruption in the society than the use of the spear.

We may now turn to an analysis of destructive magic. Let us first compare the pattern of destructive magic in several primitive societies. Destructive magic among the Maori consists essentially in destroying some part of the victim's clothing or hair or nails or even his excreta with the recital of a powerful spell. Among the Zande of Central Africa *mangu* or witchcraft is a kind of emanation from an imaginary material substance in the bodies of some persons. It is thought to be capable of being diagnosed by oracles in the living, and is said to be discovered by autopsy on the dead. To the Zande ordinary magic and witchcraft are of quite a different order. In comparing the magic of these two societies we see that among the Maori there is no use of medicine, that destructive magic and productive magic are of the same generic kind, and that destructive magic is actually practised and relies for its success on the use of objects associated with the victim. But whereas the productive magic of the Zande is very similar to that of the Maori, Zande destructive magic has an additional category to the Maori type. Side by side with the sorcery which is actually performed and follows a special technique, is witchcraft, which does not require either formulæ or exuviæ of the victim, and is not actually capable of human performance. This duality in the sphere of destructive magic is commonly found in Africa as well as in Australia and parts of Melanesia. It does not, however, appear to exist in Polynesia.

Among the Daly River people of Australia two varieties of destructive magic are actually practised: the rite to bring on storms and damage one's enemies; and the burning or burying of personal exuviæ to cause sickness and death. Also, there is a belief in and a great terror of *mamakpik*, the stealing of a living man's kidney fat with his resultant rapid decline and death. This presents the features of the Zande *mangu* in that it is never witnessed, and though a person may be accused of practising it he never admits to doing so, and its activity is diagnosed essentially by its supposed effects. But unlike the possessor of *mangu*, the practitioner of *mamakpik* has no supposed organic peculiarity of his body. In rare cases an attempt has actually been made to steal kidney fat in the prescribed fashion, but has naturally failed. In some parts of Melanesia there is a strong belief in a type of destructive magic, some of the cardinal features of which are physically impossible to carry out; yet there are people who actually profess to perform it. Such is the *vele* of Guadalcanal and the *vada* of south-eastern New Guinea, in which a magician is believed to daze his victim, extract vital organs, miraculously close the wound, and resuscitate him for a short time, though he cannot name his assailant and dies soon afterwards. The major difference of this from the Australian *mamakpik* is the existence of men who purport to practise this magic.

There is in all this destructive magic a set of common elements, though the emphasis upon each may vary from one community to another, and a fairly clear distinction can be drawn between one type, the practice of which is imaginary, and another type, where some ritual is actually performed. It is common to describe the first type as witchcraft and the second as sorcery, though these terms are not always uniformly so used.

RELIGION

A great deal of what we have said about magic also applies to religion. It is founded on assumptions from beyond the sphere of reason, it uses manual rites and verbal formulæ, and the condition of the performer is frequently held to be proper to the success of its appeal. But a number of points for distinction between them have been put forward. As examples we may mention Frazer's* formal criteria, which have been widely adopted, of magic being an assertion of man's control over Nature by the commanding power of the *spell*, and religion as his reliance on spirit powers through the appeal of the *prayer*. Then there is Malinowski's functional criteria of magic being a simple belief in the definite effects of man's power of using spell and rite, limited in technique and directed to a definite practical end; and religion as a complex set of beliefs and practices, united not in the form of its acts or subject matter, but in the function which it fulfils, self-contained, and finding its fulfillment in its very execution. Piddington, again, takes a cross-classification of religion as the ideology of the supernatural, and magic as its application to practical affairs, so that in activities which are ordinarily

*James Frazer received wide acclaim for his twelve-volume work THE GOLDEN BOUGH (1890). While Frazer was uncritical of his sources and used much unverified and unsifted data, he correctly noted that rites, taboos, and other magical practices had important meaning, over and above the literal ones. See *The Golden Bough* (T.H. Gaster, ed. Abridged version of the twelve-volume work. New York: Criterion Books, 1959).

regarded as essentially religious there would be on his definition a magical component. Other writers have stressed the difficulty of drawing such a distinction, and prefer to speak of the magico-religious sphere as a whole. Linked with this are two further points. The practices of magic are frequently individual, with one person opposing his interests and his emotions to those of his fellows, creating disharmony rather than resolving it. Those of religion are essentially social, often partaking of the ritual of a church, with the basic aim of adjusting individuals to their social environment, leading them to find peace within themselves, and reconciliation with others. From this comes the moral classification of magic as something frequently bad from the social point of view, and religion as something good and socially valuable. We speak of black magic but never of black religion.

Using any criterion singly the distinction between magic and religion can be easily drawn. But when they are considered in conjunction the two spheres cannot be so clearly demarcated. Table II shows that elements ordinarily considered to be magical can be found in rites ordinarily considered as religious, and vice versa.

Within the Christian Church prayer may be used to secure immediately practical benefits. Not so many years ago a rural dean blessed the nets of a whitebait fleet of the Thames estuary before the fishing began; the Mayor of the town helped to pull in the nets, supplies of the catch were sent to cabinet ministers, and three hundred guests attended the whitebait supper organized by the Chamber of Trade. In 1935 an Austrian cardinal blessed all motorcars assembled at St. Christosen in Lower Austria, the ceremony being attended by the Austrian Minister of Trade and the local Government. This strongly resembles the consecration of the implements of production, with the ensuing ritual feasts, that take place in many a primitive society, and is frequently classed as magic. These prayers often represent the claims of sectional as well as individual interests. When prayers for rain are recited in our churches, for instance, the answering showers are not an unmitigated blessing to all members of our society. On a wider scale sectional interests are still further represented by the national alignment of different sections of the Church in time of war. In such ways religion can be just as practical, just as closely linked with technology and economics and with the interest of specific groups, as magic.

The basic attitude in prayer is that of appeal. But many of the forms of prayer by their phraseology alone are commands, and it has been held that persistent prayer will inevitably bring a response.

Table II. Cross-Classifications in Magic and Religion

I Elements in situations commonly regarded as		PRIMARILY MAGICAL ELEMENTS WHICH ARE COMMON ALSO IN RELIGION.
	Affirmation of human control of supernatural.	
	Spell commanding obedience.	Compulsive power of words.
MAGICAL.	Rites using magical substances (medicines) which have their own powers.	Virtue of material and other symbols (the Cross), images, idols.
	Belief in supernatural power (*e.g. mana*).	Utilization for sectional or individual ends.
	Manipulation for individual interests.	
II Elements in situations commonly regarded as		PRIMARILY RELIGIOUS ELEMENTS WHICH ARE COMMON AND ALSO IN MAGIC.
		Control through spirit agencies.
	Reliance on extra-human aid.	Material interests of group.
	Prayer appealing for aid.	
RELIGIOUS.	Rites using symbols, offerings, and sacrifices.	Prayers for rain.
	Belief in spiritual beings.	Blessing of technical equipment and of economic methods and adjuncts.
	Group participation, as *e.g.* in a church.	

The idea that God answers prayer is in a way an assertion of the power of the spoken word to bring the results we desire.

In a primitive society what is ordinarily classed as magic can contain elements ordinarily regarded as religious. In Tikopia, for instance, when a man is fishing with a rod and line on the reef, he recites a formula commanding the fish to come to bite on the hook. He addresses the fish alone and brings in no spirit being. But he does not merely order the fish to obey, and he does not believe that the mere virtue of the words in themselves constrain obedience. He talks to the fish as he would to a human being, he cajoles them with tempting offers. He believes that they hear and appreciate his words, though he is not sure of this, since fish live in the depths of the sea, and he cannot observe them. But he also calls upon spiritual beings, his ancestors and guardian deities, to assist in bringing the fish to him. Here command and entreaty, belief in his own power of "spellbinding," and in the power of his spirit helpers are so closely intertwined with his practical situation, that to separate out the magical and religious elements involved would be to tear the formula apart, phrase by phrase, and almost word by word. Moreover, these same spiritual beings are invoked during the great fertility ceremonies, which represent the high point of the native ritual life, or during crises of life such as initiation, sickness, and death, and which could only be called religious on any ordinary classification.

If we look back now at our table we see that we have to deal, not with magic and religion as two exclusive spheres, but with a variety of different combinations of the elements we have discussed. In so far as a distinction can be drawn on broad lines it is in describing certain acts, and the situations in which they take place, as primarily magical at one end of the scale, and primarily religious at the other. In between lies a sphere in which the elements are so closely combined that the institutions may be termed magico-religious or religio-magical. In practice such intermediate types are commonly found.

The argument about this classification has been complicated by the view that the belief in spiritual beings is more complex than that in supernatural power and human control; that it is higher in the evolutionary scale of human progress and later in development. From this point of view difficulties are solved by speaking of any combination of elements as a transition stage. In view of our ignorance of the historical development of primitive institutions, this should be regarded as an evasion of the problem rather than a solution of it.

We may now turn to an examination of the character and

function of those aspects of primitive belief and practice which can be termed primarily religious. It is not today necessary to prove, as Tylor had to prove half a century ago, that all known peoples, however primitive, have a religion. This "religion" may not be of the type to which we are accustomed, but it is none the less real and fills an important place in their lives. It may include acts that shock and horrify us—head-hunting, cannibalism, human sacrifice, mutilation of the body. It may include beliefs that seem childish and absurd, in the powers of stones and trees to move and to talk, in veneration for animals and birds, taboos against simple ordinary habits, beliefs in contaminations which the human body can suffer. Yet it includes, too, beliefs of considerable imaginative power and even of beauty, cults of fertility and of vegetation, personification of natural phenomena, and tales about them. Strangely assorted as they may seem, these things can be found linked together in the religious life of a single people.

It appears that in every society men believe in the existence of spirit entities and spirit powers which influence human activity. This impressed Tylor so much that he based his minimum definition of religion on what he called animism, and described as a belief in spiritual beings. When we think of a religion we usually think of a god or gods. But primitive religion frequently concentrates upon beliefs in spirit powers which it is difficult to classify in this way. In Australia religious belief is concerned with ideas of pre-existing spirits, which, often through the action of superhuman tribal heroes, become embodied in living animal and plant species and in natural objects. These are sometimes linked with human artifacts such as the bull-roarer, which are treated as sacred, and become the focus of rich ceremonial and artistic practices concerned with fertility and the crises of life. In addition, as on the Daly River, there may be a belief in ghosts, and in spirits of the hobgoblin type, which come as apparitions and startle people. In most areas of Australia one supernatural being, the Rainbow Serpent, takes the dominant place as a culture-hero to whom are attributed many of the most important creative feats. From the eastern tribes there are reports of a supernatural being of the order of a god, known as Baiame or Darumulum, but the rôle of this being in the religious life is not altogether clear, and such a concept seems to be lacking in other areas of Australia that have been well studied.

A broad survey of spirit beings recognized among primitive peoples reveals two principal categories: those regarded as human in origin, and those which are non-human, though they may have human attributes.

The beliefs in the spiritual beings, powers, or principles derived from Man are diverse, and discussion of them is difficult, since the categories of them do not coincide with our own nor are they the same in all native societies. We distinguish broadly the body and the soul. But we have other concepts which represent different facets of the human individual. We speak of a person's *vitality*, thinking of something partly physiological and partly psychological. We speak also of his *personality*, as a psychological expression, though it often amounts to the equivalent of his social aura, the kind of impact which the projection of his individuality makes upon others. Something of these ideas runs through the ideas of native peoples. But since our idiom of speech and thought expresses itself in distinctions such as those of natural from supernatural, and psychological from spiritual, we are apt either to superimpose our own categories directly upon those of native peoples, or to regard these native categories as confused, perhaps even to the people themselves. We attempt to render their terms as "soul," "personality," "sub-conscious," or to classify their beliefs as a theory of multiple souls.

What in effect they have done is to take different facets of human experience and of the immaterial side of man's activities, and to combine them in ways somewhat different from ours. In translating the terms which classify native belief into our own language we have usually to be content, then, with merely rough approximations. It is not that we are incapable of understanding their beliefs, but that the luggage in our portmanteau of terms is differently distributed from that in theirs.

It is impossible to list here all the facets of human experience and individuality which native peoples distinguish. But we may refer to four of the most general. These are an immaterial essence or vital principle, a dream counterpart, a shadow counterpart, and that element which survives after death and may be termed the soul, or the ghost.[1] Often, however, some of these coincide.

---

[1]There is some discrepancy in the usage of the terms "spirit," "soul," and "ghost." By "spirit" is sometimes meant all beings or powers, human and non-human in origin; sometimes only those which are non-human. "Soul" is sometimes used for the spirit of man (and natural objects) before death, with "ghost" for his spirit after death; sometimes, however, "soul" is used for his spirit before and after death, and "ghost" for human spirits which are not at rest and impinge upon human activities.

The immaterial essence of human beings is a kind of invisible counterpart of the body, vague and formless, like some unseen fluid. On its well-being that of the body is believed to depend. If it is abstracted from the body then sickness follows, and if it is not restored the body dies. It is often thought to be subject to sorcery. For this reason the ancient Maori in leaving a seat frequently made a scooping motion with his hand behind him in order to gather up any portions of his immaterial essence which a sorcerer might work upon to his undoing. Among the Maori there were believed to be three different immaterial elements of this kind, the *mauri*, the *hau* and the *ora*, each of which was necessary to well-being and could be affected in different ways, though the relation between them is not clear to us. Natural objects can also have their immaterial essence—their soul-stuff as some writers call it. In Tikopia, when a bundle of green food is laid upon the grave of a dead man, the ancestral spirits are believed to come and to take away the essence of the food, its *ora*, leaving the material substance behind. The natives say "we do not see the spirits do this, but we know that they have taken away the *ora*, because the plants wilt."

In some societies the vital element is that which is responsible for one's dream adventures, in others the dream counterpart is different again. Dreams often play an important part in primitive life, not only in building up the theory of the soul and the spirit world, but in guiding action. They are treated as omens, giving warning of the conception of children, their sex, the locality of game sought in hunting, success in undertakings, or sickness and death, and people regulate their conduct accordingly.

Some peoples regard the shadow as a purely physical phenomenon, but others link it up with the human personality, either by giving it special powers of contagion such as the material touch of its owner gives, or by linking it up with the vital principle or even with the soul. The reflection in a mirror or a pool of water can also be an expression of one such immaterial element in personality. The projection of the individual into any visual shape, such as a sketch or a photograph, may be disliked by a primitive people because of their belief that such is a projection of an immaterial element of the individual concerned. Apart from the association with shadow or reflection, one or other of the spirit elements may be located in a definite part of the body, as the stomach, behind the eyes, or in the back. Where the last is the case, hearty back-slapping may have serious consequences.

In almost every human society there appears to be a belief that the individual does not cease to exist at the death of his body, but that he has some continuity in immaterial form. In some societies the ideas of the nature of this continuity of the destination and future of the soul are vague. Life in the next world is not always immortality. The Ila, for instance, believe that a haunting ghost of a dead person can be overcome by a medicine-man, who secures it in a vessel and throws it away on waste land to be consumed by the next grass fire, or into a river to drown. In other societies it is held that the soul lives on and cannot be destroyed. The afterworld may also be well defined, and may comprise a systematic arrangement of zones, lands, or heavens in which the souls of the dead join those of their kinsfolk in particular regions, or those of their social equals in particular ranks or departments. Rarely is there a division according to moral conduct in this world. When there is, it is the morality of the display of wealth and feasting or of bravery in war that takes pride of place, rather than that of goodness in ordinary daily life.

The belief in the persistence of the soul after death has its culmination in the institution of ancestor worship, so common in China and Polynesia and Africa. Here the spirits of the dead do not simply rest in some Elysium, but take a constant interest in the doings of their descendants, are consulted for their advice on practical problems, and even revisit their people through some human or other medium.

Consider for a moment the beliefs of two peoples in this connection, the Ila of South-East Africa and the Tikopia of Polynesia. The Ila believe in the metamorphosis of men into animals. In accordance with this, men of the lion clan may turn into lions after death, and may leave game that they have killed as a gift to people, or chase old friends for the sport of seeing them run. If the fleeing man stops and addresses the lion by its human name it will turn away and leave him. The Tikopia believe in somewhat similar fashion that the spirit of an ancestor may assume the form of a rat, a bat, a fish, or a bird, and manifest itself to men. A creature that behaves normally is "just an animal," but when it behaves in a peculiar way, keeping close to a man instead of taking to flight when he tries to scare it, then it is a spirit in this guise, and should be addressed as such. Here is a general belief, that may be termed a dogma, that the spirits of men may take on the form of animals. There are also certain facts needing explanation—that lions do not always refuse to budge from their kill, or injure people whom they chase, or bats and birds do not always fly off when shooed away. They do not behave consistently in their "natural" way, but sometimes act "unnaturally." This unnatural behaviour is reduced to principle by the native belief. The explanation of any particular incident is not itself a matter of dogma, but is an inference from the general principle. In this sense, Tylor was right in stating that animistic beliefs give an explanation of events. In these beliefs in different categories of spirit entities or aspects of the human individual, we can see not merely an intellectual response, as Tylor argued, to two philosophical problems—the nature of dreams and visions, and the difference between life and death. We see rather a complex response to needs of many kinds, to hopes and fears for oneself and for others by whom one's life is made up. Spirit mediumship, metamorphosis, transmigration of souls, reincarnation, are all ways in which the dead are believed to communicate with the living, or to participate again in the life they have left. Through such beliefs people frequently obtain a guide to decisions which they might otherwise find it difficult to take, an escape from ignorance and a feeling of being merely the playthings of chance, and an outlet for emotions.

While it is possible to say how these beliefs work, it is often impossible to say why they should have taken any particular form. The Ila believe in reincarnation; sooner or later almost every person who dies returns to earth in human form, often in that of a grandchild. Ghosts even clamour to be reborn. The precise identity of the new child in terms of its "real" personality is found by reciting the names of its ancestors when it is held to the breast of its mother. At the moment it begins to suck it is identified as being the returned spirit of the name then mentioned. The Tikopia have no theory of reincarnation. They may name a person after his dead grandfather, or father's brother, or other ancestor, but they do not believe that the living person is then the same as the dead in spirit. But they do hold that there can be a particularly close relationship between the living man and the spirit of the dead, who is appealed to by the man to help and protect him in virtue of the name which they bear in common. He and the spirit are spoken of as "linked names." In some cases the spirit may manifest himself to men by appearing in the body of his descendant, though he may choose another medium. Like the ghosts of the Ila, those of the Tikopia are believed to be eager to appear in the flesh again, though in the latter case it is not to be reborn, but merely to have the pleasures of eating and drinking, and chewing betel, and of talking. When such a spirit appears it is only for a short time, and he soon takes his leave. It is temporary habitation, not reincarnation. But both Tikopia and

Ila beliefs and practices serve to give expression to feelings of affection and interest in kinsfolk who have died, and use these feelings to add colour to the personalities of living individuals and supply them with some sort of standard by which they may act. How the respective beliefs of these two peoples have come into being is beyond our knowledge.

Spiritual beings conceived as non-human in origin are of many kinds. They include spirits of the wild and of the sea; fairies, elves, fauns, water-pixies, goblins, and many other types, in which the individual spirit usually does not receive a personal name, but is regarded as one of a crowd. Then there are spirits of the monster or ogre type, and, again, guardian spirits whose function it is to safeguard the interest of their human wards. In some societies personifications of natural phenomena play a large part in the scheme of religious belief. Some of these spiritual beings are regarded as self-creative, and from their importance in the religious scheme can be given the term of "gods." Such a god can be creator, ruler of a spirit world, or, as in much American Indian mythology, a divine trickster.

Each of these types of spiritual beings may correspond to some complex emotional disposition and set of practical problems in the life of the people who believe in them. Wood spirits, fairies, and the like give expression to the fantasy element in human psychology, provide explanation for small pieces of good fortune or mishap, for unaccountable noises heard, for the illusions of fatigue and darkness and the tendency to see in the movements of Nature analogies with human activity. Stripped of the literary form in which they are so often known nowadays, they must have provided "reasonable" explanations to a people not highly literary, and to whom the scientific attitude was not so insistently presented as it is to us nowadays. Other types of spirit being are linked with deeper emotions and broader problems. The guardian spirit of the North American Indian, as its name suggests, takes care of a person, instructs him in the way to attain wealth, social eminence, and power, and often appears to him in a vision after prolonged physical privation and searching of the heart. The personifications of natural phenomena are not just the products of a mytho-poetic fancy, but play their part in the attempts of man to control his physical environment for his own economic and social ends. The departmental gods of the Maori were invoked each in his own sphere—the god of the sea for fishing and ocean voyaging, the god of the forests for bird-snaring and canoe-building, the god of agriculture for successful planting and harvests. The creator spirit, again, not only provides intellectual explanation of the origins of the world and of man, but often gives a charter or title to social groups for the particular position that they occupy and the privileges that they exercise. The position of some of these higher gods is not always easy to define, and there has been much controversy about the definition of some of them, and the rôle that they play in native belief. Baiame and Darumulum in Australia, Io in eastern Polynesia, Leza among the Ila and other southeastern Bantu, Mbori among the Zande, have all been regarded as high gods indicating a recognition by the respective peoples of a power greater than their ordinary pantheon, and an acknowledgment, however dim, of some ultimate moral value in their universe. The position of these deities is not yet entirely clear, particularly because the classification of them as high gods has been championed especially by certain clerics who cannot be regarded as quite free from partisanship. While it is true that no investigator is entirely dispassionate, the researches of some other anthropologists point to the fact that there has been a tendency to invest these deities with attributes more clear-cut and more near to our Christian conceptions of the Godhead than are expressed in the beliefs of the native peoples. Evans-Pritchard has pointed out that to translate the Zande Mbori as Supreme Being tends to ascribe to him personality, omnipotence, benevolence, and other divine qualities which are by no means clearly formulated by the Zande themselves. When the Zande call upon Mbori it is in situations of fear, anxiety, and despair, but the doctrine about him is vague, and the concept of him overlaps their ideas about ghosts to a large degree.

From all this it would appear that primitive people are essentially polytheistic, and that a true monotheism is not characteristic of them. Native ideas about their spiritual beings are not merely expressed in the form of doctrinal statements, but are frequently embedded in an elaborate system of mythological tales. These myths are not simply stories preserved for their narrative and dramatic interest. They have a vital function to perform in providing a strongly emotional background to the body of religious belief and to ritual practices. They are an appeal to the past in justification of a great deal of action in the present. The concepts of spiritual beings and their relation to the doings of men involve ideas of supernatural power. These ideas differ from one people to another, but frequently involve beliefs in a quality of sacredness or taboo and in a principle of efficacy of more than a normal human kind. Such is the Oceanic idea of *mana* and the cognate ideas of *wakan* and *orenda* in North

America. There has been much discussion of these native terms and their meaning, but it appears as if they represent, not an idea of an all-pervasive abstract power or natural potency so much as the essential characteristic or aspect of activity which consists in the attainment of its end, in its "working." I have myself tried to elucidate the meaning of this idea in Polynesia, and could get from natives only explanations of *mana* in terms such as, "when we ask the ancestors and gods for the fish to come, or the crops to spring and ripen, and they do so, that is *mana*." "When a chief appeals for the wind to fall or the breadfruit to fruit and it happens, then he is *mana*." In brief, *mana* is that which is effective.

Religion cannot be described only in terms of belief. Human faith does not exist in a vacuum, but is applied to ends intended to be successful for human interests. Belief must be translated into rite, faith into action. Marett has said happily, "savage religion is not so much thought out as danced out"—where dancing may be taken as representative of ritual practice in general. Economic interests, desire for personal distinction, desire to protect oneself and one's associates from illness and misfortune supply the motive forces. As in magic, the rites of religion are a means of bringing belief and desire together by a set procedure. Ritual is the bridge between faith and action.

Symbols in African Ritual

by
Victor W. Turner

NO ONE WHO has lived for long in rural sub-Saharan Africa can fail to be struck by the importance of ritual in the lives of villagers and homesteaders and by the fact that rituals are composed of symbols.

A ritual is a stereotyped sequence of activities involving gestures, words, and objects, performed in a sequestered place, and designed to influence preternatural entities or forces on behalf of the actors' goals and interests. Rituals may be seasonal hallowing a culturally defined moment of change in the climatic cycle or the inauguration of an activity such as planting, harvesting, or moving from winter to summer pasture; or they may be contingent, held in response to an individual or collective crisis. Contingent rituals may be further subdivided into life-crisis ceremonies, which are performed at birth, puberty, marriage, death, and so on to demarcate the passage from one phase to another in the individual's life-cycle, and rituals of affliction, which are performed to placate or exorcise preternatural beings or forces believed to have afflicted villagers with illness, bad luck, gynecological troubles, severe physical injuries, and the like. Other classes of rituals include divinatory rituals; ceremonies performed by political authorities to ensure the health and fertility of human beings, animals, and crops in their territories; initiation into priesthoods devoted to certain deities, into religious associations, or into secret societies; and those accompanying the daily offering of food and libations to deities or ancestral spirits or both. Africa is rich indeed in ritual genres, and each involves many specific performances.

Each rural African society (which is often, though not always,

Reprinted from *Science*, vol. 179, no. 4078 (March 1973), pp. 100–105, by permission of the author. Copyright © 1973 The American Association for the Advancement of Science.

coterminous with a linguistic community) possesses a finite number of distinguishable rituals that may include all or some of the types listed above. At varying intervals, from a year to several decades, all of a society's rituals will be performed, the most important [for example, the symbolic transference of political authority from one generation to another, as among the Nyakyusa (1) of Tanzania] being performed perhaps the least often. Since societies are processes responsive to change, not fixed structures, new rituals are devised or borrowed, and old ones decline and disappear. Nevertheless, forms survive through flux, and new ritual items, even new ritual configurations, tend more often to be variants of old themes than radical novelties. Thus it is possible for anthropologists to describe the main features of a ritual system, or rather ritual round (successive ritual performances), in those parts of rural Africa where change is occurring slowly.

THE SEMANTIC STRUCTURE OF THE SYMBOL

The ritual symbol is "the smallest unit of ritual which still retains the specific properties of ritual behavior . . . the ultimate unit of specific structure in a ritual context" (2, p. 20). This structure is a semantic one (that is, it deals with relationships between signs and symbols and the things to which they refer) and has the following attributes: (i) multiple meanings (significata) —actions or objects perceived by the senses in ritual contexts (that is, symbol vehicles) have many meanings; (ii) unification of apparently disparate significata—the essentially distinct significata are interconnected by analogy or by association in fact or thought; (iii) condensation—many ideas, relations between things, actions, interactions, and transactions are represented simultaneously by the symbol vehicle (the ritual use of such a vehicle abridges what would verbally be a lengthy statement or argument); (iv) polarization of significata—the referents assigned by custom to a major ritual symbol tend frequently to be grouped at opposed semantic poles. At one pole of meaning, empirical research has shown that the significata tend to refer to components of the moral and social orders—this might be termed the ideological (or normative) pole of symbolic meaning; at the other, the sensory (or orectic) pole, are concentrated references to phenomena and processes that may be expected to stimulate desires and feelings. Thus, I have shown (2, pp. 21–36) that the mudyi-tree, or milk-tree (*Diplorrhyncus mossambicensis*), which is the focal symbol of the girls' puberty ritual of the Ndembu people of northwestern

Zambia, at its normative pole represents womanhood, motherhood, the mother-child bond, a novice undergoing initiation into mature womanhood, a specific matrilineage, the principle of matriliny, the process of learning "women's wisdom," the unity and perdurance of Ndembu society, and all of the values and virtues inherent in the various relationships—domestic, legal, and political—controlled by matrilineal descent. Each of these aspects of its normative meaning becomes paramount in a specific episode of the puberty ritual; together, they form a condensed statement of the structural and communal importance of femaleness in Ndembu culture. At its sensory pole, the same symbol stands for breast milk (the tree exudes milky latex—indeed, the significata associated with the sensory pole often have a more or less direct connection with some sensorily perceptible attribute of the symbol), mother's breasts, and the bodily slenderness and mental pliancy of the novice (a young slender sapling of mudyi is used). The tree, situated a short distance from the novice's village, becomes the center of a sequence of ritual episodes rich in symbols (words, objects, and actions) that express important cultural themes.

RITUAL SYMBOLS AND CULTURAL THEMES

Opler has defined a theme as a part of a limited set of "dynamic affirmations" that "can be identified in every culture" (3, p. 198; 4). In the "nature, expression, and relationship" of themes is to be found the "key to the character, structure, and direction of the specific culture" (3, p. 198). The term "theme" denotes "a postulate or position, declared or implied, and usually controlling behavior or stimulating activity, which is tacitly approved or openly promoted in a society" (3, p. 198). Every culture has multiple themes, and most themes have multiple expressions, some of which may be in one or more parts of the institutional culture (5, p. 164). Ritual forms an important setting for the expression of themes, and ritual symbols transmit themes. Themes have multiple expressions, and ritual symbols, such as the mudyi tree (and thousands of others in the ethnographic literature of African ritual), have multiple significata (6). The major difference between themes and symbols is that themes are postulates or ideas inferred by an observer from the data of a given culture, while ritual symbols are one class of such data. Ritual symbols are multivocal—that is, each symbol expresses not one theme but many themes simultaneously by the same perceptible object or activity (symbol vehicle). Symbols *have* significata, themes may *be* significata.

Themes, in their capacity as significata (including both conceptions and images), may be disparate or grouped, as we have seen, at opposed semantic poles. Thus the mudyi signifies aspects of female bodily imagery (milk, suckling, breasts, girlish slenderness) and conceptions about standards of womanhood and motherhood, as well as the normative ordering of these in relation to group membership, the inheritance of property, and succession to such political offices as chieftainship and village headmanship through matrilineal descent. There are rules of exclusion connected with the mudyi in this ritual context—all that is not concerned with the nurtural, procreative, and esthetic aspects of human femaleness and with their cultural control and structuring, is excluded from the semantic field of mudyi symbolism. This is a field of themes with varying degrees of concreteness, abstraction, and cognitive and orectic quality. The impulse that leads advanced cultures to the economical use of signs in mathematics finds its equivalent here in the use of a single symbol vehicle to represent simultaneously a variety of themes, most of which can be shown to be related, logically or pragmatically, but some of which depend for their association on a sensed likeness between variables rather than on cognitive criteria. One is dealing with a "mathematics" of sociocultural experience rather than with a mathematics of logical relationships.

Ritual symbols differ from other modes of thematic expression, particularly from those unformalized modes that arise in spontaneous behavior and allow for individual choice in expression (3, p. 200). Indeed, it might be argued that the more ritualized the expression, the wider the range of themes that may be signified by it. On the other hand, since a ritual symbol may represent disparate, even contradictory themes, the gain in economy may be offset by a loss in clarity of communication. This would be inevitable if such symbols existed in a vacuum, but they exist in cultural and operational contexts that to some extent overcome the loss in intelligibility and to some extent capitalize on it.

DOMINANT SYMBOLS IN RITUAL CYCLES

Rituals tend to be organized in a cycle of performances (annual, biennial, quinquennial, and so on); even in the case of contingent rituals, each is performed eventually. In each total assemblage, or system, there is a nucleus of dominant symbols, which are characterized by extreme multivocality (having many senses) and a central position in each ritual performance. Associated with this nucleus is a much larger number of enclitic (dependent) symbols. Some of these are univocal, while others, like prepositions in language, become mere relation or function signs that keep the ritual action going (for example, bowings, lustrations, sweepings, and objects indicative of joining or separation). Dominant symbols provide the fixed points of the total system and recur in many of its component rituals. For example, if 15 separate kinds of ritual can be empirically distinguished in a given ritual system, dominant symbol A may be found in 10 of them, B in 7, C in 5, and D in 12. The mudyi tree, for example, is found in boys' and girls' initiation ceremonies, in five rituals concerned with female reproductive disorders, in at least three rituals of the hunters' cults, and in various herbalistic practices of a magical cast. Other dominant symbols of Ndembu rituals, as I have shown elsewhere (seven), recur almost as frequently in the ritual round. Each of these symbols, then, has multiple referents, but on each occasion that it is used—usually an episode within a ritual performance—only one or a related few of its referents are drawn to public attention. The process of "selectivity" consists in constructing around the dominant symbol a context of symbolic objects, activities, gestures, social relationships between actors of ritual roles, and verbal behavior (prayers, formulas, chants, songs, recitation of sacred narratives, and so on) that both bracket and underline those of its referents deemed pertinent in the given situation. Thus, only a portion of a dominant symbol's full semantic wealth is deployed in a single kind of ritual or in one of its episodes. The semantic structure of a dominant symbol may be compared with a ratchet wheel, each of whose teeth represents a conception or theme. The ritual context is like a pawl, which engages the notches. The point of engagement represents a meaning that is important in the particular situation. The wheel is the symbol's total meaning, and the complete range is only exposed when the whole cycle of rituals has been performed. Dominant symbols represent sets of fundamental themes. The symbol appears in many rituals, and its meanings are emphasized separately in many episodes. Since the settings in which the themes are ritually presented vary, and since themes are linked in different combinations in each setting, members of the culture who have been exposed to the entire ritual cycle gradually learn, through repetition, variation, and contrast of symbols and themes, what the values, rules, behavioral styles, and cognitive postulates of their culture are. Even more important, they learn in what cultural domains and with what intensity in each domain the themes should apply.

POSITIONAL ROLE OF BINARY OPPOSITION

The selection of a given theme from a symbol's theme assemblage is a function of positioning—that is, of the manner in which the object or activity assigned symbolic value is placed or arranged vis-à-vis similar objects or activities. One common mode of positioning is binary opposition, the relating of two symbol vehicles whose opposed perceptible qualities or quantities suggest, in terms of the associative rules of the culture, semantic opposition. Thus when a grass hut is made at the Ndembu girls' puberty ceremony for the seclusion of the novice for several months, the two principal laths of the wooden frame are made respectively from mudyi and mukula (blood tree) wood. Both species are dominant symbols. To the Ndembu, mukula represents the husband whom the girl will marry immediately after the puberty rites, and the mudyi stands for the bride, the novice herself. Yet when mukula is considered as a dominant symbol of the total ritual system, it is found to have a wide range (what has aptly been called a "fan") of significata (8, 9). Its primary and sensory meaning is blood—the Ndembu point to the dusky red gum secreted by the tree from cracks in its bark to justify their interpretation. But some bloods, they say, are masculine and some feminine. The former include blood shed by warriors, hunters, and circumcisers in the call of duty; the latter represents blood shown at menstruation and parturition. Another binary opposition within the semantic field of blood is between running blood and coagulating blood. The latter is good, the former is dangerous. Thus, prolonged menstruation means that a woman's blood is ebbing away uselessly; it should coagulate to form fetus and placenta. But since men are the dangerous sex, the blood they cause to flow in hunting and war may be good— that is, beneficial for their own group.

Mukula symbolism is adroitly manipulated in different rituals to express various aspects of the human condition as the Ndembu experience it. For example, in the *Nkula* ritual, performed to placate the spirit of a dead kinswoman afflicting the female patient with menstrual troubles causing barrenness, mukula and other red symbols are contextually connected with symbols characteristic of the male hunting cults to convey the message: the patient is behaving like a male shedder of blood, not like a female conserver of blood, as she should be. It is her "masculine protest" that the ritual is mainly directed at overcoming and domesticating into the service of her female role (9, pp. 55–88). Mukula means many other things in other contexts, when used in religious ritual or in magical therapy. But the binary opposition of mudyi to mukula restricts the meaning of mudyi to young mature femininity and that of mukula to young mature masculinity, both of which are foundations of a hut, the prototypical domestic unit. The binding together of the laths taken from these trees is said to represent the sexual and the procreative union of the young couple. If these meanings form the sensory pole of the binary opposition as symbol, then the legitimated union by marriage represents the normative pole. In other words, even the binary opposition does not stand alone; it must be examined in the context of building the novice's seclusion hut and of the symbolic objects comprising the hut and its total meaning. There are, of course, many types of binary opposition. The members of pairs of symbols may be asymmetrical ($A > B$, $A < B$); they may be like or unlike but equal in value; they may be antithetical; one may be thought of as the product or offspring of the other; one may be active, the other passive; and so on. In this way, the Ndembu are induced to consider the nature and function of relationships as well as of the variables being related, for nonverbal symbol systems have the equivalents of grammar, syntax, accidence, and parts of speech.

Sometimes binary opposition may appear between complexes of symbol vehicles, each carrying a system of dominant and secondary symbols. Thus, in the circumcision rites of the Wiko, in Zambia (10), one group of masked dancers may mime opposition to another group; each mask and headpiece is already a combination of multivocal symbols. Yet one team may represent protectiveness and the other, aggressiveness. It is, in fact, not uncommon to find complex symbol vehicles, such as statues or shrines, with simple meanings, while simple vehicles, such as marks drawn in white or red clay, may be highly multivocal in almost every ritual situation in which they are used. A simple vehicle, exhibiting some color, shape, texture, or contrast commonly found in one's experience (such as the whiteness of the mudyi or the redness of the mukula), can literally or metaphorically connect a great range of phenomena and ideas. By contrast, a complex vehicle is already committed, at the level of sensory perception, to a host of contrasts that narrow and specify its message. This is probably why the great religious symbol vehi-

cles such as the cross, the lotus, the crescent moon, the ark, and
so on are relatively simple, although their significata constitute
whole theological systems and control liturgical and architectural
structures of immense complexity. One might almost hypothe-
size that the more complex the ritual (many symbols, complex
vehicles), the more particularistic, localized, and socially structured its message; the simpler the ritual (few symbols, simple
vehicles), the more universalistic its message. Thus, ecumenical
liturgiologists today are recommending that Christian ritual be
essentially reduced to the blessing, distribution, and partaking of
bread and wine, in order to provide most denominations with a
common ground.

ACTORS EXPERIENCE SYMBOLS AS POWERS AND AS MEANINGS

The second characteristic of ritual condensation, which com-
pensates in some measure for semantic obscurity, is its efficacy.
Ritual is not just a concentration of referents, of messages about
values and norms; nor is it simply a set of practical guidelines
and a set of symbolic paradigms for everyday action, indicating
how spouses should treat each other, how pastoralists should
classify and regard cattle, how hunters should behave in different
wild habitats, and so on. It is also a fusion of the powers
believed to be inherent in the persons, objects, relationships,
events, and histories represented by ritual symbols. It is a mobilization of energies as well as messages (11). In this respect, the
objects and activities in point are not merely things that stand for
other things or something abstract, they participate in the powers
and virtues they represent. I use "virtue" advisedly, for many
objects termed symbols are also termed medicines. Thus, scrap-
ings and leaves from such trees as the mudyi and the mukula are
pounded together in meal mortars, mixed with water, and given
to the afflicted to drink or to wash with. Here there is direct
communication of the life-giving powers thought to inhere in
certain objects under ritual conditions (a consecrated site, invocations of preternatural entities, and so on). When an object is used
analogously, it functions unambiguously as a symbol. Thus,
when the mudyi tree is used in puberty rites it clearly *represents*
mother's milk; here the association is through sight, not taste.
But when the mudyi is used as medicine in ritual, it is felt that
certain qualities of motherhood and nurturing are being communicated physically. In the first case, the mudyi is used because it is

"good to think" rather than "good to eat" (12); in the second, it is used because it has maternal power. The same objects are used both as powers and symbols, metonymically and metaphorically—it is the context that distinguishes them. The power aspect of a symbol derives from its being a part of a physical whole, the ideational aspect from an analogy between a symbol vehicle and its principal significata.

Each symbol expresses many themes, and each theme is expressed by many symbols. The cultural weave is made up of symbolic warp and thematic weft. This weaving of symbols and themes serves as a rich store of information, not only about the natural environment as perceived and evaluated by the ritual actors, but also about their ethical, esthetic, political, legal, and ludic (the domain of play, sport, and so forth in a culture) ideas, ideals, and rules. Each symbol is a store of information, both for actors and investigators, but in order to specify just which set of themes any particular ritual or ritual episode contains, one must determine the relations between the ritual's symbols and their vehicles, including verbal symbolic behavior. The advantages of communication by means of rituals in nonliterate societies are clearly great, for the individual symbols and the patterned relations between them have a mnemonic function. The symbolic vocabulary and grammar to some extent make up for the lack of written records.

THE SEMANTIC DIMENSIONS

Symbols have three especially significant dimensions: the exegetic, the operational, and the positional. The exegetic dimension consists of the explanations given the investigator by actors in the ritual system. Actors of different age, sex, ritual role, status, grade of esoteric knowledge, and so forth provide data of varying richness, explicitness, and internal coherence. The investigator should infer from this information how members of a given society think about ritual. Not all African societies contain persons who are ready to make verbal statements about ritual, and the percentage of those prepared to offer interpretations varies from group to group and within groups. But, as much ethnographic work attests (13), many African societies are well endowed with exegetes.

In the operational dimension, the investigator equates a symbol's meaning with its use—he observes what actors do with it and how they relate to one another in this process. He also records their gestures, expressions, and other nonverbal aspects of behavior and discovers what values they represent—grief, joy, anger, triumph, modesty, and so on. Anthropologists are now studying several genres of nonverbal language, from iconography (the study of symbols whose vehicles picture the conceptions they signify, rather than being arbitrary, conventional signs for them) to kinesics (the study of bodily movements, facial expressions, and so forth as ways of communication or adjuncts and intensifiers of speech). Several of these fall under the rubric of a symbol's operational meaning. Nonexegetical, ritualized speech, such as formalized prayers or invocations, would also fall into this category. Here verbal symbols approximate nonverbal symbols. The investigator is interested not only in the social organization and structure of those individuals who operate with symbols on this level, but also in what persons, categories, and groups are absent from the situation, for formal exclusion would reveal social values and attitudes.

In the positional dimension, the observer finds in the relations between one symbol and other symbols an important source of its meaning. I have shown how binary opposition may, in context, highlight one (or more) of a symbol's many referents by contrasting it with one (or more) of another symbol's referents. When used in a ritual context with three or more other symbols, a particular symbol reveals further facets of its total "meaning." Groups of symbols may be so arrayed as to state a message in which some symbols function analogously to parts of speech and in which there may be conventional rules of connection. The message is not about specific actions and circumstances, but about the given culture's basic structures of thought, ethics, esthetics, law, and modes of speculation about new experience.

In several African cultures, particularly in West Africa, a complex system of rituals is associated with myths (14). These tell of the origins of the gods, the cosmos, human types and groups, and the key institutions of culture and society. Some ritual episodes reenact primordial events, drawing on their inherent power to achieve the contemporary goals of the members of the culture (for example, adjustment to puberty and the healing of the sick). Ritual systems are sometimes based on myths. There may coexist with myths and rituals standardized schemata of interpretation that may amount to theological doctrine. But in wide areas of East and Central Africa, there may be few myths connected with rituals and no religious system interrelating myths, rituals, and doctrine. In compensation, there may be much piecemeal exegesis of particular symbols.

FOUNDATIONS OF MEANING

Most African languages have terms for ritual symbol. The Nyakyusa, for example, speak of *ififwani* (likenesses); the Ndembu use *chijikijilu* (a landmark, or blaze), which is derived from *kujikijila* (to blaze a trail or set up a landmark). The first connotes an association, a feeling of likeness between sign and signified, vehicle and concept; the second is a means of connecting known with unknown territory. (The Ndembu compare the ritual symbol to the trail a hunter blazes in order to find his way back from unexplored bush to his village.) Other languages possess similar terms. In societies that do not have myths, the meaning of a symbol is built up by analogy and association of three foundations—nominal, substantial, and artifactual—though in any given instance only one of these might be utilized. The nominal basis is the name of the symbol, an element in an acoustic system; the substantial basis is a symbol's sensorily perceptible physical or chemical properties as recognized by the culture; and its artifactual basis is the technical changing of an object used in ritual by human purposive activity.

For example: At the start of a girl's puberty ritual among the Nyakyusa of Tanzania (15), she is treated with a "medicine" called *undumila*. This medicine is also an elaborate symbol. Its nominal basis is the derivation of the term from *ukulumila*, meaning "to bite, to be painful." The substantial basis is a natural property of the root after which the medicine is named—it is pungent-tasting. As an artifact, the medicine is a composite of several symbolic substances. The total symbol involves action as well as a set of objects. Wilson writes (15, p. 87) that the root "is pushed through the tip of a funnel or cup made of a leaf of the bark-cloth tree, and salt is poured into the cup. The girl takes the tip of the root in her mouth and pulls it inward with her teeth, thus causing the salt to trickle into her mouth." The root and leaf funnel, together with their ritual use, constitute an artifact. These three bases of significance are substantiated by the Nyakyusa Wilson talked to. One woman told her (15, p. 102): "The pungent root is the penis of the husband, the cup is her vagina, the salt, also pungent, is the semen of her husband. Biting the root and eating the salt is copulation." Another woman confirmed this: "The *undumila* is put through the leaf of a bark-cloth tree, shaped into a cup, and it is a sign of man and woman, the penis in the vagina. It is similar to the plantains which we give her when we wash her. The plantains are a symbol of the husband. If we do not give her . . . the *undumila*, she constantly has periods and is barren." A third informant said: "It is the pain of periods that we symbolize in the sharpness of the *undumila* and salt." Thus *undumila* is at once a symbol of sexual intercourse, a prophylactic against pain in intercourse and against frequent or painful periods, and (according to other accounts) a ritual defense against those who are "heavy"—that is, those actively engaged in sexual intercourse, especially women who have just conceived. If a heavy person steps over the novice's footprints, the novice will not bear a child, but will menstruate continually. These explanations also demonstrate the multivocality and economy of reference of a single dominant symbol. The same symbol vehicles can represent different, even disparate, processes—marital intercourse and menstrual difficulty—although it may be argued that the Nyakyusa, at an unconscious level, regard a woman's "distaste" for intercourse as a cause of her barrenness or menorrhagia.

SYMBOLS AND COSMOLOGIES

Similar examples abound in the ethnography of subsaharan Africa, but in the great West African cultures of the Fon, Ashanti, Yoruba, Dahomeyans, and Dogon, piecemeal exegesis gives way to explicit, complex cosmologies. Among the Dogon, for example (16, 17), a symbol becomes a fixed point of linkage between animal, vegetable, and mineral kingdoms, which are themselves regarded as parts of "un gigantesque organisme humaine." The doctrine of correspondences reigns—everything is a symbol of everything else, whether in ritual context or not. Thus the Dogon establish a correspondence between the different categories of minerals and the organs of the body. The various soils in the area are conceived of as the organs of "the interior of the stomach," rocks are regarded as the bones of the skeleton, and various hues of red clay are likened to the blood. Sometimes these correspondences are remarkably precise: one rock resting on another represents the chest; little white river pebbles stand for the toes of the feet. The same *parole du monde* principles hold true for the relationship between man and the vegetable kingdom. Man is not only the grain of the universe, but each distinct part of a single grain represents part of the human body. In fact, it is only science that has emancipated man from the complex weave of correspondences, based on analogy, metaphor, and mystical participation, and that enables him to regard all relations as problematical, not preordained, until they have been experimentally tested or systematically compared.

The Dogon further conceive of a subtle and finely wrought interplay between speech and the components of personality. The body constitutes a magnet or focus for man's spiritual principles, which nevertheless are capable of sustaining an independent existence. The Dogon contrast visible and invisible ("spiritual") components of the human personality. The body is made up of four elements: water (the blood and bodily fluids), earth (the skeleton), air (breath), and fire (animal warmth). There is a continuous interchange between these internal expressions of the elements and their external aspects. The body has 22 parts: feet, shins, thighs, lumbar region, stomach, chest, arms, neck, and head make up nine parts (it would seem that Dogon reckon double parts, as they do twins, as a unit); the fingers (each counting as a unit) make up ten parts; and the male genitals make up three parts. Further numerical symbolism is involved: there are believed to be eight symbolic grains—representing the principal cereal crops of the region—lodged in the collarbones of each Dogon. These grains represent the mystical bond between man and his crops. The *body* of speech itself is, like the human body, composed of four elements: water is saliva, without which speech is dry; air gives rise to sound vibrations; earth gives speech its weight and significance; and fire gives speech its warmth. There is not only homology between personality and speech, but also a sort of functional interdependence, for words are selected by the brain, stir up the liver, and rise as steam from the lungs to the clavicles, which decide ultimately whether the speech is to emerge from the mouth.

To the 22 parts of the personality must be added the 48 types of speech, which are divided into two sets of 24. Each set is under the sign of a supernatural being, one of the androgynous twins Nommo and Yourougou. Here I must draw on Griaule and Dieterlen's extensive work on the Dogons' cosmogonic mythology (16). The twins are the creations of Amma. Yourougou rebelled against Amma and had sexual relations with his mother—he was punished by being changed into a pale fox. Nommo saved the world by an act of self-sacrifice, brought humans, animals, and plants to the earth, and became the lord of speech. Nommo's speech is human and can be heard; the Fox's is silent, a sign language made by his paw marks, and only diviners can interpret it. These myths provide a classification and taxonomy of cosmos and society; explain many details of ritual, including the forms and color symbolism of elaborate masks;

and, indeed, determine where and how houses are constructed. Other West African cultures have equally elaborate cosmologies, which are manifested in ritual and divinatory symbolism. Their internal consistency and symmetry may be related to traditions of continuous residence and farming in a single habitat, combined with exposure to trans-Saharan cultural elements, including religious beliefs, for thousands of years—ancient Egyptian, Roman, Christian, Neo-Platonic, Gnostic, Islamic. The history of West Africa contrasts with that of Central Africa, where most societies descend from groups that migrated in a relatively short period of time across several distinct ecological habitats and that were then exposed to several centuries of slave raiding and slave trading. Groups were fragmented and then combined with the social detritus of other societies into new, temporary polities. There were conquests, assimilations, reconquests, the rise and fall of "kingdoms of the savannah," and temporary centralization followed by decentralization into localized clans. Swidden (slash-and-burn) agriculture kept people constantly on the move; hunting and pastoralism compounded the mobility. Because of these circumstances, there was less likelihood of complex, integrated religious and cosmological systems arising in Central Africa than in West Africa. Yet the needs and dangers of social and personal survival provided suitable conditions for the development of rituals as pragmatic instruments (from the standpoint of the actors) for coping with biological change, disease, and natural hazards of all kinds. Social action in response to material pressures was the systematic and systematizing factor. Order, cosmos, came from purpose, not from an elaborate and articulated cosmology. It is an order that accords well with human experience at preindustrial technological levels; even its discrepancies accurately reflect the "facts of life"—in contrast to consistent and harmonious cosmologies whose symbols and myths mask and cloak the basic contradictions between wishes and facts.

THE CONTINUING EFFICACY OF AFRICAN RITUAL SYMBOLS

Nevertheless, from the comparative viewpoint, there are remarkable similarities among symbols used in ritual throughout sub-Saharan Africa, in spite of differences in cosmological sophistication. The same ideas, analogies, and modes of association underlie symbol formation and manipulation from the Senegal River to the Cape of Good Hope. The same assumptions about powers prevail in kingdoms and nomadic bands. Whether these assemblages of similar symbols represent units of complex order or the debris of formerly prevalent ones, the symbols remain extraordinarily viable and the themes they represent and embody tenaciously rooted. This may be because they arose in ecological and social experiences of a kind that still prevails in large areas of the continent. Since they are thus sustained and since there is a continuous flux and reflux of people between country and city, it is not surprising that much of the imagery found in the writings of modern African novelists and in the rhetoric of politicians is drawn from ritual symbolism—from which it derives its power to move and channel emotion.

REFERENCES

1. Wilson, M. *Communal Rituals of the Nyakyusa* (London: Oxford University Press, 1959), pp. 49–69.
2. Turner, V. W. in *Closed Systems and Open Minds: The Limits of Naivety in Social Anthropology*, M. Gluckman, ed. (Edinburgh: Oliver & Boyd, 1964), pp. 20–51.
3. Opler, M. E. *Amer. J. Sociol.*, 51 (1945), p. 198.
4. ———, *Southwest. J. Anthropol.*, 24 (1968), p. 215.
5. Watson, J. B. in *A Dictionary of the Social Sciences*, J. Gould and W. L. Kolb, eds. (London: Tavistock, 1964), pp. 163–164.
6. Turner, V. W. in *Themes in Culture*, M. D. Zamora, J. M. Mahar, H. Orenstein, eds. (Quezon City, Philippines: Kayumanggi, 1971), pp. 270–284.
7. Turner, V. W. *Ndembu Divination: Its Symbolism and Techniques* (Manchester: Manchester University Press, 1961); in *Anthropological Approaches to the Study of Religion*, M. Banton, ed. (London: Tavistock, 1966), pp. 47–84; in *Forms of Symbolic Action*, R. F. Spencer, ed. (Seattle: University of Washington Press, 1969), pp. 3–25.
8. ———, *The Forest of Symbols* (Ithaca, N.Y.: Cornell University Press, 1967), pp. 28, 31, 42, 51, 55, 213–217.
9. ———, *The Drums of Affliction* (Oxford: Clarendon Press, 1968), pp. 59–60, 68–69, 71–74, 82–87, 160, 203.
10. Gluckman, M. in *Social Structure: Studies Presented to A. R. Radcliffe-Brown*, M. Fortes, ed. (Oxford: Clarendon Press, 1949), pp. 165–167.
11. This problem of the sources of the effectiveness of symbols has been discussed by C. Lévi-Strauss, *Structural Anthropol-*

ogy (New York: Basic Books, 1963), pp. 186–205; V. W. Turner, *The Ritual Process* (Chicago: Aldine, 1969), pp. 10–43; N. Munn, in *Forms of Symbolic Action,* R. F. Spencer, ed. (Seattle: University of Washington Press, 1969), pp. 178–207.

12. See C. Lévi-Strauss's formulation regarding "totemic" objects, countering the "common-sense" view of J. Frazer and other early-twentieth-century anthropologists [*Le Totémisme Aujourd'hui* (Paris: Presses Universitaires de France, 1962)].

13. For example, M. Wilson, *Amer. Anthropol.,* 56 (1954), p. 228; A. Richards, *Chisungu* (London: Faber, 1956); M. Griaule, *Conversations with Ogotemmêli* (London: Oxford University Press, 1965); E. E. Evans-Pritchard, *Nuer Religion* (Oxford: Clarendon Press, 1956); M. Douglas, *Africa*, 27 (1955), p. 27; C. M. N. White, *Afr. Stud.*, 7 (1948), p. 146; T. O. Beidelman, *Africa*, 31 (1961), p. 250; P. Morton-Williams, W. Bascom, E. M. McClelland, *ibid.*, 36 (1966), p. 406; J. Beattie, *ibid.*, 38 (1968), p. 413.

14. Examples of African cosmological systems may be found in D. Forde, ed., *African Worlds* (London: Oxford University Press, 1954). See also T. O. Beidelman on aspects of Swazi cosmology [*Africa*, 36 (1966), p. 379].

15. Wilson, M. *Rituals of Kinship among the Nyakyusa* (London: Oxford University Press, 1957), pp. 87, 102.

16. Calame-Griaule, G. *Ethnologie et Langage: Le Parole Chez les Dogon* (Paris: Gallimard, 1966); G. Dieterlen, *Les Ames des Dogon* (Paris: Institut d'Ethnologie, 1941); *Le Renard Pale* (Paris: Institut d'Ethnologie, 1963).

17. Douglas, M. *Africa*, 38 (1968), p. 16.

VIII

POLITICS, LAW, AND WAR

Men possess a sense of the just and the unjust, and their sharing a common understanding of justice makes a polis.

Aristotle, *Politics*

Wars are caused by unprotected wealth.
General Douglas MacArthur

POLITICS IS THE art of the possible. Its purpose is the organization, distribution and manipulation of power. How is it possible to judge the strength of a political system? Some believe that a system is strong at such times as talented leaders hold the reigns of power. Others, including Marshall D. Sahlins, believe that a system's strength sits in its structure. The structure includes the roles available and the way such roles are assumed by potential office-holders. In Melanesia the "big-man" *achieves* power and status by being a "wheeler-dealer"; he is the self-made leader of a small, localized kinship group. In Polynesia, by contrast, the role of "chief" is *ascribed*; a person is born to be a chief just as some in Europe are born to be royalty. In "Poor Man, Rich Man, Big-Man, Chief" Sahlins shows that the Polynesian system could organize massive projects and was capable of handling the logistics of extensive military campaigns. Comparing the two systems, Sahlins writes, "Larger and more easily replenished than their western Melanesian counterparts, Polynesian funds of power permitted greater political regulation of a greater range of social activities on greater scale."

Roles, as noted, form a structure within which certain types of action can occur. To put it differently, roles regulate behavior. Along with roles there are always *rules*: "oughts" or obligations to behave in given ways at given times and circumstances. Rules, while basic aspects of all human society, as not well understood in the social sciences. And when social scientists, like "ordinary people," find something hard to deal with, they call it by many different names. Rules, essentially fuzzy phenomena, are therefore made yet fuzzier by being given lots of labels: fashion, manners, morals, beliefs, norms, laws, to name several. To better understand the fuzzy nature of rules consider those called "laws." Laws are rules with "teeth." Or, as the great anthropologist Adamson Hoebel put it, laws are "social norms that are maintained through the application of legal sanctions." Legal sanctions, the teeth, are more concrete and more predictable than other kinds of sanctions. However, with all their apparent power, legal sanctions are often avoided. Laws, while more concrete than other forms of rules, are still manipulable and manipulated. If rules are often avoided, what does it mean to say a rule is an "ought"? Why do humans often break rules and thereby escape from their obligations? To what extent do humans feel that they are actually obliged to follow the rules of their society? These and related questions are insightfully discussed in Raymond Firth's "Rules and Custom in 'Primitive' Society."

Sahlins and Firth discuss *internal regulation*; the roles and rules which maintain order and peaceful interaction within a society. But what of problems from outside the system? Historically, the most popular strategy for dealing with troublesome "outsiders" has been war. "War" seems like a simple term to define. Yet some serious thought, coupled with examples from the modern world, should help change the minds of many. Is the Soviet government at war with Afghanistan? Are the Vietnamese at war with Cambodia? Is Morocco at war with Algeria? Is the Republic of South Africa at war with Angola? Are the Bushmen at war with the South-West Africa People's Organization (SWAPO)? To these and similar questions John Gellner (editor of the *Canadian Defence Quarterly*) would answer yes! For according to Gellner, war is "any armed clash between sovereign states whether direct or indirect, through proxies."[1]

War has been and still remains *the way* to solve conflicts between sovereign states. For the past 3,500 years (according to the *Guinness Book of Records*) there have only been 230 years of complete peace. According to the latest edition of *World Military and Social Expenditures* (compiled by Ruth Sivard), the world is spending 550 billion dollars on arms, twice the amount it spends on food. A nuclear war which could destroy approximately eight hundred million people can be launched on the basis of a decision by a single person. There is an endless escalation of new, more deadly weapon systems: each time the U.S. or the USSR

[1]John Gellner, "A Year of Warfare in the Third World" *The Globe and Mail* (Ottawa, Canada), December 31, 1980.

develops new weapons, the rival nation follows with yet newer and more powerful systems. Over an eighteen-month period, the U.S. nuclear warning system produced 147 false indications of Soviet missile attacks. To say that making and preparing for war remains the most popular game around avoids basic and serious questions: namely, why has warfare been used so often to solve conflicts? Moreover, given the enormous risks created by modern weapon systems, why do modern states continue arming to the teeth?

A false but (for some) persuasive explanation is that humans are warlike because they are naked or killer apes. We (supposedly) have war-making in our genes. The notion that humans are naked apes stimulates public interest in evolution and seems to help increase sales of periodicals which popularize science.[2] How is it possible to explain human evolution as a process which creates "killer" animals? According to the anthropologists S. L. Washburn and C. S. Lancaster, hunting has dominated the course of human evolution for hundreds of thousands of years. Therefore, they argue "our intellect, interests, emotions and basic social life all are evolutionary products of the success of the hunting adaptation." To become good hunters, they conclude, humans had to learn to love killing:

> Men enjoy hunting and killing, and these activities are continued even when they are no longer economically necessary . . . until recently war was viewed in much the same way as hunting. Other human beings were simply the most dangerous game. War has been far too important in human history for it to be other than pleasurable for the males involved.[3]

Old men, generally, make wars and send young men to fight in them. If killing is "in" our genes, how do the old free themselves from the necessity to kill? Moreover, if killing is really fun, why do the old men allow the young men to hog all the pleasure? Hunting includes a variety of activities, including close

---

[2]For example, *Science Digest* published an article ("The First Killers," October 1981) with a headline that announced: "FEARSOME TEETH AND POWERFUL JAWS WERE TWO OF THE EVOLUTIONARY INNOVATIONS THAT LED TO THE RISE OF PREDATORS. A NEW BREED OF CREATURES THAT CULMINATED IN *HOMO SAPIENS*."

[3]See, but do not take seriously S. L. Washburn and C. S. Lancaster, "The Evolution of Hunting," in *Man the Hunter*, ed. Richard B. Lee and Irven DeVore (Chicago: Aldine, 1964).

cooperation among the men who hunt together. One could argue, quite plausibly, that hundreds of thousands of years of hunting helped to develop cooperative skills rather than a love of killing.

Naked apism is more than a misinterpretation of human history. It is more than a misrepresentation of the human essence. Naked apism is a dangerous myth. It oversimplifies human evolution and promotes a fallacious fatalism. Let me explain. It is currently faddish, in some circles, to consider humans as killer or naked apes. The fad fascinates by its fatalism and seduces by its simplicity. Fatalism fascinates because it reduces our responsibility for the future: Wars are not our fault; blame biology or the devil called "human evolutionary history"; interpersonal violence cannot be stopped; planning for peaceful compromises becomes foolish, misplaced energy; we must arm to the teeth; we must kill or be killed. Simplicity seduces because we live in the age of "instant culture." The proper way to do things is as fast as possible. Whatever the medium, the modern message is the same. The fast is exciting; the slow is a drag. Shortcuts help us to reach goals faster. In the age of instant culture, shortcuts become very valuable, and simple explanations are shortcuts to knowledge. What can be simpler than defining war as inevitable and describing humans as killer apes? As children of instant culture we must fight hard to resist instant knowledge.

David Pilbeam's "The Naked Ape: An Idea We Could Live Without" provides a scholarly and well-researched rebuttal to the postulates of naked-apism. Pilbeam's valuable essay presents our evolutionary history in proper perspective. The data used by the naked-apist clique is carefully evaluated. Pilbeam also provides other data pertinent to the question: "Is *Homo sapiens* a naked, killer ape?" Among his many valuable comments, the following really merits memorizing: "It is overly simplistic in the extreme to believe that man behaves in strongly genetically deterministic ways, when we know that apes and monkeys do not." Learning plays a significant role in human behavior. If warfare is a popular game, it is one that humans are taught. Clearly, we need to examine our teachers rather than our genes.

Teachers are ever available to socialize people in the art of war. And, as Gary Thatcher tells us in "Bushmen: The Hunters Now Hunt Guerrillas", agreeing to learn and to participate in the fighting can be a profitable decision. For example, the Bushmen are paid four hundred dollars a month for hunting guerrillas. In addition, they get free housing for their wives and children. For the Bushmen the money alone represents a staggering amount. It is well to note that these hunters must be enticed with large rewards to participate in a war. If hunters really enjoyed killing, they would require little monetary inducement to join in the fun.

Humans are taught to define certain people as "enemies": killing enemies proves that we are loyal tribesmen; refraining from killing indicates that we are cowardly traitors. But killing for pleasure does not explain human warfare, and killing because we are taught to kill only partially explains the extensiveness and frequency of armed conflict. What is left unexplained is the motivation of the teachers and the fearlessness of the taught. Why should teachers still promote this outmoded form of dispute management? Why are the students minimally concerned that modern weaponry may blow up the world? In "The Two Worlds of *Homo Sapiens*" I suggest that humans are often faced by a dilemma. This dilemma—"Shall I do it *smartly* or *properly*?" —has no simple solution. Those who often go the road of the "smart" maximize their chances of physical survival but risk the loss of dignity. For humans, life without dignity carries the risk of mental illness. Those who follow the path of the "proper" maximize personal dignity but frequently take survival risks. This thesis, put briefly, is that tensions caused by frequent and frustrating involvement with a dilemma seek an outlet. One such is warfare. War, then, is a costly catharsis, a playing out on a social level of the battle within.

The thesis that war is a catharsis for human tensions, especially those due to deciding between the "smart" and the "proper" accounts for war as well as does "naked apism." Unlike the latter, this thesis has gut validity. We all frequently choose between non-proper but more successful paths, and proper but less successful paths. And these choices leave us (often) in states of internal conflict. Few of us, however, find life wearisome because it lacks opportunities for killing humans. In my view, humans are *neurotic primates* rather than naked, killer apes. Neurotic primates need not kill. They can find catharsis by involvement with less costly games than war.

REFERENCES

Hoebel, E. Adamson. *The Law of Primitive Man.* New York: Athenaeum, 1968.

Nader, Laura and Harry F. Todd, Jr., eds. *The Disputing Process: Law in Ten Societies.* New York: Columbia University Press, 1978.

Poor Man, Rich Man,
Big-Man, Chief

by
Marshall D. Sahlins

WITH AN EYE to their own life goals, the native peoples of Pacific Islands unwittingly present to anthropologists a generous scientific gift: an extended series of experiments in cultural adaptation and evolutionary development. They have compressed their institutions within the confines of infertile coral atolls, expanded them on volcanic islands, created with the means history gave them cultures adapted to the deserts of Australia, the mountains and warm coasts of New Guinea, the rain forests of the Solomon Islands. From the Australian Aborigines, whose hunting and gathering existence duplicates in outline the cultural life of the later Paleolithic, to the great chiefdoms of Hawaii, where society approached the formative levels of the old Fertile Crescent civilizations, almost every general phase in the progress of primitive culture is exemplified.

Where culture so experiments, anthropology finds its laboratories—makes its comparisons.

In the southern and eastern Pacific two contrasting cultural provinces have long evoked anthropological interest: *Melanesia*, including New Guinea, the Bismarcks, Solomons, and island groups east to Fiji; and *Polynesia*, consisting in its main portion of the triangular constellation of lands between New Zealand, Easter Island, and the Hawaiian Islands. In and around Fiji, Melanesia and Polynesia intergrade culturally, but west and east of their intersection the two provinces pose broad contrasts in several sectors: in religion, art, kinship groupings, economics, political organization. The differences are the more notable for

Reprinted from "Poor Man, Rich Man, Big-Man, Chief: Political Types in Melanesia and Polynesia," *Comparative Studies in Society & History*, 5 (April, 1963), pp. 285–303, by permission of Cambridge University Press.

the underlying similarities from which they emerge. Melanesia and Polynesia are both agricultural regions in which many of the same crops—such as yams, taro, breadfruit, bananas, and coconuts—have long been cultivated by many similar techniques. Some recently presented linguistic and archaeological studies indeed suggest that Polynesian cultures originated from an eastern Melanesian hearth during the first millennium B.C. Yet in anthropological annals the Polynesians were to become famous for elaborate forms of rank and chieftainship, whereas most Melanesian societies broke off advance on this front at more rudimentary levels.

It is obviously imprecise, however, to make out the political contrast in broad culture-area terms. Within Polynesia, certain of the islands, such as Hawaii, the Society Islands and Tonga, developed unparalleled political momentum. And not all Melanesian polities, on the other side, were constrained and truncated in their evolution. In New Guinea and nearby areas of western Melanesia, small and loosely ordered political groupings are numerous, but in eastern Melanesia, New Caledonia and Fiji for example, political approximations of the Polynesian condition become common. There is more of an upward west to east slope in political development in the southern Pacific than a step-like, quantum progression. It is quite revealing, however, to compare the extremes of this continuum, the western Melanesian underdevelopment against the greater Polynesian chiefdoms. While such comparison does not exhaust the evolutionary variations, it fairly establishes the scope of overall political achievement in this Pacific phylum of cultures.

Measurable along several dimensions, the contrast between developed Polynesian and underdeveloped Melanesian polities is immediately striking for differences in scale. H. Ian Hogbin and Camilla Wedgwood concluded from a survey of Melanesian (most western Melanesian) societies that ordered, independent political bodies in the region typically include seventy to three hundred persons; more recent work in the New Guinea Highlands suggests political groupings of up to a thousand, occasionally a few thousand, people.[1] But in Polynesia sovereignties of two thousand or three thousand are run-of-the-mill, and the most advanced chiefdoms, as in Tonga or Hawaii, might claim ten thousand, even tens of thousands. Varying step by step with such differences, in size, of the polity are differences in territorial

[1] H. Ian Hogbin and Camilla H. Wedgwood, "Local Groupings in Melanesia," *Oceania*, 23 (1952–53), pp. 241–276; 24 (1953–54), pp. 58–76.

extent: from a few square miles in western Melanesia to tens or even hundreds of square miles in Polynesia.

The Polynesian advance in political scale was supported by advance over Melanesia in political structure. Melanesia presents a great array of social-political forms: here political organization is based upon patrilineal descent groups, there on cognatic groups, or men's club-houses recruiting neighborhood memberships, on a secret ceremonial society, or perhaps on some combination of these structural principles. Yet a general plan can be discerned. The characteristic western Melanesia "tribe," that is, the ethnic-cultural entity, consists of many autonomous kinship-residential groups. Amounting on the ground to a small village or a local cluster of hamlets, each of these is a copy of the others in organization, each tends to be economically self-governing, and each is the equal of the others in political status. The tribal plan is one of politically unintegrated segments—segmental. But the political geometry in Polynesia is pyramidal. Local groups of the order of self-governing Melanesian communities appear in Polynesia as subdivisions of a more inclusive political body. Smaller units are integrated into larger through a system of intergroup ranking, and the network of representative chiefs of the subdivisions amounts to a coordinating political structure. So instead of the Melanesian scheme of small, separate, and equal political blocs, the Polynesian polity is an extensive pyramid of groups capped by the family and following of a paramount chief. (This Polynesian political upshot is often, although not always, facilitated by the development of ranked lineages. Called *conical clan* by Kirchhoff, at one time *ramage* by Firth and *status lineage* by Goldman, the Polynesian ranked lineage is the same in principle as the so-called *obok* system widely distributed in Central Asia, and it is at least analogous to the Scottish clan, the Chinese clan, certain Central African Bantu lineage systems, the house-groups of Northwest Coast Indians, perhaps even the "tribes" of the Israelites. Genealogical ranking is its distinctive feature: members of the same descent unit are ranked by genealogical distance from the common ancestor; lines of the same group become senior and cadet branches on this principle; related corporate lineages are relatively ranked, again by genealogical priority.)

Here is another criterion of Polynesia political advance: historical performance. Almost all of the native peoples of the South Pacific were brought up against intense European cultural pressure in the late eighteenth and the nineteenth centuries. Yet only the Hawaiians, Tahitians, Tongans, and to a lesser extent the

Fijians, successfully defended themselves by evolving countervailing, native-controlled states. Complete with public governments and public law, monarchs and taxes, ministers and minions, these nineteenth-century states are testimony to the native Polynesian political genius, to the level and the potential of indigenous political accomplishments.

Embedded within the grand differences in political scale, structure and performance is a more personal contrast, one in quality of leadership. An historically particular type of leader-figure, the "big-man" as he is often locally styled, appears in the underdeveloped settings of Melanesia. Another type, a chief properly so-called, is associated with the Polynesian advance. Now these are distinct sociological types, that is to say, differences in the powers, privileges, rights, duties, and obligations of Melanesian big-men and Polynesian chiefs are given by the divergent societal contexts in which they operate. Yet the institutional distinctions cannot help but be manifest also in differences in bearing and character, appearance and manner—in a word, personality. It may be a good way to begin the more rigorous sociological comparison of leadership with a more impressionistic sketch of the contrast in the human dimension. Here I find it useful to apply characterizations—or is it caricature?—from our own history to big-men and chiefs, however much injustice this does to the historically incomparable backgrounds of the Melanesians and Polynesians. The Melanesian big-man seems so thoroughly bourgeois, so reminiscent of the free-enterprising rugged individual of our own heritage. He combines with an ostensible interest in the general welfare a more profound measure of self-interested cunning and economic calculation. His gaze, as Veblen might have put it, is fixed unswervingly to the main chance. His every public action is designed to make a competitive and invidious comparison with others, to show a standing above the masses that is a product of his own personal manufacture. The historical caricature of the Polynesian chief, however, is feudal rather than capitalist. His appearance, his bearing is almost regal; very likely he just *is* a big man—" 'Can't you see he is a chief? See how big he is?' "[2] In his every public action is a display of the refinements of breeding, in his manner always that *noblesse oblige* of true pedigree and an incontestable right of rule. With his standing not so much a personal achievement as a just social due, he can afford to be, and he is, every inch a chief.

[2]Edward Winslow Gifford, *Tongan Society* (Honolulu: Bernice P. Bishop Museum Bulletin, 61, 1926).

In the several Melanesian tribes in which big-men have come under anthropological scrutiny, local cultural differences modify the expression of their personal powers. But the indicative quality of big-man authority is everywhere the same: it is *personal* power. Big-men do not come to office; they do not succeed to, nor are they installed in, existing positions of leadership over political groups. The attainment of big-man status is rather the outcome of a series of acts which elevate a person above the common herd and attract about him a coterie of loyal, lesser men. It is not accurate to speak of "big-man" as a political title, for it is but an acknowledged standing in interpersonal relations—a "prince among men" so to speak as opposed to "The Prince of Danes." In particular Melanesian tribes the phrase might be "man of importance" or "man of renown," "generous rich-man," or "center-man," as well as "big-man."

A kind of two-sidedness in authority is implied in this series of phrases, a division of the big-man's field of influence into two distinct sectors. "Center-man" particularly connotes a cluster of followers gathered about an influential pivot. It socially implies the division of the tribe into political in-groups dominated by outstanding personalities. To the in-group, the big-man presents this sort of picture:

> The place of the leader in the district group [in northern Malaita] is well summed up by his title, which might be translated as "center-man." . . . He was like a banyan, the natives explain, which, though the biggest and tallest in the forest, is still a tree like the rest. But, just because it exceeds all others, the banyan gives support to more lianas and creepers, provides more food for the birds, and gives better protection against sun and rain.[3]

But "man of renown" connotes a broader tribal field in which a man is not so much a leader as he is some sort of hero. This is the side of the big-man facing outward from his own faction, his status among some or all of the other political clusters of the tribe. The political sphere of the big-man divides itself into a small internal sector composed of his personal satellites—rarely over eighty men—and a much larger external sector, the tribal galaxy consisting of many similar constellations.

As it crosses over from the internal into the external sector, a

---

[3]H. Ian Hogbin, "Native Councils and Courts in the Solomon Islands," *Oceania*, 14 (1943–44), pp. 258–283.

big-man's power undergoes qualitative change. Within his faction a Melanesian leader has true command ability, outside of it only fame and indirect influence. It is not that the center-man rules his faction by physical force, but his followers do feel obliged to obey him, and he can usually get what he wants by haranguing them—public verbal suasion is indeed so often employed by center-men that they have been styled "harangueutans." The orbits of outsiders, however, are set by their own center-men. " 'Do it yourself. I'm not *your* fool,' " would be the characteristic response to an order issued by a center-man to an outsider among the Siuai.[4] This fragmentation of true authority presents special political difficulties, particularly in organizing large masses of people for the prosecution of such collective ends as warfare or ceremony. Big-men do instigate mass action, but only by establishing both extensive renown and special personal relations of compulsion or reciprocity with other center-men.

Politics is in the main personal politicking in these Melanesian societies, and the size of a leader's faction as well as the extent of his renown are normally set by competition with other ambitious men. Little or no authority is given by social ascription: leadership is a creation—a creation of followership. "Followers," as it is written of the Kapauku of New Guinea, "stand in various relations to the leader. Their obedience to the headman's decisions is caused by motivations which reflect their particular relations to the leader."[5] So a man must be prepared to demonstrate that he possesses the kinds of skills that command respect—magical powers, gardening prowess, mastery of oratorical style, perhaps bravery in war and feud. Typically decisive is the deployment of one's skills and efforts in a certain direction: towards amassing goods, most often pigs, shell monies and vegetable foods, and distributing them in ways which build a name for cavalier generosity, if not for compassion. A faction is developed by informal private assistance to people of a locale. Tribal rank and renown are developed by great public giveaways sponsored by the rising big-man, often on behalf of his faction as well as himself. In different Melanesian tribes, the renown-making public distribution may appear as one side of a delayed exchange of pigs between corporate kinship groups; a marital

[4]Douglas Oliver, *A Solomon Islands Society* (Cambridge: Harvard University Press, 1955).

[5]Leopold Pospisil, *Kapauku Papuans and Their Law* (New Haven: Yale University Press, Yale University Publications in Anthropology, no. 54, 1958).

consideration given a bride's kinfolk; a set of feasts connected with the erection of a big-man's dwelling, or of a club-house for himself and his faction, or with the purchase of higher grades of rank in secret societies; the sponsorship of a religious ceremony; a payment of subsidies and blood compensations to military allies: or perhaps the giveaway in a ceremonial challenge bestowed on another leader in the attempt to outgive and thus outrank him (a potlatch).

The making of the faction, however, is the true making of the Melanesian big-man. It is essential to establish relations of loyalty and obligation on the part of a number of people such that their production can be mobilized for renown-building external distribution. The bigger the faction the greater the renown; once momentum in external distribution has been generated the opposite can also be true. Any ambitious man who can gather a following can launch a societal career. The rising big-man necessarily depends initially on a small core of followers, principally his own household and his closest relatives. Upon these people he can prevail economically: he capitalizes in the first instance on kinship dues and by finessing the relation of reciprocity appropriate among close kinsmen. Often it becomes necessary at an early phase to enlarge one's household. The rising leader goes out of his way to incorporate within his family "strays" of various sorts, people without familial support themselves, such as widows and orphans. Additional wives are especially useful. The more wives a man has the more pigs he has. The relation here is functional, not identical: with more women gardening there will be more food for pigs and more swineherds. A Kiwai Papuan picturesquely put to an anthropologist in pidgin the advantages, economic and political, of polygamy: " 'Another woman go garden, another woman go take firewood, another woman go catch fish, another woman cook him—husband he sing out plenty people come kaikai [i.e., come to eat].' "[6] Each new marriage, incidentally, creates for the big-man an additional set of in-laws from whom he can exact economic favors. Finally, a leader's career sustains its upward climb when he is able to link other men and their families to his faction, harnessing their production to his ambition. This is done by calculated generosities, by placing others in gratitude and obligation through helping them in some big way. A common technique is payment of bridewealth on behalf of young men seeking wives.

[6]Gunnar Landtman, *The Kiwai Papuans of British New Guinea* (London: Macmillan, 1927).

The great Malinowski used a phrase in analyzing primitive political economy that felicitously describes just what the big-man is doing: amassing a "fund of power." A big-man is one who can create and use social relations which give him leverage on others' production and the ability to siphon off an excess product—or sometimes he can cut down their consumption in the interest of the siphon. Now although his attention may be given primarily to short-term personal interests, from an objective standpoint the leader acts to promote long-term societal interests. The fund of power provisions activities that involve other groups of the society at large. In the greater perspective of that society at large, big-men are indispensable means of creating supralocal organization: in tribes normally fragmented into small independent groups, big-men at least temporarily widen the sphere of ceremony, recreation and art, economic collaboration, of war too. Yet always this greater societal organization depends on the lesser factional organization, particularly on the ceilings on economic mobilization set by relations between center-men and followers. The limits and the weaknesses of the political order in general are the limits and weaknesses of the factional in-groups.

And the personal quality of subordination to a center-man is a serious weakness in factional structure. A personal loyalty has to be made and continually reinforced; if there is discontent it may well be severed. Merely to create a faction takes time and effort, and to hold it, still more effort. The potential rupture of personal links in the factional chain is at the heart of two broad evolutionary shortcomings of western Melanesian political orders. First, a comparative instability. Shifting dispositions and magnetisms of ambitious men in a region may induce fluctuations in factions, perhaps some overlapping of them, and fluctuations also in the extent of different renowns. The death of a center-man can become a regional political trauma; the death undermines the personally cemented faction, the group dissolves in whole or in part, and the people re-group finally around rising pivotal big-men. Although particular tribal structures in places cushion the disorganization, the big-man political system is generally unstable over short terms: in its superstructure it is a flux of rising and falling leaders, in its substructure of enlarging and contracting factions. Secondly, the personal political bond contributes to the containment of evolutionary advance. The possibility of their desertion, it is clear, often inhibits a leader's ability to forceably push up his followers' output, thereby placing constraints on higher political organization, but there is more to it than that. If it is to generate great momentum, a big-man's quest for the summits of renown is likely to bring out a contradiction in his relations to followers, so that he finds himself encouraging defection—or worse, an egalitarian rebellion—by encouraging production.

One side of the Melanesian contradiction is the initial economic reciprocity between a center-man and his followers. For his help they give their help, and for goods going out through his hands other goods (often from outside factions) flow back to his followers by the same path. The other side is that a cumulative build-up of renown forces center-men into economic extortion of the faction. Here it is important that not merely his own status, but the standing and perhaps the military security of his people depend on the big-man's achievements in public distribution. Established at the head of a sizeable faction, a center-man comes under increasing pressure to extract goods from his followers, to delay reciprocities owing them, and to deflect incoming goods back into external circulation. Success in competition with other big-men particularly undermines internal-factional reciprocities: such success is precisely measurable by the ability to give outsiders more than they can possibly reciprocate. In well delineated big-man polities, we find leaders negating the reciprocal obligations upon which their following had been predicated. Substituting extraction for reciprocity, they must compel their people to "eat the leader's renown," as one Solomon Island group puts it, in return for productive efforts. Some center-men appear more able than others to dam the inevitable tide of discontent that mounts within their factions, perhaps because of charismatic personalities, perhaps because of the particular social organizations in which they operate. But paradoxically the ultimate defense of the center-man's position is some slackening of his drive to enlarge the funds of power. The alternative is much worse. In the anthropological record there are not merely instances of big-man chicanery and of material deprivation of the faction in the interests of renown, but some also of overloading of social relations with followers: the generation of antagonisms, defections, and in extreme cases the violent liquidation of the center-man. Developing internal constraints, the Melanesian big-man political order brakes evolutionary advance at a certain level. It sets ceilings on the intensification of political authority, on the intensification of household production by political means, and on the diversion of household outputs in support of wider political organization. But in Polynesia these constraints were breached, and although Polynesian chiefdoms also found their developmental plateau, it was not before political evolution had been carried above the Melanesian ceilings. The fundamental defects of the Melanesian plan were overcome in Polynesia. The division between small internal and larger external political sectors, upon which all big-man politics hinged, was suppressed in Polynesia by the growth of an enclaving chiefdom-at-large. A chain of command subordinating lesser chiefs and groups to greater, on the basis of inherent societal rank, made local blocs or personal followings (such as were independent in Melanesia) merely dependent parts of the larger Polynesian chiefdom. So the nexus of the Polynesian chiefdom became an extensive set of offices, a pyramid of higher and lower chiefs holding sway over larger and smaller sections of the polity. Indeed the system of ranked and subdivided lineages (conical clan system), upon which the pyramid was characteristically established, might build up through several orders of inclusion and encompass the whole of an island or group of islands. While the island or the archipelago would normally be divided into several independent chiefdoms, high-order lineage connections between them, as well as kinship ties between their paramount chiefs, provided structural avenues for at least temporary expansion of political scale, for consolidation of great into even greater chiefdoms.

The pivotal paramount chief as well as the chieftains controlling parts of a chiefdom were true office holders and title holders. They were not, like Melanesian big-men, fishers of men: they held positions of authority over permanent groups. The honorifics of Polynesian chiefs likewise did not refer to a standing in interpersonal relations, but to their leadership of political divisions— here "The Prince of Danes" *not* "the prince among men." In western Melanesia the personal superiorities and inferiorities arising in the intercourse of particular men largely defined the political bodies. In Polynesia there emerged suprapersonal structures of leadership and followership, organizations that continued independently of the particular men who occupied positions in them for brief mortal spans.

And these Polynesian chiefs did not make their positions in society—they were installed in societal positions. In several of the islands, men did struggle to office against the will and stratagems of rival aspirants. But then they came to power. Power resided in the office; it was not made by the demonstration of personal superiority. In other islands, Tahiti was famous for it, succession to chieftainship was tightly controlled by inherent rank. The chiefly lineage ruled by virtue of its genealogical connections with divinity, and chiefs were succeeded by first sons, who carried "in the blood" the attributes of leadership. The important comparative point is this: the qualities of command that had to reside in men in Melanesia, that had to be personally demonstrated in order to attract loyal followers, were in Polynesia socially assigned to office and rank. In Polynesia, people of high rank and office *ipso facto* were leaders, and by the same token the qualities of leadership were automatically lacking—theirs was not to question why—among the underlying population. Magical powers such as a Melanesian big-man might acquire to sustain his position, a Polynesian high chief inherited by divine descent as the *mana* which sanctified his rule and protected his person against the hands of the commonalty. The productive ability the big-man laboriously had to demonstrate was effortlessly given Polynesian chiefs as religious control over agricultural fertility, and upon the ceremonial implementation of it the rest of the people were conceived dependent. Where a Melanesian leader had to master the compelling oratorical style, Polynesian paramounts often had trained "talking chiefs" whose voice was the chiefly command.

In the Polynesian view, a chiefly personage was in the nature of things powerful. But this merely implies the objective observation that his power was of the group rather than of himself. His authority came from the organization, from an organized acquiescence in his privileges and organized means of sustaining them. A kind of paradox resides in evolutionary developments which detach the exercise of authority from the necessity to demonstrate personal superiority: organizational power actually extends the role of personal decision and conscious planning, gives it greater scope, impact, and effectiveness. The growth of a political system such as the Polynesian constitutes advance over Melanesian orders of interpersonal dominance in the human control of human affairs. Especially significant for society at large were privileges accorded Polynesian chiefs which made them greater architects of funds of power than ever was any Melanesian big-man.

Masters of their people and "owners" in a titular sense of group resources, Polynesian chiefs had rights of call upon the labor and agricultural produce of households within their domains. Economic mobilization did not depend on, as it necessarily had for Melanesian big-men, the *de novo* creation by the leader of personal loyalties and economic obligations. A chief need not stoop to obligate this man or that man, need not by a series of individual acts of generosity induce others to support him, for economic leverage over a group was the inherent chiefly due. Consider the implications for the fund of power of the widespread chiefly privilege, related to titular "ownership" of land, of placing an interdiction, a tabu, on the harvest of some crop by way of reserving its use for a collective project. By means of the tabu the chief directs the course of production in a general way: households of his domain must turn to some other means of subsistence. He delivers a stimulus to household production: in the absence of the tabu further labors would not have been necessary. Most significantly, he has generated a politically utilizable agricultural surplus. A subsequent call on this surplus floats chieftainship as a going concern, capitalizes the fund of power. In certain islands, Polynesian chiefs controlled great storehouses which held the goods congealed by chiefly pressures on the commonalty. David Malo, one of the great native custodians of old Hawaiian lore, felicitously catches the political significance of the chiefly magazine in his well-known *Hawaiian Antiquities*:

> It was the practice for kings [i.e., paramount chiefs of individual islands] to build store-houses in which to collect food, fish, tapas [bark cloth], malos [men's loin cloths], pa-us [women's loin skirts], and all sorts of goods. These storehouses were designed by the Kalaimoku [the chief's principal executive] as a means of keeping the people contented, so they would not desert the king. They were like the baskets that were used to entrap the *hinalea* fish. The *hinalea* thought there was something good within the basket, and he hung round the outside of it. In the same way the people thought there was food in the store-houses, and they kept their eyes on the king. As the rat will not desert the pantry . . . where he thinks food is, so the people will not desert the king while they think there is food in his store-house.[7]

Redistribution of the fund of power was the supreme art of Polynesian politics. By well-planned *noblesse oblige* the large domain of a paramount chief was held together, organized at times for massive projects, protected against other chiefdoms, even further enriched. Uses of the chiefly fund included lavish

[7]David Malo, *Hawaiian Antiquities* (Honolulu: Hawaiian Gazette Co., 1903).

hospitality and entertainments for outside chiefs and for the chief's own people, and succor of individuals or the underlying population at large in times of scarcities—bread and circuses. Chiefs subsidized craft production, promoting in Polynesia a division of technical labor unparalleled in extent and expertise in most of the Pacific. They supported also great technical construction, as of irrigation complexes, the further returns to which swelled the chiefly fund. They initiated large-scale religious construction too, subsidized the great ceremonies, and organized logistic support for extensive military campaigns. Larger and more easily replenished than their western Melanesian counterparts, Polynesian funds of power permitted greater political regulation of a greater range of social activities on greater scale.

In the most advanced Polynesian chiefdoms, as in Hawaii and Tahiti, a significant part of the chiefly fund was deflected away from general redistribution towards the upkeep of the institution of chieftainship. The fund was siphoned for the support of a permanent administrative establishment. In some measure, goods and services contributed by the people precipitated out as the grand houses, assembly places, and temple platforms of chiefly precincts. In another measure, they were appropriated for the livelihood of circles of retainers, many of them close kinsmen of the chief, who clustered about the powerful paramounts. These were not all useless hangers-on. They were political cadres: supervisors of the stores, talking chiefs, ceremonial attendants, high priests who were intimately involved in political rule, envoys to transmit directives through the chiefdom. There were men in these chiefly retinues—in Tahiti and perhaps Hawaii, specialized warrior corps—whose force could be directed internally as a buttress against fragmenting or rebellious elements of the chiefdom. A Tahitian or Hawaiian high chief had more compelling sanctions than the harangue. He controlled a ready physical force, an armed body of executioners, which gave him mastery particularly over the lesser people of the community. While it looks a lot like the big-man's faction again, the differences in functioning of the great Polynesian chief's retinue are more significant than the superficial similarities in appearance. The chief's coterie, for one thing, is economically dependent upon him rather than he upon them. And in deploying the cadres politically in various sections of the chiefdom, or against the lower orders, the great Polynesian chiefs sustained command where the Melanesian big-man, in his external sector, had at best renown.

This is not to say that the advanced Polynesian chiefdoms were free of internal defect, of potential or actual malfunctioning. The large political-military apparatus indicates something of the opposite. So does the recent work of Irving Goldman[8] on the intensity of "status rivalry" in Polynesia, especially when it is considered that much of the status rivalry in developed chiefdoms, as the Hawaiian, amounted to popular rebellion against chiefly despotism rather than mere contest for position within the ruling-stratum. This suggests that Polynesian chiefdoms, just as Melanesian big-man orders, generate along with evolutionary development countervailing anti-authority pressures, and that the weight of the latter may ultimately impede further development.

The Polynesian contradiction seems clear enough. On one side, chieftainship is never detached from kinship moorings and kinship economic ethics. Even the greatest Polynesian chiefs were conceived superior kinsmen to the masses, fathers of their people, and generosity was morally incumbent upon them. On the other side, the major Polynesian paramounts seemed inclined to "eat the power of the government too much," as the Tahitians put it, to divert an undue proportion of the general wealth toward the chiefly establishment. The diversion could be accomplished by lowering the customary level of general redistribution, lessening the material returns of chieftainship to the community at large—tradition attributes the great rebellion of Mangarevan commoners to such cause. Or the diversion might—and I suspect more commonly did—consist in greater and more forceful exactions from lesser chiefs and people, increasing returns to the chiefly apparatus without necessarily affecting the level of general redistribution. In either case, the well-developed chiefdom creates for itself the dampening paradox of stoking rebellion by funding its authority.

In Hawaii and other islands cycles of political centralization and decentralization may be abstracted from traditional histories. That is, larger chiefdoms periodically fragmented into smaller and then were later reconstituted. Here would be more evidence of a tendency to overtax the political structure. But how to explain the emergence of a developmental stymie, of an inability to sustain political advance beyond a certain level? To point to a chiefly propensity to consume or a Polynesian propensity to rebel

---

[8]Irving Goldman, "Status Rivalry and Cultural Evolution in Polynesia," *American Anthropologist*, 57 (1957), pp. 680–697; "Variations in Polynesian Social Organization," *Journal of the Polynesian Society*, 66 (1957), pp. 374–390.

is not enough: such propensities are promoted by the very advance of chiefdoms. There is reason to hazard instead that Parkinson's notable law is behind it all: that progressive expansion in political scale entailed more-than-proportionate accretion in the ruling apparatus, unbalancing the flow of wealth in favor of the apparatus. The ensuing unrest then curbs the chiefly impositions, sometimes by reducing chiefdom scale to the nadir of the periodic cycle. Comparison of the requirements of administration in small and large Polynesian chiefdoms helps make the point.

A lesser chiefdom, confined say as in the Marquesas Islands to a narrow valley, could be almost personally ruled by a headman in frequent contact with the relatively small population. Melville's partly romanticized—also for its ethnographic details, partly cribbed—account in *Typee* makes this clear enough. But the great Polynesian chiefs had to rule much larger, spatially dispersed, internally organized populations. Hawaii, an island over four thousand square miles with an aboriginal population approaching one hundred thousand, was at times a single chiefdom, at other times divided into two to six independent chiefdoms, and at all times each chiefdom was composed of large subdivisions under powerful subchiefs. Sometimes a chiefdom in the Hawaiian group extended beyond the confines of one of the islands, incorporating part of another through conquest. Now, such extensive chiefdoms would have to be coordinated; they would have to be centrally tapped for a fund of power, buttressed against internal disruption, sometimes massed for distant, perhaps overseas, military engagements. All of this to be implemented by means of communication still at the level of word-of-mouth, and means of transportation consisting of human bodies and canoes. (The extent of certain larger chieftainships, coupled with the limitations of communication and transportation, incidentally suggests another possible source of political unrest: that the burden of provisioning the governing apparatus would tend to fall disproportionately on groups within easiest access of the paramount.) A tendency for the developed chiefdom to proliferate in executive cadres, to grow top-heavy, seems in these circumstances altogether functional, even though the ensuing drain on wealth proves the chiefdom's undoing. Functional also, and likewise a material drain on the chiefdom at large, would be widening distinctions between chiefs and people in style of life. Palatial housing, ornamentation and luxury, finery and ceremony, in brief, conspicuous consumption, however much it seems mere self-interest always has a more decisive social significance. It creates those invidious distinctions between rulers and ruled so conducive to a passive—hence quite economical!—acceptance of authority. Throughout history, inherently more powerful political organizations than the Polynesian, with more assured logistics of rule, have turned to it—including in our time some ostensibly revolutionary and proletarian governments, despite every pre-revolutionary protestation of solidarity with the masses and equality for the classes.

In Polynesia then, as in Melanesia, political evolution is eventually shortcircuited by an overload on the relations between leaders and their people. The Polynesian tragedy, however, was somewhat the opposite of the Melanesian. In Polynesia, the evolutionary ceiling was set by extraction from the population at large in favor of the chiefly faction, in Melanesia by extraction from the big-man's faction in favor of distribution to the population at large. Most importantly, the Polynesian ceiling was higher. Melanesian big-men and Polynesian chiefs not only reflect different varieties and levels of political evolution, they display in different degrees the capacity to generate and to sustain political progress.

Especially emerging from their juxtaposition is the more decisive impact of Polynesian chiefs on the economy, the chiefs' greater leverage on the output of the several households of society. The success of any primitive political organization is decided here, in the control that can be developed over household economies. For the household is not merely the principal productive unit in primitive societies, it is often quite capable of autonomous direction of its own production, and it is oriented towards production for its own, not societal consumption. The greater potential of Polynesian chieftainship is precisely the greater pressure it could exert on household output, its capacity both to generate a surplus and to deploy it out of the household towards a broader division of labor, cooperative construction, and massive ceremonial and military action. Polynesian chiefs were the more effective means of societal collaboration on economic, political, indeed all cultural fronts. Perhaps we have been too long accustomed to perceive rank and rule from the standpoint of the individuals involved, rather than from the perspective of the total society, as if the secret of the subordination of man to man lay in the personal satisfactions of power. And then the breakdowns too, or the evolutionary limits, have been searched out in men, in "weak" kings or megalomaniacal dictators—always, "who is the matter?" An excursion into the field of primitive politics suggests the more fruitful conception that the gains of political developments accrue more decisively to society than to individuals, and the failings as well are of structure not men.

Rules and Custom in "Primitive" Society

by
Raymond Firth

THE RULES OF conduct in any society are difficult to classify, but, broadly speaking, they comprise rules of technique, of taste and fashion, of manners, of morals, of law, and of religion.

A distinction can be drawn in theory, and to some extent in practice, between what people actually do—the "rule" in the sense of a statistical average—and what they ought to do—the "rule" in a normative sense, of a standard to be aimed at. In practice these two kinds of rule tend to coincide. What most people in fact do is felt to be what everyone should do. . . . To go barefooted in a city is eccentric; to sit on the floor may offend one's hostess; to marry more than one wife brings down condemnation by Church and State. Yet in some societies, people eat but one meal a day, go with naked feet, sit on the floor, and marry several wives, and are expected by others to do all these things. Men, unlike other animals, have a wide choice between different ways of behaving in a given situation, and make their choice largely for social reasons. They are guided in what they do by the opinion of their fellows, and ideas of what it is proper to do—by values.

In some spheres, however, there may be a wide gap between the rule which ought to be followed and what is actually done. In spite of the fact that the English pride themselves on being a tolerably law-abiding people, returning travelers often fail to declare to the customs authorities goods that they have obtained abroad; motorists often exceed the speed limit; and business men evade income tax. The Christian theme of love for one's neighbour is in strong contrast to commercial dealing, restrictive tariffs,

Adapted from Raymond Firth, *Human Types* (New York: New American Library, 1958), 105–121.

and the building up of armaments. The discrepancy between the legal or moral rule and the actual practice is not merely due to ignorance, negligence, or individual self-interest. Loyalty to others, ideals of efficiency and practicability, beliefs in the unfairness of the law, conformity to public opinion, all help to provide a set of additional standards which allow individuals and groups to justify their departure from the admitted ideal.

For those interested in the life of Man in society a number of questions arise. Are there in other societies similar rules for the regulation of conduct? If so, how far are they clearly formulated by the people? How far are they kept, and if they are broken, for what reason? What is the reaction of other people to such a breach? Is there any machinery for enforcement of the rules? And if they are, on the whole, effective, whence comes their power? And finally, why do such rules exist at all? Let us attempt to answer at least some of these questions.

It is sometimes vaguely said that natives are children, obeying no rules and following their own fancy. Or, again, that they have their own customs which they follow blindly, and that when once they have decided to do something they can be moved by no argument. And, further, that many of their customs are "queer," that is, one can see no sensible reason for them, and therefore one is reduced to classifying them under the heading of taboos. We shall see how far these popular opinions are true. In the first place, it can be said quite definitely that in all known human communities social order is preserved to some degree. There is no wholesale violence or unrestrained aggression. But, on the other hand, there is no passive conformity to an ideal of the good of the community. The social order is not an unconscious process; it is an affair of rules, and of keeping or breaking them according to a variety of individual interests, and responding to conscious obligations and training. In each society these rules form a system. In most primitive societies they are not codified—there are no Ten Commandments, or any set scheme of numbered injunctions, nor are they always expressed as abstract principles. It is often difficult to draw from a native a general formulation, and one may hear a rule uttered only in reference to some actual incident. By such means a great deal of the education of young people is done.

Though we have spoken of primitive societies as being simple in their organization and in their technical achievements, this does not mean to say that their rules of conduct are few and simple. . . . We can see in primitive societies rules of the same order as those which we distinguish as manners, ethics, morals, law, and religion, granting that our own distinctions are not always very consciously and clearly made.

The popular notion that primitive peoples lack all the gentler forms of social intercourse is very wide of the mark. Codes of manners seem to exist in all societies, and a half-naked savage may be just as polite as a civilized European. For instance, a Polynesian once brought me a gift of green coconuts on a hot day. When I drank, and pressed him to drink also, he refused, though he admitted he was thirsty. He explained courteously, "In this land one does not partake of a gift that one has brought, lest people say, 'One who eats his own present.' " Here, then, is a delicacy of attitude that is at least as refined as our own.

Sometimes native manners seem even excessive. Baganda in olden days had a code of etiquette which included fulsome greetings and thanks even to those met by the wayside. When Europeans were seen they were politely thanked for being well dressed, or two of them might be thanked for walking in step!

Even where the greeting does not conform to our usages, nonetheless it follows rules of etiquette. The Tikopia or the Malay peasants do not say, "How do you do?" on meeting a person on the path, but ask, "Where are you going?" This is not inquisitive or rude, but is the convention. It may be answered either by a factual reply or by the vague words, "I am going for a stroll." If anything, it is as sensible as the English "How do you do?" which is not now intended as a genuine inquiry about the state of one's health, even though a naïve stranger may reply in those terms. The important thing in these modes of greeting is not the overt meaning of the words, but the fact that words are uttered, that some verbal bridge is thrown across the social gap between people coming into fresh contact.

For the European entering a native community, conformity to native manners is one of the best ways to begin cooperation. Natives often think that Europeans are rude because they make no attempt to adapt themselves. A shaping of one's own manners to those of another community is one of the easiest sacrifices to make; it does not mean giving up the more fundamental values involved in a moral code or religious belief.

Primitive peoples have their own ethical and moral judgments too. Persons are regarded as good or bad, actions as right or wrong—though not infrequently a single native term does duty for a range of ideas for which we have separate words such as "correct," "good," "right," "proper," and "virtuous." The fact that native codes of morality differ must not, however, cause us to say that some are on a "higher" level than others. The truer view is that each is adapted to particular social conditions, and should be judged according to its efficiency in maintaining social order.

By the "immorality" of savages is usually meant nothing more than that their codes are not ours. This is clearly seen in the case of sex relations. In Western Europe chastity before marriage is at least a moral ideal to those who follow the orthodox conventions. In some primitive communities such as the Manus of the Admiralty Islands, or the chiefly families of Samoa and Tonga, this is also the case. But in a great number pre-marital sex intercourse is not only common but also regarded as right. To call this immoral ignores the fact that, like other social activities, it has rules to regulate its occurrence and its consequences. It frequently exists side by side with standards of opinion which prescribe the type and degree of intercourse to be indulged in, which are critical of frequent changes of lovers, and which place strong penalties upon conception, or at least upon the birth of a child outside wedlock. Our moral judgments in this sphere often tend to overlook social realities. Condemnation of pre-marital intercourse overlooks the fact that, as Malinowski has shown for the Trobrianders, it is often an essential element in the process of education in sex matters before marriage, and of experiment in the choice of a mate. It meets to some extent the difficulty caused by a wide gap between puberty and marriage.

The much-criticized institution of child marriage in India has been defended by Hindus on the ground that one function of it is to prevent the dangers of pre-marital sex relations of girls. It has been stated to me by missionaries that one difficulty which has arisen from the success of their efforts in stopping child marriage, with its admitted evils of too early bearing of offspring and exploitation of the young, has been that now cases occur of girls bearing illegitimate children, with all the consequences of shame and family friction.

Our own conception of morality is complicated by the fact that it is so closely bound up with religion. Relations before and outside marriage are contrary to Christian rule; marriage itself is a sacrament as well as a legal contract, and in England we have seen how closely the law of divorce is scrutinized by the Church and interpreted in accordance with religious dogma. The frequent association which the Christian Church makes between sex and sin is, as we have seen, not found in many primitive societies.

So also, in general, primitive morality is quite often separate from primitive religion. It is rare to find among the sanctions of right conduct in a primitive society the belief that good and bad people go after death to separate destinations or conditions, which are regulated according to the moral quality of their behaviour on earth. Much more frequently rank, wealth, and social condition in this world give different passports to the next.

When we turn to the sphere of primitive law, we are confronted by difficulties of definition. There is usually no specific code of legislation, issued by a central authority, and no formal judicial body of the nature of a court. Nevertheless there are rules which are expected to be obeyed and which, in fact, are normally kept, and there are means for ensuring some degree of obedience. The classification of these rules and the definition of law in primitive society have become at times a matter of some argument.

The simplest basis of classification is that of the practising jurist who tends to equate law with what is decided by the courts. On this criterion most primitive peoples have no *law*, but simply a body of customs. This classification is of practical importance when primitive societies are subject to the government of European powers, and where it is a problem as to how far the traditional rules controlling native life should be taken into consideration. But for the anthropologist studying primitive societies this formal juridical approach is not very helpful, because it considers custom only in relation to what use the courts can make of it, and does not examine how it operates where there are no courts. This is not, however, the only juridical point of view. The sociological jurist, examining the concept of law from a broader standpoint, is interested in all kinds of rules that exist in a society and in the problem of their functioning. This is more in line with the anthropological approach. The major difference of opinion between anthropologists is between those represented by Malinowski, who would include in primitive law all types of binding obligation and any customary action to prevent breaches in the pattern of social conformity; and those represented by Radcliffe-Brown, who would restrict the sphere of law to the entry of the force of a politically organized society. An intermediate position has been taken up by Godfrey Wilson in his study of Nyakyusa law and custom. He takes as the criterion of legal action the entry into an issue of one or more members of a social group who are not themselves personally concerned. In this tribe it is common, for instance, for disputants to take their quarrel to a senior kinsman, a friend, or a respected neighbour for adjudication, and this Wilson treats as part of the tribal law. This would be treated by some anthropologists as private arbitration of a non-legal kind, and, indeed, to take only this element of procedure as the criterion of definition of law seems somewhat arbitrary. A great many societies in Melanesia and Australia, where there is no such appeal to a person outside the dispute, would on this basis have no law. If a definition of law which would separate it from "custom" is thought necessary, then it would seem to lie in bringing together a number of elements—rules: the degree to which they are obligatory; the degree of obedience to them; the degree of precise formulation of them; the character of the sanction for them; the type of authority with which they are enforced; and the acceptability of this authority. Law is a function of all these together, and not of any single one of them. It relates particularly to the sphere where the rules are closely formulated, highly obligatory, the sanction for them is strong and frequently negative, and the authority by which they are enforced is of an organized kind. This in effect is the standpoint of the jurist. But the need for such a definition does not seem to be great for sociological purposes. Whatever be his basis of classification the sociologist still has to remember that for the understanding of law in this sense he must be prepared to examine all these elements in the wider sense, and to specify the degree to which each enters into the situation. If a system of European law is intelligible only by reference to the changing practices of the people, their system of ethics, their institutional structure, their judges' ideas of what is "reasonable," and non-legal factors which lead them to keep it or to break it, how much more must this be so in the case of a primitive people without such a clear-cut formal scheme?

Consideration of this array of means of securing control of the behaviour of people raises the questions of the source of these means, of how judgments are passed, and by whom they are carried out. A highly organized legal system recognizes a division into legislative, judicial, and executive functions—represented in England, broadly speaking, by Parliament, the courts, and the administrative services, including the police. Such a clear-cut division is not a common feature of a system of law in a primitive society. The main body of rules does not originate through the act of any specific body appointed for the purpose, but is believed to have existed from immemorial antiquity. The force upon which their power rests is that of the tradition of the society which is the nearest equivalent to the "sovereign" in the Austinian sense. Sometimes, however, by a general agreement, new rules are introduced or an old rule interpreted to meet changing conditions, or again, common practice in such conditions imperceptibly comes to be regarded as the rule which should be observed. Schapera in his study of Tswana law gives a very clear exposition of the sources of their rules of conduct. The Tswana speak of the main body of their laws as having always existed, from the time that Man himself came into being, or as having been instituted by God or by the ancestor spirits. A further source of law is given by the judicial decisions of the native courts which in their judgments recognize and strengthen the obligatory character of most existing rules, but occasionally by distinguishing between cases give rise to new precedents. A third and mainly modern source of their law is given by the decrees of their chiefs, who have the power to abolish outgrown usages or issue new regulations for the better conduct of tribal affairs. In many primitive communities, however, there are no chiefs, and even where they exist they have no specific legislative functions. Nor again is there often any organized judicial body which can give an impetus to changes in the system of rules.

Judicial machinery, then, frequently does not exist as a separate department of primitive law. The passing of judgments is done not as an organized affair, but through the unorganized exchange of opinions among the people discussing the event. In primitive Australia, when an important rule is broken, there is no formal calling together of an assembly to discuss the matter, but it is canvassed by the group of adult men, who are normally in close contact with each other. To describe their common discussions as a legal council would be an over-statement; they certainly discuss the merits of the case, they make concessions for extenuating circumstances, and they may arrive at a decision, but there is no formal procedure, and the decision emerges out of the general talk and is not a formal pronouncement. Moreover, it is not necessarily the elders who play the most influential part. Younger, more vigorous men, assertive in personality, may dominate the opinions of the gathering, and may often precipitate a decision. Much the same is true of complex politically organized societies such as Tikopia in Polynesia. Here the decision of a chief has a final authority which may not be gainsaid, and often guides conduct or causes punishment to be visited upon an offender. But this decision, though it is controlled to a considerable extent by the advice of other men of influence and by public opinion, is not taken as the result of any formal judicial council. It may spring from his own immediate perception of an event, or from informal discussion, or be almost forced upon him by some party that goes to him and pleads for him to issue a command. The primitive societies in which the formal judicial apparatus is most highly developed are mainly in parts of Africa. Here a council of elders, or a chief in council, or a court, may proceed in quite a formal manner, admit plaintiff and defendant, call witnesses, pronounce an explicit decision, and order the execution of the judgment.

Along the same lines, a body of executive officials to carry out legal functions is often lacking. In some communities there are persons who act as "police." In Tikopia, for instance, the brothers and close cousins of a chief bear a special title—and are recognized as being primarily responsible for carrying out his decisions and for keeping order in the land. They can even serve as protection and aid to individuals who have fallen under the wrath of another man of rank. Hence their title of *maru*, "shelterers," because they afford shelter to the people as a tree casts its shade as a relief from the sun. In many societies, however, a judgment is put into effect by some of the people immediately delegated or even self-appointed from the social group as a whole.

In this chapter we are concerned primarily with the general nature and functioning of the means of regulating conduct, the forces of social control rather than the content of the rules in themselves. A number of important problems, then, including an analysis of family law and the law of property, of civil and criminal injuries, and of the procedure of adjudication and the theory of motive and responsibility, cannot be explained here.

Let us now consider the working of rules. It is a commonplace that although rules usually have some penalty attached to their non-observance, they are not observed merely because of the penalty. In primitive as in civilized society, men do not abstain from stealing simply because of the punishment for theft. Consideration of this question brings in the question of sanctions. There is no clearly agreed definition of what is meant by a sanction. The older juridical idea derived from Austin was that a sanction was the penalty probably incurred in case the rule was disobeyed. The modern jurist has broadened this to include the reward for keeping the rule, and considers sanctions as the conditions calculated to render the law effective. If these conditions are interpreted widely this is essentially the anthropologist's view. He feels it necessary to take into account not only those conditions immediately connected with the law itself, such as fines, rewards, possibility of prosecution, respect for Parliament, etc., but also the general conditions of the community life—and these not on the simple plane of acquiescence of the governed, recognition of benefits to be gained, or the inertia of habit, but the active forces of public opinion, education, the moral view of obligations. The action of any individual in respect of a rule is governed not only by his immediate personal interests and the degree of temptation which he has at the moment felt, but by his recognition of what a variety of people will say, think, feel, and believe, and by what he knows them to have done in the past. The conditions which make the law effective may then be restated as those activities and responses of individuals, whether expressed in the name of the society or not, which tend to govern the behaviour of a person in respect of a rule, and to maintain order and equilibrium in the social system.

One can view these sanctions in a number of ways, which represent cross-classification. Some are personal to the individual, as the complicated pull of his own interests, his inertia of habit, and the fullness of his recognition of the nature of the issues; others are *social*, such as domestic or public approval or disapproval, retaliation, punishment, etc. Another classification could be into *immediate* and *ultimate* sanctions; the former arise directly from the nature of the rule, such as the punishment following on its breach; the latter are of a more general character, such as the fear of being talked about, or the loss of future benefits. A further classification adopted by Radcliffe-Brown is of a more precise and factual kind. After distinguishing organized from unorganized sanctions, this proceeds from ethical and moral sanctions through sanctions of retaliation, restitution, and punishment to those of a ritual order. Those of restitution and punishment alone are considered as legal sanctions.

Without pursuing any of these classifications further, we may list here a number of the most important sanctions, particularly in primitive societies, some of them, of course, functioning also in civilized societies.

The sanction of public opinion is always extremely important. Usually unorganized, it sometimes assumes an organized character, as when in civilized society presentations are made for saving life, or meritorious exploration, or social service. Sometimes public opinion can be expressed in a crystallized form through the agency of proverbs, which have greater weight than a purely individual opinion at the moment. Among the Maori, proverbs played quite an important part as a stimulus to action or a check upon it. Ridicule in primitive societies may sometimes assume a set public form as in the taunting songs of the Eskimo or of the Tikopia. Theft in Tikopia is dealt with by tongue-lashing, and sometimes by physical violence if the culprit is known. If he is not, then the bereft owner may compose a dance song embodying his views of the thief with slighting allusions, and get it chanted in full chorus at the public dances on the beach. Primarily this relieves his feelings, but to some extent it acts as a sanction by shaming the thief before any who may know of him.

Another type of sanction often of great importance is that of reciprocity. He who breaks a rule or does not do his duty may find himself on short commons at a later date, or without necessary labour, or blocked from achieving some valued object which would give him prestige. By breach of the rule for immediate gain he wastes his assets for the future. Realization of this plays a large part in keeping many a man on the straight and narrow way of social conformity. That whole system of values which may be comprised under the head of tradition, inculcated by the complex processes of training and learning, is also of vital import. The law is often kept not because it is the law, but because it is thought right to keep that kind of rule. As we have seen, primitive people have their ethical formulations, and rely upon them.

Another group of sanctions is of the kind popularly known as superstition. This is usually a slipshod term to describe someone else's religion. But more precisely it may mean a faith in the supernatural which we regard as irrational. A taboo in the concrete sense, a bundle of leaves tied to a pole, with a backing of supernatural force, is a common means of protecting property in primitive society in Oceania. Sometimes this taboo is believed to punish an offender through its own magical power, sometimes through action by spirit beings or ancestors to whom it has been dedicated. Fear of supernatural punishment is a sanction even though no material token is set up. In many communities incest is held to be punished by the intervention of the ancestors of the guilty pair, who visit them or their offspring with sickness and death. In Tikopia this sanction and that of public opinion act alone with no sanction of any physical kind. Persons who commit incest are not punished by their social group as they are, for instance, in many African communities. A third sanction of the supernatural type is that of sorcery. Malinowski has shown that in the Trobriands the power of a chief, which is an important factor in the preservation of law and order, is maintained quite considerably by his employment, or the fear of his employment, of sorcerers. Among the Australian aborigines the fulfilment of obligations of ceremonial exchange is facilitated by a number of factors, recognition of future economic and other benefits to be obtained, wish to conform to the traditional pattern, or a desire to maintain one's reputation as a "good trading partner"; in addition, failure may involve the need to fight, and it is believed that a bad partner may have sorcery levelled against him. Ritual practices to avert the wasting sickness and death believed to be consequent on such sorcery are not infrequent. A further type of sanction is that of retaliation by physical violence upon an offender. Among the Tswana retaliation is still sometimes allowed in cases of assault, particularly on a woman. The court will instruct the injured woman to inflict upon her assailant an injury of the same kind as she herself received. Then again there is the sanction of restitution, where the breach of a rule means that the offender must hand over property to the offended party. Such a type of sanction is extremely common in native African law. Finally, there is the penal sanction where the organized force of the community working through the machinery of a chief, a court, or a council punishes an offender.

All these sanctions do not work with equal effect in every primitive society. In some the weight of public opinion is highly mobilized to secure conformity to rules, and organized restitution or punishment do not play an important part. Supernatural sanctions, again, enter much more thoroughly into the regulation of conduct in some societies than in others. There is not space here to examine the different types of conditions which give these sanctions their differential weight.

It must be observed that just as the types of rule to be kept vary from one society to another, so also does the classification of behaviour as offences. In Europe, to go through a marriage ceremony with a woman while one is still married to another is an offence in law and a sin in religion. But it is not only permissible, but is a socially desirable practice in most Muslim countries and in many primitive societies. The native belief in the rightness of polygamy has created difficulties for the Christian Church in Africa, and has even been partially responsible for the secession of native Christians from the parent mission. In England, to enter private property without leave is a trespass against which the owner can take action in law. But in Tikopia, to plant crops on the land of another person without having obtained leave is regarded as quite permissible, and the owner is not expected to have a grievance provided that a basket of the crop is given to him at the harvest. Where the same type of act is classified as an offence, the immediate sanction against it may vary considerably. The intentional killing of another person is in civilized countries a criminal offence, visited with punishment, sometimes by death. But in many parts of Africa the native rule is that homicide within the tribe is a matter not for punishment of the killer, but for the paying of compensation by him and his kin-group to the relatives of the slain person. Here, again, the difference in the sanction applied has been a cause of difficulty in the application of European law to such communities. In other communities, again, the immediate sanction does not take the form necessarily of punishment of the guilty person, but of retaliation upon his kinsfolk if he himself is not available. This concept, crystallizing in the form of the blood feud, has also increased the complexity of governing a native people by European standards. Sometimes, again, the immediate sanction for damage to a person or his property is not the exaction of compensation, but the *lex talionis* of classical times—the "eye for an eye and tooth for a tooth" of Mosaic law.

It is clear from what has just been said that there may be at the initial stage of introduction of European law to a primitive community a conflict of sanctions. One result of this is often to produce an increase of certain types of offences, which by native rule were punished much more severely than by European law. An example of this is adultery. In Malaita in the Solomon Islands the commission of adultery was normally visited with death by spearing. Nowadays, under European government, an aggrieved husband can only sue for divorce or demand compensation for alienation of affection. This to the Malaita people seems insufficient, and it is said that adultery has grown more common thereby. Another result is that acts have now become offences which were formerly not so, and people become lawbreakers in the eyes of the European governments, though they may be right according to their own traditional rules. Examples of this are the avenger of a kinsman's murder who now becomes a criminal instead of the executor of justice, and a defaulting native labourer who, in fulfilling his obligations to attend some tribal ceremony, breaks his contract with his European employer. Consideration of such cases leads us to see that the conflict between tribal ethics and compulsions on the one hand, and European law on the other, may be a very real one, disturbing to the life of a native people who have respect for their traditional rules. This is a strong argument for a close examination of the forces of social control in primitive communities, and for an attempt to incorporate into the European system of administrative justice as much as possible of the native concepts.

In a primitive society unaffected by European contacts there is no conflict to any great extent between the different types of sanction at work; the whole scheme is fairly well integrated and consistent. In civilized society, however, with its great complexity of many different types of social groups with different immediate backgrounds, such conflict is only too apparent. What is felt to be right, or at all events permissible, to an individual may clash with what the law prescribes or forbids. An outstanding example of this was the widespread breach of the Volstead Act in the United States of America, whereby large sections of the population manufactured, imported, and consumed alcoholic liquor contrary to the law. This wholesale disregard of the law obviously did not mean that a large percentage of Americans suddenly displayed criminal tendencies, but that operating against the legal sanction were strong sanctions of what may be called a moral kind. . . .

There is one difficult problem to which the sociologist has yet been able to give no satisfactory answer. In all the bewildering complexity of rules which we have seen existing in a range of primitive and civilized societies, is there any common basis to be found? Is there anything that can be termed "natural" law? The answers that have been given by philosophers and by the exponents of religious doctrine have often been quite definite. But these answers depend on certain initial assumptions concerning which there is by no means general agreement. Moreover, certain of these assumptions are definitely declared to be outside the province of science. One such assumption is that the value of human life is intrinsic, that every individual has a *right* to live, and that only in cases of extreme offence can the State decide to abrogate this right. On this assumption native practices of infanticide, which are not uncommonly resorted to as an escape from difficult social situations such as threatened embarrassment with an illegitimate child, or pressure of population on food supplies, are condemned. This judgment may be passed even when no other remedy for the difficulty can be immediately seen. In consequence, people who practice infanticide are arraigned as criminals and reprobated by the Church, even though in native eyes they have committed no wrong. Yet in civilized society the logical implications of this assumption are not rigidly followed through—except in the case of a few groups such as the Quakers. In what is deemed to be a situation of national necessity the taking of human life becomes not an offence, but a praiseworthy action. The State does its best to compel it by conscription, and the Church blesses the arms and stigmatizes the foe. Here, then, we see in our own circumstances a supreme need to abrogate the moral law, which we deny to others.

To turn from war to sport. The arguments about the merits and demerits of fox-hunting in England are too common to restate here. But there is one appendage to it which is of interest. In former years there have been several cases in which the Royal Society for the Prevention of Cruelty to Animals has prosecuted officials of hunts "for causing suffering to a fox by allowing it to be unnecessarily worried by hounds." In some of these cases the official of the R.S.P.C.A. appears to have said that he did not object to fox-hunting as such. The general assumption here is that pain should not be inflicted upon animals where it is avoidable. Here we see the curious feature of singling out for legal action one single aspect and moment of what must on any honest examination be recognized as a painful process for the fox in its entirety. It has been claimed that the fox enjoys being hunted, except presumably when he is actually being torn to pieces, but as yet we have no evidence of this. The presumption is, in fact, all the other way. The conflict of sanctions between the established institutions of fox-hunting and all its values, what the law allows and prohibits, and the humanitarian views of many sections of the people, gives rise to a position which it is hardly possible to defend on grounds of its consistency. In one defence of such a case it was stated that to say of any M.F.H. that he caused suffering to a fox would be very distressing, and that in this instance the Master's kindness to animals was "simply notorious." Instead of this intellectual refusal to see the inconsistency involved, it would be more logical to say that a fox-hunter in his pleasure in the sport, which might be justified on other grounds, is willing to forego up to a point his humanitarian interest in the avoidance of pain.

The scientist searching for some common denominator in social rules, for some basic universal quality which might be termed an absolute, is faced by much inconsistency of this kind, by much failure to examine the bases of assumption, and to employ these assumptions in a logical way in actual life. Where, perhaps, the sociologist of the future may be able to see some basic quality in the variety of rules for the regulation of conduct, is by engaging in a more precise search for the conditions of social efficiency. If men are to live together in groups, there must be some conditions for their cooperation and mutual contact. Physical violence must be restrained, aggression kept within bounds, and machinery provided to decide between interests which conflict or appear to conflict. As yet the results of this search have been expressed only in very formal abstract principles largely of an *a priori* kind, and need much more inductive, empirical inquiry to establish their validity.

Bushmen: The Hunters Now Hunt Guerrillas

by
Gary Thatcher

OMEGA BASE. CAPRIVI Strip, Namibia. The copper-colored woman looked toward the stars, holding up her infant to face the moon and praying it would be gifted with "the heart of a hunter."

Her plea, according to writer Laurens van der Post, was for the child to receive the instinct for survival in the desolate stretches of southern Africa's Kalahari Desert. Mother and child were members of the Bushman race, one of the last nomadic groups of hunters and foragers in Africa.

Now, Bushmen truly are being trained to have the "heart of a hunter." But their quarry is not free-ranging land bucks or swift duiker antelope—but men.

The South African Army is now inducting Bushmen into its ranks, teaching them to forsake traditional bows and arrows for R-1 rifles. And their phenomenal tracking skills, gleaned from centuries of stalking animals over the vast roadless stretches of southern Africa, are being employed to track down black nationalist guerrillas contesting South Africa's control of this disputed territory.

In the process, the Bushmen's way of life is being changed— perhaps permanently. And the time may come when, because of their role in a war that they little understand, the Bushmen themselves may become the hunted.

Bushmen are a unique race, their wrinkled amber skin and slight stature setting them apart from either black Africans or white settlers of this region. Along with the Khoi-Khoi (Hottentots), the Khoi-San peoples—later dubbed the "Bushmen"—are thought to be the original inhabitants of the African subcontinent. But their nomadic wanderings, coupled with their penchant for hunting—including domesticated livestock as well as wild game— clashed with both blacks and whites migrating from the north and south.

The Bushmen "refused to be tamed," as Laurens van der Post writes, and were pushed into the remote wastelands of Namibia, Botswana, and Angola.

The vast, forbidding wastelands in and around the Kalahari Desert have been their protectors, keeping black and white settlements from encroaching while grudgingly yielding enough plants and animals for subsistence.

In this shimmering, hostile environment, Bushmen have out of necessity developed tracking skills that other races hold in awe. Some Bushmen live in true symbiosis with the land, trusting snapped twigs as sentinels and animal footprints as signets on some higher plan for their race's sustenance and survival.

It is no wonder, then, that the South African Army—locked in a guerrilla war with the South-West Africa People's Organization (SWAPO) for control of Namibia—is only too happy to enlist Bushmen.

As a South African soldier explains, "Everything in this war goes according to the tracks."

Indeed, tracks have become all-important in the kind of bush war being waged here. Both SWAPO guerrillas, infiltrating from Angola and Zambia to the north, and South African soldiers on patrol leave telltale footprints: The other side often takes up the trail. A deadly stalking ensues, in which ambushes are common and a misreading of a spoor can mean injury or death.

So, in 1974, the South African Army set about attracting Bushmen into its ranks. Now, here at Omega Base in the far northeastern corner of the country, some 850 Bushmen sport the olive-brown uniforms—and the twentieth-century weaponry—of the South African Defense Force (SADF).

In return for fighting SWAPO, the Bushmen are paid about four hundred dollars per month by the South Africans—a considerable sum in these parts, and a staggering amount for people unaccustomed to cash. In addition, the SADF provides housing for some nine hundred women and fifteen hundred children of the Bushmen troops.

The military is quite proud of its efforts, and regularly steers parliamentarians, civic leaders—and sometimes journalists— through Omega Base. The Bushmen obligingly banter in their distinctive language, punctuated by soft clicks made with the tongue, and put on ''firepower demonstrations'' during which they unleash a fusillade at an imaginary band of ''terrorists.''

These demonstrations sometimes start with a mock ambush of a convoy carrying the visitors who, after getting over the shock of the initial land mine blast, usually are delighted with the spectacle of Bushmen blasting away at the brush.

Between these exhibitions the Bushmen go about the deadly serious business of soldiering, usually in north-central Namibia, ferreting out SWAPO cadres and engaging them in firefights. One South African soldier says the Bushmen's markmanship is ''a matter of debate,'' but their keen tracking skill and composure under fire is not. One Bushman has been posthumously awarded the Honoris Crux, the highest military honor in South Africa.

But as they alternate roles between attractions and artillerymen, curiosities and commandos, something is happening to the Bushmen. The South African military says they are gradually being brought into the twentieth century, with its attendant material benefits.

But Richard Lee, an anthropologist at the University of Toronto, has been quoted as saying, ''They are being ground to death in the South African war machine.'' According to Professor Lee, the very ethos of Bushman life is being threatened by their exposure to Western ways of war.

Officers here at Omega Base bristle at such suggestions, however. ''Our aim is not to try to Westernize them,'' says Lieut. Ben Wolff, a white commander, ''but to make them better Bushmen.''

The SADF's qualifications for that task are questionable, however. Only now, some six years after enlisting the first Bushmen, is the military consulting with ethnologists and anthropologists to determine the impact of soldiering on Bushman traditions and culture.

It is clear, however, that the impact is substantial. For one thing, the Bushmen here—about equally divided between the Barakwena and !Kung tribes—have forsaken the traditional nomadic life of their ancestors.

No longer do these Bushmen rove the *sandveld*, foraging for roots and tubers, felling game, pausing at hidden waterholes, and constructing simple grass lean-tos. Instead, they live in rows of identical bungalows. Food and water are trucked into the base, and there is running water from wells. The Army is even undertaking agricultural projects to teach them rudimentary farming methods.

Some of the Bushmen here cling to traditional remedies for their maladies, concocted from wild herbs, berries, and roots. However, about five hundred Bushmen turn up each month at the tin-roofed military hospital here on the base, where they receive Western-style medicines and even consultations with a physiotherapist.

The yawning gap between cultures is perhaps most strikingly evident to Bushman children, however. Since the Army has erected a cluster of classrooms on the edge of the base, the open veld has been supplanted as a school, and math problems have replaced mantises as objects for quiet, patient study. Their teachers? White South African troops.

These children do not imbibe the arcane skills of living off the land by actually doing it. Instead, they are given week-long "bushcraft" sessions by senior Bushmen officers once each month.

Late at night, some of the Bushmen here still gather around fires deep in the woodlands and perform the dances and rituals celebrating their traditional worship of the earth, animals, their ancestors, and the sky. But here at Omega Base, a young Army chaplain, Lieut. Gert van Rooyen of the Dutch Reformed Church, is busily converting them.

The base now has 159 "baptized and confessed" Christians, he says proudly.

In a small workshop near the chapel, Bushman wives sit at sewing machines making clothing, sheets, curtains, and table-cloths under the tutelage of Annatkie Botes, wife of the base commander. By selling these products and charging soldiers modest fees to mend their uniforms, Mrs. Botes explains, the women are able to earn a small salary.

Lieutenant Wolff concedes that a cash economy once baffled the Bushmen. "When they first arrived here, their sense of money was very poor," he explains.

But now, he says, they are being taught to invest their earnings. Indeed, Bushman wives are even being offered insurance plans—as a hedge against the death of their husbands in combat.

The soft clicking of the Bushman tongue is still used around Omega Base—but almost exclusively among the Bushmen themselves. In fact, among the 250 whites here only Lieutenant Wolff can converse in Bushman dialect. The official language in the classrooms, at the church, or on the battlefield is Afrikaans, the language of South Africa's dominant white Afrikaner ethnic group.

Yet the Afrikaner officers here—so fiercely protective of their own language and culture—seem untroubled that they may be contributing to the devastation of someone else's.

Lieutenant Wolff says "we are going to get civilians" to provide expert guidance in easing the impact of Westernization on Bushman life, but admits, "to date we've had nothing like that." He does acknowledge that some problems have surfaced at the base. Women, for example, are beginning to be resentful because their traditional culture demands that they marry early and bear children at age thirteen or fourteen—forcing them to drop out of school after the third grade.

Also, he says, Bushman troops sometimes yearn for unregimented ventures into the surrounding bush, and the military tries to accommodate unexpected absences or longer-than-planned leaves.

Units on patrol have to make unscheduled stops when beehives are discovered, to allow the Bushmen to indulge their proverbial passion for wild honey.

But that only underscores the growing distance between the Bushman soldier and his past. In earlier times, their predecessors might have trekked for miles across the desolate stretches of southern Africa, pursuing a honey-diviner bird or a ratel (honey badger) headed for amber-gold honeycombs. For these Bushmen, however, raiding a hive is only a brief diversion from soldierly discipline.

Anthropologist Lee, according to press reports, has protested that the Bushmen "are important for science because they represent a way of life which was previously universal."

But what may be at stake here is far more than simply a wandering way of life: in fact, the very future of the Bushmen themselves may be in question.

Lieutenant Wolff admits that the Bushmen's involvement with the Army of the white-ruled republic mean, "They will never be able to go back to Angola," the country from which many of them fled as refugees during Angola's war for independence.

And if SWAPO should come to power in Namibia, as many analysts predict, retribution against the Bushmen cannot be ruled out. Their future well-being can hardly be promoted by articles like the one which appeared in *Soldier of Fortune* magazine last year which labeled the Bushmen as "essentially mercenaries" and headlined "their SWAPO kill-ratio is 36–1."

Lieutenant Wolff admits that the Bushmen have "no political sense" and know little about the causes in the war which they are helping to fight.

Indeed, when this reporter asked a Bushman trooper why he was involved in the conflict, he replied simply, "For the money."

But sometimes, Lietuenant Wolff says, "They do ask what's going to happen to them" in the future. His answer?

"At this stage, I can't tell them anything," he says. "I'm here for the fighting part, not the talking."

The Naked Ape: An Idea We Could Live Without

by
David Pilbeam

LAST FALL CBS television broadcast a National Geographic Special, in prime time, called "Monkeys, Apes, and Man." This was an attempt to demonstrate how much studies of primates can tell us about our true biological selves. In a recent *Newsweek* magazine article, Stewart Alsop, while discussing problems of war, stated that nations often quarrel over geopolitical real estate when national boundaries are poorly defined; his examples were culled from areas as diverse as the Middle East, Central Europe, and Asia. One of his introductory paragraphs included the following:

> The animal behaviorists—Konrad Lorenz, Robert Ardrey, Desmond Morris—have provided wonderful insights into human behavior. Animals that operate in groups, from fish up to our ancestors among the primates, instinctively establish and defend a territory, or turf. There are two main reasons why fighting erupts between turfs—when the turfs are ill-defined or overlapping; or when one group is so weakened by sickness or other cause as to be unable to defend its turf, thus inviting aggression.

Here Alsop is taking facts (some of them are actually untrue facts) from the field of ethology—which is the science of whole animal behavior as studied in naturalistic environments—and extrapolating directly to man from these ethological facts as though words such as *territoriality, aggression*, and so forth describe the same phenomena in all animal species, including man.

Reprinted from *Discovery* (Peabody Museum, Yale University), 7, 2, (1972), by permission of the publisher.

Both these examples from popular media demonstrate nicely what can be called "naked apery." When Charles Darwin first published *The Origin of Species* and *The Descent of Man*, over a hundred years ago, few people believed in any kind of biological or evolutionary continuity between men and other primates. Gradually the idea of man's physical evolution from ape- or monkey-like ancestors came to be accepted; yet the concept of human behavioral evolution was always treated with scepticism, or even horror. But times have changed. No longer do we discriminate between rational man, whose behavior is almost wholly learned, and all other species, brutish automata governed solely by instincts.

One of the principal achievements of ethologists, particularly those who study primates, has been to demonstrate the extent to which the dichotomy between instinct and learning is totally inadequate in analyzing the behavior of higher vertebrate species—especially primates. Almost all behavior in monkeys and apes involves a mixture of the learned and the innate; almost all behavior is under some genetic control in that its development is channelled—although the amount of channelling varies. Thus, all baboons of one species will grow up producing much the same range of vocalizations; however, the same sound may have subtly different meaning for members of different troops of the same species. In one area, adult male baboons may defend the troop; those of the identical species in a different environment may habitually run from danger. Monkeys in one part of their species range may be sternly territorial; one hundred miles away feeding ranges of adjacent groups may overlap considerably and amicably. These differences are due to learning. Man is the learning animal par excellence. We have more to learn, take longer to do it, learn it in a more complex and yet more efficient way (that is, culturally), and have a unique type of communication system (vocal language) to promote our learning. All this the ethologists have made clear.

Studies of human behavior, at least under naturalistic conditions, have been mostly the preserve of social anthropologists and sociologists. The anthropological achievement has been to document the extraordinary lengths to which human groups will go to behave differently from other groups. The term "culture," a special one for the anthropologist, describes the specifically human type of learned behavior in which arbitrary rules and norms are so important. Thus, whether we have one or two spouses, wear black or white to a funeral, live in societies that have kings or lack chiefs entirely, is a function not of our genes but of learning; the matter depends upon which learned behaviors we deem appropriate—again because of learning. Some behaviors make us feel comfortable, others do not; some behaviors may be correct in one situation and not in another—forming a line outside of a cinema as opposed to the middle of the sidewalk, for example; singing rather than whistling in church; talking to domestic animals but not to wild ones. The appropriate or correct behavior varies from culture to culture; exactly which one is appropriate is arbitrary. This sort of behavior is known as "context dependent behavior" and is, in its learned form, pervasively and almost uniquely human. So pervasive is it, indeed, that we are unaware most of the time of the effects on our behavior of context dependence. It is important to realize here that although a great deal of ape and monkey behavior is learned, little of it is context dependent in a cultural, human sense.

In the past ten years there has been a spate of books—the first of the genre was Robert Ardrey's *African Genesis* published in 1961—that claim first to describe man's "real" or "natural" behavior in ethological style, then go on to explain how these behaviors have evolved. In order to do this, primate societies are used as models of earlier stages of human evolution; primates are ourselves, so to speak, unborn. *African Genesis, The Territorial Imperative, The Social Contract*, all by Ardrey, *The Naked Ape* and *The Human Zoo* by Desmond Morris, Konrad Lorenz's *On Aggression*, the exotic *The Descent of Woman*, by Elaine Morgan, plus Antony Jay's *Corporate Man*, without exception, for some reason approach the bestseller level. All purport to document the supposedly surprising truth that man is an animal. The more extreme of them also argue that his behavior—particularly his aggressive, status-oriented, territorial and sexual behavior—is somehow out of tune with the needs of the modern world, that these behaviors are under genetic control and are largely determined by our animal heritage, and that there is little we can do but accept our grotesque natures; if we insist on trying to change ourselves, we must realize that we have almost no room for maneuver, for natural man is far more like other animals than he would care to admit. Actually, it is of some anthropological interest to inquire exactly why this naked apery should have caught on. Apart from our obsessive neophilia, and the fact that these ideas are somehow "new," they provide attractive excuses for our unpleasant behavior toward each other.

However, I believe these general arguments to be wrong; they are based upon misinterpretation of ethological studies and of the rich variety of human behavior documented by anthropologists.

At a time when so many people wish to reject the past because it has no meaning and can contribute nothing, it is perhaps a little ironic that arguments about man's innate and atavistic depravity should have so much appeal. The world *is* in a mess; people *are* unpleasant to each other; that much is true. I can only suppose that argument about the inevitability of all the nastiness not only absolves people in some way of the responsibility for their actions, but allows us also to sit back and positively enjoy it all. Let me illustrate my argument a little.

Take, for example, one particular set of ethological studies— those on baboons. Baboons are large African monkeys that live today south of the Sahara in habitats ranging from tropical rain forest to desert. They are the animals that have been most frequently used as models of early human behavior; a lot of work has been done on them, and they are easy to study—at least those living in the savannah habitats thought to be typical of the hunting territories of early man. They are appealing to ethologists because of their habitat, because they live in discrete and structured social groups, and because they have satisfied so many previous hypotheses.

Earlier reports of baboon behavior emphasized the following. Baboons are intensely social creatures, living in discrete troops of thirty to fifty animals, their membership rarely changing; they are omnivorous, foraging alone and rarely sharing food. Males are twice as big as females; they are stronger and more aggressive. The functions of male aggression supposedly are for repelling predators, for maintaining group order, and (paradoxically) for fighting among themselves. The adult males are organized into a dominance hierarchy, the most dominant animal being the one that gets his own way as far as food, grooming partners, sex, when to stop and eat, and when and where the troop should move are concerned. He is the most aggressive, wins the most fights, and impregnates the most desirable females. Females, by the way, do little that is exciting in baboondom, but sit around having babies, bickering, and tending to their lords. Adult males are clearly the most important animals—although they cannot have the babies—and they are highly status conscious. On the basis of fighting abilities they form themselves into a dominance hierarchy, the function of which is to reduce aggression by the controlling means of each animal knowing its own place in the hierarchy. When groups meet up, fighting may well ensue. When the troop moves, males walk in front and at the rear; when the group is attacked, adult males remain to fight a rearguard action as females and young animals flee to safety in the trees.

Here then we have in microcosm one view of the way our early ancestors may well have behaved. How better to account for the destructiveness of so much human male aggression, to justify sex differences in behavior, status seeking, and so forth. I exaggerate, of course, but not too much. But what comments can be made?

First, the baboons studied—and these are the groups that are described, reported, and extrapolated from in magazine articles, books, and in CBS TV specials—are probably abnormal. They live in game parks—open country where predators, especially human ones, are present in abundance—and are under a great deal of tension. The same species has been studied elsewhere—in the open country and in forest too, away from human contact—with different results.

Forest groups of baboons are fluid, changing composition regularly (rather than being tightly closed); only adult females and their offspring remain to form the core of a stable group. Food and cover are dispersed, and there is little fighting over either. Aggression in general is very infrequent, and male dominance hierarchies are difficult to discern. Intertroop encounters are rare, and friendly. When the troop is startled (almost invariably by humans, for baboons are probably too smart, too fast, and too powerful to be seriously troubled by other predators), it flees, and, far from forming a rearguard, the males—being biggest and strongest—are frequently up the trees long before the females (encumbered as they are with their infants).

When the troop moves it is the adult females that determine when and where to; and as it moves adult males are not invariably to be found in front and at the rear. As for sexual differences, in terms of functionally important behaviors, the significant dichotomy seems to be not between males and females but between adults and young. This makes good sense for animals that learn and live a long time.

The English primatologist Thelma Rowell, who studied some of these forest baboons in Uganda, removed a troop of them and placed them in cages where food had to be given a few times a day in competition-inducing clumps. Their population density went up and cover was reduced. The result? More aggression, more fighting, and the emergence of marked dominance hierarchies. So, those first baboons probably were under stress, in a relatively impoverished environment, pestered by humans of various sorts. The high degree of aggression, the hierarchies, the rigid sex-role differences, were in a sense abnormalities. In one respect, troop defense, there is accumulating evidence that male threats directed toward human interlopers occur only after troops become habituated to the observers, and must therefore be treated as learned behavior too.

Studies on undisturbed baboons elsewhere have shown other interesting patterns of adult male behaviors. Thus in one troop an old male baboon with broken canines was the animal that most frequently completed successful matings, that influenced troop movements, and served as a focus for females and infants, even though he was far less aggressive than, and frequently lost fights with, a younger and more vigorous adult male. Here, classical dominance criteria simply do not tie together as they are supposed to.

The concept of dominance is what psychologists call a unitary motivational theory; there are two such theories purporting to explain primate social behavior. These are that the sexual bond ties the group together, and that social dominance structures and orders the troop. The first of these theories has been shown to be wrong. The second we are beginning to realize is too simplistic. In undisturbed species in the wild, dominance hierarchies are hard to discern, if they are present at all; yet workers still persist in trying to find them. For example, Japanese primatologists describe using the "peanut test" to determine "dominance" in wild chimpanzees by seeing which chimp gets the goodies. Yet what relevance does such a test have for real chimp behavior in the wild where the animals have far more important things to do—in an evolutionary or truly biological sense—than fight over peanuts? Such an experimental design implies too the belief that "dominance" is something lurking just beneath the surface, waiting for the appropriate releaser.

Steven Gartlan, an English primatologist working in the Cameroons, has recently suggested a different way of analyzing behavior, in terms of function. Each troop has to survive and reproduce, and in order to do so it must find food, nurture its mothers, protect and give its young the opportunity to learn adult skills. There are certain tasks that have to be completed if successful survival is to result. For example, the troop must be led, fights might be stopped, lookouts kept, infants fed and protected; some animals must serve as social foci, others might be needed to chase away intruders, and so on. Such an attribute list can be extended indefinitely.

If troop behavior is analyzed in a functional way like this, it immediately becomes clear that different classes of animals perform different functions. Thus, in undisturbed baboons, adults, particularly males, police the troop; males, especially the subadults and young adults, maintain vigilance; adult females determine the time and direction of movement; younger animals, especially infants, act as centers of attention.

Thus a particular age-sex class performs a certain set of behaviors that go together and that fulfill definite adaptive needs. Such a constellation of behavioral attributes is termed a role. Roles, even in nonhuman primates, are quite variable. (Witness the great differences between male behaviors in normal baboon troops and those under stress.) If dominance can come and go with varying intensities of certain environmental pressures, then it is clearly not innately inevitable, even in baboons. Rigid dominance hierarchies, then, seem to be largely artifacts of abnormal environments.

What is particularly interesting in the newer animal studies is the extent to which aggression, priority of access, and leadership are divorced from each other. Although a baboon may be highly aggressive, what matters most is how other animals react to him; if they ignore him as far as functionally important behaviors such as grooming, mating and feeding are concerned, then his aggression is, in a social or evolutionary sense, irrelevant.

I want to look a little more closely at aggression, again from the functional point of view. What does it do? What is the point of a behavior that can cause so much trouble socially?

The developmental course of aggressive behavior has been traced in a number of species; among primates it is perhaps best documented in rhesus macaques, animals very similar to baboons. There are genetical and hormonal bases to aggressive behavior in macaques; in young animals males are more aggressive, on the average, than females, and this characteristic is apparently related to hormonal influences. If animals are inadequately or abnormally socialized, aggressive behaviors become distorted and exaggerated. Animals that are correctly socialized in normal habitats, or richly stimulating artificial ones, show moderate amounts of aggression, and only in certain circumstances. These would be, for example, when an infant is threatened, when a choice item is disputed, when fights have to be interrupted, under certain circumstances when the troop is threatened, and occasionally when other species are killed for food.

Under normal conditions, aggression plays little part in other aspects of primate social life. The idea that the function of maleness is to be overbearingly aggressive, to fight constantly, and to be dominant, makes little evolutionary sense.

How about extrapolations from primates to man that the "naked-apers" are so fond of? Take, for example, dominance. Everything that I have said about its shortcomings as a concept in analyzing baboon social organization applies to man, only more so. Behaviors affecting status-seeking in man are strongly influenced by learning, as we can see by the wide variation in human behavior from one society to another. In certain cultures, status is important, clear-cut, and valued; the emphasis placed on caste in Hindu society is an obvious example. At the opposite extreme, though—among the Bushmen of the Kalahari Desert, for example—it is hard to discern; equality and cooperativeness are highly valued qualities in Bushman society, and hence learned by each new generation.

I've used the term "status-seeking" rather than "dominance" for humans, because it describes much better the kind of hierarchical ordering one finds within human groups. And that points to a general problem in extrapolating from monkey to man, for "status" is a word that one can't easily apply to baboon or chimp society; status involves prestige, and prestige presupposes values—arbitrary rules or norms. That sort of behavior is cultural, human, and practically unique.

As we turn to man, let's consider for a while human groups as they were before the switch to a settled way of life began a mere—in evolutionary terms—ten thousand years ago. Before that our ancestors were hunters and gatherers. Evidence for this in the form of stone tool making, living areas with butchered game, camp sites, and so on, begins to turn up almost 3 million years ago, at a time when our ancestors were very different physically from us. For at least two and one-half to three million years, man and his ancestors have lived as hunters and gatherers. The change from hunting to agricultural-based economies began, as I said, just over ten thousand years ago, a fractional moment on the geological time scale. That famous (and overworked) hypothetical visiting Martian geologist of the twenty-first century would find remains of hunters represented in hundreds of feet of sediments; the first evidence for agriculture, like the remains of the thermonuclear holocaust, would be jammed, together, in the last few inches. Hunting and gathering has been a highly significant event in human history; indeed, it is believed by most of us interested in human evolution to have been an absolutely vital determinant, molding many aspects of human behavior.

There are a number of societies surviving today that still live as hunters and gatherers. Congo pygmies, Kalahari Bushmen, and Australian Aborigines, are three well-known examples. When comparisons are made of these hunting societies, we can see that certain features are typical of most or all of them, and these features are likely to have been typical of earlier hunters.

In hunting societies, families—frequently monogamous nuclear families—are often grouped together in bands of twenty to forty individuals; members of these hunting bands are kinsmen, either by blood or marriage. The band hunts and gathers over wide areas, and its foraging range often overlaps those of adjacent groups. Bands are flexible and variable in composition—splitting and reforming with changes in the seasons, game and water availability, and whim.

Far from life being "nasty, brutish, and short" for these peoples, recent studies show that hunters work on the average only three or four days each week; the rest of their time is leisure. Further, at least ten percent of Bushmen, for example, are over sixty years of age, valued and nurtured by their children. Although they lack large numbers of material possessions, one can never describe such peoples as savages, degenerates, or failures.

The men in these societies hunt animals while the women gather plant food. However, women often scout for game, and in some groups may also hunt smaller animals, while a man returning empty-handed from a day's hunting will almost always gather vegetable food on his way. Thus the division of labor between sexes is not distinct and immutable; it seems to be functional, related to mobility: the women with infants to protect and carry simply cannot move far and fast enough to hunt efficiently.

Relations between bands are amicable; that makes economic sense as the most efficient way of utilizing potentially scarce resources, and also because of exogamy—marrying out—for adjacent groups will contain kinsmen and kinsmen will not fight. Within the group, individual relations between adults are cooperative and based upon reciprocity; status disputes are avoided. These behaviors are formalized, part of cultural behavior, in that such actions are positively valued and rewarded. Aggression between individuals is generally maintained at the level of bickering; in cases where violence flares, hunters generally solve the problem by fission: the band divides.

Data on child-rearing practices in hunters are well known only in Bushmen, and we don't yet know to what extent Bushmen are typical of hunters. (This work on Bushman child-rearing has been done by Patricia Draper, an anthropologist at the University of New Mexico, and I am grateful to her for permitting me to use her data.) Bushman children are almost always in the company of adults; because of the small size of Bushman societies, children rarely play in large groups with others of their own age. Aggression is minimal in the growing child for two principal reasons. First, arguments between youngsters almost inevitably take place in the presence of adults and adults always break these up before fights erupt; so the socialization process gives little opportunity for practicing aggressive behavior. Second, because of the reciprocity and cooperativeness of adults, children have few adult models on which to base the learning of aggressiveness.

Thus, the closest we can come to a concept of "natural man" would indicate that our ancestors were, like other primates, capable of being aggressive, but they would have been socialized culturally in such a way as to reduce as far as possible the manifestation of aggression. This control through learning is much more efficient in man than in other primates, because we are cultural creatures—with the ability to attach positive values to aggression-controlling behaviors. Thus Bushmen value and thereby encourage peaceful cooperation. Their culture provides the young with nonviolent models.

Other cultures promote the very opposite. Take, for example, the Yanomamö Indians of Venezuela and Brazil; their culture completely reverses our ideals of "good" and "desirable." To quote a student of Yanomamö society: "A high capacity for rage, a quick flash point, and a willingness to use violence to obtain one's ends are considered desirable traits." In order to produce the appropriate adult behaviors, the Yanomamö encourage their children, especially young boys, to argue, fight, and be generally belligerent. These behaviors, I should emphasize, are learned, and depend for their encouragement upon specific cultural values.

Our own culture certainly provides the young with violent, though perhaps less obtrusive, models. These I should emphasize again, are to a great extent learned and arbitrary, and we *could* change them should we choose to do so.

So far we have seen that fierce aggression and status-seeking are no more "natural" attributes of man than they are of most monkey and ape societies. The degree to which such behaviors are developed depends very considerably indeed upon cultural values and learning. Territoriality, likewise, is not a "natural" feature of human group living; nor is it among most other primates.

As a parting shot, let me mention one more topic that is of great interest to everyone at the moment—sex roles. Too many of us have in the past treated the male and female stereotypes of our particular culture as fixed and "natural": in our genes so to speak. It may well be true that human male infants play a little more vigorously than females, or that they learn aggressive behaviors somewhat more easily, because of hormonal differences. But simply look around the world at other cultures. In some, "masculinity" and "femininity" are much more marked than they are in our own culture; in others the roles are blurred. As I said earlier, among Bushmen that are still hunters, sex roles are far from rigid, and in childhood the two sexes have a very similar upbringing. However, among those Bushmen that have adopted a sedentary life devoted to herding or agriculture, sex roles are much more rigid. Men devote their energies to one set of tasks, women to another, mutually exclusive set. Little boys learn only "male" tasks, little girls exclusively "female" ones. Maybe the switch to the sedentary life started man on the road toward marked sex roles differences. These differences are almost entirely learned, and heavily affected by economic factors.

So much of human role behavior is learned that we could imagine narrowing or widening the differences almost as much or as little as we wish.

So, what conclusions can be drawn from all this? It is overly simplistic in the extreme to believe that man behaves in strongly genetically deterministic ways, when we know that apes and monkeys do not. Careful ethological work shows us that the primates closely related to us—chimps and baboons are the best known—get on quite amicably together under natural and undisturbed conditions. Learning plays a very significant part in the acquisition of their behavior. They are not for the most part highly aggressive, obsessively dominance-oriented, territorial creatures.

There is no evidence to support the view that early man was a violent status-seeking creature; ethological and anthropological evidence indicates rather that pre-urban men would have used their evolving cultural capacities to channel and control aggression. To be sure, we are not born empty slates upon which anything can be written; but to believe in the "inevitability of beastliness" is to deny our humanity as well as our primate heritage—and, incidentally, does a grave injustice to the "beasts."

The Two Worlds of *Homo Sapiens*: Yet Another Explanation for War

by
Morris Freilich

DO WE LIVE IN "CULTURE," "SOCIETY," OR BOTH?

HUMANS ARE OFTEN described as animals who live in and with culture. This description, although correct, is both incomplete and fuzzy. To get rid of the fuzziness, "culture" must be better understood. To get rid of the incompleteness we must add: humans are animals that (also) live in *society*. Humans, in short, are sociocultural animals. Sociocultural animals live in two worlds with distinctly different adaptational problems. Two-world life produces conflicts, dilemmas, and tensions which humans and only humans experience. Such conflicts, I suggest, produce a peculiar primate termed *Homo sapiens*, a primate that is necessarily neurotic. Is this primate also necessarily warlike? Or can this large-brained, neurotic primate create less costly games which have similar cathartic functions? To approach an answer to these gargantuan questions we need a stronger grasp of two concepts: "culture" and "sociocultural."

WHAT DOES "CULTURE" REALLY MEAN?

· For anthropologists "culture" has magical properties; the frequent repetition of culture begets prestige from other tribal members. Other social scientists use culture to display ethnological sophistication. No one currently provides useful information

Adapted from "The Meaning of 'Sociocultural,'" in B. Bernado, ed., *The Concept and Dynamic of Culture*. (The Hague: Mouton, 1978), pp. 89–101, by permission of the publisher.

by adding "culture" to a sentence. Yet culture has great utility for science as Kluckhohn and Kelly showed long ago (Kluckhohn and Kelly, 1945): "By culture we mean all those *historically created designs for living*, explicit and implicit, rational and *irrational*, and *non-rational*, which exist at any given time as *potential guides* for the behavior of men."

Let us focus on the words I have emphasized. Culture is a *design for living*, a set of *potential guides* which at any given time may or may not be followed. As a guidance system maps routes for all kinds of projectiles, so culture maps routes for human life. However, in each case all kinds of environmental factors enter, impeding a one-to-one relationship between the guidance system and behavior. Culture, therefore, must not be confused with behavior, nor with any of the material consequences of systematic action: digging sticks, canoes, huts, etc. Culture is information; behavior is action. Information is "invisible," hence its presence or absence is not easily demonstrated. Behavior, by contrast, is very visible, rarely escaping notice by one or more of our five senses.

Within a given semantic domain two types of connections exist between culture and behavior. The behavior may be consistent with the cultural guide—it is "proper"—or the behavior may be inconsistent with the cultural guide—it is "non-proper." For reasons only vaguely understood human behavior is often non-proper. For example, in analyzing land-inheritance data for a ninety-year period for thirty-two East Indian families in Trinidad I found that the "proper" was never done. Although land was always divided among the sons of the deceased, not once was it divided equally as "culture" there dictates! Every fieldworker has similar information which only infrequently is published.[1] Humans are proud of their culture, yet often they avoid its dictates. Stranger yet, non-proper behavior generally escapes negative sanction and is generally predictable by other members of the actor's community. How do we know what is likely to happen when cultural guides are avoided? Clearly culture is but one of many guidance systems which influence human behavior. Those who belong to the same community know what guides tend to replace culture on given occasions.

---

[1] See discussions in my *Marginal Natives at Work: Anthropologists in the Field* (Schenkman, 1977) and *The Meaning of Culture* (Schenkman, 1982).

CULTURE AND OTHER GUIDANCE SYSTEMS

As already implied, culture belongs to the family "guidance systems." A guide is a bit of information (I_g) which makes one type of behavior (B_g) more probably than its opposite. Our basic drives, hunger, thirst, sex, etc., are obvious guides to action. Equally obvious guides are phenomena such as temperature, humidity, rainfall and altitude. Other guides include population size and density, body type and personality. In brief, a guide is an influence or determination of behavior.

People who share space—members of the same geographic community—share a number of additional guides. In analyzing human guides I will distinguish *natural guides* (body drives, climate, etc.) from *standards* (guides which are man-made and developed as a by-product of social interaction). Culture as a member of the family guidance system belongs to the subfamily *standards* (phenomena with "qualities or attributes required by law or established by custom . . . having recognized and permanent value . . . substantially uniform . . ." [*Webster's Dictionary*, 1963 edition]). My view of culture, thus far, is in complete agreement with Goodenough's definition. "Culture," he writes, "is that which is learned . . . [that which] one needs to know in order to meet the standards of others" (Goodenough, 1971).

While culture is indeed a set of standards, all standards are not culture. Cultural standards have a history (they are "historically created designs for living") and it is this aging process which gives to culture its unique quality. Time works on standards the way it works on most other phenomena; it erodes function and highlights form. Cultural standards have no obvious function (they may be irrational or non-rational) hence their essential meaning lies in their form: the manner in which one standard interrelates with other standards. We can no more easily demonstrate the functionality of matrilateral cross-cousin marriage than we can show the utility of Mona Lisa's smile. Both examples belong to the same realm, aesthetics. Cultural standards are then *conventions* or *logical standards*: phenomena given meaning within a logical system.

Common experience testifies to our constant reference to a second guidance system, one which is less abstract, less consistent but more practical and more oriented to function. Sociologists, at times, refer to what people tend to do as social norms, however, norms is (like culture) a cliché-concept and therefore best avoided. I will refer to the pragmatic guides we use as empirical standards. A knowledge of the empirical standards of the system is the key factor which distinguishes the veteran from the novice in any system. The veteran, in American slang, "knows the ropes," she knows the real boundaries of the system; the empirical standards which often rule in place of the logical standards (culture).

We usually learn logical standards from people around us whose status is higher than ours. Empirical standards are learned by living in a system and slowly putting together the operational rules for getting things done. Learning the empirical standards of a system is much like what a child does when he learns to speak (Goodenough, 1971):

> The actual process of language learning is a complicated one that is still imperfectly understood. But we know that the individual learner plays an active role, the standards he arrives at . . . being his own creation. Other people, of course, have their standards for him and correct them when he fails to meet them. But they do not recite to him the principles to which their own speech conforms. These principles are something they know only subjectively in that they have a feel for them. Unless they are grammarians, they have not objectified these principles to themselves.

Because empirical standards are rarely codified, some sociologists refer to them as forming an *informal structure*. Thus Page writes (1946–47):

> . . . codes which govern the navy's operation to the most detailed activities . . . [constitute] the *formal structure* of the navy . . . [such codes] fail to include a very significant part of the organization which is vital in any functional analysis. This aspect shall be termed the *informal structure*. Like the formal it consists of rules, groupings, and sanctioned systems of procedure. They are informal because they are never recorded in the codes of official blueprints and because they are generated and maintained with a degree of spontaneity always lacking in the activities which make up the formal structure.

Empirical standards are indeed informal and maintained "with a degree of spontaneity" not found in culture or logical standards. These characteristics are necessary because empirical standards carry the burden of function; they help us to adapt to space. It is quite simple therefore to distinguish between culture (logical standards) which teaches proper behavior and empirical standards from which we learn how to do "the smart thing." All we need is the child's question "Why?" Take, for example, the following two standards:

S_1 Look to the right and to the left before crossing the street.
S_2 Avoid your wife's mother.

S_1 is clearly an empirical standard because the answer to "Why should I follow S_1?" is empirically obvious. Not looking before crossing is often followed by not living after crossing. This empirical standard gives pedestrians practical advice on how to reach their destinations and escape the homicidal impulses hidden in the psyche of the typical automobile driver. S_2 may help us live better; it all depends on a host of situational variables. But basically there is no empirically obvious answer to why one should avoid his wife's mother; in the same way no empirically obvious answer exists to such similar logical standards as, "Bishops move along the diagonals in chess."

To summarize thus far: *culture* belongs to the universe "guidance systems," within the family standards and within the subfamily logical standards. *Logical standards*—including rules of games, the conventions in various forms of mathematics, and culture—are not easily analyzed in functional terms. Satisfactions derived from the use of logical standards are well described in aesthetic terms, such as beauty, simplicity, pattern, rhythm and balance. Logical standards of the subtype culture, or, more simply, *cultural standards*, do not teach us how to live "better"; rather they instruct in how to live "differently" in ways the system defines as "proper." *Empirical standards* are generalizations concerning how the system actually works. Each actor has his own set of empirical standards which only approximate those of other community members. Empirical standards instruct us to behave in ways the system defines as "smart."

As noted, the child's question "Why?" is the acid test for distinguishing *empirical* from *logical* standards. However, a number of additional criteria exist which require formal presentation.

Empirical standards are:

1. *empirical*—based (largely) on the shared experiences of community members.
2. *pragmatic*—used because they work. The focus is on function, which "creates" forms for its purposes.

3. *"smart"*—a community's definition of what is strategic or effective.
4. *new*—recently developed generalizations and ideas.
5. *falsifiable*—can be proven to be false or non-smart.
6. *emotionally light*—lacking strong emotional ties to users.
7. *instrumentally meaningful or meaningful as "signs"*—meanings are primarily influenced by utility. Something is done because we are really interested in something else. The "something else" is where the heavy, symbolic meaning lies (cf. Polanyi and Prosch, 1975).
8. *learned rather than taught*—primarily learned informally, "where the action is."
9. *freely accepted*—primarily accepted because of its usefulness.
10. *fast-changing*—being emotionally light and meaningful mainly as an instrument; changes occur when required for pragmatic purposes.
11. *simple in purpose*—the minimal goal is survival; maximal goals include comfort, status, and power.
12. *not uniquely human*—found among (at least) the higher primates.

Logical standards are:

1. *theoretical*—taken altogether, logical standards present a theory of "the good life."
2. *aesthetic*—used (in part) because of consistency, elegance, logic, and beauty. Forms here "pick up" functions.
3. *"proper"*—a community's definition of the human way to do things; the way which provides dignity and differentiates us from the animals.
4. *old*—generalizations and ideas which come out of the past as "tradition."
5. *unfalsifiable*—this theory of "the good life" (like all other theories) cannot be directly falsified.
6. *emotionally heavy*—these standards do more than guide action; they are also "containers" for storing sentiments considered appropriate for given situations, times, and interactions.
7. *symbolically meaningful*—these standards are also "containers" for storing meanings which have been traditionally assigned to things, events, and people.
8. *taught*—generally taught by "superiors" (parents, teachers, etc.) to "inferiors."
9. *accepted with the help of sanctions*—fear of the clout and displeasure of superiors and embarrassment at the loss of

dignity are among the sanctions which protect logical
standards.

10. *slow changing*—protected by myths, unfalsifiability, rituals,
emotional attachments, symbolic meaning and dignity needs.

11. *complex in purpose*—minimal goals include maintaining
"face"; maximal goals include having sanity and a meaningful life.

12. *uniquely human*—found, as a system of logical standards
for properness, only among humans.

DUALISTIC STANDARDS AND OTHER DUALISMS

Human life, as Chinese philosophers long ago taught and as
structuralists now teach, is dualistic. For me the basic duality is
not Yin/Yang, nor nature versus culture but rather cultural standards (logic) and empirical standards (experience). The empirical
and experiential aspect of human life is illustrated by the word
"social" while the more abstract logical standards we develop
are summarized by the word "culture." When put together and
shortened into "sociocultural" we find a conflict. That conflict
is an essential ingredient of human life is clear to any student of
history and equally clear to anyone who has read this morning's
(or any morning's) newspaper. Somehow much cultural theory,
tied as it has been to functionalism for so long, has managed to
avoid dealing with the obvious.

Anthropological theory, until recently, managed to bypass
man's dualisms and it was left to philosophers, among others, to
present a more complete picture of human existence. For example "the main trend of Platonic thought and the tradition of
Plato's school were dualistic, emphasizing the conflict between
the reasonable and the sensual" (Tillich 1965, 3). Similar duali-
ties are found in the works of Descartes (time vs. matter),
Bergson (time vs. space), Spengler (history vs. politics), Polanyi
(aesthetics of reason vs. aesthetics of senses), Whitehead (living
in history vs. living in nature) and Frye (symbols vs. signs).

Taken as one unit organizational theorists provide us with
another dualism: reason vs. adaptation to nature. The school
which developed from the work of Max Weber considers man to
be a rational being, hence the organizations which man creates
have a high degree of rationality. Goals are clearly and precisely
formalized and means are developed to reach them efficiently.
The school which developed from the work of August Comte
focuses on man's spontaneity and his need to adapt to changing

environmental conditions. Organizations are here seen in less formal terms; goals are not always clear-cut and means are constantly modified to meet environmental pressures.

The rational model hides man's animality and his primary goal: survival. Yet much of life must avoid the cool logic of culture in favor of less reasonable but more adaptive strategies of survival. To maintain the image of human superiority over the less endowed life forms it is tempting to dissect the human race into those who typify human excellence and the rest. Falling prey to this temptation, Friedrich Nietzsche gave us those with master morality as against those with slave morality. More correctly, Robert Louis Stevenson showed that the two faces of "human" are part of every human animal, not just Dr. Jekyll and Mr. Hyde.

The pervasive nature of dualistic thought has been well documented in Lévi-Strauss' extensive work on myth. Nature vs. culture, human vs. animal, life vs. death, raw vs. cooked, are but a few of the "conflicting" ideas identified in hundreds of myths. The point is no longer debatable; human life is dualistic (cf. Lévi-Strauss, 1970). The question which remains is: Why? When answered, this question will lead to a host of other questions—all connected to that complex word "sociocultural."

TO KNOW MAN *(HOMO SAPIENS)* WE MUST KNOW HISTORY

In an ingenious little paper entitled "The Necessity for Historical Trajectories," Gilbert Shapiro demonstrated that a historical perspective is essential in order to fully understand any phenomena (1982). Human history, therefore, holds one of the keys to unlocking the secrets of human duality. Before man was human (and here we must of course piece together incomplete evidence) he was, as now, a social animal. That is, our ancestors probably lived in small-group settings, adapting to space by means of instinctive responses and by means of shared information. As our ancestral line continued to evolve, instinct played an ever smaller and learning an ever larger role in their lives. Utilizing, in modified form, a creative synthesis of paleontological, archaeological, and ethnological data (Watson and Watson, 1969) I will describe the course of human evolution in terms of four critical stages: non-human primate, protohuman, linguistic, and cultural.

In the non-human primate stage a group-living, dominance-ranked animal, generally described as "generalized" in formal structure, developed a unique specialization. With a large (compared to other mammals) cerebral cortex, with an opposable thumb providing the ability to grasp and examine even small objects, and with stereoscopic color vision, the non-human primate specialized in the collection and analysis of information. The typical form of this stage utilized about two dozen vocalizations to express pleasure and pain. These vocalizations were used in the community as signs providing general environmental information. That is, a non-intentional communication system was in existence; without intending to do so, animals sent each other messages concerning danger, fright, tension, sexual aggression, satisfactions from grooming, from copulating, from nourishment, etc. By taking these non-intentional communications as signs of body states, and by observing other behaviors and environmental conditions coexisting with these signs, community members shared considerable information. The community, we could say, shared information or "owned" a set of empirical standards. The empirical standards, we should note, were indeed "standards." All these animals did not behave in precisely the same way when faced with similar situations. Hence what they learned from each other was types of responses to types of situations rather than a response to a situation.

The absence of intention in the non-human primate stage of communication (i.e. the absence of symbolic communication) meant that this system lacked the process we call teaching. Yet some kind of pseudo-self-teaching through vocal signs did exist, for the system included total feedback of vocalizations. An animal heard itself make instinctive vocalizations, it heard itself copy vocalizations of other community members and it "observed" environmental conditions at such times as well as its own state. The fact that the vocalizations stood for something, and that that something was being communicated could not long escape an animal whose brain was evolving toward an ever stronger specialization in information. Perhaps an animal first accidentally made a pleasurable vocalization and noticed that the vocalization itself had pleasant consequences. From accidental vocalizations may have come vocalizations for their own sake: a kind of babbling stage of semi-intentional communication. Then as the babbling of one animal is noticed to have consequences for others a stage of intentional communication is entered. It is this stage that I refer to as the protohuman.

For many scholars intentional communication by use of vocalizations indicates the presence of a language. I believe otherwise. Although a language is a symbolic (i.e., intentional and hence conventionalized) system of communication, it is more than that. A language is a communication system which has the characteristic of displacement. To invent symbols which have the displacement characteristic, an animal must have the concept of time. Time is a far more complex concept than intentionality; hence it is reasonable to assume that a stage with intentional communication preceded a stage with time. My logic is strengthened by the fact that intentionality includes a vague appreciation of a time realm. One can easily imagine how an animal with a limited communication system—just the ability to send messages concerning immediately visible phenomena—can reach true language. Experience with intentionality is actually experience with causal analysis: doing A so that B will occur. The protohuman stage was then an experimental, prelinguistic stage where animals played with space symbols (empirical phenomena which were present in the immediate environment) and constantly invented new symbols to represent various aspects of the environment. From at most thirty-five to fifty vocalizations which developed in the non-human stage one can reasonably imagine a protohuman population with several hundred space symbols. The ability both to invent new symbols and to make the many sounds that this space-symbolic system demanded was due to animals of this stage having a brain size of around nine hundred to one thousand cubic centimeters. Going along with this bigger brain was more cortical area devoted to such sound makers as the lips, the tongue, and the larynx. The social environment of protohumans, it should be noticed, was becoming quite complex. Whatever else may have developed—simple tools, simple familial and associational arrangements, etc.—a large symbolic environment existed, making for a considerably enlarged set of empirical standards. Any individual with intelligence far below the mode would have had great survival problems. And periodically, with competition between protohuman communities and with attacks from other types of animals, given communities must have lost large numbers of their membership—just as modern communities do. Under the conditions here outlined it is probably true that the more intelligent protohumans tended to survive such crises more often than did the less intelligent. Lacking culture—concepts concerned with properness—protohumans either followed their empirical standards (and did what was "smart" for the community) or acted in terms of personal ideas or by instinct (and did what was "smart" for the individual). In either case, ideas such as trying to save less able fellows for reasons of honor, charity or religious duty were absent from the system. In the protohuman stage the less intelligent must have been quickly weeded out as the system developed a stronger focus on information collection and information distribution. And the typical protohuman animal must have had a passion for information and a brain size to satisfy this hunger.

The linguistic stage probably did not require a greatly increased brain size. It did require a full understanding of the logic of space symbols. If A, the intentional vocalization of an animal, leads to B, a given change in the environment, then A causes B. That is, A, something which happened ''before,'' causes B, something which happened ''after.'' The linguistic stage—the stage which includes as its major advance the invention of time—is for many scholars also the stage of culture. I believe otherwise. Standards for properness or culture grew out of an understanding of time; just as time grew out of an understanding of intentionality. To postulate that culture is a child of time is to tie cultural theory more closely to general evolutionary theory.

The road leading into time has been shown as a series of logical steps which follow once an animal has specialized in information, has considerable intelligence, and emits vocal signs. The road into time is a slow one-way journey and once the new world of time is reached none but the insane can escape its demands. Once locked into time—once a system includes the notions of past and future—a whole series of novel states of consciousness develops. Now there is a future to live in and imaginations have the freedom to wander where no animal wandered before.

Purpose is discovered in time as goals get pushed ever forward and it is necessary to give the prime goal a label. The unraveling of the many aspects of cause-and-effect relationships leads later into the stage of culture but meanwhile whets appetites for more information. More information means the possibility of greater control over an ever more understandable environment. Living in time leads to associations between a given time and a given activity. It becomes noted, for example, that it is smart to hunt at a certain time, perhaps when the sun has just risen. Or it is noted that food left to bake in the sun for a certain time tastes sweeter. Time begins to pick up a whole set of labels for itself as more and more associations with time make living more pleasurable and make work more efficient.

Living in time has created the first wall between linguistic animals and non-linguistic animals. This wall is built out of long-range planning, more complex technology (due to a fuller appreciation of cause-and-effect relationships) and a communication system with infinite possibilities of message sending. As time continues to be used as a marker for activities and as it becomes habitual to hunt at a certain time, eat at a certain time, pick wild fruits at a certain time, and so forth, uneasy feelings develop when special times are missed. Let us note that it is not that it is smart to eat, say, at a given time; rather it is comfortable— some kind of aesthetic emotion has gotten attached to a natural activity. Once firmly linked to time, eating is no longer just a natural activity; it is something else as yet vaguely understood by this linguistic animal. In order to avoid the uneasy feelings and to hold onto the pleasures which come when things are done at special times, some general concept such as "proper" first got associated with important activities. "Proper" originally only referred to time—that is, there were only proper "whens" in this system. Soon more and more activities got a proper time and hence, so to speak, an aesthetic cover. From properness of time a small logical jump led to properness of place. Soon there was a proper place for eating, sleeping, meeting with friends, and so on. As properness spread through the social life of the linguistic animal, leaving nothing untouched by its strange quality (not even its inventor), the second wall was erected between what was now *Homo sapiens* and the rest of the animal world. *Homo sapiens*, locked into the world of time and surrounded by properness, was now firmly pushed out of nature and into culture.

Two walls, time and culture, separate *Homo sapiens* from his animal ancestry. Yet *Homo sapiens* lives in space. Humans are still animals that need personal space to maintain their separateness from other community members and they still need a "range" within which to find the wherewithal for subsistence. Is *Homo sapiens* in space with its demands of smartness or is he time's child marching to the beat of properness? The answer—he is both—is the paradox known as human life.

SPACE, TIME AND WAR

Humans live in two distinct worlds. Like the blue-green algae found in stagnant ponds we, too, are halfway creatures. Blue-green algae are part plant and part animal. Humans are part animal and part X. Our inability to grasp the essential nature of X gives us both conceptual problems and war!

Theologians tell us we are partly human (animal-like?) and partly divine. Moralists tell us we are partly good and partly evil. Similar information from scholarship since the beginning of written history has been of little help to social science or to man. Perhaps we can get further by saying that we live partly in space and partly in time. The adaptive problems of space-life lead to solutions belonging to the category "smartness"; while the adaptive problems of time-life lead to solutions belonging to the category "properness." Smartness and properness belong to distinctly different sets of phenomena; and the behavioral requirements of these two systems are often completely contradictory. The modal state of the human psyche must then be "tension." Social conflict (of any type) must then be a release of tension, a catharsis for the strange animal called *Homo sapiens*. Conflict is therapeutic, for it gives a behavioral expression to what the system experiences. Conflict is a drama which devours the energy which is pushing us in two different directions.

Intuitively we know that the essence of human existence is conflict because we use the term sociocultural to describe our life. Not fully social and following the empirical standards of other natural animals, nor fully cultural and flourishing with our own logical standards, we exist in a constant state of disharmony. Historically, we have been quick to follow anyone who would lead us into bloody conflict (war) and promised to bring us back safely. The world of time gave us concepts with which to hide our true motives, both from ourselves and from others; we had honor, glory, duty and loyalty. Historically, we have utilized other, less costly means to express the tension which rages within us. We responded to the thesis of our neighbor with an antithesis, and spectators watching this battle of wits sat back and smiled. Here, too, was catharsis. Dualistic thinking kept multiplying, not because our minds have the same structure as digital computers as some scholars maintain, but rather because our minds are forced to live in two separate worlds.

Our tremendous fascination with games of all kinds is further proof of our passionate involvement with conflict and is similarly explained by our two-world existence. Young and old, strong and weak, brilliant and stupid—all of mankind enjoys conflict. Our ancestral line specialized in information, a harmless enough specialty that could have led in various directions. Information seeking led to a life-in-time and a dualistic existence. Our new specialization—conflict—is not as harmless as information. Like our previous specialization this one, too, can lead in many directions, among which is the total destruction of this planet. What can we do to harness the energy provided by our specialization toward productive ends? What kinds of games can we invent that will have the same cathartic effects as war, but will define the harming of another human as against the rules?

These difficult problems will need our combined efforts even to approach a solution that could work. One thing, however, is certain: we must resist hiding our true condition before no condition exists to be hidden.

REFERENCES

Freilich, Morris, ed. *Marginal Natives at Work: Anthropologists in the Field*. Cambridge, Mass.: Schenkman, 1977.

———. *The Meaning of Culture*. Cambridge, Mass.: Schenkman, 1982.

Goodenough, Ward. *Culture, Language and Society*. McCaleb Module in Anthropology. Reading, Mass.: Addison-Wesley, 1971.

Kluckhohn, Clyde, and W. H. Kelly. "The Concept of Culture." In *The Science of Man in the World of Crisis*, ed. Ralph Linton. New York: Columbia University Press, 1945.

Lévi-Strauss, Claude. *The Raw and the Cooked*. New York: Harper and Row, 1970.

Page, Charles. "Bureaucracy's Other Face." *Social Forces*, 25 (1946–47), pp. 88–94.

Polanyi, Michael, and Harry Prosch. *Meaning*. Chicago: University of Chicago Press, 1975.

Shapiro, Gilbert. "The Importance of History." In *The Meaning of Culture*, ed. Morris Freilich. Cambridge, Mass.: Schenkman, 1982.

Tillich, Paul. *The Courage to Be*. New Haven: Yale University Press, 1965.

Watson, R. A., and P. J. Watson. *Man and Nature: An Anthropological Essay in Human Ecology*. New York: Harcourt, Brace and World, 1969.

The Study of Man from SIGNET and MENTOR Books

(0451)

☐ **KOSTER: Americans In Search of Their Past by Stuart Struever, Ph.D. and Felicia Antonelli Holton.** A lively narrative describing the ten-year archaeological dig in a cornfield in west central Illinois conducted in 1968 by the author. His find turned out to be a village dating back to 6,500 B.C. that shed light on settlements in prehistoric America. "Should have wide appeal; strongly recommended."—*Library Journal* (091981—$2.95)

☐ **FATU-HIVA by Thor Heyerdahl.** The fascinating story of Heyerdahl's first Pacific adventure; there were no white inhabitants and no contact with the outside world. "An enormous literary event . . . a work of awesome inspiration . . . simply and beautifully written, engrossing and entertaining."—*Newsday* (086821—$2.25)

☐ **THE *RA* EXPEDITIONS by Thor Heyerdahl.** The gripping, day-by-day account of Heyerdahl's epic voyages in papyrus boats across the Atlantic, voyages which created plausible links between the ancient civilization of the Mediterranean and the Americas. Illustrations. (051211—$1.95)

☐ **THE FIRST AMERICAN: A Story of North American Archaeology by C.W. Ceram.** One of the most popular archaeological writers of our time pieces together the recent discoveries of early American man with "grisly detail, fascinating testimony from diggers and scholars . . ."—*Christian Science Monitor*. Bibliography, Index, and Notes. (618629—$2.95)

MENTOR and SIGNET Books of Special Interest

Buy them at your local

bookstore or use coupon

on next page for ordering.

Technology Today and Tomorrow from MENTOR ar SIGNET

(045

☐ **THE COMMUNICATIONS REVOLUTION by Frederick W liams.** Revised edition. Your irreplaceable guide to grasping the va possibilities of present and future technological breakthroughs in t communications field, and their implications—for better or worse— society and you. "An excellent introduction to a complex and quicl changing field."—*Choice* (622111—$3.9

☐ **MICROELECTRONICS AND SOCIETY: A Report to the Club Rome edited by Guenter Friedrichs and Adam Schaff.** Born the union of the calculator, the transistor, and the silicon chip, micr electronics will alter the world almost beyond recognition in the comi decades. The role of this new technology has been explored a assessed by leading world experts resulting in the first true total pictu of where we are going—and what we can do about it.
(622375—$4.50

☐ **UNDERSTANDING MICROCOMPUTERS: An Introduction the New Personal Computers by Rose Deakin.** Now this con prehensive guide—written in plain English—takes the mystery out computers, making them accessible to anyone willing to take t relatively short time it requires to understand and master them.
(124278—$3.50

☐ **KEN USTON'S GUIDE TO HOME COMPUTERS by Ken Usto** In language you can understand—the most accessible and up-to-da guide you need to pick the personal computer that's best for yo Leading video game and home computer expert Ken Uston takes tl mystery out of personal computers as he surveys the ever-growin often confusing home computer market. (125975—$3.5

*Prices slightly higher in Canada
†Not available in Canada